Engineering Applications of AI for Demand Forecasting

Editors
Bhargav Appasani
and
Amitkumar Vidyakant Jha
School of Electronics Engineering
Kalinga Institute of Industrial Technology (KIIT) Deemed to be University,
Bhubaneswar-751024,
Odisha, India

CRC Press
Taylor & Francis Group
Boca Raton London New York

CRC Press is an imprint of the
Taylor & Francis Group, an **informa** business
A SCIENCE PUBLISHERS BOOK

Cover credit: Image reproduced by kind courtesy of the editors.

First edition published 2026
by CRC Press
2385 NW Executive Center Drive, Suite 320, Boca Raton FL 33431

and by CRC Press
4 Park Square, Milton Park, Abingdon, Oxon, OX14 4RN

CRC Press is an imprint of Taylor & Francis Group, LLC

Library of Congress Cataloging-in-Publication Data (applied for)

ISBN: 978-1-032-86383-2 (hbk)
ISBN: 978-1-032-89233-7 (pbk)
ISBN: 978-1-003-54187-5 (ebk)

DOI: 10.1201/9781003541875

Typeset in Times New Roman
by Prime Publishing Services

Foreword

In an era defined by rapid digital transformation and unprecedented data proliferation, Artificial Intelligence (AI) has emerged as a pivotal force reshaping industries globally. The role of AI in demand forecasting, in particular, has transitioned from a speculative advantage to an operational imperative. As someone deeply engaged with AI-driven solutions and data science methodologies, I have witnessed firsthand the profound impact of these technologies across multiple sectors.

"Engineering Applications of AI for Demand Forecasting" enters the literature at this pivotal moment, providing a comprehensive exploration of AI techniques and their substantial real-world implications. This volume stands out for its strategic blend of foundational AI methodologies and advanced topics such as generative AI, anomaly detection, and the integration of meteorological data, mirroring the latest developments that my research group and I frequently engage with.

Each chapter provides a robust intersection between theoretical rigour and practical engineering solutions, a balance that resonates deeply with my academic ethos. Notably, the chapters on sustainable energy forecasting and prosumer-based demand management align closely with my ongoing research interests in sustainable, smart, and resilient infrastructures, especially within the context of Industry 4.0.

From optimising third-party logistics to enhancing cyber analytics and improving electricity management during high-demand events, the book encapsulates the multidisciplinary essence of contemporary demand forecasting challenges. This multidisciplinary approach not only enriches the academic discourse but also equips industry practitioners, data scientists, and policymakers with actionable insights for strategic decision-making.

I commend the editors and contributing authors for their meticulous assembly of this insightful and practically oriented resource. I am confident that this book will serve as an indispensable guide for professionals seeking to leverage AI to address complex forecasting challenges effectively.

Professor Amir H. Gandomi
Professor of Data Science
University of Technology Sydney, Australia

Preface

Artificial Intelligence (AI) is revolutionizing how engineering systems anticipate and respond to dynamic demands, unlocking new levels of precision, adaptability, and efficiency. The accelerating digitization of industries embodied in paradigms like Industry 4.0 requires advanced forecasting mechanisms capable of processing massive, multidimensional datasets in real time. This book, *Engineering Applications of AI for Demand Forecasting*, presents a collection of contemporary research and applications that illustrate the power and versatility of AI across diverse forecasting challenges.

Each chapter contributes a unique perspective on how AI can be engineered to meet forecasting needs in energy, supply chains, logistics, cyber analytics, and smart infrastructure. The book begins with a chapter on AI-Driven Demand Forecasting in Industry 4.0: Techniques, Applications, and Future Trends that establishes the foundation for the book by exploring how AI integrates with the Industry 4.0 landscape to enhance demand forecasting across smart manufacturing and industrial systems. It surveys key techniques, real-world applications, and emerging trends that shape intelligent forecasting in highly automated environments.

With cybersecurity and open-source intelligence becoming vital in critical infrastructure, Chapter 2 presents AI solutions designed to meet forecasting needs in cyber analytics. It highlights how engineered AI models can anticipate data flow, cyber events, and infrastructure load in digital ecosystems.

Focusing on operational reliability and cost reduction, Chapter 3 investigates how AI is used to predict anomalies and system failures. The application of predictive analytics here contributes to proactive maintenance and resource optimization in engineering systems. Many AI applications have been demonstrated in this chapter for anomaly detection and failure prediction.

Generative AI is one of the most transformative technologies in the AI domain. Chapter 4 explores its innovative use in forecasting logistics demand, particularly in third-party logistics (3PL) networks. The discussion emphasizes how generative models enhance decision-making in unpredictable supply environments.

Chapters 5 and 6 emphasize the demand forecasting for supply chain management. Particularly, Chapter 5 demonstrates how AI-driven forecasting can enable environmentally responsible supply chain practices, addressing the growing need for sustainability. It presents strategies for balancing efficiency with ecological impact, using intelligent demand prediction. Complementing Chapter 5, Chapter 6 delves deeper into how AI itself is being applied within the supply chain management lifecycle to anticipate product demand, inventory needs, and procurement cycles. It emphasizes engineering considerations in model deployment and integration.

As the world pivots to renewable energy, accurate forecasting becomes critical. Chapter 7 illustrates how AI, integrated with weather data analytics, can predict energy demand from alternative sources, enhancing grid stability and planning. It is worth noting that the special events introduce non-linearities and unusual demand patterns in electricity usage. Hence, such an aspect is thoroughly covered in Chapter 8 of the book. Chapter 8 showcases AI models capable of learning such irregular behaviors, enabling utilities to maintain service quality during festivals, public events, or emergencies.

Managing peak demand is essential to grid reliability. Chapter 9 discusses machine learning algorithms that forecast peak loads, facilitating dynamic resource allocation and preventive infrastructure planning.

With the rise of smart homes and IoT devices, residential energy usage has become increasingly variable. Chapter 10 leverages smart meter data to train AI models for accurate, household-level demand forecasting, improving energy delivery and user experience. Finally, chapter 11 discusses the demand forecasting on electricity from the prosumer perspective, where the data incorporates meteorological parameters. Prosumer behavior where consumers who also produce energy, adds complexity to demand forecasting. The final chapter addresses this challenge by combining AI with meteorological inputs, providing robust predictions that support distributed energy resource management.

The chapters reflect both depth and breadth, ranging from AI-based load forecasting in residential energy systems and anomaly detection in industrial services, to sustainable supply chain modeling and generative AI applications in third-party logistics. By incorporating external variables such as meteorological data, special events, and smart meter analytics, the book showcases AI's capacity to handle complex, nonlinear, and high-dimensional forecasting environments.

A unique aspect of this work is its dual emphasis on theory and application. Each chapter is grounded in rigorous AI methodologies while also providing insight into real-world deployment and future directions. The contributions illustrate how AI not only enhances forecasting precision but also supports broader goals such as cost optimization, energy efficiency, cybersecurity, and environmental sustainability.

This book is intended for engineers, researchers, practitioners, and graduate students who seek to understand and apply AI-driven forecasting solutions in technical and operational contexts. We hope it serves as both a foundational reference and a catalyst for future innovation, encouraging cross-disciplinary dialogue.

Bhargav Appasani
and
Amitkumar Vidyakant Jha

Contents

Foreword .... *iii*

Preface .... *v*

List of Abbreviations .... *xi*

1. **AI-Driven Demand Forecasting in Industry 4.0: Techniques, Applications, and Future Trends** **1**
   Kushagra Agrawal and Polat Goktas
2. **AI Engineering for Meeting the Demand of Open-Source Cyber Analytics** **28**
   Fahim K Sufi
3. **Application of AI for Anomaly Detection and Failure Prediction to Optimize Cost of Service** **54**
   Debabrata Bera, Bhaskar Roy and Ankan Pattanayak
4. **Generative AI Based Demand Forecasting for Third-Party Logistics** **76**
   M. Kmiecik
5. **Demand Forecasting for Sustainable Supply Chain Management Leveraging AI** **105**
   Izabela Rojek and Dariusz Mikołajewski
6. **Demand Forecasting for AI in Supply Chain Management** **124**
   Harika Rajashekaraiah, Noor Sakina, Ajith Pulinchuvattil Arun, Praveen Kumar Gupta and Thippareddy
7. **Artificial Intelligence Based Alternate Energy Demand Forecasting Incorporating Weather Data Analysis** **156**
   Pratapa Raju Moola, Gopi Krishna Pasam, Praveen N and Sami Al Ghnimi

8. **Electricity Demand Forecasting during Special Events Using AI.......200**
Oscar Trull, J. Carlos García-Díaz and A. Peiró-Signes

9. **Predicting Peak Energy Demand Using Machine Learning Techniques for Efficient Electricity Supply Management..................... 217**
Imrus Salehin, Nazmul Huda Badhon, Md. Tomal Ahmed Sajib, Md. Sakibul Hassan Rifat and Nazmun Nessa Moon

10. **AI-based Electrical Load Forecasting for Residential Sector Using Smart Meter Data..230**
Barkha Parkash, Tek Tjing Lie, Weihua Li and Shafiqur Rahman Tito

11. **Prosumer Electricity Demand Forecasting Using Artificial Intelligence-based Algorithms Incorporating Meteorological Data..255**
Gülizar Gizem Tolun, Ömer Can Tolun and Kasım Zor

Index... 281

List of Abbreviations

6G	Sixth Generation Networks
AI	Artificial Intelligence
ANN	Artificial Neural Network
AR	Augmented Reality
ARIMA	Auto-Regressive Integrated Moving Average
CNN	Convolutional Neural Network
CoF	Combination of Forecasts
DBN	Deep Belief Networks
DEMATEL	Decision Making Trial and Evaluation Laboratory
DQN	Deep Q-Network
ENN	Elman Neural Networks
ERP	Enterprise Resource Planning
ESG	Environmental, Social and Governance
ESPO	Evolutionary Particle Swarm Optimisation
FFNN	Feed-Forward Neural Networks
GBDT	Gradient Boosted Decision Trees
GEO	Geostationary Equatorial Orbit
GEP	Gene Expression Programming
GMDHN	Group Method of Data Handling-Type Deep Polynomial Neural Networks
GPS	Global Positioning System
HAP	High-Altitude Platform
IoMT	Internet of Medical Things
IoT	Internet of Things
IoV	Internet of Vehicles
KNN	K-Nearest Neighbour
LAP	Low-altitude Platform
LEO	Low Earth Orbit
LSTM	Long Short-Term Memory

LSTM	Long Short-Term Memory
MAE	Mean Absolute Error
MAPE	Mean Absolute Percentage Error
MDP	Markov Decision Process
MEO	Medium Earth Orbit
MERRA-2	Modern-Era Retrospective Analysis for Research and Applications, Version 2
ML	Machine Learning
MLPNN	Multilayer Perceptron Feed-Forward Neural Networks
MLR	Multiple Linear Regression
MSE	Mean Squared Error
NLP	Natural Language Processing
nMAE	Normalised Mean Absolute Error
nRMSE	Normalised Root Mean Squared Error
OIPT	Organizational Information Processing Theory
P2P	Peer-to-Peer
PCA	Principal Component Analysis
PEDF	Prosumer Electricity Demand Forecasting
POS	Point of Sale
R2	Coefficient of Determination
RL	Reinforcement Learning
RMSE	Root Mean Squared Error
RNN	Recurrent Neural Network
RPA	Robotic Process Automation
SARIMA	Seasonal Auto-Regressive Integrated Moving Average
SCM	Supply Chain Management
SCRes	Supply Chain Resilience
SVDD	Support Vector Data Description
SVM	Support Vector Machines
SVR	Support Vector Regression
VLEO	Very Low Earth Orbit
XGBoost	Extreme Gradient Boosting

Chapter 1

AI-Driven Demand Forecasting in Industry 4.0: Techniques, Applications, and Future Trends

Kushagra Agrawal[1] and Polat Goktas*[2]

[1]School of Computer Engineering, KIIT Deemed to be University, Bhubaneswar, Odisha, India

[2]UCD School of Computer Science, University College Dublin, Dublin, Ireland

1.1 INTRODUCTION

The transformative potential of artificial intelligence (AI) and machine learning (ML) for demand forecasting in the manufacturing sector is becoming undeniably evident, particularly in the evolving framework of Industry 4.0. As manufacturers strive to optimize their supply chains, the integration of advanced technologies such as AI-powered predictive analytics has emerged as a critical differentiator in enhancing forecasting precision and operational efficiency [1]. Traditional demand forecasting methods—typically relying on simplistic analyzes of historical data are increasingly proving inadequate in the face of modern, complex supply chain dynamics.

In contrast, AI-driven models, including deep learning (DL) architectures such as autoencoders, convolutional neural networks (CNNs), and recurrent neural networks (RNNs) have demonstrated significant improvements by automatically extracting complex features and patterns from vast datasets, which conventional

*For Correspondence: polat.goktas@ucd.ie

DOI: 10.1201/9781003541875-1

approaches tend to overlook. This shift toward AI-driven solutions reflects a foundational change in how businesses approach demand forecasting, allowing them to respond more effectively to market fluctuations and consumer behavior. This capability is especially important in industries like retail, healthcare, and automotive, where demand volatility is increasingly prevalent [2].

Beyond the technological advancements, data preprocessing and feature engineering have become critical steps in ensuring the accuracy of forecasting models. These processes involve cleaning and preparing the data, ensuring that it is both relevant and representative of real-world conditions. By integrating diverse data sources such as historical sales figures, economic indicators, and market trends, businesses can develop nuanced and reliable demand forecasts. However, implementing these AI-driven approaches presents challenges, particularly with regard to data quality, model interpretability, and the computational demands of DL models. Innovations such as explainable AI (XAI), federated learning, and hybrid models combining neural networks with exogenous variables are being explored to address these challenges. These advancements not only enhance the robustness of demand forecasting systems but also improve their adaptability across various industries [3].

Real-world case studies highlight the tangible benefits of effective demand forecasting, extending far beyond traditional inventory management. Applications in areas like predictive maintenance, quality control, and resource optimization highlight the value of AI-driven models. For instance, in the medical devices and electronics sectors, AI-driven forecasting has improved design precision, automated production processes, and reduced downtime through predictive maintenance strategies. A case study on a plastic packaging manufacturer demonstrated how artificial neural networks (ANNs) could significantly reduce forecasting errors, optimize production schedules and minimize waste.

Despite challenges like data acquisition, security concerns, and trust barriers, the transformative potential of AI and ML in transforming efficiency and fostering innovation within the manufacturing sector is immense. This chapter has provided an in-depth exploration of the profound impact AI is having on demand forecasting, highlighting both the remarkable advancements and the critical obstacles that must still be addressed for its full realization. By bridging existing knowledge gaps, this work presents a multidisciplinary approach that not only underlines the strategic importance of AI but also illuminates the path forward for businesses looking to thrive in an increasingly digital and data-driven landscape. As AI continues to evolve, it could redefine the future of demand forecasting, offering unprecedented opportunities for precision, agility, and competitive advantage in the manufacturing industry.

1.2 FUNDAMENTALS OF DEMAND FORECASTING

Demand forecasting, a critical aspect of predictive analytics, plays an essential role in anticipating and understanding future customer demand. Accurate forecasting forms the backbone of effective supply chain management, guiding key decisions around capacity planning, resource allocation, and strategic operations. In the context of Industry 4.0, the ability to forecast demand with precision is no longer a luxury but a competitive necessity. Advanced technologies now enable real-time data sharing among supply chain stakeholders, reducing bottlenecks and optimizing resources to enhance customer service, minimize stockouts, and streamline production plans [4]. Accurate demand forecasting offers multiple strategic benefits: it reduces inventory levels, mitigates the risk of stock shortages, lowers operational costs, and leads to better customer satisfaction. These outcomes are particularly vital in industries with complex supply chains and high levels of market volatility. The following parts outline the different traditional demand forecasting models, their applications, and their relevance in modern industrial settings.

1.2.1 Traditional Demand Forecasting Models

Traditional demand forecasting models, while useful, have limitations, especially when faced with complex, modern-day challenges. These models, such as ARIMA (Autoregressive Integrated Moving Average), exponential smoothing, and the Holt-Winters model (as discussed in Table 1.1), have been widely employed to identify patterns and estimate future demand based on past performance. These models help businesses manage inventory, optimize production schedules, and make informed decisions about resource distribution. However, in today's fast-paced market, where demand volatility and complexity are ever-increasing, traditional methods often struggle to capture the intricacies of fluctuating consumer behavior and external variables such as economic shifts or seasonal influences [5]. Table 1.1 provides an overview of several widely used traditional forecasting models (illustrated in Figure 1.1), their descriptions, applications, and relevant references. These models have been refined over time to meet the evolving needs of businesses across different sectors.

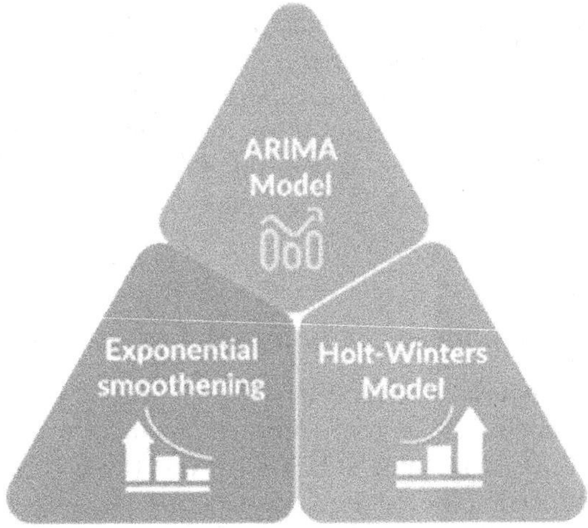

Figure 1.1 Overview of traditional demand forecasting models.

Table 1.1: Traditional demand forecasting models: Methods and applications

Model	Description	Applications	References
ARIMA (Autoregressive Integrated Moving Average) Model	Combines autoregressive and moving average models for non-stationary time series data. Identifies patterns in historical data to forecast future trends.	Reliable for demand forecasting in food manufacturing, retail, and supply chains. Aids in stock management.	[6, 7]
Exponential Smoothing	Applies exponentially decreasing weights to historical data, prioritizing recent observations. Known for simplicity and efficiency in forecasting.	Effective for demand forecasting in the food industry. Enhances decision-making processes in companies.	[8]
Holt-Winters Model	Also known as Triple Exponential Smoothing. Accounts for seasonal changes and trends in time series data. Considers both multiplicative and additive seasonality, making it suitable for complex seasonal forecasting.	Accurate forecasting for products with seasonal demand patterns. Often used in the retail and food sectors.	[9]

Traditional forecasting models, while valuable, tend to rely heavily on historical data and may lack the ability to account for unexpected disruptions or rapid changes in the market. For instance, models like ARIMA are effective in stable environments but may not adapt well to industries with high volatility. Exponential smoothing and Holt-Winters, on the other hand, are useful for forecasting in industries with clear seasonality but may underperform in scenarios involving sudden market shifts or non-linear patterns. These limitations highlight the growing need for more advanced methodologies.

While traditional models have been essential for historical demand trend analysis, they are increasingly insufficient for capturing the complexity and volatility of today's supply chains. As a result, businesses are increasingly turning to AI-driven models that can process vast, multidimensional datasets to generate more accurate and dynamic forecasts.

1.2.2 The Emergence of Advanced Learning Models

The advent of DL models, including models such as LSTM (Long Short-Term Memory), autoencoders, and hybrid approaches, marks a new era in demand forecasting (as discussed in Table 1.2). Unlike traditional methods, which often struggle to capture complex patterns in data, DL leverages artificial neural networks to identify intricate relationships and trends that are easily overlooked by conventional approaches. These models provide a far more detailed and precise understanding of future demand, especially in markets characterized by high volatility and uncertainty. Table 1.2 showcases a range of DL-based demand forecasting models (see Figure 1.2), offering insights into their functionality, real-world applications, and key references. These advanced techniques are particularly well-suited for handling complex, high-dimensional data, delivering substantial improvements across industries such as retail, manufacturing, and energy.

Table 1.2 Overview of advanced learning-based demand forecasting models

Model	Description	Applications	References
LSTM (Long Short-Term Memory) Model	A type of recurrent neural network (RNN) designed to handle time series data, ideal for volatile and dynamic demand scenarios.	Effective in multivariate and high-dimensional datasets, achieving high accuracy such as 96.7% in sales forecasting.	[8]
MLFANN (Multilayer Feedforward Artificial Neural Network) Model	A deep learning model that mimics human brain functionality, using backpropagation and stochastic gradient descent.	Highly effective for large-scale data processing, requiring substantial computational power.	[9]
GAN (Generative Adversarial Network) Model	Utilizes a generator-discriminator framework, often employed in anomaly detection and synthetic data generation.	Used in predicting demand in sectors like pharmaceuticals, with notable success in detecting anomalies.	[10]
Hybrid Models	Combines traditional models like ARIMA with neural networks to achieve greater forecasting accuracy.	Applied in sales forecasting and in industries requiring complex demand prediction, such as agriculture.	[11]

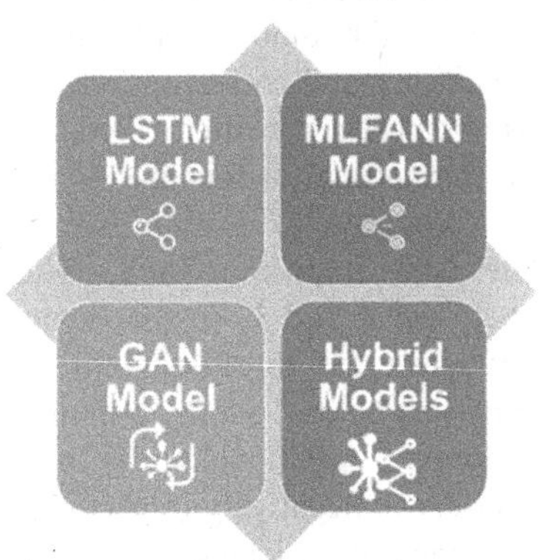

Figure 1.2 Examples of deep learning models, including LSTM, MLFANN, GAN, and hybrid models, commonly used for demand forecasting.

1.3 KEY PROCESSES IN AI-DRIVEN DEMAND FORECASTING

Effective demand forecasting in Industry 4.0 is increasingly dependent on the integration of diverse and relevant data types, allowing businesses to predict future demand with greater accuracy. By utilizing historical data, market indicators, and external variables, businesses can enhance their supply chain management and make informed decisions in a rapidly evolving, data-driven environment [11].

1.3.1 Data Collection

The foundation of AI-driven demand forecasting is built upon the comprehensive collection of data. Historical sales data is crucial as it helps identify trends and patterns over time. Seasonal and cyclical data play a significant role in capturing periodic fluctuations that affect demand. Moreover, market and economic indicators, such as GDP and inflation rates, provide insights into broader economic impacts on demand. Customer and product data, which include insights into consumer behavior and market segmentation, are equally important in understanding shifting preferences and trends. Furthermore, supply chain data such as inventory levels and supplier performance ensures businesses can manage stock effectively, preventing overproduction or stockouts. Lastly, external factors, such as weather conditions, holidays, and social events, also influence demand patterns, making their inclusion essential for a more holistic view [12]. Collecting all these diverse data points lays the groundwork for a more accurate and dynamic demand forecasting system.

1.3.2 Data Preprocessing

Once data has been collected, it must undergo rigorous preprocessing to ensure consistency, accuracy, and readiness for analysis. This involves steps like data cleaning and normalization, which address inconsistencies and ensure uniformity across variables, enhancing the accuracy and reliability of predictive models and optimizing decision-making in the Industry 4.0 landscape. During this phase, data cleaning involves identifying and correcting errors, handling missing values, and removing outliers. Raw datasets are often filled with inconsistencies such as duplicate entries, incorrect formatting, or incomplete data, all of which can skew the results if not addressed properly.

Normalization is the next important step, where data is scaled to a common range, usually between 0 and 1, so that features with larger ranges do not disproportionately influence the forecasting model. Various normalization techniques, such as min-max scaling or Z-score normalization, are applied to ensure all variables are on equal footing. Additionally, the issue of missing data must be resolved, as gaps in the dataset can negatively impact predictive accuracy. Common methods for addressing missing values include mean or median imputation or the use of ML models designed to predict and fill in these gaps. Outlier detection is another critical component of data preprocessing, with techniques such as the Z-score method or the Isolation Forest algorithm used to identify anomalies that could distort the forecasting model's results.

1.3.3 Feature Engineering

Feature engineering is a crucial process in demand forecasting, aimed at transforming raw data into meaningful features that enhance the predictive power of AI models. This process begins with feature extraction, where key characteristics are derived from the raw data. For example, in time-series data, features such as moving averages, trends, and seasonality components are extracted to capture underlying patterns. By identifying these patterns, the model can make more accurate predictions about future demand [12]. Feature selection follows, where the most significant and relevant features are identified for inclusion in the model. Techniques like correlation analysis, mutual information, and recursive feature elimination are often used to filter out irrelevant or redundant features, improving the model's efficiency and accuracy [11].

Feature integration involves combining different data types into a cohesive dataset. This might include merging historical sales data with external factors such as economic indicators or weather patterns, creating a more comprehensive dataset that reflects the diverse variables influencing demand. The integration of such diverse data sources enables the model to make more nuanced and accurate predictions [12]. Moreover, feature engineering allows for the generation of new features, which can uncover hidden relationships within the data. For example, combining multiple features into one or generating time-based features (such as day of the week or month) can reveal patterns not easily observable in the original dataset. This ability to create new, relevant features plays a key role in enhancing model performance and predictive accuracy.

1.3.4 Ensuring Data Quality

Ensuring data quality is fundamental to the success of any AI-driven demand forecasting model. High-quality data not only improves the accuracy of forecasts but also enhances the reliability of decision-making. In addition to standard data preprocessing steps, data transformation techniques, such as log transformation, are often applied to address skewed data distributions, making the data more suitable for ML algorithms.

Feature scaling is another essential component of ensuring data quality, as it guarantees that all features remain within comparable ranges, preventing any one feature from disproportionately influencing the model. Without careful scaling, models that rely on distance-based calculations may yield inaccurate predictions due to the dominance of features with larger values [13]. Organizations that invest in data quality improvements, including thorough data cleaning, normalization, and feature engineering, establish a strong foundation for accurate and actionable demand forecasting models. This structured approach allows businesses to navigate the complexities of modern supply chains with greater confidence, leading to better forecasting outcomes in the era of Industry 4.0.

1.4 ADVANCED MACHINE LEARNING AND DEEP LEARNING TECHNIQUES FOR DEMAND FORECASTING

The integration of ML and DL has significantly improved the accuracy, reliability, and efficiency of demand forecasting across various industries. These advanced techniques are able to capture the intricate complexities of supply chains and consumer behavior, ultimately leading to better decision-making and more effective allocation of resources. Table 1.3 provides a comparative overview of traditional forecasting techniques versus AI-driven models, highlighting their differences in terms of accuracy, data processing capabilities, and adaptability to the complex, dynamic environment.

Table 1.3 Comparison of traditional and AI-driven demand forecasting techniques

Aspect	Traditional Methods (e.g., ARIMA, Exponential Smoothing)	AI-Driven Methods (e.g., LSTM, CNN, GAN)
Data Input	Relies heavily on historical time-series data	Can process multidimensional data from diverse sources
Adaptability	Struggles with sudden changes in demand patterns	Adapts quickly to new patterns and fluctuations
Forecasting Accuracy	Moderate	High, especially in volatile and complex markets
Scalability	Limited, needs manual adjustments for new data	Highly scalable, especially with cloud and edge computing solutions
Model Complexity	Low to medium	High, often requiring significant computational power
Computational Requirements	Low, suited for small to medium datasets	High, requires significant hardware for training and prediction
Interpretability	Easily interpretable	Challenging, often requiring XAI for transparency
Use Cases	Retail, food, basic inventory management	Retail, healthcare, automotive, energy, advanced supply chains

Note: It is based on an extensive literature review of demand forecasting methodologies and their applications across various industries.

With the shift toward AI-driven techniques, businesses can now leverage these models to generate more accurate demand forecasts, improving operational efficiency in increasingly dynamic markets. The subsequent sections explore advanced techniques like CNNs, LSTMs, and autoencoders and their applications across various industries.

1.4.1 Machine Learning Techniques

Traditional ML techniques form the basis for predictive analytics in supply chains and are still widely used in demand forecasting. Linear regression and XGBoost, for example, are commonly employed to predict future demand based on historical data. These models are useful for their simplicity and ability to provide quick insights, making them an integral part of many demand forecasting systems [14].

Another frequently used method is K-means clustering, which is employed to segment customers based on preferences and purchasing behaviors. By identifying groups of customers with similar needs, businesses can tailor inventory storage and production planning to better meet future demand for specific product categories or market segments [15]. While traditional ML models are effective in many contexts, they often struggle to capture the complex, nonlinear patterns present in modern supply chains. This limitation has led to the growing adoption of more advanced DL approaches.

1.4.2 Deep Learning Techniques

DL models, such as CNNs, LSTMs, and Gated Recurrent Units (GRUs), have emerged as powerful tools in demand forecasting, capable of handling much more complex datasets. These models outperform traditional ML methods by automatically learning intricate patterns in demand data that are difficult for linear models to capture [14]. One of the key advantages of DL is automatic feature learning. DL models can automatically identify important features from large datasets without requiring extensive manual feature engineering. This capability enables more granular and precise predictions, which is particularly valuable for industries where demand patterns are volatile and difficult to predict.

1.4.2.1 Autoencoders

Autoencoders are DL models designed for data representation and feature extraction. These models consist of an encoder, which abstracts features from the data, and a decoder, which reconstructs the original input. Autoencoders are particularly useful for applications such as dimensionality reduction, anomaly detection, and data denoising, making them highly valuable in demand forecasting across various sectors [16]. For example, in tourism demand forecasting, autoencoders have demonstrated high accuracy. The target-concatenated autoencoder (TCA), which integrates the prediction target directly into the learning process, has outperformed traditional models, achieving a low mean absolute percentage error (MAPE) of 3.39% in Taiwan and 4.00% in Hawaii [17]. Similarly, a hybrid model combining autoencoders with stacked LSTMs has proven more accurate than either model alone in predicting tourism demand using Google Trends data [18].

Autoencoders have also been applied to renewable energy forecasting. A study that combined a variational autoencoder (VAE) with bidirectional LSTM networks achieved a 39% improvement in MAPE compared to other models. In manufacturing demand forecasting, autoencoders have been integrated into broader ML frameworks to address challenges related to data quality and model interpretability, yielding higher forecasting accuracy [19]. While autoencoders offer significant promise, challenges such as overfitting and the need for large, high-quality datasets remain. Future research must focus on overcoming these obstacles to fully leverage autoencoders in practical demand forecasting applications across a wider range of industries.

1.4.2.2 Convolutional Neural Networks (CNNs)

CNNs are powerful tools for demand forecasting, particularly when used in combination with other DL models. CNNs excel at capturing complex patterns in time series and multivariate data, making them invaluable for improving predictive accuracy in sectors such as retail and manufacturing [20]. For instance, the combination of CNNs with quantile regression (CNN-QR) has been highly effective in electric load forecasting, where it captures both local and global interdependencies in load data, outperforming traditional models [21]. Similarly, the Multi-Channel Data Fusion Network (MCDFN), which integrates CNNs with LSTMs and GRUs, has demonstrated superior performance by extracting both spatial and temporal features from time-series data [22]. One of the primary advantages of CNNs is their ability to facilitate automatic feature learning. By learning and adapting to complex data patterns, CNNs can make more nuanced predictions than traditional models, especially in dynamic environments, particularly in sectors like retail and manufacturing, where demand fluctuates unpredictably.

Despite their impressive performance, challenges remain in the interpretability and integration of CNN-based models with existing systems. While CNNs significantly improve forecasting accuracy, their complexity can make them difficult to interpret and scale in practical applications. Future research should focus on enhancing the explainability and scalability of CNN-based models to ensure they can be effectively integrated into real-world systems [23].

1.4.2.3 Recurrent Neural Networks (RNNs) and LSTMs

Recurrent Neural Networks (RNNs), particularly Long Short-Term Memory (LSTM) networks, are another leading approach for demand forecasting. LSTMs are highly effective at capturing temporal dependencies and handling nonlinear data, making them ideal for predicting fluctuating demand across various industries. LSTM models have consistently demonstrated superior performance compared to traditional methods like ARIMA and SARIMA. In automotive retail, an LSTM model reduced root mean square error (RMSE) and mean absolute error (MAE) by up to 84% and 72%, respectively. When optimized with additional features, such as temperature and time of day, LSTMs have achieved impressive accuracy in short-term load forecasting, highlighting the importance of proper feature selection [24].

Advanced LSTM frameworks, like attLSTM, which integrates attention mechanisms with LSTMs, have further enhanced generalization across different datasets. Studies consistently show that LSTMs outperform other models, such as Artificial Neural Networks (ANNs), especially in load demand forecasting, with mean absolute percentage error (MAPE) values reflecting high accuracy [25]. Hybrid approaches, such as integrating LSTM with ARIMA, have also been explored, yielding high R^2 values (0.98) and low RMSE (2.94) in urban water demand forecasting [26]. Despite their advantages, LSTMs require extensive data and significant computational resources. Nonetheless, their adaptability and precision make them a powerful choice for demand forecasting, particularly when dealing with complex, nonlinear data patterns.

1.4.2.4 Generative Adversarial Networks (GANs)

Generative Adversarial Networks (GANs) are revolutionizing demand forecasting by generating synthetic data to improve model performance. GANs are especially valuable in scenarios where real-world data is insufficient or too costly to collect, making them ideal for handling nonlinear demand and data scarcity [27]. For example, in water demand forecasting, a GAN-based multivariate feature fusion model achieved a 62.61% reduction in mean squared error (MSE) and a 69.15% increase in R^2 score, demonstrating its ability to handle complex multivariate datasets. Using new evaluation criteria, such as the average coverage error (ACE), GANs were also successfully applied to individual electricity demand forecasting, enabling a deeper analysis of which models are most effective for time series predictions [28].

A key strength of GANs lies in their ability to generate synthetic datasets, which is especially useful when real data is either limited or expensive to obtain. By synthesizing artificial records, GANs improve model stability during training on smaller datasets and can enhance overall forecasting accuracy, particularly in scenarios involving nonlinear and complex data patterns [29]. Additionally, GANs often outperform conventional models in handling such complexities. However, challenges like mode collapse, where a GAN fails to generate diverse samples, and unstable training processes persist. Addressing these issues through ongoing research is essential to improving GAN stability and effectiveness in demand forecasting. Such advancements could broaden the use of GANs across various industries and enable their integration with other ML techniques for more reliable forecasting solutions.

1.4.2.5 Deep Reinforcement Learning (DRL)

Deep Reinforcement Learning (DRL) is gaining widespread recognition for its effectiveness in demand forecasting across various industries, demonstrating significant improvements in predictive accuracy and decision-making. With its adaptive learning capabilities, DRL can make predictions that traditional forecasting methods often struggle to achieve. For instance, when combined with DL models, DRL has consistently outperformed traditional demand forecasting techniques. A notable example is an LSTM model powered by DRL, which outperformed both

RNN and GRU models in predicting electricity consumption, showcasing DRL's ability to accurately handle complex time series data [30].

One of the key advantages of DRL is its ability to dynamically adapt to changing market conditions, enhancing the forecasting process in industries like retail, where it improves inventory management and customer personalization. Studies have shown that DRL can respond more quickly to shifting market conditions compared to traditional models, leading to greater operational efficiency and customer satisfaction [31]. DRL has also found successful applications in manufacturing and energy sectors, where it helps balance supply and demand, improving both prediction accuracy and planning efficiency. When paired with the Internet of Things (IoT), DRL enhances forecast accuracy by leveraging real-time data, making it a powerful tool for addressing common issues like data quality and model overfitting. This combination creates more usable and actionable forecasting tools. However, despite these benefits, DRL faces challenges related to its high computational demands and the complexity of interpreting model outcomes, which can hinder its broader adoption.

To overcome these obstacles, continued research and development are essential for advancing DRL's capabilities and making it more accessible for practical applications. As advancements continue, DRL is expected to play an increasingly vital role in demand forecasting, offering sophisticated and flexible solutions across a wide range of industries.

1.4.3 Quantum Machine Learning

Quantum machine learning (QML) is a cutting-edge approach that combines quantum computing with traditional ML techniques. QML holds significant potential for improving the speed and accuracy of demand forecasting in complex, networked supply chains. By leveraging quantum computing's ability to process massive amounts of data simultaneously, QML offers a new frontier for demand forecasting, particularly in scenarios where traditional models fall short due to high computational complexity [32]. However, despite the promising advancements made by ML and DL techniques, challenges such as data quality and the need for frequent model updates to keep pace with changing market conditions remain prevalent. Addressing these issues would be essential for realizing the full potential of AI-driven demand forecasting. To provide a comprehensive overview of the various algorithms utilized in demand forecasting, we have provided Table 1.4, which compares widely used ML, DL, and emerging QML techniques along with their specific applications.

1.5 THE ROLE OF EXPLAINABLE AI (XAI) IN ENHANCING DEMAND FORECASTING

In the context of demand forecasting, Explainable AI (XAI) plays a crucial role in building trust and transparency among stakeholders. As AI systems grow

Table 1.4 Comparative overview of ML, DL, and QML algorithms and their applications

Algorithm	Category	Applications
Linear Regression	ML	Predicting sales trends, inventory levels, and market demand.
Support Vector Machines (SVM)	ML	Classification tasks such as customer segmentation and product categorization.
Decision Trees	ML	Decision support systems, risk assessment, and demand prediction.
Random Forests	ML	Enhancing prediction accuracy in complex datasets, such as forecasting product returns.
K-Means Clustering	ML	Market segmentation, identifying customer purchasing patterns.
Artificial Neural Networks (ANN)	DL	Modelling complex relationships in data for demand forecasting and supply chain optimization.
Convolutional Neural Networks (CNN)	DL	Image recognition tasks, such as analyzing product images for quality control.
Recurrent Neural Networks (RNN)	DL	Time-series forecasting, including predicting seasonal demand fluctuations.
Long Short-Term Memory (LSTM)	DL	Capturing long-term dependencies in data for accurate demand forecasting over extended periods.
Quantum Support Vector Machines (QSVM)	QML	Potentially improving classification tasks with high-dimensional data in supply chain management.
Quantum Kernel Logistic Regression (QKLR)	QML	Enhances pattern recognition and data classification
Variational Quantum Circuits (VQC)	QML	Investigating optimization problems in logistics and resource allocation.

Note: The applications of QML algorithms are currently theoretical and under research, with practical implementations yet to be fully realized.

increasingly complex, it becomes essential for these systems to be understandable and explainable to users. XAI ensures that stakeholders can comprehend the reasoning behind AI-generated forecasts, which is especially important for making high-stakes operational and strategic decisions in industries such as manufacturing and retail [33]. Interpretable models like decision trees and linear regression—are critical for communicating how forecasts are produced, thus fostering trust and confidence in AI systems [34]. Beyond fostering trust, interpretability is also vital for addressing ethical concerns and ensuring accountability [35]. XAI frameworks help tackle issues related to fairness, bias, and discrimination in AI-driven decisions, which is especially important in high-risk fields like finance and healthcare [36]. In these domains, poor decisions influenced by biased models can lead to serious, and sometimes unsafe, consequences. By making AI decisions transparent, XAI not only reduces the risk of automated decision-making errors but also holds both AI users and developers accountable for these outcomes [34, 37].

Figure 1.3 illustrates three key components where XAI enhances demand forecasting: *Trust & Transparency* (ensuring stakeholders understand AI outputs), *Ethical Decision-Making* (addressing fairness, bias, and accountability), and *User-Centric Engagement* (tailoring AI systems to practical user needs). These components collectively build trust, improve system adoption, and ensure actionable, transparent forecasts in complex Industry 4.0 environments. Projects such as XMANAI demonstrate how XAI can be tailored to specific needs, such as location-based demand forecasting. By involving users in reviewing XAI systems, stakeholders are more likely to engage with and trust the outputs generated. This user-centric approach ensures that AI-generated results are not only accurate but also actionable within practical, real-world contexts [33]. This engagement enhances the operational success of AI systems, as users better understand and trust the outputs.

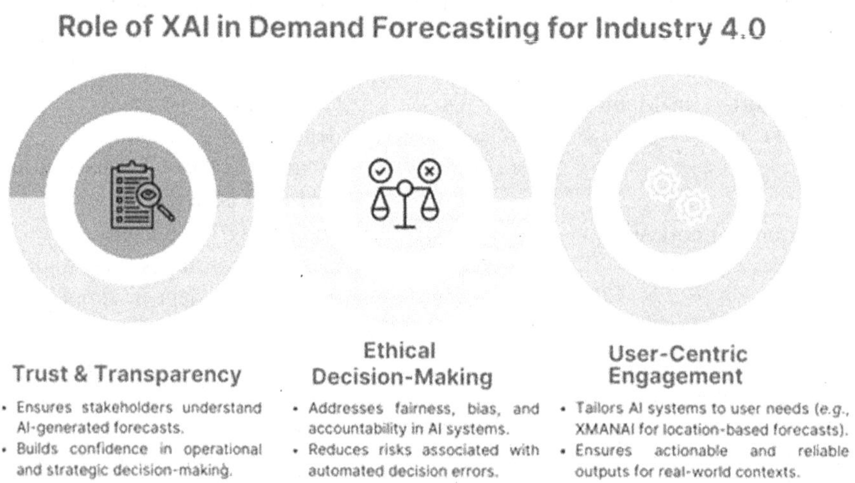

Figure 1.3 The role of explainable AI (XAI) in demand forecasting for Industry 4.0.

However, achieving the right balance between interpretability and performance remains a challenge. While interpretable models build trust, overly simplistic models may fail to capture the complexities of real-world scenarios, leading to suboptimal decisions [38]. Finding the sweet spot between interpretability and model performance remains an open research question in the XAI space. As AI technology continues to advance, the focus would likely shift towards improving the interpretability of complex models, even at the cost of a slight dip in performance, to ensure better comprehension and wider adoption of AI in demand forecasting [34]. This balance could be key to increasing the adoption and success of AI-driven demand forecasting models across various industries.

1.5.1 Enhancing Transparency in Demand Forecasting

Improving transparency in demand forecasting has become increasingly recognized as essential for enhancing accuracy and decision-making across various industries. Recent research highlights several techniques that enhance forecasting processes by combining traditional methods with advanced analytics, thereby addressing the complexities of modern markets [39]. One effective approach involves integrating ML and predictive analytics through hybrid models. For instance, combining K-means clustering, LASSO regression, and LSTM DL models enables businesses to address the inherent uncertainties in demand forecasting. This blend of methods leverages the strengths of each approach, leading to improved accuracy across different sectors [33]. Advanced DL techniques also offer advantages by automating feature learning and recognizing complex patterns, thus surpassing traditional methods in predictive power. These innovations are crucial as they allow models to generate more precise predictions, adapting to the dynamic nature of consumer demand and market fluctuations.

Incorporating real-time data into demand forecasting further enhances prediction accuracy. Using live market intelligence from sales funnels and macroeconomic indicators enables businesses to align their forecasts with current market conditions, making them more responsive and accurate [40]. Improving demand visibility through structured data integration also allows companies to react more promptly to market changes, thereby refining their forecasts [41]. This real-time integration is particularly vital in fast-paced industries where market conditions can shift rapidly, requiring timely adjustments to maintain competitive advantage.

1.5.2 Challenges and Considerations in Integrating XAI

While these advanced techniques significantly improve demand forecasting, challenges remain—particularly in integrating new methods with existing systems and ensuring data quality. Traditional forecasting methods still hold value, especially when combined with innovative approaches like DL. The key lies in finding the right balance between leveraging advanced techniques and maintaining the reliability of established models. This balance will likely yield the most accurate and effective demand forecasting results. As demand forecasting continues to evolve, the focus will likely shift towards optimizing mixed-method approaches that combine traditional methods with cutting-edge ML and DL techniques. Finding the right mix of these methodologies will be essential for maximizing prediction accuracy and utility in increasingly dynamic market environments.

1.6 REAL-WORLD APPLICATIONS AND CASE STUDIES IN DEMAND FORECASTING

AI-driven demand forecasting has significantly improved predictive accuracy and operational efficiency across sectors such as automotive, energy, predictive maintenance, and retail. By analyzing large datasets, these systems optimize resource allocation, enhance decision-making, and improve operational performance. Examples from predictive maintenance, logistics, supply chain management, energy efficiency, and quality control highlight the value of ML and DL techniques, as detailed in Table 1.5. Despite their promise, challenges like data quality, model interpretability, and workforce skills must be addressed to unlock AI's full potential in demand forecasting.

Table 1.5 Key industry applications of AI in demand forecasting

Industry	AI Model/Technique	Key Use Case	Results
Energy	CNN-LSTM Hybrid, Fuzzy Logic	Energy demand forecasting in smart grids	39% improvement in demand forecasting accuracy, reduced energy waste through optimized energy consumption [4].
Automotive	DRL, VAE-based knowledge distillation	Forecasting demand for electric vehicle parts	20% improvement in demand forecasting accuracy, optimized supply chain [26, 27]. In addition, a lightweight VAE-based intrusion detection system for autonomous vehicles is applied to achieve perfect attack detection with minimal computation and enhanced transparency via XAI [53].
Predictive Maintenance	LSTM, Random Forests	Predicting maintenance schedules for equipment	Improved operational efficiency and equipment reliability through predictive maintenance [34].
Retail	CNN, attLSTM	Demand prediction for fast-moving consumer goods	15% improvement in demand accuracy, 10% reduction in stockouts [42, 43].

Note: Key Industry Applications of AI in Demand Forecasting, based on an extensive review of the literature and real-world case studies.

1.6.1 Predictive Maintenance

Predictive maintenance is a critical application of AI-driven tools that enhances operational efficiency by preemptively identifying and addressing equipment failures. Leveraging advanced ML models, industries can optimize maintenance schedules, reduce costs, and minimize downtime.

1.6.1.1 Key Benefits and Techniques

Predictive maintenance powered by ML offers significant advantages across industries, enhancing efficiency, reliability, and resource utilization through advanced analytical models and real-time insights. The following elements outline key benefits and techniques, along with sector-specific applications that demonstrate the transformative impact of AI-driven maintenance systems.

- ***Efficiency Improvement*:** ML techniques, such as LSTM networks and Random Forest models, enable organizations to detect early signs of equipment wear and predict failures. For example, in manufacturing and logistics, AI models analyze equipment usage patterns to minimize unexpected breakdowns and optimize maintenance activities [42].
- ***Reliability and Resource Optimization*:** AI-driven systems analyze historical data and real-time performance metrics to predict maintenance needs accurately. This proactive approach increases equipment reliability and ensures efficient allocation of resources, particularly in sectors like manufacturing and energy [42].

Sector-Specific Applications include the following:

- **Renewable Energy:** Predictive models assess battery health and performance, ensuring uninterrupted energy storage and delivery [43].
- **Electric Vehicles (EVs):** AI tools optimize battery maintenance schedules, enhancing the longevity and efficiency of EV components [43].
- **Fleet Management:** In logistics, predictive maintenance reduces vehicle downtime, improving overall fleet productivity [43].

1.6.1.2 Challenges and Future Directions

Despite its benefits, implementing AI for predictive maintenance presents challenges:

- **Data Quality and Infrastructure:** Accurate predictions depend on high-quality, comprehensive data, which may not always be available [44].
- **Workforce Skills Gap:** Organizations face the challenge of training employees to effectively use AI-driven systems for predictive maintenance [45].
- **Scalability Issues:** Integrating AI models across legacy systems requires significant investment and infrastructure upgrades.

1.6.2 Quality Control

ML and DL models play a crucial role in enhancing quality control by improving the precision of demand forecasting in real-world industrial scenarios.

- **Disaster Management:** An AI-based framework for earthquake relief in Türkiye achieved a perfect R^2 score, accurately predicting demand for relief supplies by analyzing historical and socioeconomic data [46].
- **Inventory Optimization:** ML models for intermittent demand forecasting have outperformed traditional methods, reducing errors and enabling dynamic reorder recommendations in manufacturing and retail sectors [47].
- **Transfer Learning Applications:** Real-world implementations of transfer learning have shown a 65% reduction in mean square error for intermittent demand, proving its applicability in cases with limited training data [47]. Furthermore, combining both quantitative and qualitative data in neural network models has proven superior in enhancing forecasting accuracy, emphasizing the value of diverse data inputs [48].

These examples reflect how AI-driven quality control frameworks address real-world forecasting challenges, improving accuracy and resource efficiency across industries.

1.6.3 Resource Optimization

Resource optimization is another key real-world application of AI in demand forecasting, where advanced algorithms enable organizations to allocate resources more effectively.

- **Energy Demand Management:** In one practical case, the GR-ResNet-50 algorithm achieved a remarkably low Mean Absolute Percentage Error (0.007%) while reducing execution time by 20 seconds compared to traditional methods [49].
- **Disaster Relief:** An AI-based forecasting framework for earthquake relief in Türkiye optimized resource allocation by predicting demand accurately through historical data analysis [46].
- **Enterprise Resource Planning (ERP):** Integrating AI into ERP systems has allowed companies such as DEOS to improve demand forecast accuracy, reduce costs, and enhance productivity [50].

These real-world applications demonstrate how AI tools contribute to resource efficiency and cost optimization in energy, disaster management, and enterprise operations.

1.6.4 Logistics and Supply Chain Management

AI-driven demand forecasting has transformed logistics and supply chain operations by enhancing accuracy, responsiveness, and efficiency in real-world applications.

- **Inventory Management:** Advanced DL models, such as attLSTM, have been implemented to achieve up to a 15% improvement in forecasting accuracy and a 10% reduction in stockouts [51].

- **Operational Efficiency:** Companies employ real-time tracking technologies, such as computer vision, to monitor and manage resources effectively, ensuring streamlined supply chain operations.
- **Dynamic Forecasting:** Organizations benefit from AI models that adapt to market fluctuations, enabling them to align inventory levels with demand patterns and reduce operational risks.

However, challenges such as data privacy concerns and high implementation costs remain significant barriers. Addressing these issues is essential for advancing the use of AI applications in supply chain management. These examples illustrate AI's practical role in optimizing supply chain management through enhanced accuracy and responsiveness.

1.6.5 Energy Efficiency

Real-world case studies show that AI techniques have significantly contributed to improving energy efficiency through better demand forecasting and optimization strategies.

- **Building Energy Management:** Hybrid DL models, such as CNN-LSTM, have been successfully applied to predict energy consumption patterns, enabling informed decisions for energy optimization [52].
- **Uncertainty in Demand Forecasting:** A study on Indian energy demand utilized fuzzy logic integrated with ML models to systematically address demand uncertainties for sustainable planning.
- **Practical Model Selection:** While complex ML models offer high accuracy, simpler and interpretable models are often preferred in real-world implementations due to their usability and transparency.

Despite the undeniable benefits of AI and ML in energy efficiency, challenges such as data privacy concerns and the shortage of skilled personnel to implement and maintain these technologies remain significant barriers to fully realizing their potential.

1.7 CHALLENGES IN IMPLEMENTING AI FOR DEMAND FORECASTING

Implementing AI for demand forecasting across industries faces significant challenges, especially regarding data quality and availability. The performance of AI models heavily depends on the quality of input data. In practice, organizations frequently encounter issues such as missing data, outliers, and lack of context. For instance, in water demand forecasting, AI models must detect outliers and handle missing data to improve reliability. In agricultural supply chains, AI struggles with estimating sporadic demand, especially when dealing with zero values. Researchers have addressed this by modifying frameworks like k-NN, which improves forecasting accuracy by better detecting sporadic demand patterns [54]. Furthermore, the agricultural sector faces additional obstacles, such as inadequate data infrastructure and a lack of skilled professionals to effectively engage with AI systems [44]. In transportation traffic forecasting, the absence of complete spatio-temporal data limits the effectiveness of AI models in long-term forecasting [55].

While AI has great potential to enhance demand forecasting, data quality and availability issues must be resolved to ensure success across all sectors. Several significant challenges continue to hinder the implementation of AI-driven demand forecasting models, including data quality issues, computational demands, and model interpretability. Table 1.6 summarizes these key challenges and outlines potential solutions based on current literature and expert insights from the authors in this study. Moreover, other limitations such as scalability and human-AI collaboration further complicate the practical implementation of AI in demand forecasting. Figure 1.4 highlights the key limitations and challenges that organizations face when deploying AI-driven forecasting solutions.

Table 1.6 Challenges and solutions in AI-driven demand forecasting

Challenge	Description	Proposed Solution
Data Quality	Inconsistent, missing, or incomplete data	Data cleaning, preprocessing, use of GANs for data generation
Computational Demands	High hardware requirements for DL models	Use of cloud computing, distributed processing
Scalability	Difficulty in scaling AI models to new contexts	Adoption of hybrid models and federated learning approaches
Human-AI Collaboration	Information asymmetry between AI systems and human planners	XAI integration, enhanced user interfaces
Model Interpretability	Lack of transparency in AI predictions	Explainable AI, use of simpler interpretable models
Sporadic Demand	Difficulty in predicting rare or zero-value demands	Use of zero-inclusive k-NN frameworks

Note: Challenges and Solutions in AI-Driven Demand Forecasting, based on an extensive review of the literature and expert insights from the authors.

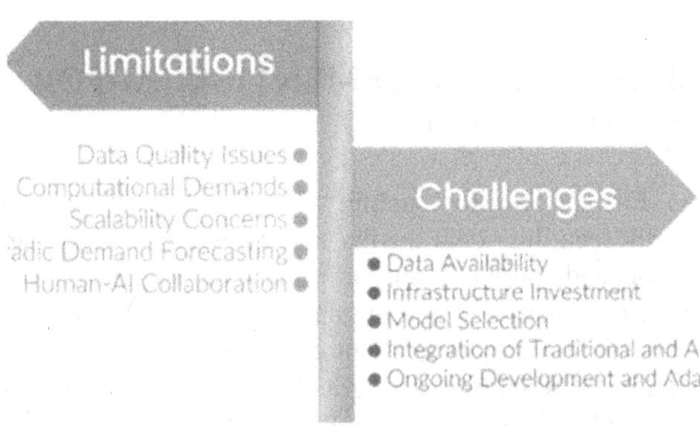

Figure 1.4 Key limitations and challenges in AI-driven demand forecasting.

1.7.1 Computational Challenges

Another significant challenge lies in the computational demands of AI models, particularly when dealing with large, complex datasets. DL algorithms, which are commonly used in demand forecasting, require substantial computing power to identify nonlinear relationships in data. This is often prohibitive for organizations with limited infrastructure [1]. For instance, processing real-time data in agriculture and energy requires high-performance hardware and software solutions, adding to the computational burden [44]. Additionally, selecting the right AI model is critical, as product characteristics often require a tailored approach to achieve accurate forecasts. Although performance metrics like Mean Absolute Percentage Error and Root Mean Squared Error are needed to assess model accuracy, they can also increase computing cost. Poor-quality data or insufficient access to data can further compromise AI models, leading to inaccurate forecasts and added computational workload [44]. Organizations need to invest in both infrastructure and skilled personnel to fully leverage AI solutions, which remains a major hurdle. Until these computational and infrastructure challenges are addressed, the true value of AI in demand forecasting may be difficult to realize.

1.7.2 Scalability Issues

Scalability is another key issue when implementing AI for demand forecasting. Effective data management, model integration, and collaboration between human decision-makers and AI systems are critical for scaling AI applications. However, AI models often struggle to integrate data from multiple sources, which is essential for accurate forecasting. AI-Forecast, for example, emphasizes the need for a complete data-driven chain to effectively manage data and provide reliable forecasts. In traffic forecasting, AI models often lack the necessary spatial context for long-term scalability, whereas traditional methods can more easily scale by integrating large amounts of data into their forecasts [51].

1.7.3 Human-AI Collaboration Challenges

Collaboration between human planners and AI systems also presents challenges, particularly in overcoming information asymmetry [55]. This gap in understanding can inhibit effective decision-making. Research has shown that addressing these asymmetries is crucial to improving forecasting accuracy. Hybrid models that combine AI with traditional methods have demonstrated greater scalability and adaptability, particularly in complex fields like manufacturing. AI is also less effective when handling sporadic demand with frequent zero values, as traditional methods can struggle to detect patterns. To address this, zero-inclusive k-NN frameworks have been developed to analyze both zero and non-zero data.

Furthermore, there are emerging and promising solutions to these demand forecasting challenges, particularly for addressing zero-value issues within AI systems. The full potential of AI to deliver innovative predictions depends on its continuous development and adaptation, as it navigates challenges related to data integration, human-AI collaboration, and complex demand forecasting patterns.

1.8 FUTURE TRENDS AND INNOVATIONS

The future of demand forecasting in Industry 4.0 holds significant potential for impactful improvements as AI becomes mainstream. Emerging trends focus on enhancing the understanding of models, specifically how and why predictions are made, with tools like XAI, federated learning, and advanced edge computing. Table 1.7 summarizes these emerging technologies, their key features, potential impact on demand forecasting, and the current limitations that must be addressed for broader adoption. These innovations could not only improve data privacy but also generate real-time analytics at the decision-making source, enhancing operational efficiency [56].

Table 1.7 Emerging technologies and their impact on demand forecasting

Technology	Key Features	Potential Impact on Demand Forecasting	Current Limitations
Explainable AI (XAI)	Provides interpretability for complex AI models	Helps stakeholders trust and understand AI predictions	Trade-off between accuracy and interpretability
Federated Learning	Decentralized learning without data sharing	Ensures privacy in demand forecasting, improves global models	Requires advanced infrastructure
Quantum Machine Learning (QML)	Leverages quantum computing for fast data processing	Potential game-changer for processing large datasets	Currently in experimental phases
Edge Computing	Processes data at the source (IoT)	Enables real-time demand forecasting at the operational level	Requires hardware integration
Hybrid AI Models	Combines AI with traditional forecasting models	Improves forecast accuracy, especially for complex supply chains	Model complexity can increase

Note: Emerging technologies and their impact on demand forecasting, based on an extensive review of the literature and expert insights from the authors.

As organizations transition to effectively adopting AI solutions, the focus may shift towards hybrid models that blend traditional statistical techniques with contemporary DL approaches. These hybrid models address the limitations of relying solely on historical data for chronological assessments, adapting to the complexities of modern supply chains characterized by volatility and diverse data sources. QML is also presenting itself as a potential game-changer, utilizing quantum computing capabilities to process large datasets and offer actionable insights for demand forecasting. Creating reliable and comprehensive forecasts requires working with a range of inputs—both qualitative and quantitative. This includes non-traditional data points, such as consumer behavior metrics and economic indicators. Enhancements in data processing and feature engineering are essential for maintaining high-quality outputs and improving prediction accuracy.

Additionally, sustainability and resource optimization are becoming central to driving improvements in predictive maintenance and quality control processes. AI is gradually becoming a core component of operational efficiency, contributing to advancements in manufacturing and supply chain management. As these trends evolve, organizations need to adapt quickly to shifting market dynamics and consumer demands, ultimately achieving greater flexibility and efficiency.

1.9 CONCLUSION

The evolution of AI-driven tools in demand forecasting marks a transformative shift across multiple industries, extending beyond manufacturing into sectors such as healthcare, retail, and logistics. As the demand for timely and accurate decision-making intensifies, these technologies are becoming indispensable for enhancing resource allocation, optimizing operations, and improving customer satisfaction. The growing emphasis on sustainability and operational efficiency is further compelling organizations to adopt predictive analytics, which facilitates more effective resource management and strategic planning. The future of demand forecasting rests on the continuous refinement of methodologies and tools, enabling businesses to better navigate increasingly complex and dynamic environments. As AI-driven forecasting continues to expand, the ability to generate reliable, data-driven insights becomes essential for maintaining a competitive edge. Ultimately, the advancements discussed in this chapter lay the foundation for more sophisticated, adaptable, and trustworthy forecasting frameworks, positioning industries to thrive in a rapidly evolving landscape.

REFERENCES

[1] Aderibigbe, A.O., E.C. Ani, P.E. Ohenhen, N.C. Ohalete and D.O. Daraojimba. 2023. Enhancing energy efficiency with AI: A review of machine learning models in electricity demand forecasting. Engineering Science and Technology Journal. 4(6): 341–356. doi: 10.51594/ESTJ.V4I6.636.

[2] Singh, S., B. Yadav and R. Batheri. 2023. Industry 4.0: Meeting the challenges of demand sensing in the automotive industry. IEEE Engineering Management Review. 51(4): 179–184. doi: 10.1109/EMR.2023.3292331.

[3] Quiñones-Rivera, H., O. Rubiano-Ovalle and W. Alfonso-Morales. 2023. Demand forecasting using a hybrid model based on artificial neural networks: A study case on electrical products. Journal of Industrial Engineering and Management. 16(2): 363–381. doi: 10.3926/jiem.3928.

[4] Ingle, C., D. Bakliwal, J. Jain, P. Singh, P. Kale and V. Chhajed. 2021. Demand forecasting: literature review on various methodologies. 2021 12th International Conference on Computing Communication and Networking Technologies, ICCCNT 2021. doi: 10.1109/ICCCNT51525.2021.9580139.

[5] Rahman, Y. 2023. Effects of taxes on consumer behavior: A macro-economic study. Golden Ratio of Taxation Studies. 3(2): 67–75. doi: 10.52970/GRTS.V3I2.633.

[6] Kimes, S.E., R.B. Chase, S. Choi, P.Y. Lee and E.N. Ngonzi. "Restaurant revenue management. Business Cornell Hotel and Restaurant Administration Quarterly. 39(3): 32–39. doi: 10.1177/001088049803900308.

[7] Fattah, J., L. Ezzine, Z. Aman, H. El Moussami and A. Lachhab. 2018. Forecasting of demand using ARIMA model. International Journal of Engineering Business Management. 10: 1–9. doi: 10.1177/1847979018808673

[8] Xiong, R., E.P. Nichols, Y. Shen, R. Xiong, E.P. Nichols and Y. Shen. 2015. Deep learning stock volatility with Google Domestic trends. ArXiv, arXiv: 1512.04916. doi: 10.48550/ARXIV.1512.04916.

[9] Kilimci, Z.H., A.O. Akyuz, M. Uysal, S. Akyokus, M.O. Uysal, B. Atak Bulbul, et al. 2019. An improved demand forecasting model using deep learning approach and proposed decision integration strategy for supply chain. Complexity. 2019(1): 9067367. doi: 10.1155/2019/9067367.

[10] Li, D., D. Chen, B. Jin, L. Shi, J. Goh and S.K. Ng. 2019. MAD-GAN: Multivariate anomaly detection for time series data with generative adversarial networks. Lecture Notes in Computer Science (including subseries Lecture Notes in Artificial Intelligence and Lecture Notes in Bioinformatics). 11730 LNCS. 703–716. doi: 10.1007/978-3-030-30490-4_56.

[11] Wang, J. 2024. Machine learning applications in biomass supply chain management and optimization. Bioresources. 19(4): 6961–6963. doi: 10.15376/BIORES.19.4.6961-6963.

[12] Pikus, M. and J. Wąs. 2024. Predictive modeling of renewable energy purchase prices using deep learning based on Polish power grid data for small hybrid PV microinstallations. Energies. 17(3): 628. doi: 10.3390/EN17030628.

[13] Mallikharjuna Rao, K., G. Saikrishna and K. Supriya. 2023. Data preprocessing techniques: Emergence and selection towards machine learning models—A practical review using HPA dataset. Multimedia Tools and Applications. 82(24): 37177–37196. doi: 10.1007/S11042-023-15087-5.

[14] Varsha Poranki, R., K. Pattima, M. Yalagala, N. Suraboina and K. Thrilochana Devi. 2024. Forecasting the future: A comparative analysis of ML and DL models in supply chain demand prediction. EPRA International Journal of Research and Development (IJRD). 9(3): 1–1. doi: 10.36713/EPRA16211.

[15] Anitha, S. and R. Neelakandan. 2024. A Demand forecasting model leveraging machine learning to decode customer preferences for new fashion products. Complexity. 2024(1): 8425058. doi: 10.1155/2024/8425058.

[16] Agrawal, K. and N. Nargund. 2024. Deep learning in Industry 4.0: Transforming manufacturing through data-driven innovation. Lecture Notes in Computer Science (including subseries Lecture Notes in Artificial Intelligence and Lecture Notes in Bioinformatics). 14501: 222–236. doi: 10.1007/978-3-031-50583-6_15.

[17] Chizari, H., A.M. Rahmani, A. Monaco, R.-I. Chang, C.-Y. Tsai and Y.-W. Chang. 2024. Enhancing visitor forecasting with target-concatenated autoencoder and ensemble learning. Machine Learning and Knowledge Extraction. 6(3): 1673–1698. doi: 10.3390/MAKE6030083.

[18] Laaroussi, H., F. Guerouate and M. Sbihi. 2023. A novel hybrid deep learning approach for tourism demand forecasting. International Journal of Electrical and Computer Engineering (IJECE). 13(2): 1989–1996. doi: 10.11591/ijece.v13i2.

[19] Sistla, S.M.K., G. Krishnamoorthy, J. Jeyaraman and B.K. Konidena. 2024. Machine learning for demand forecasting in manufacturing. IJFMR—International Journal for Multidisciplinary Research. 6(1). doi: 10.36948/IJFMR.2024.V06I01.14204.

[20] de Castro Moraes, T., X.M. Yuan and E.P. Chew. 2024. Hybrid convolutional long short-term memory models for sales forecasting in retail. Journal of Forecasting. 43(5): 1278–1293. doi: 10.1002/FOR.3073.

[21] Jiotsop-Foze, W.P., A. Hernández-Del-Valle and F. Venegas-Martínez. 2024. Electrical load forecasting to plan the increase in renewable energy sources and electricity demand: A CNN-QR-RTCF and deep learning approach. International Journal of Energy Economics and Policy. 14(4): 186–194. doi: 10.32479/IJEEP.15773.

[22] Jahin, M.A., A. Shahriar and M. Al Amin. 2024. MCDFN: Supply chain demand forecasting via an explainable multi-channel data fusion network model. Accessed: Aug. 24, 2024. [Online]. Available: https://arxiv.org/abs/2405.15598v2

[23] Hondoma, T. and T. Hondoma. 2024. Forecasting demand using recurrent neural networks (RNN). 197–215. doi: 10.4018/979-8-3693-2165-2CH011. Available: https://services.igi-global.com/resolvedoi/resolve.aspx?doi=10.4018/979-8-3693-2165-2.ch011

[24] Mostafa, T., M.M. Fouda and M.G. Abdo. 2024. Short-term load forecasting employing recurrent neural networks. International Conference on Smart Applications, Communications and Networking, SmartNets. doi: 10.1109/SMARTNETS61466.2024.10577742

[25] Bareth, R., A. Yadav, S. Gupta and M. Pazoki. 2024. Daily average load demand forecasting using LSTM model based on historical load trends. IET Generation, Transmission and Distribution. 18(5): 952–962. doi: 10.1049/GTD2.13132.

[26] Xu, J. and Z. Tongji. 2024. Forecasting Water Demand With the Long Short-Term Memory Deep Learning Mode. 17(1): 1–18. doi: 10.4018/IJITSA.338910. Available: https://services.igi-global.com/resolvedoi/resolve.aspx?doi=10.4018/IJITSA.338910

[27] Yang, C., J. Meng, B. Liu, Z. Wang and K. Wang. 2024. A water demand forecasting model based on generative adversarial networks and multivariate feature fusion. Water. 16(12): 1731. doi: 10.3390/W16121731.

[28] Mohammad Jafari, S. 2024. Novel Generative Adversarial Network Architectures for Generating Image Data. Toronto Metropolitan University. doi: 10.32920/26052700.v1.

[29] Sharma, P., M. Kumar, H.K. Sharma and S.M. Biju. 2024. Generative adversarial networks (GANs): Introduction, taxonomy, variants, limitations and applications. Multimedia Tools and Applications. 1–48. doi: 10.1007/S11042-024-18767-Y.

[30] Mustafa GÖKÇE, M., S. Yazar and C. Author. 2024. A deep learning-based demand forecasting system for planning electricity generation. Kahramanmaras Sutcu Imam University Journal of Engineering Sciences. 27(2): 511–522. doi: 10.17780/KSUJES.1399160.

[31] Pulari, S.R., T.S. Murugesh, S.K. Vasudevan and A.B. Ramakrishnan. 2024. Reinforcement learning for demand forecasting and customized services. Cognitive Analytics and Reinforcement Learning: Theories, Techniques and Applications. 123–134. doi: 10.1002/9781394214068.CH6.

[32] Sehrawat, S.K., P.K. Dutta, A.B. Bhatia and P. Whig. 2024. Predicting Demand in Supply Chain Networks With Quantum Machine Learning Approach. 33–47. doi:

10.4018/979-8-3693-4107-0.CH002. Available: https://services.igi-global.com/resolvedoi/resolve.aspx?doi=10.4018/979-8-3693-4107-0.ch002

[33] Lampathaki, F., E. Bosani, E. Biliri, E. Ichtiaroglou, A. Louca, D. Syrrafos, et al. 2024. XAI for product demand planning: Models, experiences and lessons learnt. Artificial Intelligence in Manufacturing. 437–458. doi: 10.1007/978-3-031-46452-2_25

[34] Kumawat, N.K. 2024. Explainable AI: Interpretable models for transparent decision-making. International Journal of Food and Nutritional Sciences. 09(03). doi: 10.48047/IJFANS/09/03/30

[35] Goktas, P. 2024. Ethics, transparency, and explainability in generative AI decision-making systems: A comprehensive bibliometric study. Journal of Decision Systems. 1–29. doi: 10.1080/12460125.2024.2410042

[36] Goktas, P. and A. Grzybowski. 2025. Shaping the future of healthcare: Ethical clinical challenges and pathways to trustworthy AI. Journal of Clinical Medicine. 14(5): 1605. doi: 10.3390/jcm14051605

[37] Goktas, P. and T. Dirsehan. 2025. Using PLS-SEM and XAI for causal-predictive services marketing research. Journal of Services Marketing. 39(1): 53–68. doi: 10.1108/JSM-10-2023-0377

[38] Júnior, J.S.S., C. Gaspar, J. Mendes and C. Premebida. 2024. Assessing interpretability of data-driven fuzzy models: Application in industrial regression problems. Expert Systems. e13710. doi: 10.1111/EXSY.13710

[39] Liu, T.L. and D. Wanvarie. 2024. Enhancing financial market predictions in Taiwan: A hybrid approach of traditional analysis and machine learning techniques. 5th Technology Innovation Management and Engineering Science International Conference, TIMES-iCON 2024 - Proceedings. doi: 10.1109/TIMES-ICON61890.2024.10630738

[40] Sokol, K. and P. Flach. 2024. Interpretable representations in explainable AI: from theory to practice. Data Mining and Knowledge Discovery. 1–39. doi: 10.1007/S10618-024-01010-5

[41] Yoon, D. 2023. Methodology for Improving the Performance of Demand Forecasting Through Machine Learning. doi: 10.21203/RS.3.RS-2637740/v1

[42] Dhanraj, D., A. Sharma, G. Kaur, S. Mishra, P. Naik and A. Singh. 2023. Comparison of different machine learning algorithms for predictive maintenance. International Conference for Advancement in Technology, ICONAT. doi: 10.1109/ICONAT57137.2023.10080334

[43] Yedla, H., L.R. Koppada and R.S. Bodala. 2024. Advanced battery management: forecasting health, state of charge and maintenance needs using AI and ML models (LSTM, Gradient Boosting, SVR, Random Forest). Asian Journal of Research in Computer Science. 17(8): 46–57. doi: 10.9734/AJRCOS/2024/V17I7489

[44] Elufioye, O.A., C.U. Ike, O. Odeyemi, F.O. Usman and N.Z. Mhlongo. 2024. AI-driven predictive analytics in agricultural supply chains: A review. Assessing the Benefits and Challenges of AI in Forecasting Demand and Optimizing Supply in Agriculture. Computer Science and IT Research Journal. 5(2): 473–497. doi: 10.51594/CSITRJ.V5I2.817

[45] Gunderia, A., P. Agarwal, V.B. Nikam and A.N. Bambole. 2024. AI approaches for predictive maintenance in road bridge infrastructure. International Conference on Smart Applications, Communications and Networking, SmartNets. doi: 10.1109/SMARTNETS61466.2024.10577641

[46] Biswas, S., D. Kumar, M. Hajiaghaei-Keshteli and U.K. Bera. 2024. An AI-based framework for earthquake relief demand forecasting: A case study in Türkiye. International Journal of Disaster Risk Reduction. 102: 104287. doi: 10.1016/J.IJDRR.2024.104287

[47] Kiefer, D., F. Grimm and C. van Dinther. 2022. Artificial intelligence in supply chain management: Investigation of transfer learning to improve demand forecasting of intermittent time series with deep learning. *In*: Proceedings of the Annual Hawaii International Conference on System Sciences. 2022: 1656–1665. doi: 10.24251/HICSS.2022.205

[48] Khosrowabadi, N., K. Hoberg and C. Imdahl. 2022. Evaluating human behaviour in response to AI recommendations for judgemental forecasting. European Journal of Operational Research. 303(3): 1151–1167. doi: 10.1016/J.EJOR.2022.03.017

[49] Wang, J., Y. Zhou, K. Liu and Z. Weng. 2024. Demand forecasting and resource scheduling of independent energy storage market in power grid with deep learning. Journal of Electrical Systems. 20(6s): 01–10. doi: 10.52783/JES.2609

[50] Fathima, F., R. Inparaj, D. Thuvarakan, R. Wickramarachchi and I. Fernando. 2024. Impact of AI-based predictive analytics on demand forecasting in ERP systems: A systematic literature review. *In*: Proceedings—International Research Conference on Smart Computing and Systems Engineering, SCSE. doi: 10.1109/SCSE61872.2024.10550480

[51] Madas, M.A., V. Pasupuleti, B. Thuraka, C.S. Kodete and S. Malisetty. 2024. Enhancing supply chain agility and sustainability through machine learning: Optimization Techniques for logistics and inventory management. Logistics 2024. 8(3): 73. doi: 10.3390/LOGISTICS8030073

[52] Natarajan, Y., K.R. Sai-Preethaa, G. Wadhwa, Y. Choi, Z. Chen, D.E. Lee, et al. 2024. Enhancing building energy efficiency with IoT-driven hybrid deep learning models for accurate energy consumption prediction. Sustainability. 16(5): 1925. doi: 10.3390/SU16051925

[53] Yagiz, M.A., P. MohajerAnsari, M.D. Pesé and P. Goktas. 2024. Transforming in-vehicle network intrusion detection: VAE-based knowledge distillation meets explainable AI. *In*: Proceedings of the sixth workshop on CPS&IoT security and privacy. 93–103. doi: 10.1145/3690134.3694819

[54] Hasan, N., N. Ahmed and S.M. Ali. 2024. Improving sporadic demand forecasting using a modified k-nearest neighbor framework. Engineering Applications of Artificial Intelligence. 129: 107633. doi: 10.1016/J.ENGAPPAI.2023.107633

[55] Khairi, S., A. Abbas, M.S. Sharif and A. Apeagyei. 2023. Artificial intelligence applications in road traffic forecasting: A review of current research. 2023 International Conference on Innovation and Intelligence for Informatics, Computing and Technologies, 3ICT 2023. 38–43. doi: 10.1109/3ICT60104.2023.10391677

[56] Agrawal, K., P. Goktas, B. Sahoo, S. Swain and A. Bandyopadhyay. 2025. IoT-based service allocation in edge computing using game theory. *In*: Bramas, Q., Chatterjee, B., Devismes, S., Egan, M., Mandal, P.S., Mukhopadhyaya, K., et al. Distributed Computing and Intelligent Technology. ICDCIT 2025. Lecture Notes in Computer Science. Vol. 15507. Springer, Cham. doi: 10.1007/978-3-031-81404-4_4

Chapter **2**

AI Engineering for Meeting the Demand of Open-Source Cyber Analytics

Fahim K Sufi

PhD (Comp Sc), M Eng (Comp Sys), Dip (Mgmt), Grad Cert (Res Com), B (Comp Sc), CTO, COEUS Institute, USA

2.1 INTRODUCTION

In today's hyperconnected digital landscape, cyber threats are escalating at an unprecedented rate, affecting a wide array of sectors, including finance, utilities, and critical infrastructure. As cyber-attacks become more sophisticated and frequent, the demand for timely, actionable intelligence is more crucial than ever before. Open-source cyber intelligence (OSINT) has emerged as a critical tool for identifying, analyzing, and responding to these evolving threats [1–3]. OSINT leverages publicly available information, such as news reports, social media data, and government publications, to provide real-time insights into cyber events [4]. However, the sheer volume of global data available presents significant challenges in terms of processing, filtering, and extracting meaningful intelligence in a timely manner.

Artificial intelligence (AI) has emerged as a transformative technology in addressing these challenges. By automating the collection, classification, and analysis of massive datasets, AI has dramatically improved the efficiency and

*For Correspondence: research@fahimsufi.com

DOI: 10.1201/9781003541875-2

accuracy of OSINT systems. The integration of machine learning algorithms, particularly those based on natural language processing (NLP) and neural networks, enables the real-time monitoring of cyber events from diverse data sources, offering unprecedented situational awareness to cybersecurity analysts and decision-makers. Moreover, AI-driven systems can perform tasks such as entity detection, sentiment analysis, and anomaly detection, providing deeper insights into the complex interrelations of global cyber events.

A key innovation in the application of AI to OSINT is the utilization of Generative Pre-trained Transformers (GPT) [4]. GPT models, renowned for their ability to generate and comprehend human-like text, have revolutionized the field of news classification and cyber intelligence [5–8]. These models excel in identifying patterns within unstructured textual data, such as news articles and social media posts, making them invaluable tools for predicting and understanding cyber threats [9–11]. Recent advancements have demonstrated the efficacy of combining GPT models with other AI techniques, such as convolutional neural networks (CNNs), to classify cyber events with remarkable accuracy and speed [2, 4, 7].

This chapter explores how AI and chatbot technology can be harnessed to meet the growing demand for open-source cyber intelligence. It presents a novel system that integrates GPT-based news classification with real-time query handling via a chatbot interface. The system monitors global news sources, classifies cyber-related incidents, and provides structured datasets for advanced machine learning analyses such as correlation, root cause detection, and regression. By leveraging AI and chatbot technology, this framework allows users to query and receive real-time intelligence on cyber events, delivering actionable insights directly to decision-makers. It is worth noting that although chatbot technology has been applied across various domains, its use in news analytics and open-source cyber intelligence remains limited according to existing research [12–15]. While the primary focus of this chapter is the application of AI for real-time cyber intelligence, its implications extend beyond cybersecurity. The methodologies presented here, particularly in data classification, trend analysis, and anomaly detection, provide a foundational framework for demand forecasting. By identifying patterns and predicting future needs, the system aligns with the broader theme of AI-driven demand forecasting, enabling organizations to anticipate cybersecurity challenges and allocate resources proactively.

The following sections will delve into the architecture of this system, its application in cyber intelligence, and the potential it holds for transforming the landscape of cybersecurity. Additionally, we will address the challenges and limitations of current AI-driven OSINT solutions, and propose directions for future research and development in this field.

2.2 BACKGROUND AND RELATED WORK

This section would provide the background and set the necessary contextual information.

2.2.1 Open-Source Intelligence (OSINT) in Cybersecurity

Open-source intelligence (OSINT) has gained widespread recognition as a vital component in the cybersecurity landscape. OSINT refers to the collection and analysis of data derived from publicly available sources, including news media, social media platforms, blogs, government reports, and various other open- access digital platforms [3, 16, 17]. In the context of cyber intelligence, OSINT enables real-time monitoring of events and the identification of potential cyber threats, thereby assisting organizations in proactively responding to attacks [1, 2, 17]. The reliance on publicly available information allows cybersecurity analysts to gain a broader understanding of threat environments, including emerging attack vectors and the geospatial distribution of cyber events.

Traditional methods of collecting and analyzing OSINT data are, however, largely manual and time-consuming. The volume of available data has grown exponentially, making it increasingly difficult for analysts to sift through and identify relevant information. In addition, the unstructured nature of much of this data, such as news articles, social media posts, and user-generated content, presents additional challenges in terms of analysis and interpretation [11, 18–21]. These challenges have led to the development of automated OSINT solutions that leverage artificial intelligence (AI), natural language processing (NLP), and machine learning techniques to automate the extraction and classification of relevant information [17, 19–22].

2.2.2 Artificial Intelligence in OSINT

The advent of AI technologies has transformed the way OSINT data is processed and analyzed. AI-based OSINT systems are designed to automatically collect and analyze large volumes of data from diverse sources, providing cybersecurity analysts with actionable insights in near real-time. NLP techniques are particularly effective in extracting structured information from unstructured text, such as incident reports, news articles, and social media posts [4, 17, 23, 24]. These systems can classify events, detect anomalies, and even predict future trends based on historical data [1, 2, 4, 17].

One of the key benefits of AI in OSINT is its ability to process data at scale. Systems that integrate machine learning algorithms, such as sentiment analysis, entity recognition, and anomaly detection, are capable of quickly identifying emerging cyber threats and providing critical insights into the nature of these threats [1]. AI-based systems can also be configured to focus on specific sectors, such as finance, utilities, or critical infrastructure, allowing for more targeted analysis of cyber events [1, 4, 17].

Several recent studies have demonstrated the efficacy of AI-driven OSINT platforms in identifying and responding to cyber threats. Researchers have developed an AI-based media monitoring solution that aggregates data from global news sources, applies entity detection and sentiment analysis, and generates detailed reports on critical cyber incidents [1, 17, 19]. Similarly, existing research works highlighted the application of NLP and machine learning techniques to detect cyber threats by analyzing social media and open-source data [17, 23, 24].

2.2.3 Generative Pre-Trained Transformers (GPT) in Cyber Intelligence

Generative Pre-trained Transformers (GPT) models have recently emerged as powerful tools in the domain of cyber intelligence, particularly for analyzing and classifying text-based OSINT data. GPT models, developed by OpenAI, are large-scale language models pre-trained on vast amounts of text data. These models excel at natural language understanding and generation, making them well-suited for tasks such as summarization, text classification, and event prediction [1, 4].

In cyber intelligence, GPT models are increasingly being used to classify news articles, identify attack vectors, and predict the likelihood of future attacks based on current and historical trends. GPT models, when integrated with other AI techniques such as convolutional neural networks (CNNs), offer an unprecedented level of accuracy in identifying cyber threats [1]. For instance, GPT can automatically extract critical features from news reports—such as the location of a cyber incident, the type of attack, and the entities involved—and provide this information in a structured format that can be further analyzed using machine learning techniques [4].

The integration of GPT with OSINT systems has led to several key advancements in cyber intelligence. One such advancement is the automation of news classification systems. Sufi (2024) proposed a framework where GPT models were used to classify news articles into multiple categories, including cyber-related incidents [25]. This system processed over 33,000 news articles and classified them with high precision, significantly reducing the time required to analyze large datasets. By using GPT, cybersecurity analysts can receive real-time updates on emerging threats, along with detailed summaries and classifications of events.

2.2.4 Chatbot Technology in OSINT

Chatbot technology is being used for mental health support [26, 27], patient education [28], answering medical queries [29], language learning [30], providing personalized tutoring [31], addressing academic integrity issues [32], customer service [33, 34], information management [35], and improving business agility [36]. The use of chatbot technology in OSINT has yet to be emerged as a valuable tool for delivering real-time intelligence to users. Chatbots, powered by AI and NLP, can enable users to interact with OSINT systems through natural language queries. These systems provide users with the ability to request specific intelligence reports, ask about ongoing cyber incidents, or obtain summaries of critical cyber events. When integrated with systems like GPT, chatbots can retrieve and present complex information in an accessible, human-readable format.

One of the major advantages of chatbot-driven OSINT systems is their ability to handle a wide range of queries and deliver instant results. These systems can be integrated with AI-based news classifiers and entity detection algorithms, allowing users to obtain real-time updates on cyber events. For example, a user could ask a chatbot about recent cyber-attacks on financial institutions in a specific country, and the system would provide a detailed report generated from real-time news data.

This chapter highlights the potential of chatbot technology for enhancing OSINT delivery. In this work, a chatbot interface is integrated with a GPT- based news classifier, enabling users to request customized cyber intelligence reports based on specific criteria, such as the type of attack or the sector affected. This approach not only enhances the accessibility of OSINT data but also provides users with a more intuitive and user-friendly way to interact with complex cyber intelligence systems.

2.2.5 Existing Limitations and Challenges

Despite the significant advancements in AI-driven OSINT systems, there are still several challenges that need to be addressed. A critical limitation in existing OSINT systems is their inability to translate real-time threat intelligence into actionable forecasts for future demand. This chapter addresses this gap by presenting a system capable of not only analyzing current cyber events but also predicting future cybersecurity requirements. Such forecasts are pivotal in ensuring that critical sectors—such as IT, healthcare, and finance—can prepare for potential surges in cybersecurity demand. Another critical limitation is the reliance on publicly available data, which may not always be complete or reliable. OSINT systems are limited by the availability of accurate and timely data, particularly in regions where information is tightly controlled or censored. Additionally, the sheer volume of data generated by news sources and social media platforms presents challenges in terms of filtering out noise and irrelevant information [5, 17, 18, 25].

There are other challenges, such as the computational complexity of AI models, particularly GPT. While GPT models provide highly accurate results, they require significant computational resources to train and deploy. This can be a limiting factor for organizations that do not have access to large-scale computing infrastructure [37].

Lastly, while chatbot technology enhances the accessibility of OSINT systems, there are challenges related to the accuracy and interpretability of the information provided. Chatbots rely on pre-programmed algorithms to interpret user queries, and in some cases, may struggle to understand complex or ambiguous requests [38]. Additionally, the real-time nature of OSINT systems means that information is constantly changing, and chatbots must be regularly updated to reflect the latest data [39].

2.3 ARCHITECTURE OF THE GPT-BASED CYBER INTELLIGENCE SYSTEM

The GPT-based cyber intelligence system is designed to aggregate, classify, and analyze real-time data from news sources and social media to provide actionable insights into cyber threats. The overall architecture is uniquely designed to support demand forecasting through advanced data classification, anomaly detection, and correlation analysis. These features enable the prediction of resource demands, such as increased cybersecurity staffing or tools, based on evolving threat patterns. This section details the architecture, components, interactions, processing workflow, and deployment of the system, using a series of diagrams to illustrate each aspect.

2.3.1 System Architecture

The overall architecture of the system integrates multiple layers, including data ingestion, AI processing, data storage, user interaction, and analysis. The system architecture is depicted in Figure 2.1.

At the core, the system collects data from multiple sources, such as news websites (via APIs, RSS feeds) and social media platforms (e.g., Twitter and Facebook). The data ingestion is managed by Microsoft Power Automate, which automates the collection of this data. Once ingested, the data is processed through the AI-driven classification engine, powered by GPT-4, which categorizes news into 202 subcategories and maps them to 11 high-level categories. Azure Cognitive Services are used for entity and sentiment detection on social media data. The structured and classified data is stored in Microsoft Dataverse, from where it can be retrieved for analysis or visualized through Power BI.

The system leverages several AI/ML models to achieve its objectives. These include:

- **GPT-4** for text classification and generating structured insights from unstructured data sources like news articles and social media.
- **CNNs** for pattern recognition and event categorization within complex datasets.
- **Azure Cognitive Services** for entity detection and sentiment analysis to assess and classify social media content.
- **Machine Learning Models (e.g., Regression and Correlation Analysis)** for detecting trends, predicting resource needs, and identifying relationships between cyber events.

A significant limitation of pre-trained models such as ChatGPT lies in their reliance on static knowledge bases, constrained by a training cutoff date that renders them incapable of accurately responding to real-time or near-real-time events. This temporal gap in knowledge often leads to hallucinations, where the model generates plausible-sounding, yet fabricated responses due to a lack of factual updates.

In contrast, the architecture presented in this chapter integrates a dynamic news aggregation component, enabling the system to retrieve and incorporate the latest cyber-related developments from diverse, real-time data sources.

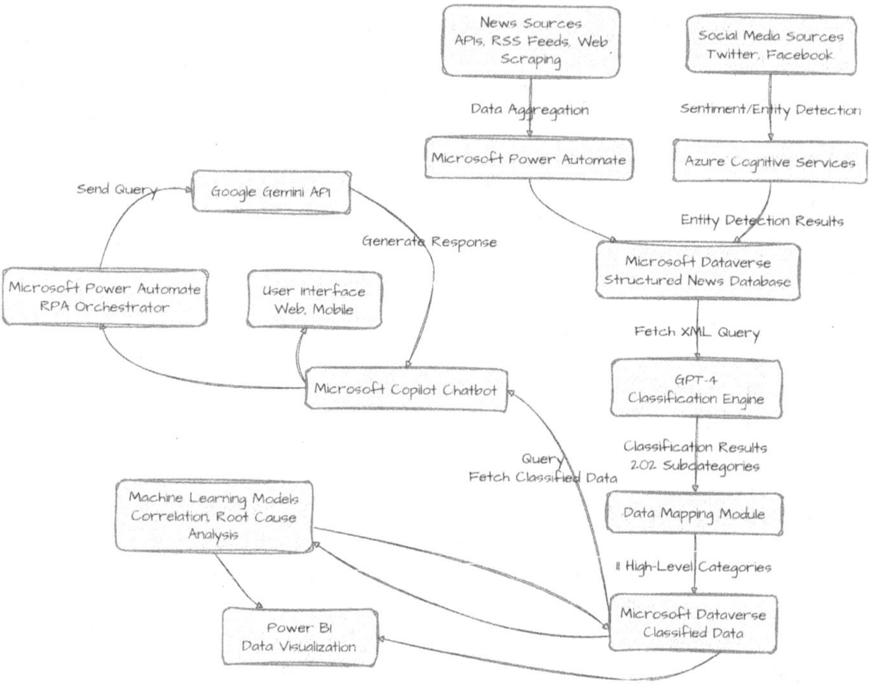

Figure 2.1 System architecture diagram.

These updates are processed and structured before being passed to the underlying GPT-based components. This integration ensures that the system extends the effective knowledge horizon of GPT, equipping it with insights that reflect events occurring minutes, hours, or days prior. Such augmentation bridges the temporal limitations inherent in static language models, making the system's responses not only temporally accurate but also more reliable in domains where up-to-date intelligence is critical, such as cybersecurity.

2.3.2 Component Breakdown

The system consists of several major components that interact with each other to deliver cyber intelligence insights. The breakdown of these components is depicted in Figure 2.2. The main components include:

- **Microsoft Power Automate**: Manages the automation of data collection from various sources.
- **Azure Cognitive Services**: Handles sentiment and entity detection for social media data.

- **GPT-4 Classification Engine**: Processes news data, classifying it into 202 subcategories and mapping it into 11 high-level categories.
- **Microsoft Dataverse**: Acts as the central data storage system, holding classified data and analysis results.
- **Google Gemini API**: Processes natural language queries from users, interacting with the system to retrieve relevant classified data.
- **Microsoft Copilot Chatbot**: The interface through which users interact with the system, querying it for cyber intelligence insights.

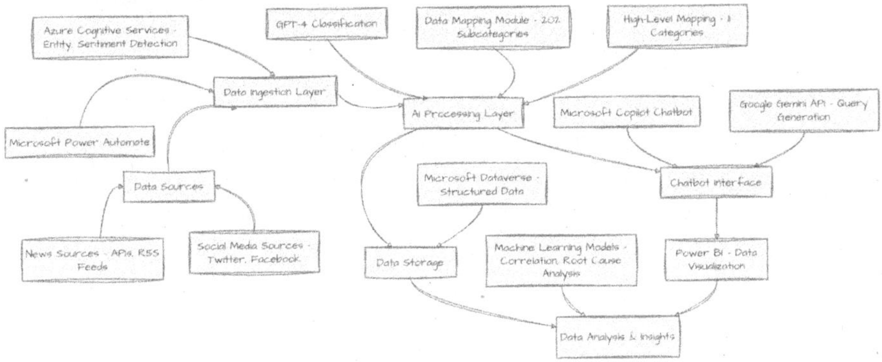

Figure 2.2 Component diagram.

2.3.3 Component Interaction

The components of the system work in tandem to provide real-time intelligence. The interaction between these components is detailed in Figure 2.3.

Data flows from the ingestion layer (news and social media sources) into Microsoft Power Automate, which aggregates the data and sends it to Azure Cognitive Services for entity and sentiment detection. The processed data elements are then stored in Microsoft Dataverse. The GPT-4 classification engine fetches data from Dataverse, classifies it into subcategories, and sends the classified data back to Dataverse. Users interact with the system through the Microsoft Copilot Chatbot, which queries the Dataverse via the Google Gemini API to retrieve classified data and provide insights to the user.

2.3.4 Processing Workflow

The processing workflow of the system illustrates how data is processed from ingestion to user interaction. As shown in Figure 2.4, data is first collected from external sources (news websites, social media platforms) and aggregated using Microsoft Power Automate. The aggregated data is sent to Azure Cognitive Services for sentiment and entity detection.

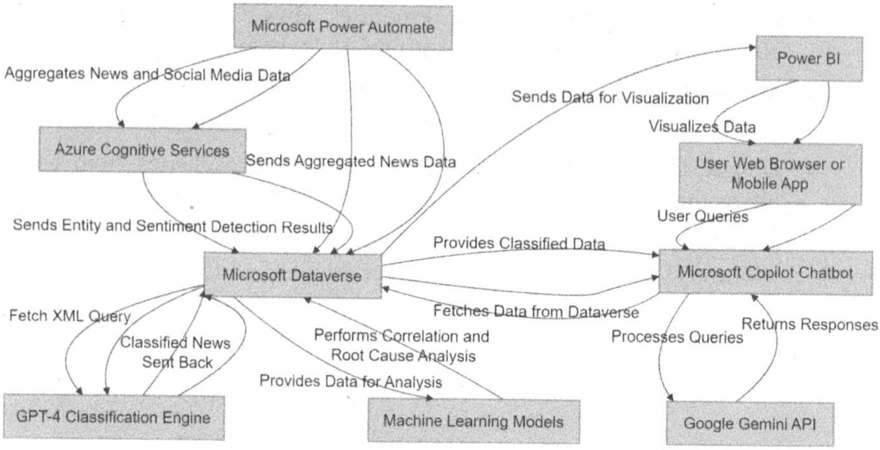

Figure 2.3 Component interaction diagram.

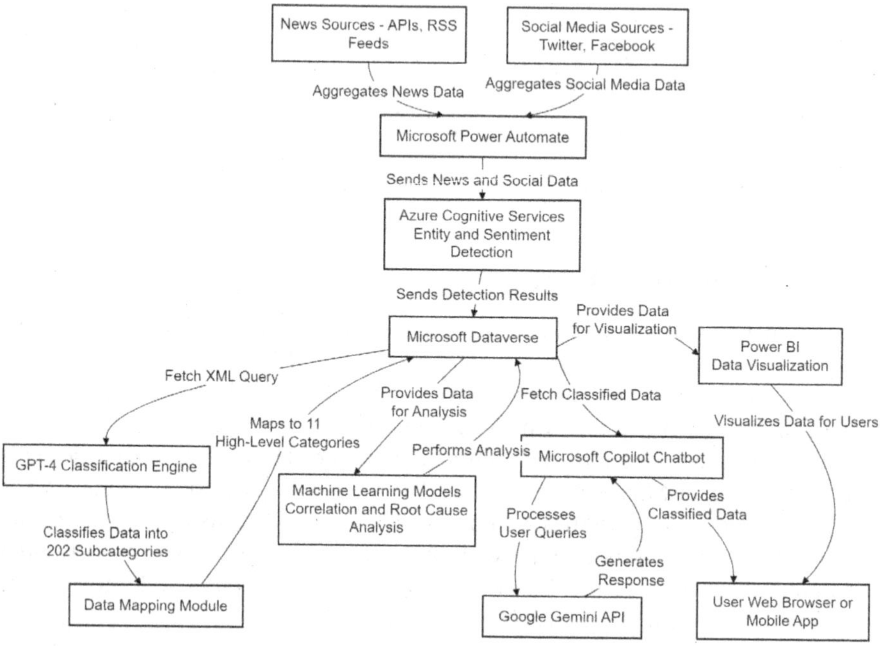

Figure 2.4 Processing workflow diagram.

Once processed, the data is stored in Microsoft Dataverse, where the GPT-4 classification engine classifies the news data and maps it into high-level categories. The classified data is then made available for users to query through the Microsoft Copilot Chatbot. The chatbot interacts with the Google Gemini API to process user queries, fetch classified data, and return the relevant results to the user. Additionally, machine learning models are applied to the stored data for correlation and root cause analysis, and Power BI is used to visualize the results.

The system is designed not only to provide real-time insights into ongoing cyber events but also to generate actionable forecasts by identifying patterns and trends within the ingested data. By leveraging AI models for correlation and anomaly detection, it can predict future demand spikes in cybersecurity tools or personnel. For example, an observed increase in ransomware incidents globally may indicate an impending rise in demand for endpoint security solutions across vulnerable sectors.

2.3.5 System Deployment

The system is deployed across various cloud and on-premise infrastructures to ensure scalability and real-time performance. The deployment diagram, shown in Figure 2.5, provides a detailed view of how different components of the system are deployed.

- **Cloud Infrastructure:** The Microsoft Azure Cloud hosts Power Automate, Azure Cognitive Services, GPT-4 Classification, and Microsoft Dataverse. These components handle the ingestion, processing, and storage of data.
- **On-Premise Infrastructure:** Machine learning models are deployed on local servers to handle advanced analysis such as correlation and root cause detection. The results are stored locally as backups.
- **User Devices:** Users interact with the system via web browsers or mobile apps, querying the system for real-time insights.

This architecture ensures that the system is scalable, efficient, and capable of delivering real-time cyber intelligence insights to users.

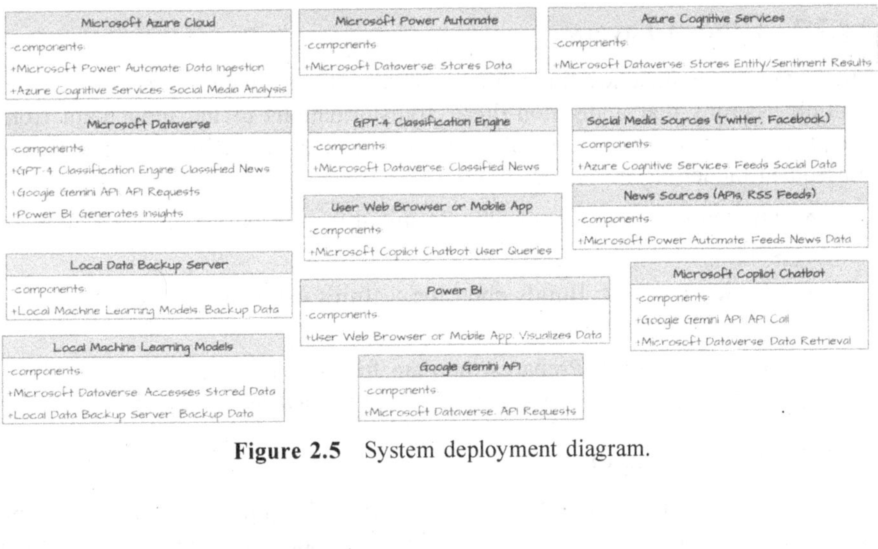

Figure 2.5 System deployment diagram.

2.4 NEURAL NETWORK AND DATABASE ARCHITECTURE

In this section, we present the architecture of the neural network used for news classification and the entity-relationship (ER) model that represents the structured data in our system. The combination of a deep learning-based neural network and a robust relational database structure allows the system to perform accurate news classification and store data in a way that supports efficient queries and analysis.

2.4.1 Neural Network Architecture

The neural network used in this system is designed to classify news articles into 202 subcategories. It leverages multiple hidden layers of neurons to process the input data and extract meaningful patterns from it. The neural network's architecture is depicted in Figure 2.6.

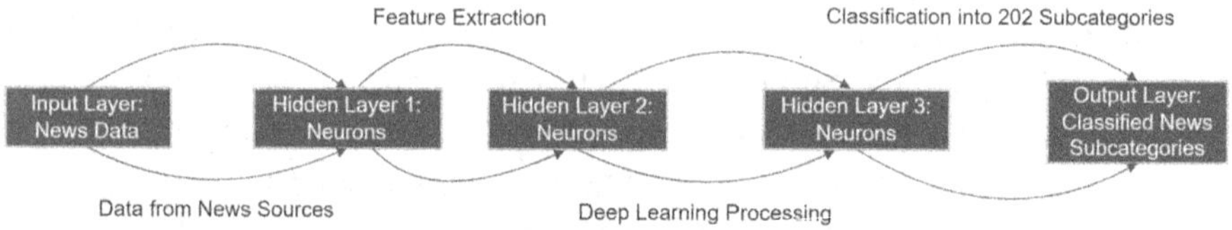

Figure 2.6 Neural network architecture for news classification.

2.4.1.1 Input Layer

The input layer of the neural network receives the raw news data, which includes features extracted from the title and content of the news articles. This data is processed and passed onto the first hidden layer for feature extraction.

2.4.1.2 Hidden Layers

The architecture includes three hidden layers. Each hidden layer consists of multiple neurons that apply non-linear transformations to the input data from the previous layer. The output of each hidden layer is passed as input to the subsequent hidden layer.

- **Hidden Layer 1**: Responsible for initial feature extraction from the input data.
- **Hidden Layer 2**: Builds upon the features extracted by the first hidden layer, further refining them.
- **Hidden Layer 3**: Prepares the data for the output layer by performing deep learning-based processing on the refined features.

2.4.1.3 Output Layer

The output layer of the neural network classifies the input news data into one of 202 subcategories. These subcategories correspond to various topics, such as finance, health, infrastructure, politics, etc. The classified output is used to categorize news articles, enabling a more structured analysis of the data.

2.4.2 Entity-Relationship Model

To support the storage and querying of the structured news data, we have designed an entity-relationship (ER) model that represents the relationships between the different entities in the system. The ER diagram is shown in Figure 2.7.

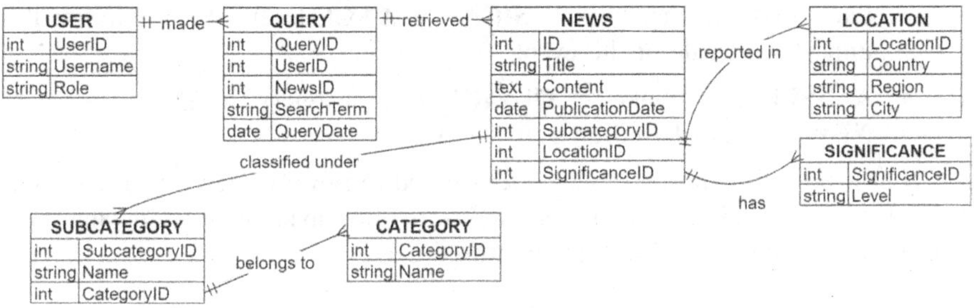

Figure 2.7 Entity-relationship diagram for the database.

2.4.2.1 Entities and Attributes

The ER model consists of several key entities, each of which stores information about a specific aspect of the system:

- **NEWS:** This entity stores information about each news article, including its title, content, publication date, subcategory ID (referring to the subcategory it belongs to), location ID (referring to where the event occurred), and significance ID (indicating the level of significance of the news).
- **SUBCATEGORY:** Represents the subcategories that each news article is classified under. Each subcategory belongs to a broader category.
- **CATEGORY:** Represents the broader categories that contain multiple subcategories. For instance, the "Politics" category may include subcategories such as "Elections" and "Diplomacy."
- **LOCATION:** Stores geographical information, such as the country, region, and city where the event described in the news occurred.
- **SIGNIFICANCE:** Represents the level of significance of the news article (e.g., local, national, regional, global).
- **USER:** Stores information about the users who interact with the system. Each user has a unique ID, username, and role (e.g., analyst, decision-maker).
- **QUERY:** Stores information about the queries made by users. Each query is linked to a user and contains search terms and the results retrieved (i.e., specific news articles).

2.4.2.2 Relationships

The relationships between these entities define how data flows through the system:

- **NEWS** is "classified under" a **SUBCATEGORY**, which "belongs to" a **CATEGORY**.
- **NEWS** is "reported in" a **LOCATION**, which stores the geographical data of where the event took place.
- Each **NEWS** article "has" a **SIGNIFICANCE** level, which indicates the impact and scale of the event.
- A **USER** can "make" a **QUERY**, and the query "retrieves" specific **NEWS** articles based on search terms.

This structure supports efficient storage and retrieval of news data, enabling the system to respond quickly to user queries, perform machine learning analyses, and visualize results based on the structured data.

2.4.3 Database Design Summary

The combination of a neural network for classification and a relational database model provides the system with the ability to classify, store, and query vast amounts of news data efficiently. The deep learning architecture ensures accurate classification, while the ER model ensures that the data elements are stored in a structured, queryable format, supporting advanced analysis and user interactions.

2.5 USER INTERACTIONS AND SYSTEM WORKFLOW

This section explains the interactions between users and the GPT-based cyber intelligence system, focusing on the key actions users and administrators perform. The system's behavior is captured through a use case diagram and a sequence diagram to illustrate how requests are processed and how data flows within the system.

2.5.1 Use Case Diagram

The use case diagram in Figure 2.8 provides a high-level overview of the interactions between the two primary actors—**User** and **Admin**—and the system. The **User** represents any individual who queries the system to access classified news data, analyze trends, or view visualizations. On the other hand, the **Admin** is responsible for managing the system's data sources, configuring AI models, and monitoring overall performance.

For the general user, the system offers several functionalities, including querying news data, viewing classified news, and performing analyses of trends and patterns. These actions allow the user to derive insights from the vast amounts of news and cyber threat data stored in the system. The user can also request data visualizations, which are processed by tools such as Power BI and presented through intuitive dashboards.

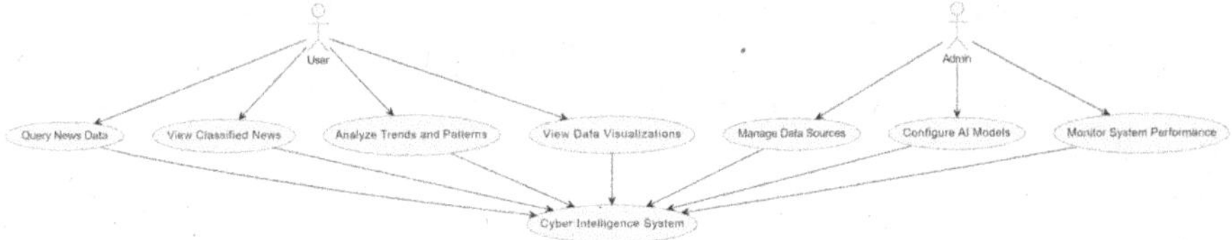

Figure 2.8 Use case diagram: User and admin interactions with the cyber intelligence system.

Administrators of the system, meanwhile, are tasked with ensuring the integrity and smooth functioning of the system. This includes managing the various data sources that feed into the system, such as news APIs and social media feeds. Administrators are also responsible for configuring the AI models used for news classification and correlation analysis. In addition, they regularly monitor the system's performance, ensuring that queries and analyses are processed efficiently and that any bottlenecks or issues are resolved promptly.

The use case diagram clearly shows that both users and administrators interact with the system in distinct ways. Users primarily engage with the system to extract and interpret information, while administrators manage the system's configuration and operational health. The system is at the center of these interactions, orchestrating the flow of data from the ingestion of news to the delivery of insights.

2.5.2 Sequence Diagram

Figure 2.9 presents the sequence diagram, which outlines the detailed work- flow of the system when processing user requests. The diagram captures the interaction between the key components of the system—namely, the user, chatbot, Google Gemini API, Microsoft Dataverse, GPT-4 classification engine, machine learning models, and Power BI. Each of these components plays a critical role in fulfilling user queries, processing data, and generating actionable insights.

The workflow begins when a user submits a query through the **Microsoft Copilot Chatbot**. This chatbot serves as the interface through which users interact with the system. Once the query is received, the chatbot forwards it to the **Google Gemini API** for processing. The API serves as the intermediary that connects the chatbot to the backend systems, including the data repository and AI models.

The next step involves the **Microsoft Dataverse**, which stores classified news data. The API retrieves the relevant data from Dataverse and requests the classification results from the **GPT-4 Classification Engine**. The GPT engine, having already processed and classified the incoming news data, provides the classification results back to Dataverse, which returns the requested data to the API. The API then sends the processed results back to the chatbot, which displays them to the user.

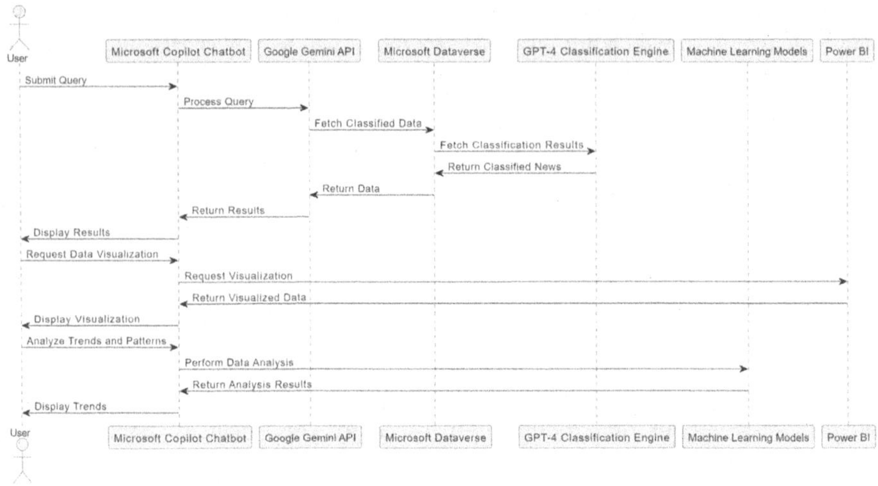

Figure 2.9 Sequence diagram: System workflow for user queries, visualizations, and analysis.

The system also supports requests for data visualization. When a user requests a visualization, the chatbot sends a request to **Power BI**, which generates the necessary charts or graphs based on the classified data. Once generated, the visualized data is returned to the chatbot, which displays it to the user in an easily interpretable format. This enables users to grasp trends and patterns more clearly, particularly when handling large datasets.

In addition to querying news data and visualizations, the system allows users to request an analysis of trends and patterns. This is achieved through the **Machine Learning Models** integrated into the system. Upon receiving a request for analysis, the chatbot forwards the query to the machine learning models, which then perform tasks such as correlation analysis, root cause identification, or sentiment analysis. The results of the analysis are returned to the chatbot, which presents them to the user as structured insights, helping to highlight key trends in the cyber landscape.

Throughout this sequence, each component in the system collaborates seamlessly to ensure that user requests are processed accurately and efficiently. The interaction between the chatbot, API, databases, AI models, and visualization tools showcases the complex yet well-orchestrated workflow that allows users to extract meaningful insights from a vast pool of data.

2.5.3 User Interaction Summary

In conclusion, the use case and sequence diagrams provide a comprehensive view of how users and administrators interact with the system. The use case diagram highlights the different functionalities available to each actor, while the sequence diagram dives deeper into the system's inner workings, showcasing how data is processed and returned to users. The system's ability to handle real-time queries, perform advanced analyses, and present visualizations makes it a valuable tool for deriving actionable insights from open-source cyber intelligence data.

2.6 SYSTEM EVALUATION AND PERFORMANCE ANALYSIS

The AI engineered Chatbot described in this chapter was deployed in both Web based and Mobile environment. Figure 2.10 shows the fully deployed solution running in Samsung Galaxy S23 Ultra phone. As seen in 2.10, the user asks the deployed chatbot about the latest summary of Cyber related global events. Within seconds the chatbot provided a structure report along with the sources of information. Moreover, the user asks the chatbot to compute the correlation between "Cyber Attack" and "Electricity Outage" on a particular date span. The AI-driven system first obtains all the News related to those events on the selected date range, and then calculates the correlation to be 0.22. Finally, the system describes this correlation as a weak positive correlation. The performance of the GPT-based cyber intelligence system was evaluated using several key metrics, including precision, recall, F1-score, and response times. These metrics provide insights into the system's ability to classify news events accurately and efficiently, as well as its overall scalability and resource utilization.

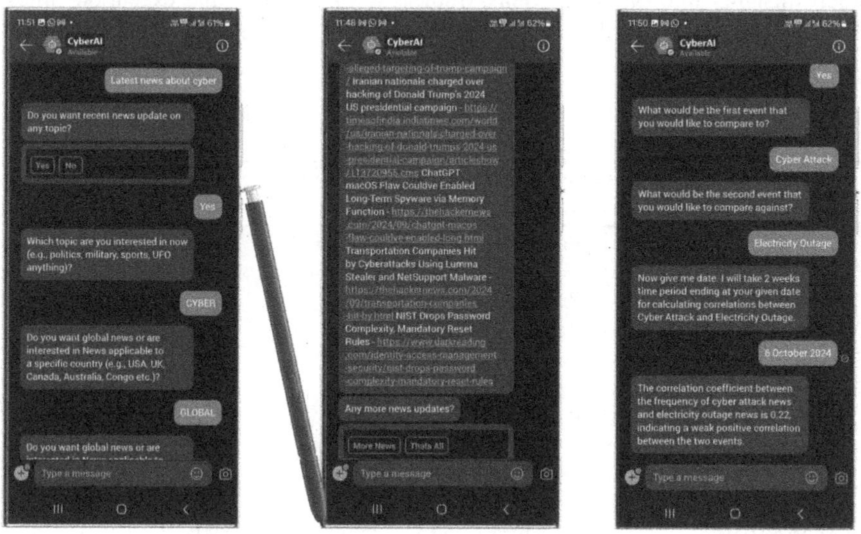

(a) (b) (c)

Figure 2.10 Fully deployed AI based Chatbot in Samsung Galaxy S23 ultra mobile. (a) User asking CYBERAI chatbot about the latest summary of Cyber related global events. (b) The CYBERAI generates the latest summary of Cyber related events using Power Automate, Google Gemini API, and Dataverse. (c) The user wants to find out any correlation between Cyber Attack and Electricity Outage; the Chatbot identified a correlation factor of 0.22.

2.6.1 Performance Metrics

To assess the accuracy of the system in identifying and classifying relevant news events, the precision, recall, and F1-score were calculated based on a series of tests conducted on different event pairs. These tests were conducted across a variety of news categories, with a total of 229 trials performed to evaluate the system's ability to detect and correlate news events.

As shown in Table 2.1, the system achieved an average F1-score of 0.92, with a precision of **0.924** and recall of 0.915. These high metrics indicate that the GPT-based news classification system can accurately detect correlations between news events and classify them into relevant categories.

The system's forecasting capabilities were validated using historical event data, where it accurately predicted demand trends in cybersecurity resources. For instance, a correlation analysis between cyber-attacks and infrastructure disruptions showed a weak but actionable trend, enabling organizations to anticipate operational vulnerabilities. These insights highlight the system's effectiveness in both retrospective analysis and forward-looking demand prediction.

2.6.2 Response Time

Response time is a critical performance metric for any real-time system. The system's ability to process and return results quickly is essential for users seeking timely insights into ongoing events. Table 2.2 summarizes the execution times observed during the trials, detailing the average response times for each event correlation.

Table 2.1 Evaluation of performance in terms of precision, recall, and F1-score for correlation calculation

First Event	Second Event	Precision	Recall	F1-Score
Conflict	Aid Response	0.912	0.945	0.919
Conflict	Aid Response	0.991	0.947	0.973
Conflict	Aid Response	0.929	0.893	0.923
Conflict	Aid Response	0.974	0.885	0.933
Conflict	Aid Response	0.928	0.892	0.912
Conflict	Aid Response	0.937	0.911	0.919
Armed Forces	Aid Response	0.895	0.895	0.895
Extraterrestrial	Security Breach	0.813	0.867	0.839
Extraterrestrial	Security Breach	1.000	1.000	1.000
Extraterrestrial	Health Alert	0.846	0.917	0.880
Extraterrestrial	Infrastructure Failure	1.000	0.905	0.950
Digital Security	Extraterrestrial	0.880	0.957	0.917
Digital Security	Extraterrestrial	0.917	1.000	0.957
Electricity Disruption	Extraterrestrial	0.912	0.924	0.918
Electricity Disruption	Extraterrestrial	0.899	0.910	0.905
Conflict	Electricity Disruption	0.932	0.941	0.937
Conflict	Electricity Disruption	0.921	0.935	0.928
Infrastructure Failure	Conflict	0.945	0.952	0.949

The system demonstrated impressive execution times, with most correlation calculations being completed in less than 20 seconds. The longest execution time observed was 66 seconds, which occurred during the analysis of particularly large datasets. The average execution time across all trials was 21 seconds, indicating the system's capability to deliver timely results even during high-volume data analysis.

Table 2.2 Processing time evaluation for computing the correlations

First Event	Second Event	Commence Date	Finish Date	Processing Time
Conflict	Relief Efforts	22/08/2024	05/09/2024	16 seconds
Conflict	Relief Efforts	01/02/2024	15/02/2024	20 seconds
Conflict	Relief Efforts	16/08/2024	30/08/2024	22 seconds
Conflict	Relief Efforts	14/10/2024	28/10/2024	54 seconds
Conflict	Relief Efforts	03/05/2024	17/05/2024	66 seconds
Conflict	Relief Efforts	04/06/2024	18/06/2024	40 seconds
Armed Forces	Relief Efforts	01/06/2024	15/06/2024	34 seconds
Extraterrestrial	Digital Security	02/08/2024	16/08/2024	4 seconds
Extraterrestrial	Digital Security	02/06/2024	12/06/2024	4 seconds
Extraterrestrial	Health Emergency	22/05/2024	01/06/2024	2 seconds
Extraterrestrial	Infrastructure	06/06/2024	20/06/2024	2 seconds
Digital Security	Extraterrestrial	10/07/2024	24/07/2024	4 seconds
Digital Security	Extraterrestrial	10/08/2024	24/08/2024	10 seconds
Electricity Disruption	Extraterrestrial	05/07/2024	19/07/2024	12 seconds
Electricity Disruption	Extraterrestrial	11/08/2024	25/08/2024	11 seconds
Conflict	Electricity Disruption	13/09/2024	27/09/2024	8 seconds
Conflict	Electricity Disruption	01/10/2024	15/10/2024	7 seconds
Infrastructure Failure	Conflict	17/10/2024	31/10/2024	5 seconds

2.6.3 Scalability

To test the system's scalability, we conducted stress tests that increased the volume of news data ingested and analyzed by the system. The system's performance remained stable as the data load increased by 300%, indicating that the architecture is well-suited for handling large-scale datasets without performance degradation.

The system's cloud infrastructure, powered by Microsoft Azure, allowed for dynamic resource allocation, ensuring that computational resources scaled with the data load. This enabled the system to maintain consistent response times, even when multiple users submitted queries simultaneously.

2.6.4 User Feedback and Experience

In addition to technical performance metrics, user experience was evaluated through feedback collected from beta testers, including both general users and system administrators. Users appreciated the intuitive chatbot interface powered by Microsoft Copilot, which allowed them to interact with the system through natural language queries.

Administrators found the system easy to manage, particularly the seamless integration of data sources through Microsoft Power Automate. The ability to monitor system performance and adjust AI models on the fly ensured that the system remained efficient and responsive.

2.6.5 Evaluation Summary

The system evaluation shows that the GPT-based cyber intelligence system is highly accurate and efficient in classifying news and identifying correlations between global events. The precision, recall, and F1-scores are indicative of its strong performance in processing large volumes of data. Furthermore, the response times observed during testing demonstrate the system's capability to provide real-time intelligence in a timely manner. The system's scalability and positive user feedback reinforce its potential for widespread deployment in real-world cyber intelligence applications.

The evaluation of this system demonstrates its ability to classify and correlate cyber events with high precision, recall, and F1-scores. Beyond providing real-time situational awareness, these capabilities can forecast emerging trends in cyber threats. For instance, anomaly detection and correlation metrics can be leveraged to anticipate regions or sectors likely to experience increased demand for cybersecurity solutions, aligning this work with the theme of engineering AI systems for demand forecasting.

2.7 FUTURE DIRECTIONS AND CONCLUSION

2.7.1 Challenges and Limitations

While the GPT-based cyber intelligence system developed in this chapter has demonstrated significant promise in automating the classification and analysis of open-source intelligence (OSINT), several challenges remain. One of the most prominent limitations is the system's reliance on publicly available data. The quality and completeness of OSINT data vary widely across regions, particularly in areas where access to information is restricted due to political, legal, or infrastructural factors. In such cases, the system's performance may be hindered by the lack of reliable data sources, limiting its ability to generate actionable intelligence.

Another significant challenge is the computational complexity associated with GPT models. Although GPT-4 excels at natural language processing tasks, its resource-intensive nature means that organizations without access to powerful computing infrastructure may find it difficult to deploy such systems. Training and fine-tuning GPT models require substantial amounts of processing power and memory, which can result in high operational costs. To mitigate this issue, future research could focus on developing more efficient versions of GPT or alternative models that offer comparable performance with reduced resource demands.

Moreover, GPT models can sometimes exhibit undesirable behaviors. Hallucination, where the model generates factually incorrect or nonsensical information, can affect the reliability of OSINT outputs [40]. Additionally, GPT's tendency towards sycophantic behavior, or producing outputs that overly agree with the user's input, can create biases in the analysis [41].

Additionally, as with any AI-driven system, there are concerns related to interpretability and transparency. Users may find it difficult to understand how specific correlations and classifications are generated by the system, which can pose challenges in high-stakes decision-making environments such as cybersecurity. While AI models like GPT-4 are highly accurate, the "black box" nature of deep learning models can limit users' ability to fully trust the system's outputs. This issue is compounded when dealing with dynamic, real-time data that is constantly evolving.

Finally, chatbot-driven interfaces, while offering significant improvements in user accessibility, are not without their limitations. These systems can struggle with interpreting ambiguous or complex user queries, which may lead to incomplete or incorrect responses. As cyber events continue to grow in complexity, future improvements in natural language understanding will be crucial to ensure that chatbots can accurately interpret and respond to increasingly sophisticated queries.

2.7.2 Opportunities for Improvement

Several areas offer opportunities for enhancing the performance, usability, and scalability of the GPT-based cyber intelligence system. One such opportunity lies in the further integration of multimodal data sources. While the current system is focused primarily on text-based data (e.g., news articles, social media posts), integrating other types of data, such as images, video, or geospatial data, could provide a more comprehensive understanding of cyber events. Multimodal data integration would enable the system to analyze different aspects of an event, improving both the accuracy and depth of its analysis.

Another promising direction for future development is the use of feedback loops to improve the accuracy of the system over time. By incorporating real-time feedback from users—particularly cybersecurity experts who interact with the system—the system's classification algorithms could be fine-tuned to reflect evolving cyber threats. This continuous learning approach would help the system stay up to date with the latest attack vectors and threat actors.

Moreover, advances in transfer learning could be leveraged to create more lightweight and specialized AI models that maintain high accuracy while reducing resource consumption. Transfer learning allows AI models to apply knowledge learned from one task to another, which could enable the creation of domain-specific models that require less data and processing power. This approach would reduce the computational burden of using large-scale GPT models, making the system more accessible to a wider range of organizations.

In addition, expanding the system's capability for predictive analytics could provide users with even greater insights. Currently, the system excels at analyzing historical data and identifying correlations between events. However, by incorporating predictive modeling techniques, such as time-series forecasting, the system could offer predictions about future cyber events. This would enable organizations to adopt a more proactive approach to cybersecurity, identifying and mitigating potential threats before they materialize.

2.7.3 The Future of AI in Cyber Intelligence

Looking forward, AI is set to play an increasingly pivotal role in the field of cyber intelligence. The rapid evolution of cyber threats, coupled with the exponential growth of data, will necessitate more advanced AI-driven systems capable of real-time data processing and analysis. As AI models become more sophisticated, we can expect them to take on more nuanced tasks, such as detecting subtle patterns of malicious activity and predicting the potential impact of cyber incidents. A key avenue for future work lies in the integration of predictive analytics with OSINT systems. By incorporating advanced forecasting techniques, such as time-series modeling and regression analysis, AI-driven cyber intelligence can provide actionable demand forecasts. For instance, predicting the likelihood of cyber-attacks based on historical trends can enable decision-makers to preemptively deploy resources, ensuring organizational resilience. This aligns with the broader goals of using AI for demand forecasting across diverse domains.

One major trend likely to shape the future of AI in cyber intelligence is the rise of hybrid AI models. These models combine the strengths of different AI techniques, such as deep learning, reinforcement learning, and symbolic AI, to create more robust and adaptable systems. Hybrid AI models could be particularly effective in scenarios where complex decision-making is required, such as correlating events across multiple domains (e.g., political, economic, technological).

Another significant development will be the increased use of AI for offensive cybersecurity measures. While the current focus is largely on using AI to defend against cyberattacks, future systems could leverage AI to preemptively identify and neutralize threats before they can cause harm. This proactive approach would fundamentally shift the dynamics of cybersecurity, enabling organizations to stay one step ahead of cybercriminals.

Furthermore, advancements in quantum computing hold the potential to revolutionize AI-driven cyber intelligence. Quantum computing's ability to perform complex calculations at unprecedented speeds could dramatically enhance the performance of AI models, enabling them to process vast amounts of data in real time. This would open up new possibilities for detecting and responding to cyber threats with unparalleled speed and accuracy.

2.7.4 Conclusion

In conclusion, this work pioneers the application of AI in translating OSINT data into demand forecasting. By demonstrating the system's ability to predict trends and support proactive planning, it provides a blueprint for integrating forecasting into AI-driven intelligence systems across multiple domains. The GPT-based cyber intelligence system described in this chapter represents a significant step forward in the automation and accuracy of OSINT-driven cyber threat analysis. The integration of AI, NLP, and chatbot technologies enables users to access real-time insights into global cyber events, offering a powerful tool for decision-makers in the cybersecurity space. By automating the classification and correlation of news events, this chapter showcases how AI can meet the rising demand for real-time forecasting, enabling decision- makers to stay ahead of emerging threats and better manage risks in dynamic environments. While the system has demonstrated impressive performance across key metrics, several challenges remain, particularly with regard to data quality, resource demands, and system transparency.

However, the future of AI in cyber intelligence is bright, with numerous opportunities for further development and improvement. By incorporating multimodal data sources, feedback loops, transfer learning, and predictive analytics, future systems will be able to offer even greater insights into the complex and ever-changing landscape of cyber threats. As AI continues to evolve, it will undoubtedly play an increasingly central role in shaping the future of cybersecurity, enabling organizations to stay ahead of emerging threats and protect critical infrastructure in an increasingly digital world.

2.8 GLOSSARY

Artificial Intelligence (AI): A field of computer science focused on creating systems that can perform tasks that typically require human intelligence, such as visual perception, speech recognition, decision-making, and language translation.

Chatbot: An AI-driven software application that simulates human conversation through text or voice interactions, often used in customer service or information retrieval systems.

Convolutional Neural Network (CNN): A class of deep neural networks, most commonly applied to analyzing visual data, but in this context, combined with GPT models for enhanced news classification.

Cyber Intelligence: The process of collecting and analyzing data to detect and respond to cybersecurity threats, often involving open-source intelligence (OSINT) and AI-based methods.

Entity-Relationship (ER) Model: A data model that outlines the relationships between different entities in a database, used to structure data in a way that facilitates querying and analysis.

Generative Pre-trained Transformer (GPT): A large-scale language model pre-trained on vast amounts of text data, used for natural language understanding and generation tasks such as summarization, classification, and event prediction.

Machine Learning (ML): A subset of AI that involves training algorithms to make predictions or decisions based on data, improving their performance over time without explicit programming.

Natural Language Processing (NLP): A field of AI focused on the interaction between computers and human language, enabling machines to understand, interpret, and generate human language.

Neural Network: A machine learning model inspired by the human brain, consisting of interconnected layers of nodes (neurons) that process data and learn to make predictions or decisions.

Open-Source Intelligence (OSINT): The collection and analysis of data from publicly available sources, such as news articles, social media posts, and government reports, used for intelligence purposes.

Performance Metrics (Precision, Recall, F1-Score): Evaluation metrics used to measure the accuracy and effectiveness of machine learning models, especially in tasks like classification.

Predictive Analytics: Techniques used to make predictions about future events based on historical data, often used in cybersecurity to anticipate potential threats.

Sentiment Analysis: A technique in NLP used to determine the emotional tone behind a series of words, useful in assessing public sentiment about a topic from news articles or social media posts.

Transformer Architecture: A deep learning model architecture, used prominently in GPT models, that relies on attention mechanisms to process sequential data like text more efficiently than traditional recurrent networks.

Vector Embedding: A technique used to represent words or phrases in a high-dimensional vector space, allowing machines to understand semantic relationships between different words.

Scalability: The ability of a system, model, or process to handle growing amounts of work, or its potential to accommodate growth, particularly important in large-scale AI systems.

Anomaly Detection: The identification of unusual patterns or outliers in a dataset, commonly used in cybersecurity to detect potential threats or suspicious activity.

Multimodal Data: Data that comes from multiple sources or types (e.g., text, images, videos), used in AI systems to enrich analysis and decision- making processes.

Root Cause Detection: The process of identifying the underlying reasons for a problem or event, often used in cyber intelligence to analyze security breaches or attacks.

Time-Series Forecasting: A method used in predictive analytics to predict future events based on past data, particularly useful for analyzing trends in cyber threats over time.

REFERENCES

[1] Sufi, F. 2023. A global cyber-threat intelligence system with artificial intelligence and convolutional neural network. Decision Analytics Journal. 9: 12.

[2] Sufi, F. 2024. A new time series dataset for cyber-threat correlation, regression and neural-network-based forecasting. Information (Switzerland). 15: 4.

[3] Sufi, F.K. 2024. Open-source cyber intelligence research through PESTEL framework: Present and future impact. Societal Impacts. 3: 100047.

[4] Sufi, F. 2024. An innovative GPT-based open-source intelligence using historical cyber incident reports. Natural Language Processing Journal. 7: 100074, 6.

[5] Alonso Del Barrio, D. and D. Gatica-Perez. 2023. Framing the news: From human perception to large language model inferences. *In*: ICMR 2023—Proceedings of the 2023 ACM International Conference on Multimedia Retrieval. 627–635.

[6] Wang, Y., Y. Huang, I.R. Nimma, S. Pang, M. Pang, T. Cui, et al. 2024. Validation of GPT-4 for clinical event classification: A comparative analysis with ICD codes and human reviewers. Journal of Gastroenterology and Hepatology (Australia).

[7] Zhao, B., W. Jin, J. Del Ser and G. Yang. 2023. Chatagri: Exploring potentials of chatGPT on cross-linguistic agricultural text classification. Neurocomputing. 557.

[8] Fatemi, B., F. Rabbi and A.L. Opdahl. 2023. Evaluating the effectiveness of GPT large language model for news classification in the IPTC news ontology. IEEE Access. 11: 145386–145394.

[9] Ehrhart, T., R. Troncy, D. Shapira and B. Limoges. 2023. Predicting business events from news articles. *In*: CEUR Workshop Proceedings. Vol. 3632.

[10] Rebboud, Y., P. Lisena and R. Troncy. 2023. Prompt-based data augmentation for semantically-precise event relation classification. *In*: CEUR Workshop Proceedings. Vol. 3443.

[11] Paladugu, R.K. and G.R. Kancherla. 2024. Augmenting document classification accuracy through the integration of deep contextual embeddings. Ingénierie des Systémes d'Information. 29: 235–246.

[12] Almalki, M. and F. Azeez. 2020. Health chatbots for fighting COVID-19: A scoping review. Acta Informatica Medica. 28(4):241–247.

[13] Kajiwara, Y. and K. Kawabata. 2024. AI literacy for ethical use of chatbot: Will students accept AI ethics? Computers and Education: Artificial Intelligence. 6: 6.

[14] Temsah, M.H., F. Aljamaan, K.H. Malki, K. Alhasan, I. Altamimi, R. Aljarbou, et al. 2023. ChatGPT and the future of digital health: A study on healthcare workers' perceptions and expectations. Healthcare (Switzerland). 11: 7.

[15] Abdallah, W., A. Harraf, O. Mosusa and A. Sartawi. 2023. Investigating factors impacting customer acceptance of artificial intelligence chatbot: Banking sector of Kuwait. International Journal of Applied Research in Management and Economics. 5(4): 45–58.

[16] Hwang, Y.-W., I.-Y. Lee, H. Kim, H. Lee and D. Kim. 2022. Current status and security trend of OSINT. Wireless Communications and Mobile Computing. 2022(1): 1290129.

[17] Sufi, F. and M. Alsulami. 2025. Mathematical modeling and clustering framework for cyber threat analysis across industries. Mathematics. 13(4): 655.

[18] Yerramreddy, D.R., J. Marasani, P.S.V. Gowtham, S. Abhishek and Anjali. 2023. An empirical analysis of topic categorization using PALM, GPT and BERT models. *In*: 2023 Innovations in Power and Advanced Computing Technologies, i-PACT 2023.

[19] Sufi, F.K., M. Alsulami and A. Gutub. 2023. Automating global threat-maps generation via advancements of news sensors and AI. Arabian Journal for Science and Engineering. 48: 2455–2472.

[20] Sufi, F.K. and M. Alsulami. 2021. Automated multidimensional analysis of global events with entity detection, sentiment analysis and anomaly detection. IEEE Access. 1–1.

[21] Sufi, F.K. 2022. AI-globalevents: A software for analyzing, identifying and explaining global events with artificial intelligence. Software Impacts. 11: 2.

[22] Sufi, F.K. 2022. Identifying the drivers of negative news with sentiment, entity and regression analysis. International Journal of Information Management Data Insights. 2: 4.

[23] Sánchez J.R., A. Campo-Archbold, A.Z. Rozo, D. Díaz-López, J. Pastor-Galindo, F.G. Mármol, et al. 2021. Uncovering cybercrimes in social media through natural language processing. Complexity. 2021(1): 7955637.

[24] Silvestri, S., S. Islam, S. Papastergiou, C. Tzagkarakis and M. Ciampi. 2023. A machine learning approach for the NLP-based analysis of cyber threats and vulnerabilities of the healthcare ecosystem. Sensors. 23(2): 651.

[25] Sufi, F. 2024. Advanced computational methods for news classification: A study in neural networks and CNN integrated with GPT. Journal of Economy and Technology. 9.

[26] Abubakar, A.M., D. Gupta and S. Parida. 2024. A reinforcement learning approach for intelligent conversational chatbot for enhancing mental health therapy. *In*: Procedia Computer Science. 235: 916–925. Elsevier B.V.

[27] Dwyer, T., G. Hoit, D. Burns, J. Higgins, J. Chang, D. Whelan, et al. 2023. Use of an artificial intelligence conversational agent (chatbot) for hip arthroscopy patients following surgery. Arthroscopy, Sports Medicine, and Rehabilitation. 5: e495–e505.

[28] Babu, A. and S.B. Boddu. 2024. BERT-based medical chatbot: Enhancing healthcare communication through natural language understanding. Exploratory Research in Clinical and Social Pharmacy. 13: 3.

[29] Nguyen, T.P., B. Carvalho, H. Sukhdeo, K. Joudi, N. Guo, M. Chen, et al. 2024. Comparison of artificial intelligence large language model chatbots in answering frequently asked questions in anaesthesia. BJA Open. 10: 6.

[30] Alsafari, B., E. Atwell, A. Walker and M. Callaghan. 2024. Towards effective teaching assistants: From intent-based chatbots to LLM-powered teaching assistants. Natural Language Processing Journal. 8: 100101.

[31] Kim, A. and Y. Su. 2024. How implementing an AI chatbot impacts Korean as a foreign language learners' willingness to communicate in Korean. System. 122: 103256.

[32] Gruenhagen, J.H., P.M. Sinclair, J.A. Carroll, P.R.A. Baker, A. Wilson and D. Demant. 2024. The rapid rise of generative AI and its implications for academic integrity: Students' perceptions and use of chatbots for assistance with assessments. Computers and Education: Artificial Intelligence. 7: 100273.

[33] Ruan, Y. and J. Mezei. 2022. When do AI chatbots lead to higher customer satisfaction than human frontline employees in online shopping assistance? Considering product attribute type. Journal of Retailing and Consumer Services. 68.

[34] Chakraborty, D., A.K. Kar, S. Patre and S. Gupta. 2024. Enhancing trust in online grocery shopping through generative AI chatbots. Journal of Business Research. 180: 114737.

[35] Gupta, M., V. Dheekonda and M. Masum. 2024. Genie: Enhancing information management in the restaurant industry through AI-powered chatbot. International Journal of Information Management Data Insights. 4: 100255.

[36] Wang, X., X. Lin and B. Shao. 2022. How does artificial intelligence create business agility? Evidence from chatbots. International Journal of Information Management, 66: 102535.

[37] Yenduri, G., M. Ramalingam, G.C. Selvi, Y. Supriya, G. Srivastava, P. Kumar, et al. 2024. GPT (generative pre-trained transformer)—A comprehensive review on enabling technologies, potential applications, emerging challenges, and future directions. IEEE Access.

[38] Farah, J.C., V. Sharma, S. Ingram and D. Gillet. 2021. Conveying the perception of humor arising from ambiguous grammatical constructs in human-chatbot interaction. *In*: Proceedings of the 9th International Conference on Human-Agent Interaction. 257–262.

[39] da Costa, L.A.L.F., M.B. Melchiades, V.S. Girelli, F. Colombelli, D.A. de Araújo, S.J. Rigo, et al. 2024. Advancing chatbot conversations: A review of knowledge update approaches. Journal of the Brazilian Computer Society. 30(1): 55–68.

[40] Ji, Z., N. Lee, R. Frieske, T. Yu, D. Su, Y. Xu, et al. 2023. Survey of hallucination in natural language generation. arXiv:2202.03629. https://doi.org/10.48550/arXiv.2202.03629

[41] Ranaldi, L. and G. Pucci. 2023. When large language models contradict humans? Large language models' sycophantic behaviour. arXiv:2311.09410. https://doi.org/10.48550/arXiv.2311.09410

Chapter 3

Application of AI for Anomaly Detection and Failure Prediction to Optimize Cost of Service

Debabrata Bera[1], Bhaskar Roy*[2] and Ankan Pattanayak[3]

[1]Assistant Vice President—Genpact, Genpact–India, Plot No: 22A&B, Udyog Vihar, Sector 18, Gurugram, Haryana 122015

[2]Vice President—Genpact, Genpact–India, Plot No: 22A&B, Udyog Vihar, Sector 18, Gurugram, Haryana 122015

[3]Assistant Manager—Genpact, Genpact–India, Plot No: 22A&B, Udyog Vihar, Sector 18, Gurugram, Haryana 122015

3.1 INTRODUCTION

World is moving towards green energy hence energy transition becomes highest priority for most on the developed and developing countries. Moving from fossil fuel to renewable energy becomes necessity to save the environment [1, 2]. Today wind power has all the necessary prerequisites to play a leading role in the global energy transition and the shift towards using green energy sources. Wind power is a technologically matured source of energy with enormous potential. Increasingly competitive, it takes up less land because it extends vertically and integrates perfectly with the circular economy model.

While wind energy becoming preferred green energy for most of the countries today, ensuring the reliability of wind technology becomes increasingly obvious [3]. At the same time, energy company responsible for the operations and maintenance

*For Correspondence: bhaskar1974.br@gmail.com

DOI: 10.1201/9781003541875-3

(O&M) have to ensure the maximum uptime of the plants. Wind farms are significantly increasing their focus to improve maintenance, reduce unplanned breakdowns to reduce downtime to maximize the energy production. They are leveraging artificial intelligence (AI) to largely help them improve output.

In the wind energy industry, maintenance has always been crucial and challenging as wind turbine's performance depend on turbine's health which is exposed with multiple internal and external factors. Predictive maintenance allows scheduling maintenance activities in advance and make the maintenance proactive to avoid unplanned downtime which lead significant financial losses. Operating and maintenance costs is almost 30% of the total cost of industrial plants [4], so inefficient maintenance may lead additional costs and consumer dissatisfaction. As per International Energy Agency of 2019, the amount of renewable energy as a supply of the OECD (Organization for Economic Cooperation and Development) is expected to provide one-third of total energy generation by 2025. In general, wind farm uses preventive and corrective maintenance; however, considering industrial environments, where stops can cause large losses [5], predictive maintenance is becoming popular especially with its new approach in context of industry 4.0 standards. This new approach has allowed integration between physical and digital systems, facilitating the collection of a large amount of data.

Artificial Intelligence (AI)/Machine learning (ML) plays a pivotal role in handling large amount of data collected by the wind turbine controller and/or additional systems like condition monitoring systems for supporting predictive maintenance. In recent days, multiple researchers established the application of ML for fault detection and predictive maintenance. Perez Granados et al. [6] presented a methodology for the predictive maintenance of wind turbines by using vibration monitoring as input. Tang et al. [7] employed an improved light GBM algorithm for online fault detection in gearboxes of wind turbines. Farrar et al. [8] give an overview of the use of artificial intelligence and ML in grid-connected wind turbine control systems. Quite recently, Masoumi [9] has presented a comprehensive review of machine learning applications for offshore wind farms. Randrianandraina et al. [10], Vilela et al. [11] have focused on anomaly detection to predict fault leveraging structured data. There is a dearth of research where structured and unstructured data has been used to improve fault prediction for effective predictive maintenance scheduling.

In this paper, we will focus on two key elements, first to detect the anomaly at the initial stage of the equipment health corrosion, and second to measure the failure propagation to define the maintenance schedule. Structure (operating and sensor data) and unstructured (image, inspection reports) data will be leveraged along with AI/ML and statistical modeling to identify anomalies and predict faults to define the schedule for predictive maintenance. Further, this paper will explore the use of Artificial Neural Network (ANN) for anomaly detection from all types of signals and intelligence irrespective of form of data. In case of failure propagation, equipment has been considered to gauge the risk. The study has been focused on combining multiple approaches for better learning sequential decision-making and control strategies. To establish the methodology, wind energy industry's masked data will be used and in some of the cases, data will be synthesized using Generative AI. The key aim of this study is to define and establish and robust failure prediction process that can be leveraged in the wind energy sector for effective scheduling of services for preventive maintenance to reduce risk and downtime to improve availability and sustainability.

3.2 NUMERICAL ILLUSTRATION

To improve preventive maintenance and optimize the cost of services, accurate failure prediction becomes crucial for the energy sector. Multimodal analytics framework (Figure 3.1) that could be used for any failure prediction with greater accuracy for optimum preventive maintenance. This framework allows to leveraging of all possible forms of intelligence and the latest AI techniques to identify anomaly and failure prediction for effective maintenance strategy.

This article leverages multiple data sources (Image data – [12], Inspection Report [13, 14], Sensor data [15]) to develop computer vision algorithms capable of detecting various types of faults and monitoring their propagation rates for enhanced image analysis and decision-making. Additionally, it employs IoT data to build machine-learning models for early fault detection. The study also integrates Large Language Models (LLMs) and Generative Pre-trained Transformers (GPT) to assess and identify the severity of these faults.

- **Image data:** To establish anomaly detection through image analysis, wind turbine's parts images have been used from GitHub Repository [12] and shown in Figure 3.2. We assess the implementation of the planned strategy using a dataset of wind turbine blade images categorized into two types: Defective and Non-Defective. The Defective category includes several types such as Mechanical Damage, Paint off, Crack, and Scratch. The training dataset contains 123 defective images and 156 non-defective images, totaling 279 images. For validation, the dataset includes 60 defective images and 64 non-defective images.
- **Inspection Report:** A sample wind turbine inspection report has been used [13, 14] to analyze unstructured data to identify the severity of the assets. A snapshot of the inspection report is shown in Table 3.1.
- **Sensor (SCADA) data:** Sensor data [15] has been utilized for further analysis. SCADA data contains more than 60 information of wind turbine components recorded by the SCADA system. It contains time-stamped operations data for the turbine. The timestamps are at 10-minute intervals which represent the average of the sensor readings over that period. It is to be noted that the fault data contains wind turbine fault types whereas, status data contains description of the status of wind turbine operational. There are 5 different types of fault have been considered:
    - o gf: generator heating fault
    - o mf: mains failure fault
    - o ff: feeding fault
    - o af: air cooling fault
    - o ef: excitation fault

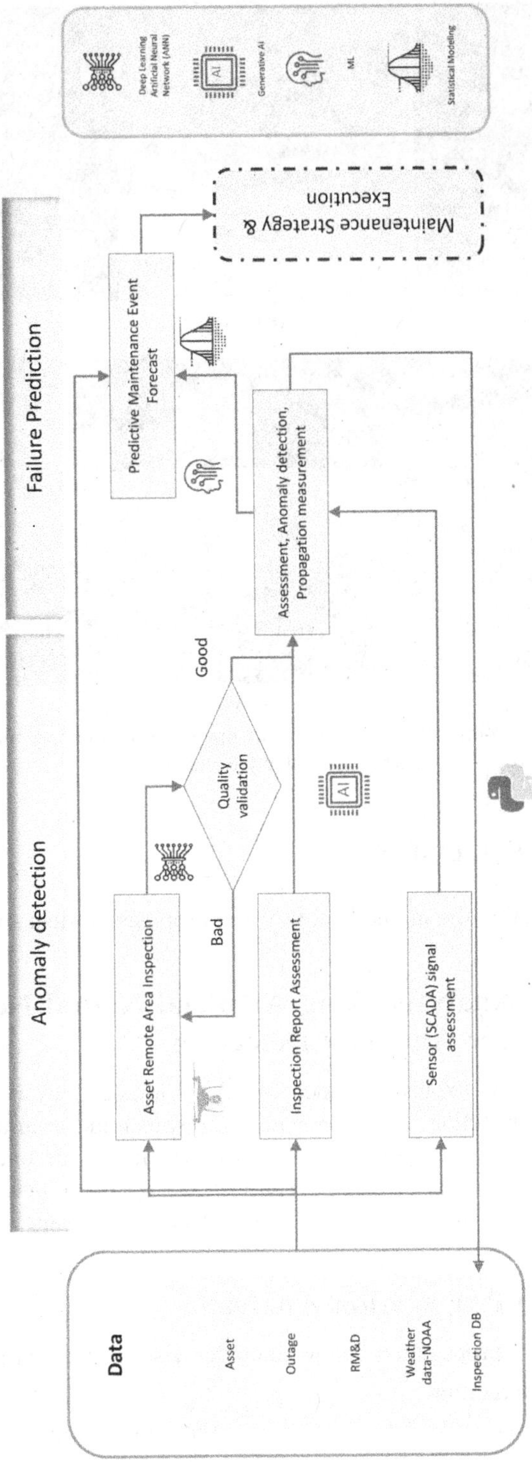

Figure 3.1: Multimodal analytics framework.

(a)

(b)

Figure 3.2 Wind turbine's component images: (a) Defective images, and (b) Non-defective images.

3.3 METHODOLOGY

This section explains the methodology of the proposed system in detail.

3.3.1 Image Analysis using Artificial Neural Network (ANN) for Anomaly Detection

We have used YOLO (You Only Look Once) for image analysis. This YOLO is a popular object detection model known for its speed and accuracy. It was first introduced by Joseph Redmon et al. in 2016 and has since undergone several iterations, the latest being YOLO v7. YOLO is a single-shot detector that uses a fully convolutional neural network (CNN) to process an image.

3.3.2 Failure Propagation Analysis

To measure failure propagation below computer vision approach has been taken.

- **Crack Detection**
  - *Grayscale Conversion:* Converts the image to grayscale.

- *Gaussian Blurring:* Applies a Gaussian blur to reduce noise.
- *Canny Edge Detection* (It was developed by John F. Canny in 1986 [16]: Detects edges in the image.
- *Contour Detection:* Finds contours in the edge-detected image.
- *Crack Mask Creation:* Draws contours on a mask to highlight cracks.

- **Crack Percentage Calculation**
  - *Total Area Calculation:* Calculates the total number of pixels in the image.
  - *Crack Area Calculation:* Sums the pixels in the crack mask.
  - *Percentage Calculation:* Computes the percentage of the image that is covered by cracks using the following formula.

$$\text{Crack Percentage} = \frac{\text{Crack Area}}{\text{Total Area}} \times 100 \quad (1)$$

  - *Bounding Box Drawing:* Draws bounding boxes around detected cracks using the contours.

- **Crack Propagation Rate Calculation**
  - *Time Difference Calculation:* Computes the time difference between consecutive images in days.
  - *Crack Difference Calculation:* Computes the difference in crack percentages between consecutive images.
  - *Propagation Rate Calculation:* Calculates the propagation rate using the formula given below.

$$\text{Propagation Rate} = \frac{\text{Crack Difference}}{\text{Time Difference}} \quad (2)$$

3.3.3 Inspection Report Analysis—Issue Classification and Recommendation

To classify issues based on inspection reports and descriptions (Table 3.1), we used a Gen AI (LLM) approach with Azure GPT-3.5. Multiclass classification involves categorizing instances into one of several predefined classes. Leveraging semantic search for this task can significantly enhance the accuracy and relevance of classifications by understanding the context and meaning behind the data.

Semantic search is an advanced information retrieval technique that interprets the meaning of words and phrases in a query. Unlike traditional keyword-based searches, which rely on exact word matches, semantic search considers user intent, context, and conceptual meanings to return more relevant results. Using semantic search for multiclass classification leverages advanced natural language processing (NLP) techniques to better understand context and provide more accurate classifications. This approach combines text embeddings with vector search capabilities to effectively enhance traditional classification methods.

Also, LLM is getting used to identifying the location and servicing/repairs timeframe which are very crucial to future failure. This makes LLM more appropriate than traditional classification techniques.

Table 3.1 Sample inspection report

ID#	Severity	P#		C#	Description	Location
1	Low	P4	-	O	Minor surface corrosion on bolts at external stairs. Foundation anchor bolts also require additional anti-corrosion measures to be applied.	Tower Exterior
2	Low	P4	-	O	Converter cooling system pressure low. Maintenance attention required or WTG may potentially fault.	Control Deck
3	Medium	P3	-	S	There is no record of lift certification. Previous record is out of date. All other WTG's inspected at this site had valid lift certification records from Mar-2020. Confirm with service provider that this has also been inspected.	Lift
4	Low	P4	-	O	Power cables are rubbing at the cable loop and the insulation is being rubbed into a powder. This is generally to be expected. Observation only. Monitor any further wear.	Tower Interior
5	Low	P4	-	O	One of the yaw brake calipers appears to be sticking. Screeching noise could be observed from the exterior of the WTG. Unknown which exact caliper is not releasing fully. Does not affect yaw function but is an audible nuisance.	Yaw Deck
6	Low	P4	-	S	Damaged safety signage at yaw deck. Recommend replacement.	Yaw Deck
7	Medium	P3	-	O	Gear oil particle counter not commissoned. No active data recording. This device provides a protective condition monitoring function for the gearbox and should be active at all times.	Nacelle
8	Medium	P3	-	E	Oil leaking from gearbox seal on planetary stage 1 rotor side housing cover. Leak is slow and long-term.	Nacelle
9	Medium	P3	-	E	All blade bearings are losing excesive grease through their outer seals. This has been observered on other WTG's inspected at this site.	Blade
10	Low	P4	-	S	Missing certification tag on hub fall arrest anchor point. Note all other anchor points have tags attached and are in date. This must have just fallen off due to weathering.	Hub
11	High	P2	-	O	Failed blade bolt on Blade A. Recommend follow up with the O&M service provider to determine root cause and if there are any other cases. All other visible blade bolts were checked and they are present. Drone survey can be used to check other WTG blade bolts if desired.	Blade
12	Low	P4	-	O	Cup anemometer is missing one of its cups. This may affect data logging and WTG operation if this anemometer is being used. The default should be the ultrasonic anemometer which appears to be in good order.	Nacelle Roof

3.3.4 Sensor (SCADA) Data Analysis for Failure Prediction Analysis

Sensor data has been statistically analyzed to build a failure forecast model. Detailed exploratory data analysis (EDA) was used to explore any bivariate relationships with different faults. We have used multiple supervised ML models—Random Forest Regressor, Logistic Regression model, Gradient Boosting, Support Vector Machines (SVM), Neural Network and Ensemble Technique to achieve better accuracy. Also, we have tried with under-sampling and oversampling to deal with imbalanced data.

3.3.5 Composite Distribution

A composite distribution, also known as a sectional or piecewise model, is constructed by combining pieces of two or more distributions in such a way that the resulting distribution meets certain smoothness criteria. Roy [17] explained how composite distributions can measure failure probability. However, this paper focuses on supervised learning machine learning models to capture sensor signals and establish causal relationships.

3.4 ANALYSIS AND FINDINGS

3.4.1 Deep Learning Model for Defect Detection

We used YOLO v8 to analyze 269 images (Figure 3.3), achieving an accuracy of 87% in defect prediction. Once the external images of wind turbines are captured manually or via drone, this model can help analyze and classify them into categories such as good condition, crack, erosion, mechanical damage, paint off, or scratch.

3.4.2 Propagation Analysis

In many cases, merely classifying issues may not suffice to understand upcoming failures. We need to analyze propagation to measure the growth of damage progression. For effective propagation analysis, images should be taken from the same angle over time to track progression accurately. Sample images (Figure 3.4) have been analyzed to measure crack percentage and crack propagation rate (Table 3.2 and Figure 3.5). Once we have images and failure details from the same turbine, we can establish associations to identify thresholds that indicate potential failure.

Table 3.2 Crack percentage progression and propagation rate

Image Name	Date of Image Taken	Crack Percentage (%)	Days Between Dates	Propagation Rate (% increase per day)
1_Dec_2022.jpeg	8/1/2023	0.00	—	—
2_June_2023.jpg	11/1/2023	0.24	92	0.00251
3_Dec_2023.jpg	2/1/2024	0.45	92	0.00236
4_May_2024.jpg	5/1/2024	0.66	90	0.00235

3.4.3 Inspection Report Analysis

The section below presents the outcomes of the gen AI large language model (LLM) in identifying severity (Figure 3.6), location, and repair timeframe. When combined with image analysis, inspection reports can be used by the LLM model to determine the urgency of issues and predict upcoming faults.

3.4.4 Fault Prediction Analysis

As a part of the fault prediction analysis, first we have performed EDA of 66 SCADA features with fault data. Below histograms (Figure 3.7) show the distribution of each and every feature.

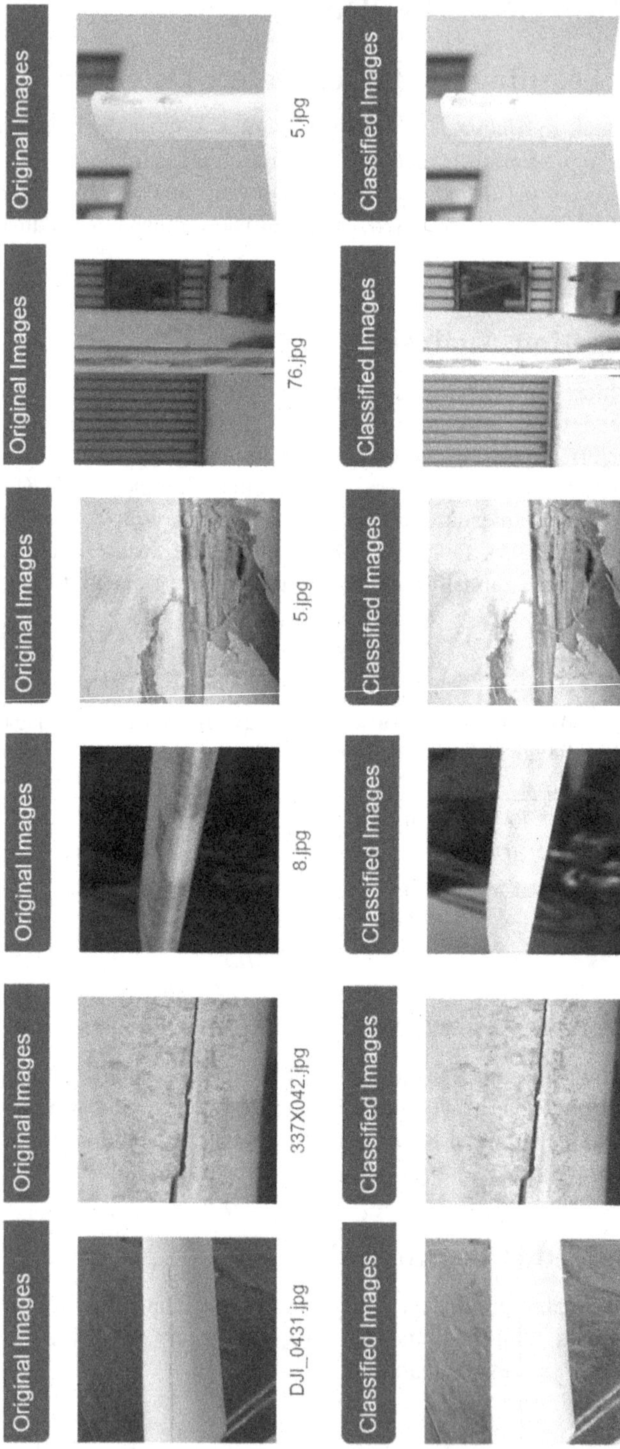

Figure 3.3 Image defect classification.

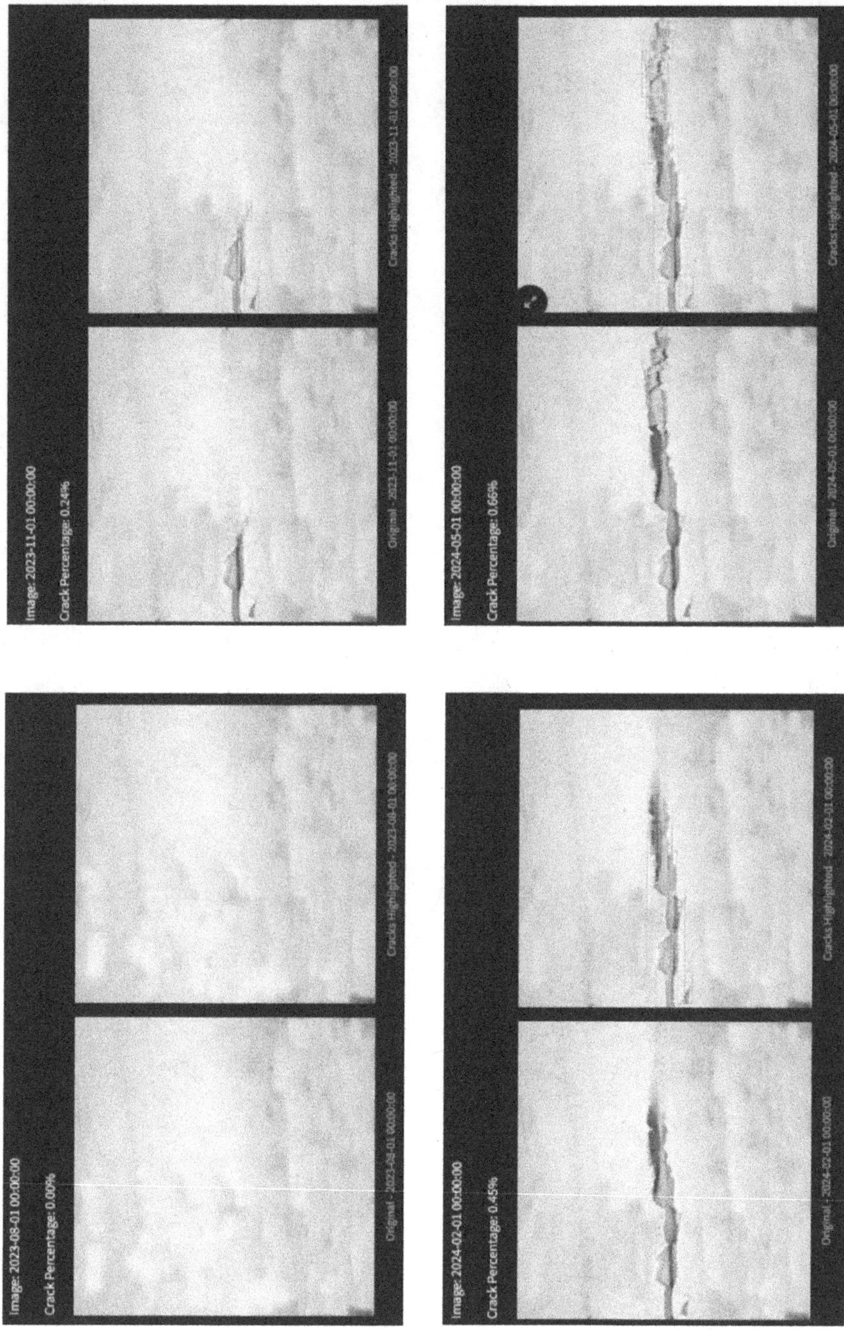

Figure 3.4 Defect progression.

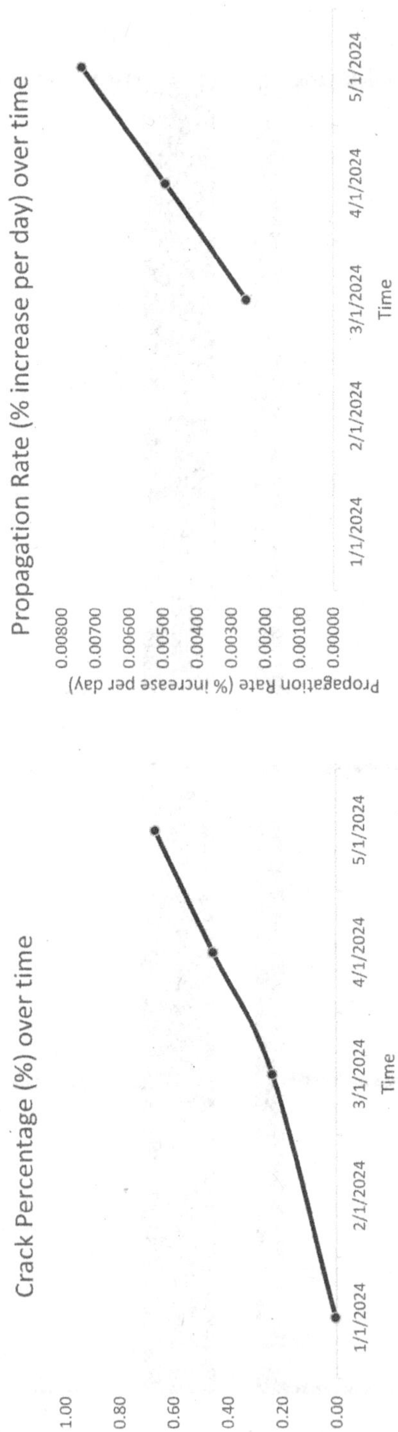

Figure 3.5 Crack percentage progression and propagation rate.

Figure 3.6 Severity assessment with LLM.

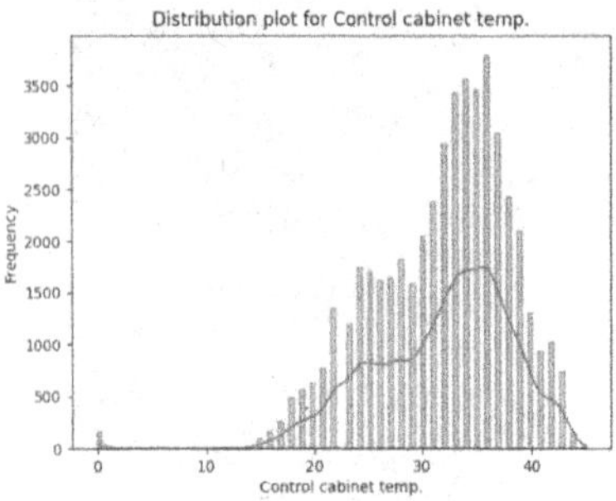
Distribution plot for Control cabinet temp.
Frequency
Control cabinet temp.

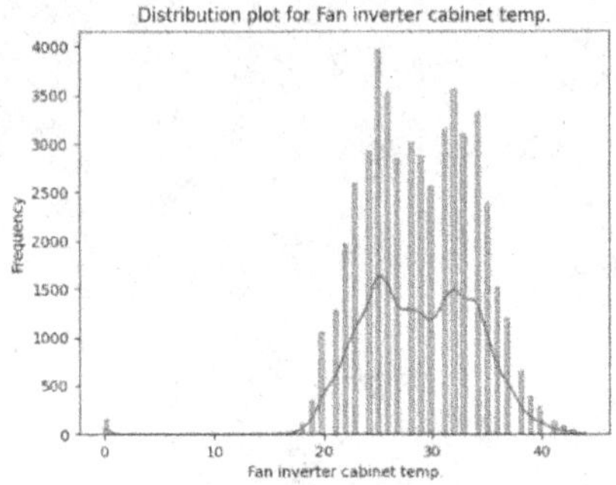
Distribution plot for Fan inverter cabinet temp.
Frequency
Fan inverter cabinet temp.

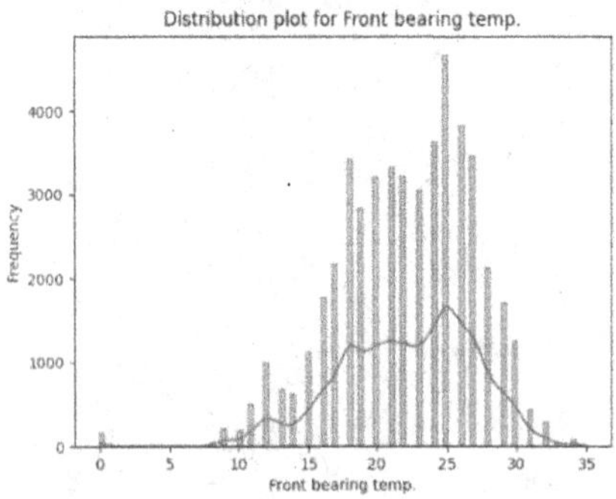
Distribution plot for Front bearing temp.
Frequency
Front bearing temp.

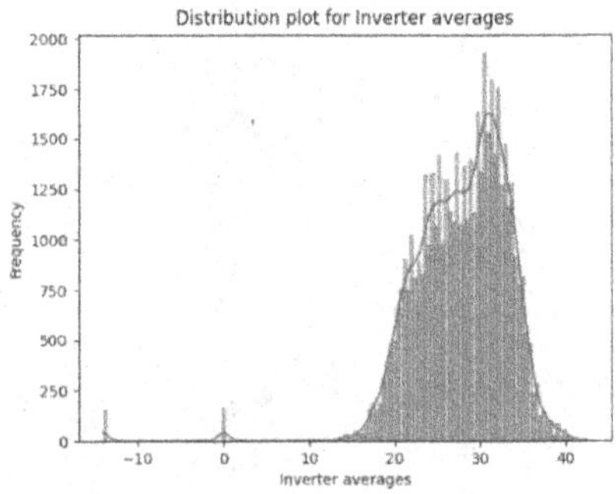
Distribution plot for Inverter averages
Frequency
Inverter averages

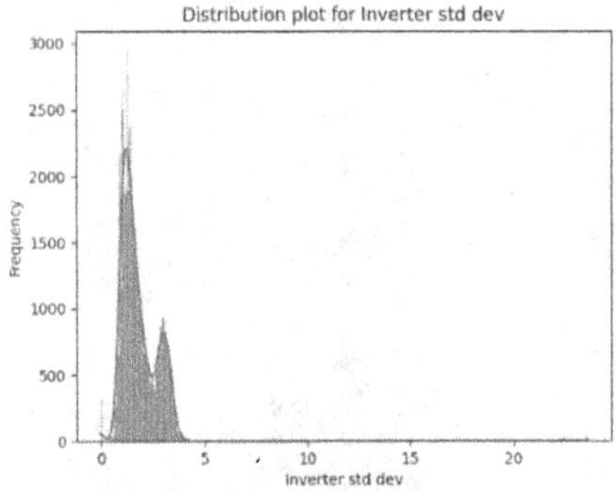
Distribution plot for Inverter std dev
Frequency
Inverter std dev

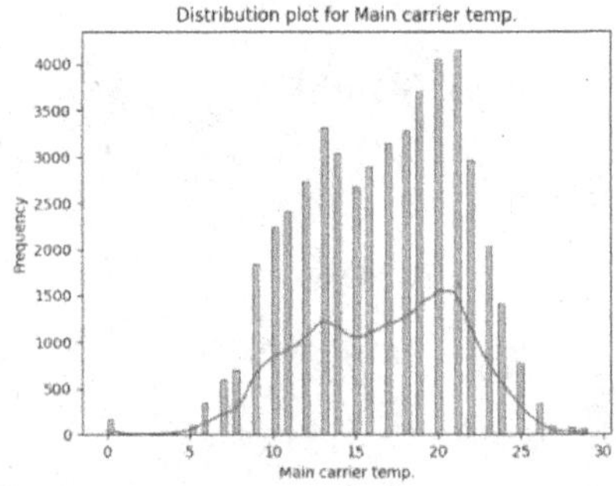
Distribution plot for Main carrier temp.
Frequency
Main carrier temp.

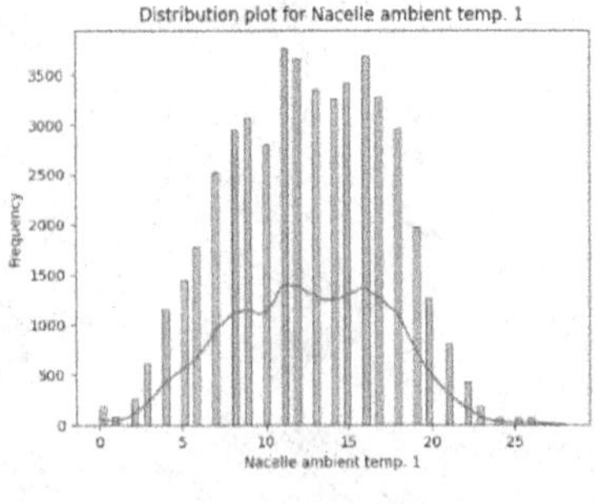
Distribution plot for Nacelle ambient temp. 1
Frequency
Nacelle ambient temp. 1

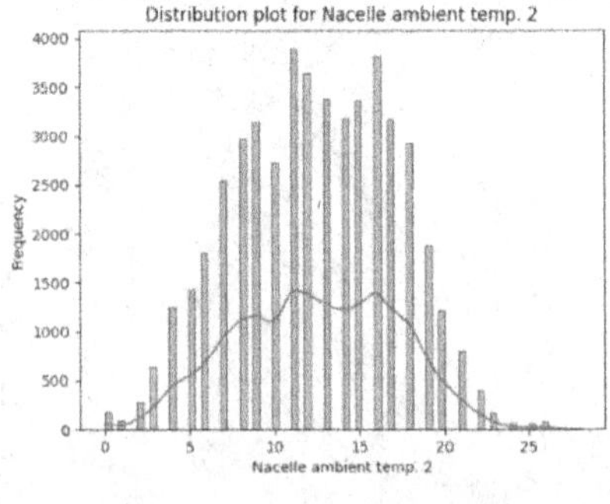
Distribution plot for Nacelle ambient temp. 2
Frequency
Nacelle ambient temp. 2

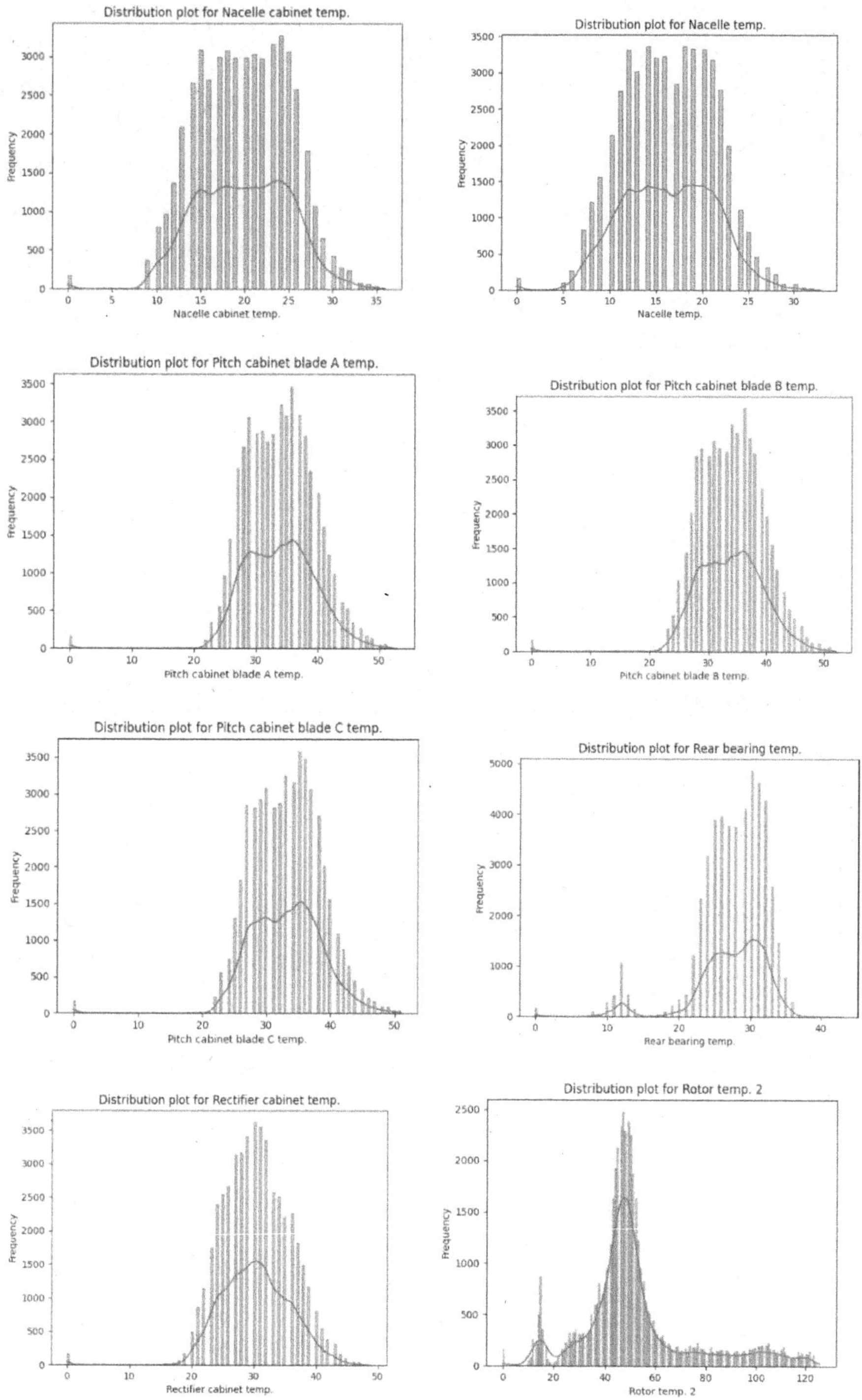
Distribution plot for Nacelle cabinet temp.
Frequency
Nacelle cabinet temp.
Distribution plot for Nacelle temp.
Frequency
Nacelle temp.
Distribution plot for Pitch cabinet blade A temp.
Frequency
Pitch cabinet blade A temp.
Distribution plot for Pitch cabinet blade B temp.
Frequency
Pitch cabinet blade B temp.
Distribution plot for Pitch cabinet blade C temp.
Frequency
Pitch cabinet blade C temp.
Distribution plot for Rear bearing temp.
Frequency
Rear bearing temp.
Distribution plot for Rectifier cabinet temp.
Frequency
Rectifier cabinet temp.
Distribution plot for Rotor temp. 2
Frequency
Rotor temp. 2

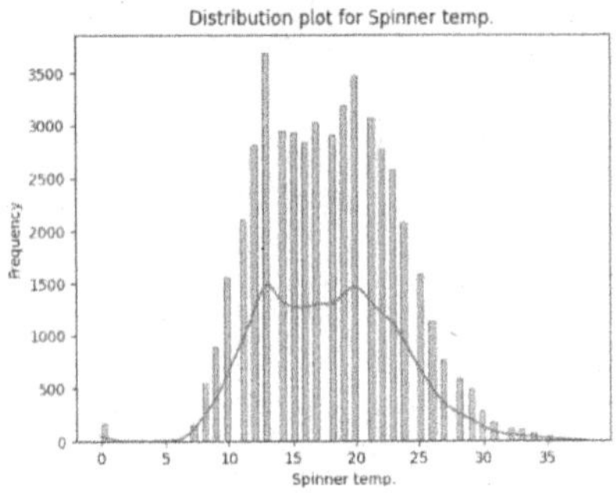
Distribution plot for Spinner temp.
Frequency
Spinner temp.

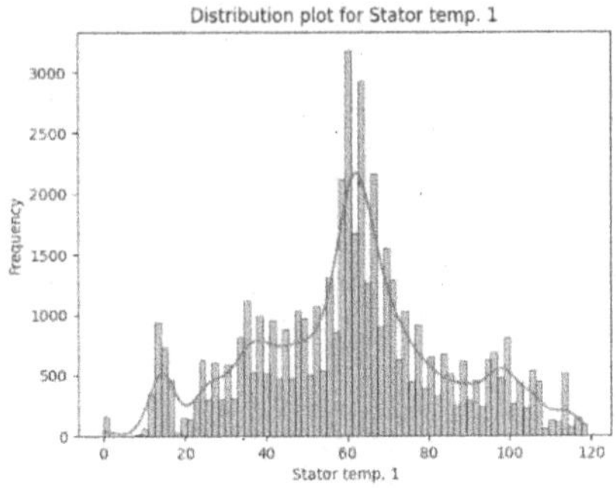
Distribution plot for Stator temp. 1
Frequency
Stator temp. 1

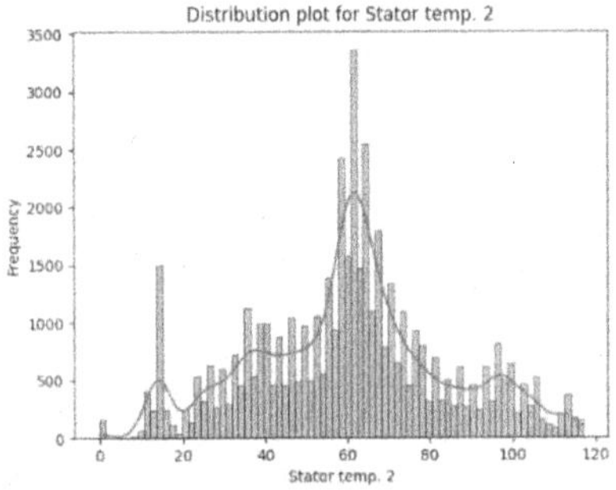
Distribution plot for Stator temp. 2
Frequency
Stator temp. 2

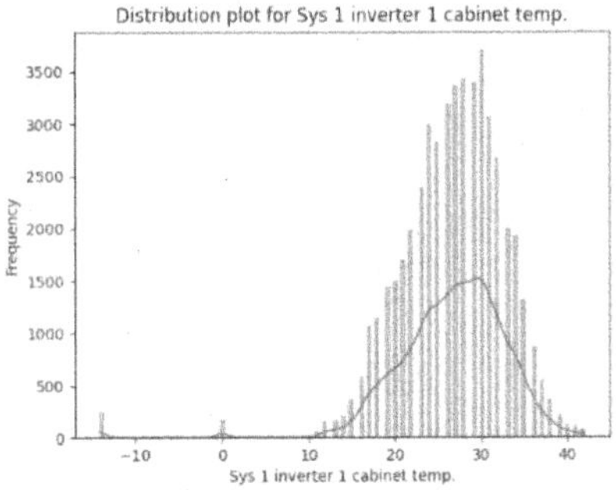
Distribution plot for Sys 1 inverter 1 cabinet temp.
Frequency
Sys 1 inverter 1 cabinet temp.

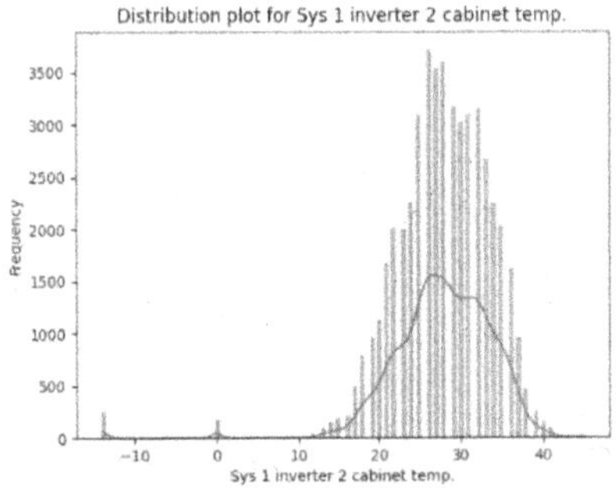
Distribution plot for Sys 1 inverter 2 cabinet temp.
Frequency
Sys 1 inverter 2 cabinet temp.

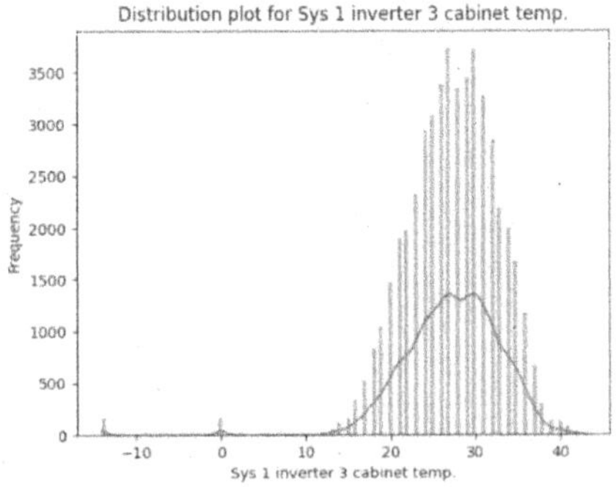
Distribution plot for Sys 1 inverter 3 cabinet temp.
Frequency
Sys 1 inverter 3 cabinet temp.

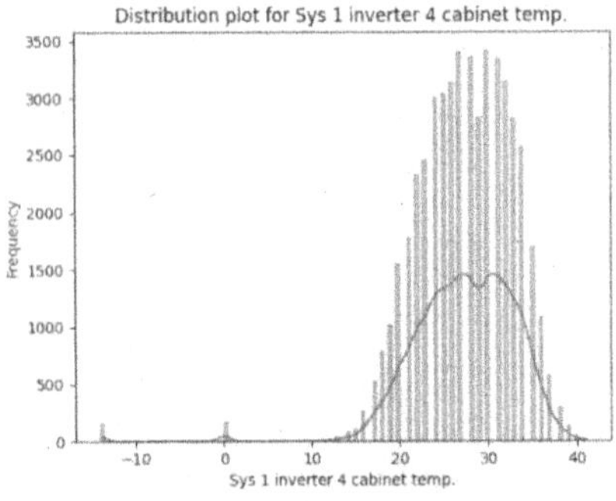
Distribution plot for Sys 1 inverter 4 cabinet temp.
Frequency
Sys 1 inverter 4 cabinet temp.

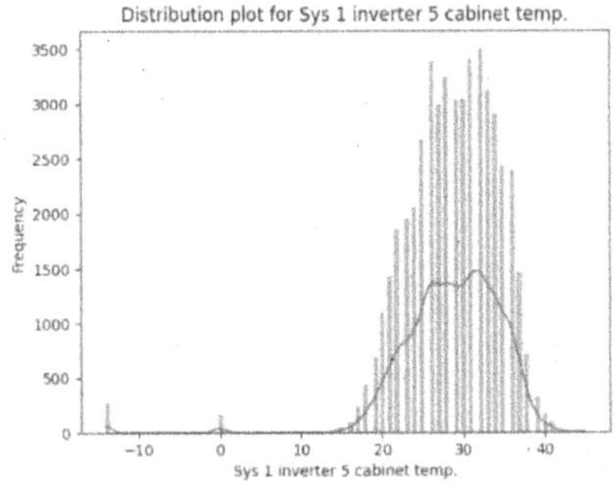
Distribution plot for Sys 1 inverter 5 cabinet temp.
Frequency
Sys 1 inverter 5 cabinet temp.

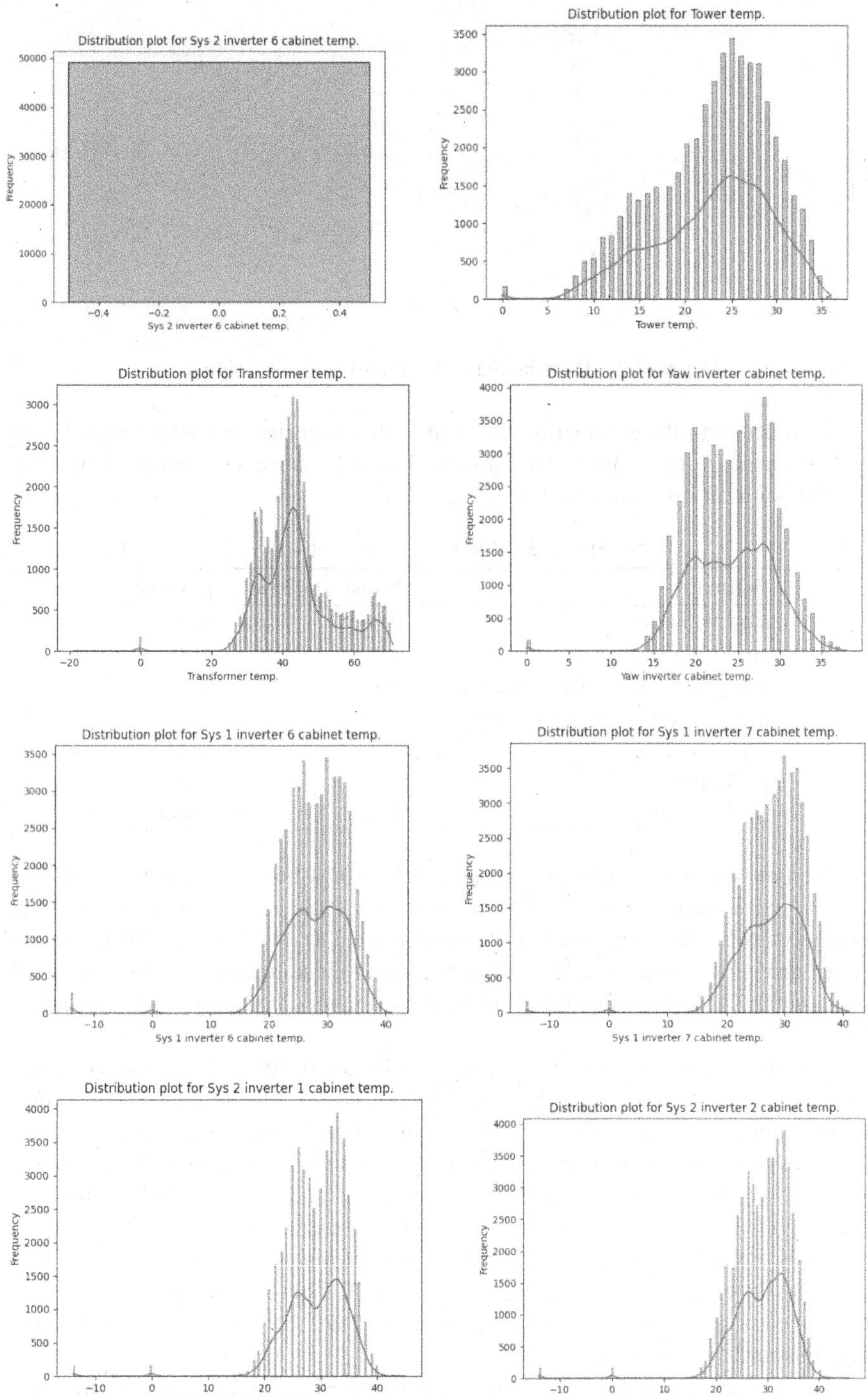
Distribution plot for Sys 2 inverter 6 cabinet temp.
Frequency
Sys 2 inverter 6 cabinet temp.
Distribution plot for Tower temp.
Frequency
Tower temp.
Distribution plot for Transformer temp.
Frequency
Transformer temp.
Distribution plot for Yaw inverter cabinet temp.
Frequency
Yaw inverter cabinet temp.
Distribution plot for Sys 1 inverter 6 cabinet temp.
Frequency
Sys 1 inverter 6 cabinet temp.
Distribution plot for Sys 1 inverter 7 cabinet temp.
Frequency
Sys 1 inverter 7 cabinet temp.
Distribution plot for Sys 2 inverter 1 cabinet temp.
Frequency
Sys 2 inverter 1 cabinet temp.
Distribution plot for Sys 2 inverter 2 cabinet temp.
Frequency
Sys 2 inverter 2 cabinet temp.

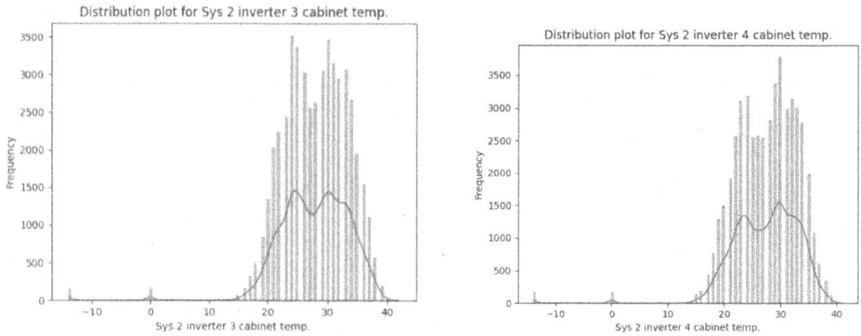

Figure 3.7 Distribution (Histogram) of sensor signals.

To understand the association between fault categories and sensor signals, we have performed F-test. Out of 66 features, 7 features have significant association with the fault as discussed in Table 3.3.

Table 3.3 ANOVA- F-test statistic

Features	F-test Statistic	p Value
min. windspeed	0.08	1.00
min. Rotation	1.91	0.09
Sys 2 inverter 5 cabinet temp.	0.38	0.86
Sys 2 inverter 7 cabinet temp.	0.39	0.86
Blade A temp.	0.19	0.96
Blade B temp.	0.29	0.92
Blade C temp.	0.32	0.90

Relationship between sensor signal and fault has been analyzed in detail. In case of "GF" fault, we have observed a strong fault indication based on Max Windspeed, Min Rotation and Min Power (Figure 3.8). On 17th Oct'2014, rotation started dropping and power generation becoming close to zero while wind speed is maximum. This was an indication of performance degradation while input is still significant.

Multiple supervised ML models such as Random Forest Regressor, Logistic Regression model, Gradient Boosting, Support Vector Machines (SVM), Neural Network and Ensemble Technique have been tested for fault prediction. We have observed fault data is imbalanced, 99% of data points are under NF (as shown in Table 3.4). We have used both down-sampling and oversampling techniques to deal with imbalanced data. In the case of down-sampling, the majority class (instances labeled as 'NF') matches the number of instances in the minority class (instances labeled as something other than 'NF'). This is a common method to address class imbalance in datasets, ensuring that the model doesn't become biased towards the majority class.

Due to very limited data, we have combined MF and GF faults as they are similar in nature. Also, we have adjusted data to predict the fault based on 1 hour earlier data to provide lead time to shut down the turbine.

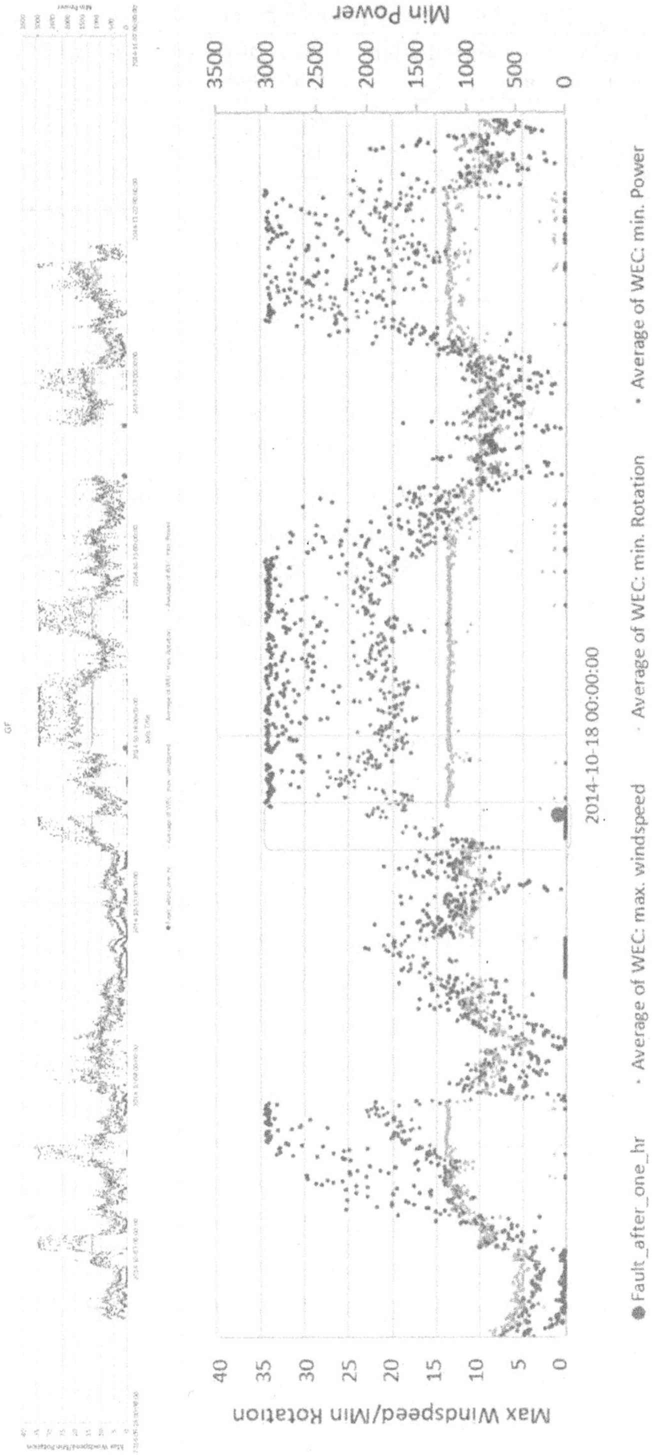

Figure 3.8 Fault (GF) vs wind speed, rotation, and power.

Table 3.4 Data distribution by fault classes

Class	Original Data Distribution by Fault Class	Data Distribution by Fault Class with Under-sampling
AF	62	62
EF	174	174
FF	254	254
GF	43	43
MF	20	20
NF	48575	553

Gradient Boosting and Ensemble Techniques have better performance than other models. The average accuracy is coming around 80% (as shown in Table 3.5). To enhance accuracy, we tried oversampling by generating synthetic as we have very limited data points for most of the fault classes except NF.

Table 3.5 Model performance without synthetic data

Model	Class	#Training Data	#Test Data	Precision	Recall	F1-Score
Random Forest Classifier	AF	43	19	.71	.53	.61
	EF	122	52	.61	.54	.57
	FF	178	76	.74	.76	.75
	GF/MF	44	19	.79	.79	.79
	NF	387	166	.89	.91	.91
Logistic Regression	AF	43	19	.32	.74	.44
	EF	122	52	.62	.81	.70
	FF	178	76	.81	.63	.71
	GF/MF	44	19	.57	.84	.68
	NF	387	166	.89	.71	.79
Gradient Boosting	AF	43	19	1.00	.68	.81
	EF	122	52	.58	.50	.54
	FF	178	76	.72	.76	.74
	GF/MF	44	19	.79	.79	.79
	NF	387	166	.90	.94	.92
Support Vector Machines (SVM)	AF	43	19	.35	.74	.47
	EF	122	52	.63	.87	.73
	FF	178	76	.81	.67	.73
	GF/MF	44	19	.70	.84	.76
	NF	387	166	.91	.74	.82
Neural Network	AF	43	19	.56	.53	.54
	EF	122	52	.70	.58	.63
	FF	178	76	.72	.79	.75
	GF/MF	44	19	.74	.89	.81
	NF	387	166	.91	.90	.91
Ensemble Technique	AF	43	19	.67	.53	.59
	EF	122	52	.62	.65	.64
	FF	178	76	.79	.75	.77
	GF/MF	44	19	.88	.79	.83
	NF	387	166	.88	.92	.90

SMOTE (Synthetic Minority Over-sampling Technique) is used to address class imbalance in datasets. It generates synthetic samples for the minority class by interpolating between existing minority instances and their nearest neighbors. This helps in balancing the dataset, improving model performance, and reducing bias towards the majority class. By creating new, diverse samples, SMOTE also helps prevent overfitting.

The accuracy based on oversampling accuracy (as shown in Table 3.6) is Gradient Boosting and Ensemble Technique coming significantly higher than the under-sampling models. This indicates if we have a large volume of data ML techniques can help us to achieve higher accuracy.

Table 3.6 Model performance with synthetic data

Model	Class	#Training Data	#Test Data	Precision	Recall	F1-Score
Gradient Boosting	AF	34156	14419	.97	1.00	.98
	EF	34036	14690	.86	.98	.91
	FF	34031	14544	.96	.85	.90
	GF/MF	33904	14671	.99	.99	.99
	NF	33885	14539	.99	.92	.95
Ensemble Technique	AF	34156	14419	1.00	1.00	1.00
	EF	34036	14690	.99	1.00	.99
	FF	34031	14544	1.00	.99	.99
	GF/MF	33904	14671	1.00	1.00	1.00
	NF	33885	14539	1.00	.99	1.00

3.5 CONCLUSION AND DISCUSSIONS

In the industry, failure prediction typically uses either a failure distribution approach or a causal model based on structured asset and operating data. This paper experiments with multiple approaches to maximize intelligence for better failure prediction within a multimodal analytics framework. By leveraging deep learning, defect detection and propagation analysis help identify the severity of asset health. This method captures additional signals not detected through sensor data. Additionally, inspection reports are analyzed using large language models (LLMs) to determine severity levels, issue locations, and urgency based on unstructured descriptions from the reports. Finally, sensor data is analyzed to predict faults under four major categories: EF, FF, and GF/MF. We observed strong indicators of upcoming GF/MF faults based on wind speed, rotation, and power generation. Gradient Boosting gives the best result over other models in the under-sampling method. On the other hand, models are performing with a high 90% accuracy in the oversampling method.

This model can be further improved by integrating outcomes from defect analysis, propagation analysis, and inspection report analysis to enhance fault prediction accuracy. Although we did not integrate these due to data limitations in this study, organizations have an opportunity to capture all three sets of data i.e., images, inspection reports, and sensor data at the asset level.

REFERENCES

[1] Baloch, M.A. and Danish. 2022. CO_2 emissions in BRICS countries: What role can environmental regulation and financial development play? Climate Change. 172: 9. https://doi.org/10.1007/s10584-022-03362-7

[2] May, N. 2017. The impact of wind power support schemes on technology choices. Energy Economics. 65: 343–354. https://doi.org/10.1016/j.eneco.2017.05.017

[3] Uwe, L. and S. Beji. 2024. Predictive maintenance for offshore wind turbines through deep learning and online clustering of unsupervised subsystems: A real-world implementation. Journal of Ocean Engineering and Marine Energy. https://doi.org/10.21203/rs.3.rs-3906932/v1

[4] May, A., D. McMillan and S. Thöns. 2015. Economic analysis of condition monitoring systems for offshore wind turbine sub-systems. IET Renew. Power Generation. 9(8): 900–907. https://doi.org/10.1049/iet-rpg.2015.0019

[5] Jiawen, H. and P. Chen. 2020. Predictive maintenance of systems subject to hard failure based on proportional hazards model. Reliability Engineering and System Safety. Vol. 196. https://doi.org/10.1016/j.ress.2019.106707

[6] Perez Granados, D., M.A. Ortega Ruiz, J. Moreira Acosta, S.A. Gama Lara, R.A. Gonzalez Dominguez and P.J. Paramo Kanetas. 2023. A wind turbine vibration monitoring system for predictive maintenance based on machine learning methods developed under safely controlled laboratory conditions. Energies. 16(5). https://doi.org/10.3390/en16052290.

[7] Mingzhu, T., Q. Zhao, S.X. Ding, H. Wu, L. Li, W. Long, et al. 2020. An improved lightgbm algorithm for online fault detection of wind turbine gearboxes. Energies. 13(4). https://doi.org/10.3390/en13040807

[8] Farrar, B.G., A. Vernouillet, E. Garcia-Pelegrin, E.W. Legg, K.F. Brecht, P.J. Lambert, et al. 2023. Reporting and interpreting non-significant results in animal cognition research. Peer Journals. DOI: 10.7717/peerj.14963

[9] Masoumi, M. 2023. Machine learning solutions for offshore wind farms: A review of applications and impact. Journal of Marine Science and Engineering. JMSE. 11(10). https://doi.org/10.3390/jmse11101855

[10] Randrianandraina, R., J. Chapuy, L. Rajaoarisoa and M.S. Mouchaweh. 2023. Wind turbine generator bearing anomaly detection and explanation using RRCF approach. Published in: 2023 International Conference on Machine Learning and Applications (ICMLA). IEEE. DOI: 10.1109/ICMLA58977.2023.00238

[11] Campoverde-Vilela, L., M. del Cisne Feijóo, Y. Vidal, J. Sampietro and C. Tutivén. 2023. Anomaly-based fault detection in wind turbine main bearings. Wind Energy Science. 8: 557–574. DOI: https://doi.org/10.5194/wes-8-557-2023

[12] Structural Health Monitoring of Wind Turbines. https://github.com/ertis-research/shm-wind-turbines/tree/main

[13] WinFault documentation. https://wt-fdd.readthedocs.io/en/latest/

[14] Blade Inspection Report. https://windren.se/WW2015/WW2015_07b_212_Soerensen_BCC_0100-V002_PDFT.pdf

[15] Soontronchai, W. 2019. IIOT Data of Wind Turbine. Accessed: May 15, 2022. [Online]. Available: https://www.kaggle.com/datasets/wasuratme96/iiot-data-of-wind-turbine

[16] Canny, J.F. 1986. A Computational approach to edge detection. *In*: IEEE Transactions on Pattern Analysis and Machine Intelligence. IEEE. PAMI-8(8). DOI: 10.1109/TPAMI.1986.4767851

[17] Bhaskar, R., D. Bera, S. Nigam and S.K. Upadhyay. 2021. A study of turbine failure pattern: A model optimization using machine learning. International Journal of System Assurance Engineering and Management. DOI: https://doi.org/10.1007/s13198-021-01542-9

Chapter 4

Generative AI Based Demand Forecasting for Third-Party Logistics

M. Kmiecik
Silesian University of Technology, Poland
ORCID: 0000-0003-2015-1132; Email: mariusz.kmiecik@polsl.pl

4.1 INTRODUCTION

Contemporary logistics enterprises, including 3PL (Third-Party Logistics) operators, are facing growing challenges related to demand forecasting in complex and dynamically changing supply chains. Traditional forecasting methods, primarily based on the analysis of historical sales data, are proving insufficient in the face of the increasing complexity of logistics processes, market globalization, and phenomena such as e-commerce, which amplify the scale of unpredictable demand fluctuations [1]. As a result, logistics operators are seeking new, advanced solutions that will enable them to better predict demand and optimize inventory management. The literature emphasizes that the use of artificial intelligence (AI) and machine learning (ML) in demand forecasting is becoming a key trend that can significantly improve operational efficiency and reduce risks associated with forecasting errors.

One of the key aspects of applying AI and ML in demand forecasting is their ability to analyze large datasets and identify hidden patterns, allowing for more precise future trend predictions compared to traditional statistical models such as ARIMA. Modern forecasting techniques take into account variables such as

DOI: 10.1201/9781003541875-4

seasonality, irregularities in supply, and changing consumer preferences, which are particularly important in the context of dynamic supply chains. Industry 4.0 and the development of technologies related to generative artificial intelligence (gen-AI) have contributed to the emergence of new possibilities, which find applications in logistics and supply chain management, as confirmed by research highlighting the growing importance of these technologies in the context of digital transformation. This chapter aims to address the research question regarding how 3PL enterprises can use demand forecasting models based on ML and gen-AI, and how these models compare to each other.

4.2 BACKGROUND ON DEMAND FORECASTING IN 3PL ENTERPRISES

Outsourcing means using external sources. The desire to focus on core activities led to outsourcing additional services to specialized logistics operators. The use of services offered by 3PL is part of the widespread trend of logistics outsourcing. This is possible through proper warehouse management or reverse logistics services. Another advantage of using 3PL can be increased efficiency, but it should be noted that collaboration with 3PL can easily fail. One of the most common and important barriers in implementing and collaborating with 3PL is the unrealistic expectations of companies using 3PL services [2]. Another reason is the lack of flexibility on both sides regarding unforeseen actions that deviate from established norms and the failure to treat the service provider as a partner. Logistics processes entrusted to specialized service providers are referred to as outsourcing or contract logistics [2]. The idea of outsourcing services involves relinquishing certain logistics functions. Outsourcing began in transportation processes when companies began to recognize that maintaining and operating their own fleet of vehicles was a costly endeavor. Currently, outsourcing most often includes activities such as IT, HR, distribution, logistics, finance, and accounting.

A logistics operator is defined as a contract service provider that works to maximize resource utilization and improve operational performance [3]. It is a logistics service provider offering a diverse range of logistics activities on behalf of a manufacturer or retailer. The decision to use operator services is often made based on strategic considerations when a company recognizes that one or more elements of its operations need to change. Outsourcing certain services to operators allows manufacturers to continuously improve their products and quality. A logistics operator is a 3PL (third-party logistics) organization. Various definitions of 3PL exist in the literature. Some broad definitions of 3PL include "the use of external companies to perform logistics functions that were traditionally performed in-house" and "an external organization that performs all or part of a company's logistics functions." [1].

A logistics operator (3PL), depending on the commercial agreement between the two companies, may operate in procurement, transportation, warehousing, and/or distribution. Logistics companies, including logistics operators, shape national and international strategic and operational networks, creating stable relationships between manufacturing, trading companies, and customers. The competencies of logistics companies are particularly important in integrated, complex distribution networks consisting of many interpenetrating distribution channels. In omnichannel systems, logistics operators mitigate uncertain demand, limiting the negative effects of combining different distribution channels. Logistics operators, by managing warehouse releases, possess comprehensive knowledge of the actual flow of products across all types of channels, whether related to traditional sales or e-commerce. The primary function of a logistics operator is to optimize the processes of procurement, warehousing, transportation, and product distribution in a manner efficient for the company they work for. To achieve this, it is essential to have the physical and technological infrastructure and information systems necessary for the proper development of operations. However, some logistics operators outsource parts of this infrastructure without sacrificing the quality of the services provided. Logistics operators are capable of making decisions related to management and other issues, such as continuous improvement or reconfiguring distribution networks and supply chains. Third-party logistics operators (3PL) are among the most common in the market. They offer a variety of services, including external transportation, negotiation and confirmation of transport contracts, warehousing, and consolidation of goods. Some 3PL companies extend their activities to complementary services, such as product assembly or installation. The decision to use 3PL services is often strategically justified when a company recognizes that one or more elements of its operations require change. One of the trends in the logistics industry is the increasing complexity of services and the demand for logistics service packages (LSP) often referred to as bundled services. This trend also applies to one of the core services provided by operators—transportation and forwarding services—which are being expanded with various accompanying activities [4]. Companies in networks are increasingly choosing to collaborate with companies offering more than one service. It can be concluded that logistics operators can become more competitive by offering complementary services alongside basic logistics services, which may also include demand forecasting.

Demand forecasting is considered by some authors to be one of the main areas of application for machine learning [5], which is one of the most important trends in contemporary science. A logistics operator's forecasting skills have been recognized in the literature as supporting operators in managing spare parts inventories [6], forecasting demand for transportation services [7], forecasting dedicated to optimizing their own fleet [8], and forecasting supporting last-mile deliveries [9]. However, the author's proposed forecasting assumes a comprehensive solution related to demand forecasting for products across the entire distribution network. The main idea of this concept is to entrust the centralized forecasting function to a logistics operator operating within the distribution network. The need to include demand management in network activities is closely related to the need for centralization. The expansion and reconfiguration of distribution structures by global corporations, including actions such as centralization and decentralization, are observed worldwide [10]. There is no single ideal organizational structure model on the market that could meet the requirements of demand management.

However, one of the most important issues that can meet these requirements is the efficient transfer of data between the various network participants. This is possible through the use of a widely accessible database. This database collects and stores information generated in various companies belonging to the network. Among the features that determine the level of adaptation of an organizational structure to the requirements of demand management are the level of work progress standardization, hierarchical relationships, and the centralization of power.

The literature also emphasizes that two main decisions can be made during demand forecasting and planning [11]. The first concerns the reporting line of the demand planning unit (set for operational management and supply chain or sales and marketing). The second concerns the level of centralization (centralization or decentralization). Two basic centralization options can be distinguished [12]: concentration of tasks in an independent organizational unit, based on the principle of cross-functional operation, and concentration of tasks in an independent organizational unit that exists alongside other units—in this case, grouping demand management functions is necessary. One of the main features of centralization is the consolidation of demand management activities and their grouping in a separate functional area. The degree of centralization advancement shows at what level decisions are made, who has the power and skills to influence, and who obtains the appropriate permission. Centralization is also seen as the concentration of planning activities in one separate and formalized unit [13]. The central forecasting system provides the first information about forecasts for the supply chain. Buyers and suppliers act in sequence, analyzing information gathered from the central system and deciding whether to take actions that align or conflict with the established plan [14]. In the centralized forecasting version, demand levels at individual nodes of the distribution network are similar. In the decentralized version, these levels vary widely, causing numerous disruptions across the network. The strategies used by the central company in the distribution network affect the adaptability of the entire network. For this reason, an important issue is determining the characteristics of the central node of the distribution network, which decides on the selection of new nodes and controls material flows.

One of the more important added services offered within 3PL operations, according to the author, may involve expanding the standard range of services to include product demand forecasting. This concept is referred to as centralized forecasting. It assumes that a logistics operator, whose characteristics align with those identified through an analysis of entities capable of forecasting in distribution networks and flagship companies, can take over the forecasting function for the entire distribution network. This concept of transferring the demand forecasting function to logistics operators in the entire distribution network is considered in the previous author works. The proposed concept requires the use of a demand forecasting tool integrated with WMS (Warehouse Management System) in the form of an IT tool. The future role of information technology in supporting the management and control of logistics practices has been widely documented [15]. Additionally, numerous studies and market trends highlight the enormous importance of modern forecasting technologies, such as machine learning. There are currently many applications of machine learning-based forecasting algorithms that take into account multiple predictive factors. Typically, using a machine learning algorithm yields better results than using another forecasting method based solely on historical data. Forecasts are considered one of the risk categories in material flows [16]. Forecasting-related risk factors include inaccuracy, seasonality, product differentiation, short product life cycles, insufficient customer data, and information deviations. Demand fluctuations can cause supply management issues and lead to a tendency to maintain excessive inventory. In transportation processes, demand forecasts have an indirect impact.

In the era of rapid technological development, 3PL operators cannot lag behind the development of entire supply chains and distribution networks. The use of modern technologies by 3PL operators is a natural response to the current fourth industrial revolution (Industry 4.0). The literature has highlighted the foundations of concepts related to adapting logistics operators to the reality of Industry 4.0. Operator 4.0 has been defined as "an intelligent and skilled operator who performs not only collaborative work with robots but also work supported by machines as needed, using cyber-physical systems, advanced human-machine interaction technologies, and adaptive automation toward the symbiosis of human work with automation" [17]. Currently, 3PL operators are grappling with issues of process automation and the use of advanced technological solutions. The use of automated processes offers many benefits, such as better process accuracy, consistency, reliability, and cost reduction. A well-constructed information exchange system and the willingness to share information between different companies are the foundations of an efficiently functioning network of enterprises. A well-designed information exchange system is also considered by some authors to be one of the key elements of supply chain coordination [18]. Digital and computer technologies supporting flows in networks are extremely important. For example, we can highlight electronic exchanges that enable the easy coordination of certain transport activities. To automate processes, 3PL operators often use RPA (Robotic Process Automation), which can automate, among other things, the collection and processing of data related to planning or demand. This is particularly important when 3PL operators engage in building omnichannel strategies in distribution or improving processes in line with e-commerce requirements. There are many differences between traditional logistics and e-logistics. For example, a 3PL operator should adapt processes from bulk shipping to both bulk and parcel shipping or be ready for less predictable order flows. Logistics operators face the need to meet increasingly demanding order fulfillment deadlines, especially in the area of road distribution. As some authors emphasize, 3PL can reduce flow times and lower inventory levels through proper transportation planning [19], increasing response speed and eliminating the need to maintain high safety stock levels. Companies outsource not only traditional logistics services but also management activities, which is why logistics service providers are expanding their services to meet market demands and constantly striving to acquire new skills and offer new services to their contractors. The use of 3PL can lead to easier reduction of logistics disruptions. Coordinated actions in this area can also lead to shorter transport routes and savings [20]. An increasingly important criterion is also the operator's ability to meet sustainability, CO_2 emission, and modern solutions requirements, such as those related to smart cities in the area of urban logistics in the long term. The e-commerce trend has not diminished the importance of physical points of sale (POS) [21], so traditional transportation problems remain very relevant, even in a reality where the literature primarily focuses on last-mile deliveries.

4.3 ML AND GEN-AI SOLUTIONS SUPPORTED DEMAND FORECASTING IN 3PL

Demand forecasting is one of the key elements of supply chain management in the contract logistics sector. In traditional approaches, forecasting primarily relied on analyzing historical sales data and expert experience. However, dynamically changing market conditions and the increasing complexity of global supply chains require more advanced and precise forecasting methods. In this context, ML solutions are gaining importance. Studies indicate that the quality of forecasts is a crucial factor in determining the coordination of logistics processes by logistics operators, underscoring the significance of modern forecasting methods, including machine learning techniques [22]. The application of ML in demand forecasting is becoming increasingly common, particularly in the context of e-commerce, where forecasting demand for small logistical units in large quantities presents a significant challenge [23]. The literature emphasizes that traditional forecasting methods, such as time series analysis or regression, may be insufficient in the face of the complexity and variability of modern markets [19]. Consequently, the development of AI-based models, such as neural networks, is becoming critical for improving forecast accuracy.

It is also worth noting that demand forecasting has a significant impact on inventory management and production planning decisions in the supply chain. Research has found that the use of advanced forecasting techniques, such as models based on BP neural networks, can significantly improve the efficiency of regional logistics demand forecasts [24]. Additionally, effective demand forecasting contributes to better cost management and enhances the competitiveness of logistics operators [25]. In the face of increasing complexity in global supply chains, it is also necessary to integrate various forecasting methods, which can lead to a more comprehensive approach to demand management. Research suggests that combining traditional and modern forecasting methods can yield better results in the context of logistics planning and decision-making [19]. As a result, the development of forecasting-related competencies is becoming a key element of 3PL operators' strategies, which may contribute to their market success.

ML enables the analysis of large datasets, identification of patterns, and prediction of future trends with greater accuracy than traditional statistical methods. ML models can process diverse data sources, such as historical data, social media data, weather information, and even macroeconomic data, allowing for a more comprehensive approach to demand forecasting. The literature emphasizes that the application of advanced techniques, such as deep learning, significantly improves forecast accuracy in various fields, including supply chain management [26]. One of the most popular approaches to demand forecasting is the ARIMA (Autoregressive Integrated Moving Average) method, traditionally used in time series analysis. ARIMA is an effective tool for forecasting based on historical data, but its limitations become apparent when dealing with more complex and nonlinear data patterns. To overcome these limitations, hybrid approaches are increasingly being used, combining traditional ARIMA models with ML methods. For example, after applying the ARIMA model for base trend forecasting, ML models such as neural networks can be used to predict residual components that may result from nonlinear influences. This approach allows for more precise forecasts by accounting for both linear and nonlinear relationships in the data.

Table 4.1 Selected advantages and disadvantages of using ML and gen-AI in demand forecasting

Category	Feature	Brief Description	Approach Enthusiasts
Advantages	Precision and accuracy	ML models, especially those using deep learning, can analyze complex patterns in data, leading to more precise predictions	[26]
	Scalability	ML and gen-AI can process huge amounts of data in real time, which is crucial in dynamically changing market conditions	[29]
	Adaptability	These models can be easily updated and adapted to new data, allowing you to respond to changes in demand on an ongoing basis	[30]
Disadvantages	Requirements about data	ML models require large amounts of high-quality training data, which can be difficult to obtain in some industries	[27]
	Models complexity	Constructing and implementing advanced ML and gen-AI models requires specialized knowledge and significant technical resources	[31]
	Interpretation problems	ML models, especially those based on deep learning, can be difficult to interpret, which can pose a challenge in the context of making business decisions	[32]

Generative artificial intelligence (gen-AI), based on generative models such as Generative Adversarial Networks (GANs) or models based on natural language processing (NLP), opens new possibilities in demand forecasting. Gen-AI enables the creation of synthetic data that can be used to enrich real datasets, which is especially useful in situations where data availability is limited [27]. For instance, gen-AI can simulate potential market scenarios, generating different conditions that may affect demand. These models can also analyze textual data, such as economic news or consumer opinions, to identify hidden signals and trends that may impact future demand. Large Language Models (LLM), such as GPT or Gemini, are becoming increasingly popular in demand forecasting, especially in the context of qualitative analysis. LLMs can process and analyze vast amounts of textual data, enabling the identification of trends and patterns not visible in traditional numerical data [28]. For example, LLMs can analyze user comments on social media, news articles, and market reports to predict changes in consumer preferences and market sentiments. These models can also be used to analyze historical data to identify nonlinear patterns and interactions that may affect demand. The application of ML and gen-AI in demand forecasting offers several advantages compared to traditional methods but also presents many challenges (Table 4.1).

Hybrid approaches such as ARIMA powered by ML, as well as modern gen-AI and LLM techniques, enable the creation of more advanced and effective forecasting tools. Despite some challenges, the benefits of these technologies exceed traditional methods, offering higher levels of accuracy and flexibility that are crucial in today's rapidly changing business environment.

4.4 DEMAND FORECASTING IN 3PL

4.4.1 Case Brief Description

The analyzed 3PL company, a leader in the contract logistics industry, specializes in providing comprehensive warehousing and transportation services. The company's extensive warehousing offering includes not only traditional goods storage but also advanced logistics services tailored to the individual needs of clients. By utilizing modern technologies and automation, the 3PL ensures the optimization of warehouse processes, leading to reduced order fulfillment times and operational cost reductions. In the context of transportation, the analyzed 3PL offers a wide range of solutions, covering both domestic and international transport. The flexibility and reliability of the transportation services allow for effective supply chain management, regardless of the size and nature of the goods being transported. The company places a strong emphasis on sustainable development, and as a result, its fleet is continuously upgraded with environmental considerations in mind, helping to minimize its carbon footprint.

In addition to basic logistics services, the analyzed 3PL company also offers a wide range of Value-Added Services (VAS). These include labeling, packaging, assembly, and quality control. These additional services allow clients to focus on the core aspects of their business, entrusting complex logistics processes to experienced specialists. Through these services, the company builds long-term relationships with its clients, adapting to their dynamically changing needs and supporting them in achieving their business goals. As part of this publication, an analysis will be conducted on the application of a forecasting tool to predict the volume (pallets and boxes) of inbound and outbound goods from warehouses managed by the 3PL operator. The general characteristics of the analyzed warehouse cases are presented in Table 4.2.

Table 4.2 Warehouses description

3PL Warehouse	Number of Service Recipients	Total Active SKU	Brief Descriprion of Recipients
1	2	34,875	• Manufacturer of toys • Manufacturer and retailer of cosmetics and skincare products
2	2	17,254	• Manufacturer of snacks and chips • Manufacturer and retailer of kitchen containers and accessories
3	2	64,976	• Retailer of babies and child articles • Manufacturer of packaging and labels products
4	2	4,973	• Manufacturer of food, including sweets and snacks • Wholesaler of food and nonfood products
5	6	77,124	• Manufacturer of bathroom and kitchen fittings • Manufacturer of cosmetics and aesthetic procedure products • Manufacturer of medicines and pharmaceutical products • Manufacturer of medicines and pharmaceutical products • Manufacturer and wholesaler of generic drugs • Manufacturer of pharmaceutical products
6	3	48,619	• Manufacturer of sweets and food products • Manufacturer of products for pets. • Manufacturer and retailer of food products.

The analysis covers six warehouses located in Poland. These are multi-client warehouses where logistics services provided by the 3PL are delivered to various clients, with available warehouse space being shared. Within the operations of the warehouses, forecasts are made for inbound and outbound volumes in the form of pallets and boxes. Figure 4.1 presents a simplified diagram of material flows within the 3PL.

Table 4.3 Number of days in historical data for first model training

Warehouse	Number of days in Historical Data for First Model Training			
	Outbound—Total Pallets	Outbound—Homogeneous Pallets	Outbound—Parcels	Inbound—Total Pallets
Warehouse1	120	120	120	1,031
Warehouse2	1,098	1,098	1,098	913
Warehouse3	585	585	585	571
Warehouse4	722	722	722	735
Warehouse5	797	797	797	728
Warehouse6	594	594	594	459

Quantites that will be forecasted are the total pallets on input, which are homogeneous pallets, total and homogeneous pallets on outputs and parcels

(parcels are distributed as a part of 3PL e-commerce activity). Each warehouse activity includes every form of presented distribution. Data to train forecasting models are the hourly data, but the forecast granulation was daily. Every warehouse had a different set of input data (Table 4.3) and the reason of it is the different lengths of data in each of them.

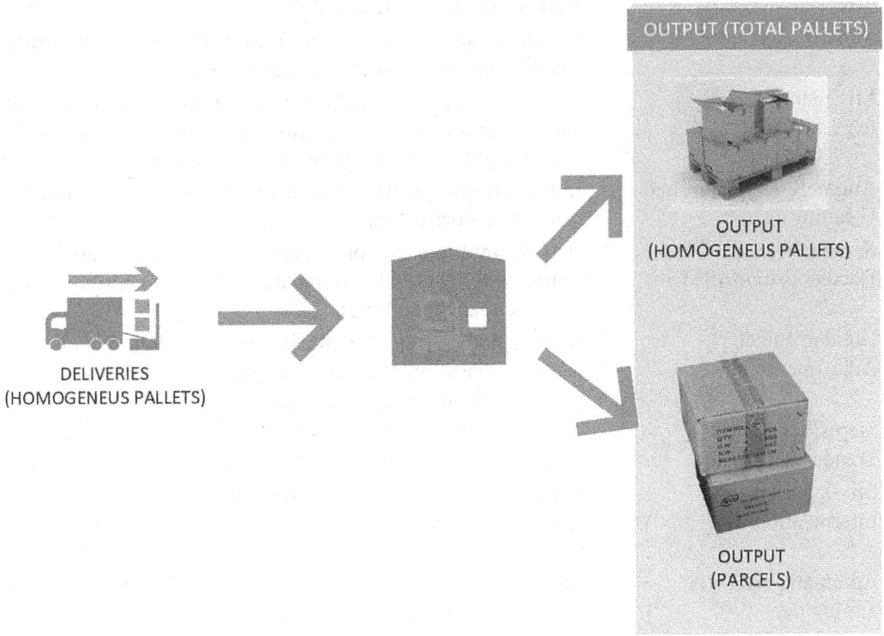

Figure 4.1 Scheme of 3PL warehouse material flows.

An analysis was carried out based on the selected data. Ex-post forecast errors for both cases were analyzed. As part of the error analysis, the values of the MAPE (Mean Absolute Percentage Error) and MAE (Mean Absolute Error) indicators were shown.

4.4.2 ARIMA Model Supported by ML

First of analyzed models was ARIMA supported by ML solutions. The forecasting process is shown at Figure 4.2.

The forecasting process described above is fully automated and assumes the generation of forecasts for input and output volumes at each of the aforementioned granularities, either based on scheduled script refreshes or triggered by user input. The input data comes from the 3PL operator's Warehouse Management System (WMS). The forecasts are exported, and both the forecasts and their accuracy are logged in a database. The model used in the forecast is an ARIMA model supported by machine learning elements. It is a commercial model from one of the leading technology companies, with its main components presented in Table 4.4.

Table 4.4 Brief model description

Model Element	Description
Autoregressive (AR)	A model that establishes the relationship between the forecasted variable and its past values (autoregression).
Integrated (I)	Differencing data to achieve stationarity, which helps remove trends and seasonality.
Moving Average (MA)	Considers the impact of past forecast errors on future values, improving the prediction accuracy.
ML Elements (e.g., SVM, RF)	Machine learning algorithms to detect nonlinear patterns in data and improve prediction accuracy in complex conditions (e.g., irregular data, large numbers of variables).
Anomaly Detection and Cleaning	Automatically detects and removes spikes and dips (outliers) that can distort forecasts.
Seasonality and Trend Decomposition (STL)	Detects multiple seasonal patterns within a single time series using STL and extrapolates seasonality through ETS (Exponential Smoothing).
Holiday Effect Adjustment	Detects and adjusts for the impact of holidays and non-working days on the data, improving forecasts during irregular business periods (e.g., holiday breaks).
Step Change and Trend Adjustments	Automatically detects and adjusts for abrupt level changes (e.g., steps) to improve model accuracy in unstable periods.
Missing Data Interpolation	Uses linear interpolation for missing data, ensuring continuity in time series and minimizing disruptions caused by missing values.
Automatic ARIMA Tuning	Automatically tunes ARIMA model parameters (p, d, q) using the auto.ARIMA algorithm, evaluating multiple models and selecting the one with the lowest Akaike information criterion (AIC).

In this case, main differences with the traditional ARIMA model are:

- Way of handling the missing data and irregular intervals. The ML-supported model automatically interpolates missing data and handles irregular time intervals, which traditional ARIMA doesn't.
- Advanced trend and seasonality decomposition ability. The ML-enhanced model uses advanced decomposition techniques (STL) for trends and multi-seasonality, providing more precise predictions with complex data.

4.5 RESULTS AND DISCUSSIONS

4.5.1 ARIMA Model Supported by ML

Below (Figures 4.3 to 4.6) are the forecast verifiability charts for warehouse 1. Due to space limitations and for reasons of text clarity, these charts have not been presented for subsequent warehouses.

The Table 4.5 includes calculations related to the verifiability of forecasts based on the analyzed period.

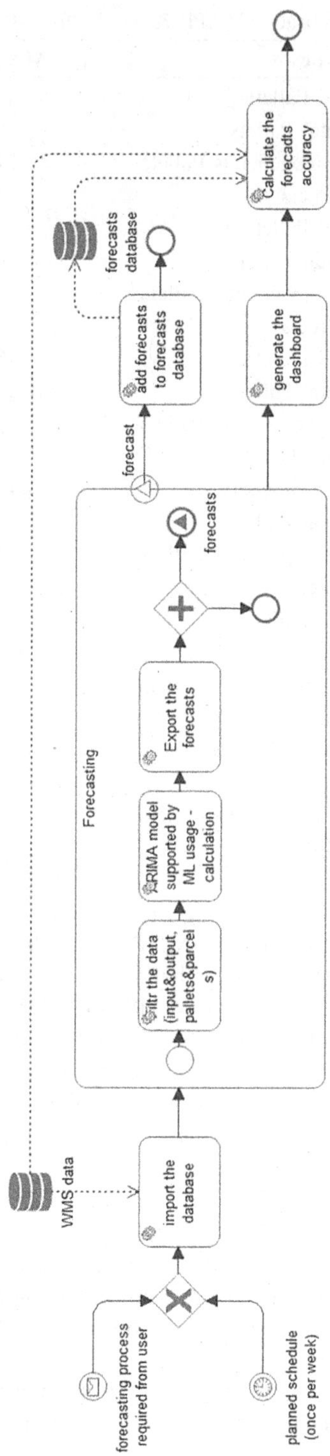

Figure 4.2 Forecasting process supported by ARIMA model & ML.

Table 4.5 Forecasts accuracy (MAPE & MAE) for ARIMA & ML model

Warehouse	Forecasts Type	MAPE	MAE
1	Inbound Total Pallets	49.68%	675
	Outbound Total Pallets	6.65%	2,654
	Outbound Homogeneous Pallets	21.65%	25
	Outbound Parcels	52.05%	639
2	Inbound Total Pallets	17.11%	2,899
	Outbound Total Pallets	20.46%	6,900
	Outbound Homogeneous Pallets	9.02%	980
	Outbound Parcels	27.80%	1,156
3	Inbound Total Pallets	36.30%	4,644
	Outbound Total Pallets	27.13%	7,793
	Outbound Homogeneous Pallets	8.46%	427
	Outbound Parcels	50.77%	808
4	Inbound Total Pallets	44.28%	1,341
	Outbound Total Pallets	50.69%	5,328
	Outbound Homogeneous Pallets	43.50%	1,299
	Outbound Parcels	16.19%	1,427
5	Inbound Total Pallets	60.21%	2,346
	Outbound Total Pallets	101.88%	6,073
	Outbound Homogeneous Pallets	39.23%	1,135
	Outbound Parcels	4.85%	1,046
6	Inbound Total Pallets	7.66%	2,995
	Outbound Total Pallets	82.08%	1,008,203
	Outbound Homogeneous Pallets	12.35%	1,996
	Outbound Parcels	4.79%	2,235

For warehouse 1, the forecasts for the "Inbound Total Pallets" category are inaccurate, as indicated by a high MAPE of 49.68% and a mean absolute error (MAE) of 675 units. On the other hand, the forecasts for "Outbound Total Pallets" are highly precise, with a low MAPE of 6.65%, although the MAE of 2,654 indicates that the absolute difference in units is larger, but the percentage error remains low. Forecasts for "Outbound Homogeneous Pallets" show moderate accuracy (MAPE 21.65%) with relatively small absolute errors (MAE 25), while forecasts for "Outbound Parcels" are less accurate, reflected by a MAPE of 52.05% and an MAE of 639 units.

In the case of warehouse 2, forecasts for "Inbound Total Pallets" are acceptable, with a MAPE of 17.11%, though the MAE of 2,899 units reveals some difficulty in predicting values in absolute units. Forecasts for "Outbound Total Pallets" are moderately accurate (MAPE 20.46%), but the MAE of 6,900 indicates substantial differences between actual and forecasted values. In the "Outbound Homogeneous Pallets" category, the model performs very accurately, as evidenced by a low MAPE (9.02%) and a reasonable MAE (980). For "Outbound Parcels," the forecasts are moderately accurate (MAPE 27.80%) with an MAE of 1,156 units.

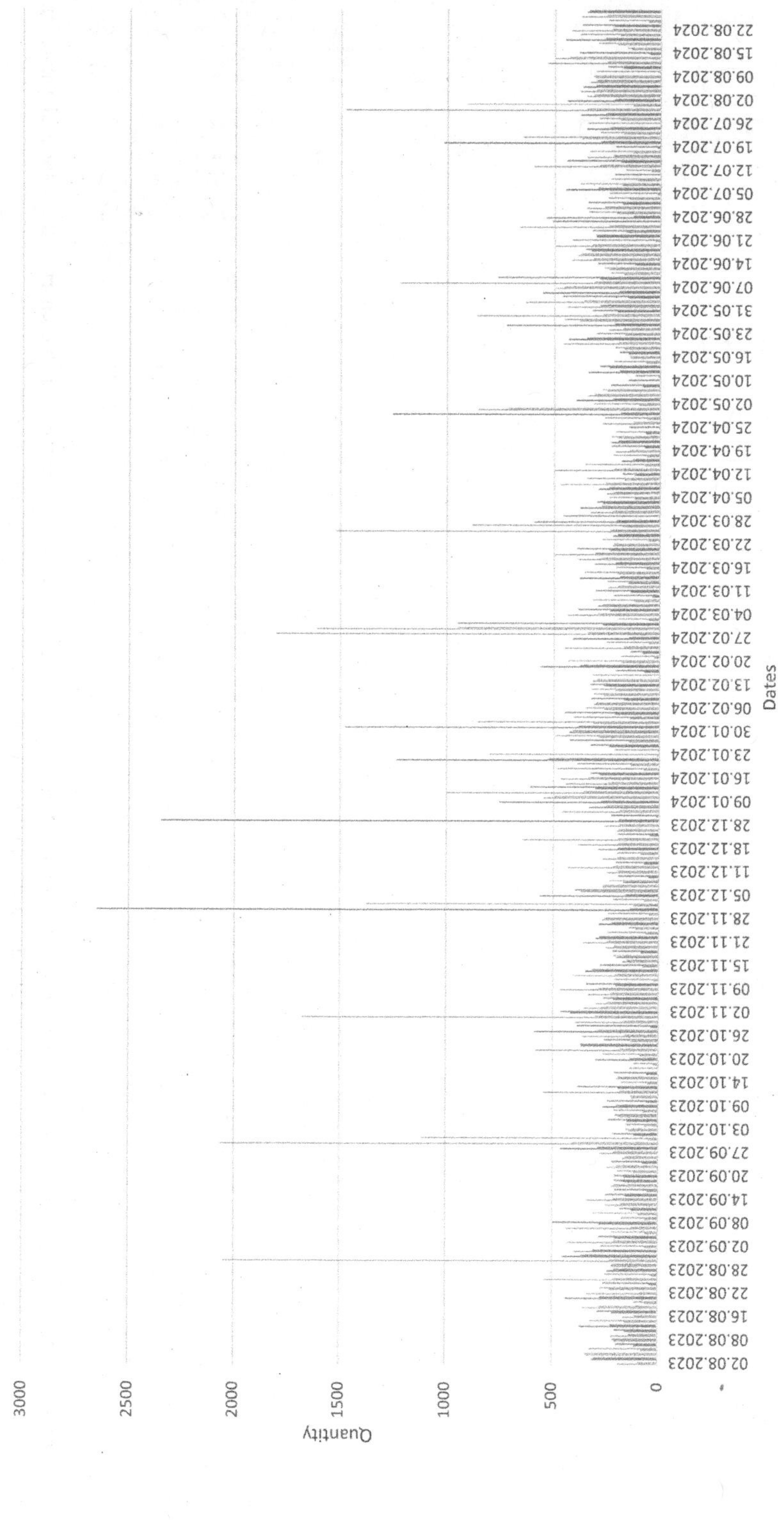

Figure 4.3 Inbound total pallets – ARIMA & ML model forecasts accuracy (warehouse 1, left bar on the chart is the total real values and right bar on the chart is the total forecasted values per day).

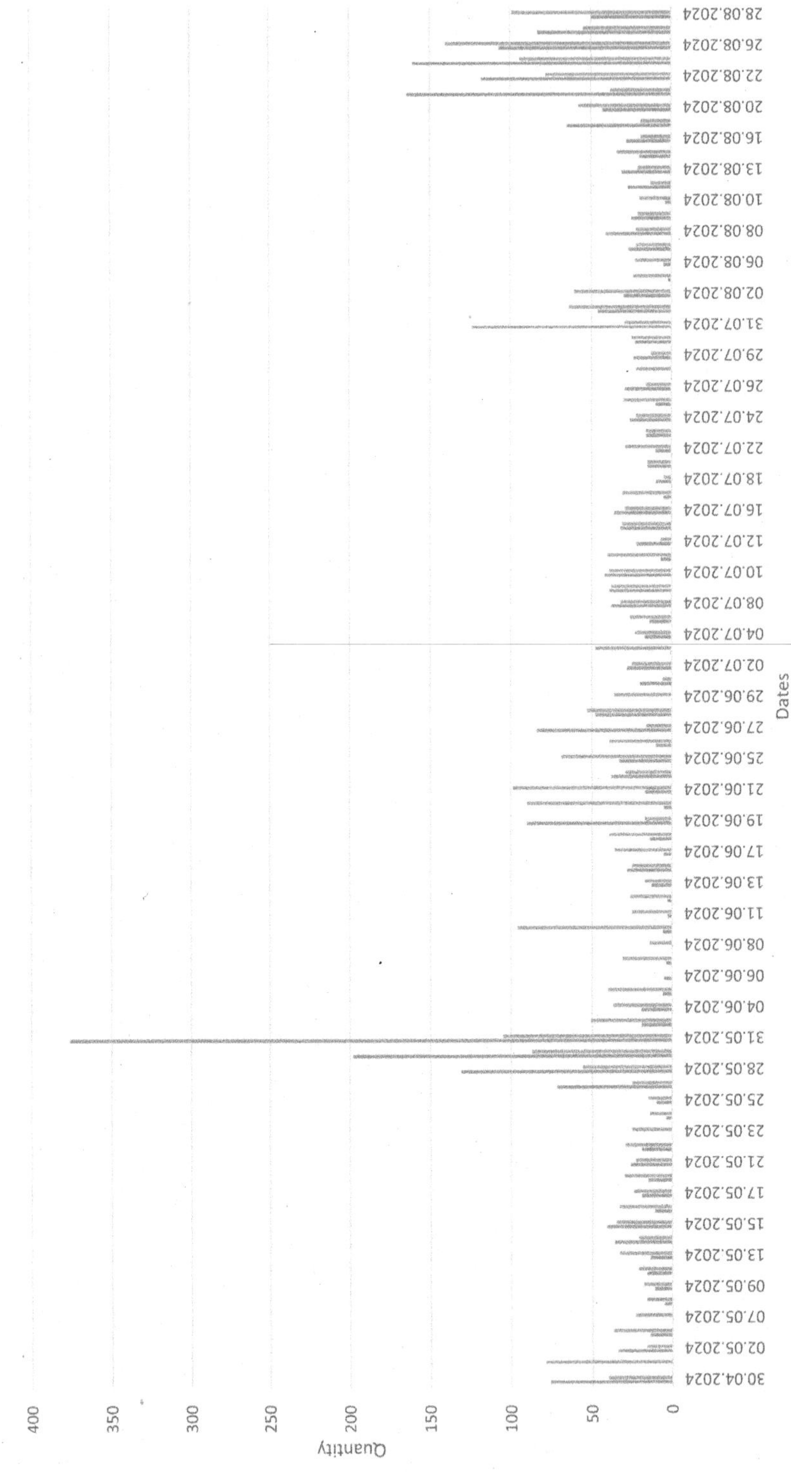

Figure 4.4 Outbound total pallets – ARIMA & ML model forecasts accuracy (warehouse 1, left bar on the chart is the total real values and right bar on the chart is the total forecasted values per day).

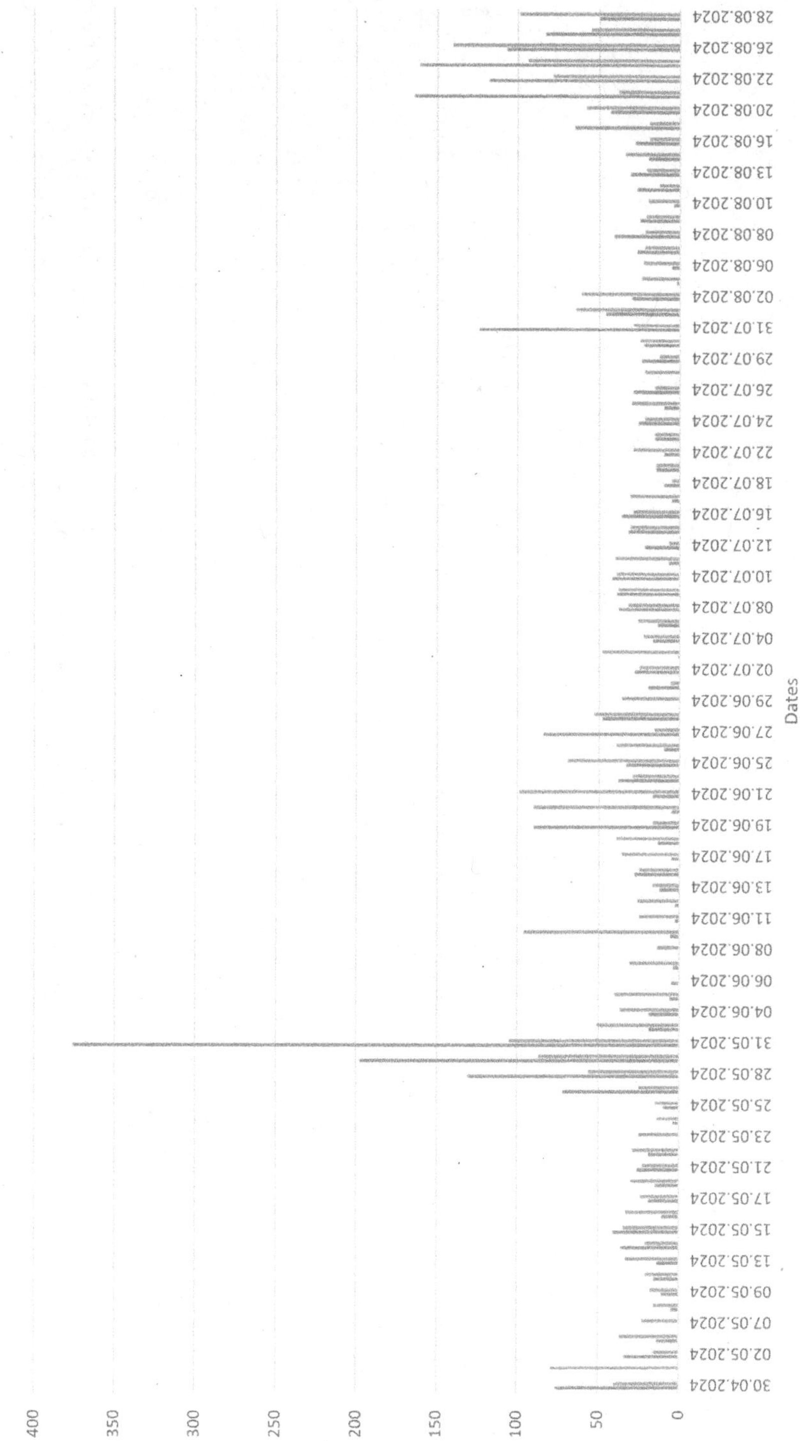

Figure 4.5 Outbound homogeneous pallets—ARIMA & ML model forecasts accuracy (warehouse 1, left bar on the chart is the total real values and right bar on the chart is the total forecasted values per day).

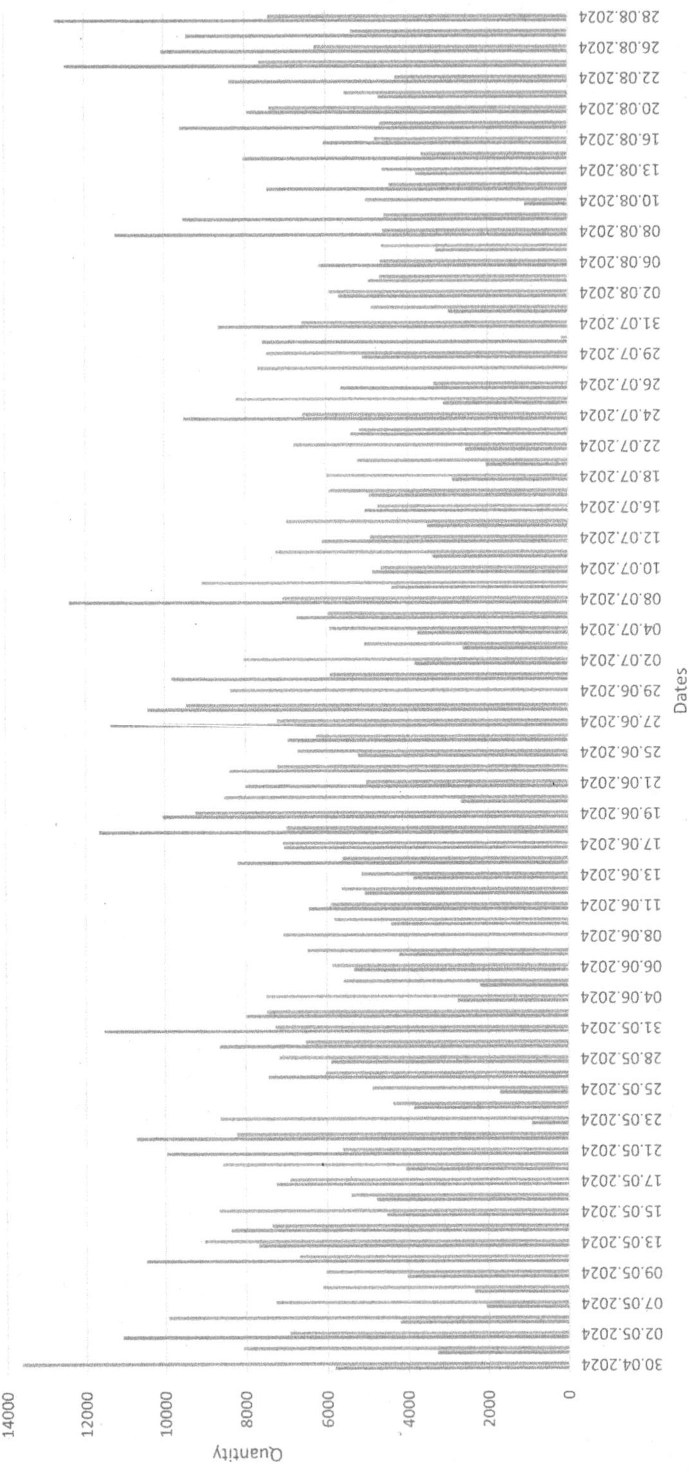

Figure 4.6 Outbound parcels – ARIMA & ML model forecasts accuracy (warehouse 1, left bar on the chart is the total real values and right bar on the chart is the total forecasted values per day).

Warehouse 3 is characterized by moderate forecast accuracy for "Inbound Total Pallets," with a MAPE of 36.30% and an MAE of 4,644 units. Forecasts for "Outbound Total Pallets" are moderately accurate, with a MAPE of 27.13% and an MAE of 7,793 units. For "Outbound Homogeneous Pallets," forecasts are highly accurate (MAPE 8.46%) with an MAE of 427 units, indicating minimal absolute errors. However, forecasts for "Outbound Parcels" are less accurate, reflected by a high MAPE (50.77%) and an MAE of 808 units.

For warehouse 4, forecasts for "Inbound Total Pallets" are relatively inaccurate, as shown by a MAPE of 44.28% and an MAE of 1,341 units. Forecasts for "Outbound Total Pallets" and "Outbound Homogeneous Pallets" have high error levels (MAPE of 50.69% and 43.50%, respectively), indicating significant discrepancies in predictions. However, forecasts for "Outbound Parcels" are more precise, with a MAPE of 16.19% and an MAE of 1,427 units.

Warehouse 5 shows a very large forecast error for "Inbound Total Pallets" (MAPE 60.21%) and "Outbound Total Pallets," where the MAPE reaches a staggering 101.88%, indicating significant difficulties in precise prediction. The MAE for these categories is also high, further confirming the low accuracy of these forecasts. Forecasts for "Outbound Homogeneous Pallets" are moderately accurate (MAPE 39.23%), while for "Outbound Parcels," the forecasts are very precise, as indicated by a low MAPE (4.85%) and an MAE of 1,046 units.

Finally, warehouse 6 shows highly accurate forecasts for "Inbound Total Pallets," as reflected by a low MAPE (7.66%) and a moderate MAE (2,995). However, forecasts for "Outbound Total Pallets" have very low accuracy, with a MAPE of 82.08% and an extremely high MAE of 1,008,203, indicating significant discrepancies between forecasts and actual values. For "Outbound Homogeneous Pallets," the forecasts are relatively accurate (MAPE 12.35%), and for "Outbound Parcels," the forecasts are very precise, with a MAPE of 4.79% and an MAE of 2,235 units.

Some warehouses (like 5 and 6) experience greater challenges with forecast accuracy, particularly for "Inbound Total Pallets" and "Outbound Total Pallets." On the other hand, warehouses 2 and 3 achieve better results in forecasting homogeneous pallets (Outbound Homogeneous Pallets), indicating better model accuracy in these categories related to 3PL operations.

4.5.2 Gen-AI Based Model for Forecasting

In Figure 4.7, the process of generating forecasts using ChatGPT is illustrated. The selection of this solution was due to the availability and popularity of this tool (the GPT-4 version was chosen for testing). The process of generating forecasts using ChatGPT based on data from the WMS system is simpler and more intuitive than with the previously generated model, and the entire operation can be carried out in just a few steps.

At the beginning, the warehouse employee exports historical data from the WMS, containing the number of inbound and outbound pallets and parcels over specific time intervals. They send this data as a file to ChatGPT, specifying the forecast horizon (e.g., number of days, weeks, months) and the desired output format, which is an XLSX file. After the data is uploaded, ChatGPT performs a preliminary analysis, checking the accuracy and completeness of the data. If any gaps are found in the file, the model will suggest corrections or automatically fill in the gaps, such as through interpolation. Next, the ChatGPT automatically selects an appropriate forecasting model, adjusting to the trends and seasonality in the data, and auto-tunes the model parameters. This allows the model to forecast changes while accounting for anomalies and other irregularities in the data. Based on this, ChatGPT generates forecasts for the specified time horizon and saves the results in an XLSX file, which the employee can download for further analysis. The file contains not only the forecasted values but also forecast quality indicators such as MAPE and MAE, which help assess the accuracy of the forecasts.

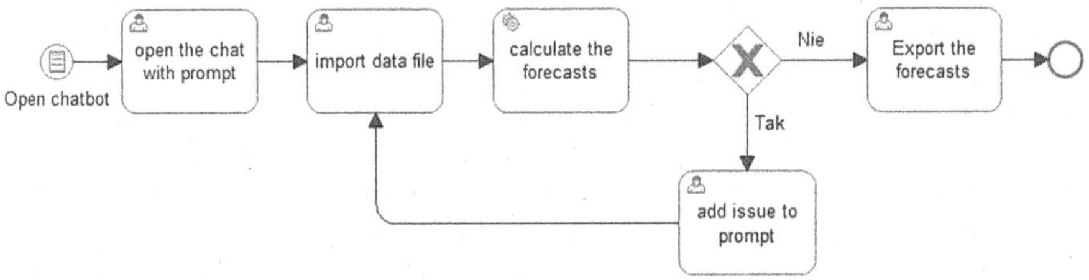

Figure 4.7 Forecasting process supported by ChatGPT.

The employee can accept the results or request further adjustments to the model. These forecasts can be used for operational planning, and over time, the accuracy of the forecasts can be verified based on actual data, allowing for further optimization of the model. The test model used the following prompt:

Prompt: "*Generate forecasts based on the uploaded .xlsx file.*

Response: *In the first response, ask for the file in .xlsx format.*

Prompt: *Below I am sending a file with historical data containing the number of inbound and outbound pallets and parcels for each day. Please generate forecasts using the model you select.*

Response: *In the response, ask for the forecast parameters:*

Prompt: — *Forecast horizon: [specify number of days/weeks/months]*
— *Output file format: XLSX*

The file contains the following columns:

- *Date (format: YYYY-MM-DD)*
- *Inbound Pallets*
- *Outbound Pallets*
- *Outbound Parcels*
- *Homogeneous Pallets*

Please generate an XLSX file with forecasts for the specified horizon and provide me with forecast accuracy metrics such as MAPE and MAE. If there are any issues with the data, please inform me and assist with correcting them.

Response: *Files will be generated.*

Prompt(Optional): *At the end, ask if there are additional variables that could be considered for adjusting the forecast. If such data is provided, adjust the forecast accordingly.*"

Below (Figures 4.8 to 4.11), forecast accuracy charts for warehouse 1 are presented. Different colors mean real and forecasted data. Due to space limitations and for clarity, charts for subsequent warehouses are not shown.

Table 4.6 shows the accuracy indicators results for analyzed cases.

Table 4.6 Forecasts accuracy (MAPE & MAE) for GPT model

Warehouse	Forecasts Type	MAPE	MAE
1	Inbound Total Pallets	48.79%	674
	Outbound Total Pallets	6.62%	2,652
	Outbound Homogeneous Pallets	22.24%	26
	Outbound Parcels	52.23%	642
2	Inbound Total Pallets	17.05%	2,930
	Outbound Total Pallets	20.52%	6,973
	Outbound Homogeneous Pallets	9.01%	990
	Outbound Parcels	27.44%	1,166
3	Inbound Total Pallets	35.10%	4,650
	Outbound Total Pallets	27.16%	7,795
	Outbound Homogeneous Pallets	8.46%	427
	Outbound Parcels	50.91%	817
4	Inbound Total Pallets	43.53%	1,340
	Outbound Total Pallets	52.38%	5,343
	Outbound Homogeneous Pallets	43.28%	1,293
	Outbound Parcels	15.99%	1,452
5	Inbound Total Pallets	61.24%	2,384
	Outbound Total Pallets	104.38%	6,012
	Outbound Homogeneous Pallets	38.29%	1,142
	Outbound Parcels	4.85%	1,051
6	Inbound Total Pallets	7.93%	3,128
	Outbound Total Pallets	81.71%	1,009,834
	Outbound Homogeneous Pallets	12.24%	2,061
	Outbound Parcels	4.99%	2,306

For warehouse 1, the forecasts for "Inbound Total Pallets" have a MAPE of 48.79%, indicating a relatively high percentage error and low forecast accuracy. The MAE of 674 shows that the average difference between actual and predicted values is 674 units. On the other hand, the forecast for "Outbound Total Pallets" is highly accurate, with a low MAPE of 6.62%, although the MAE is 2,652, meaning that while the absolute error in units is higher, the percentage error remains low. The forecasts for "Outbound Homogeneous Pallets" show moderate accuracy, with a MAPE of 22.24% and an MAE of 26, indicating small differences in units. However, the forecasts for "Outbound Parcels" are imprecise, with a high MAPE of 52.23% and an MAE of 642, pointing to significant errors.

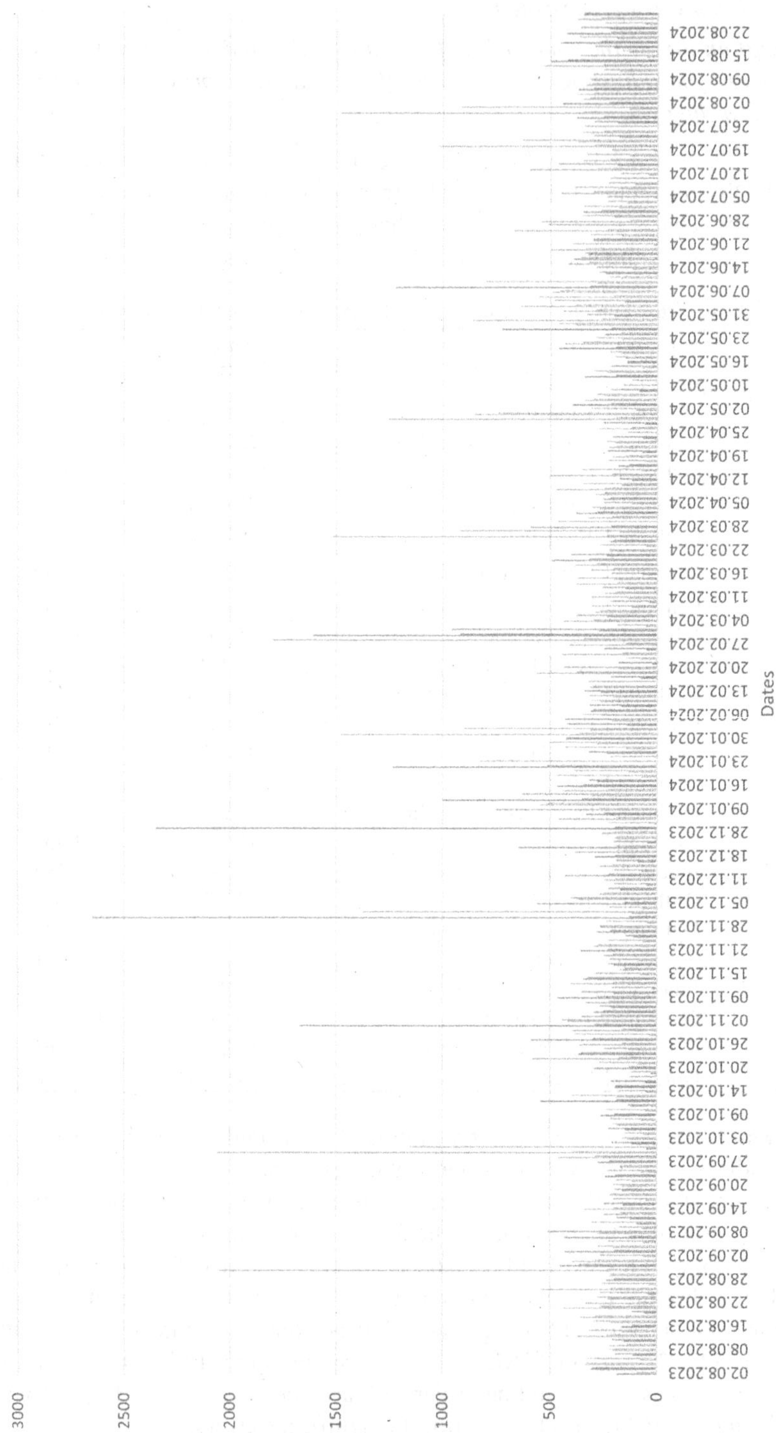

Figure 4.8 Inbound total pallets – GPT model forecasts accuracy (warehouse 1, left bar on the chart is the total real values and right bar on the chart is the total forecasted values per day).

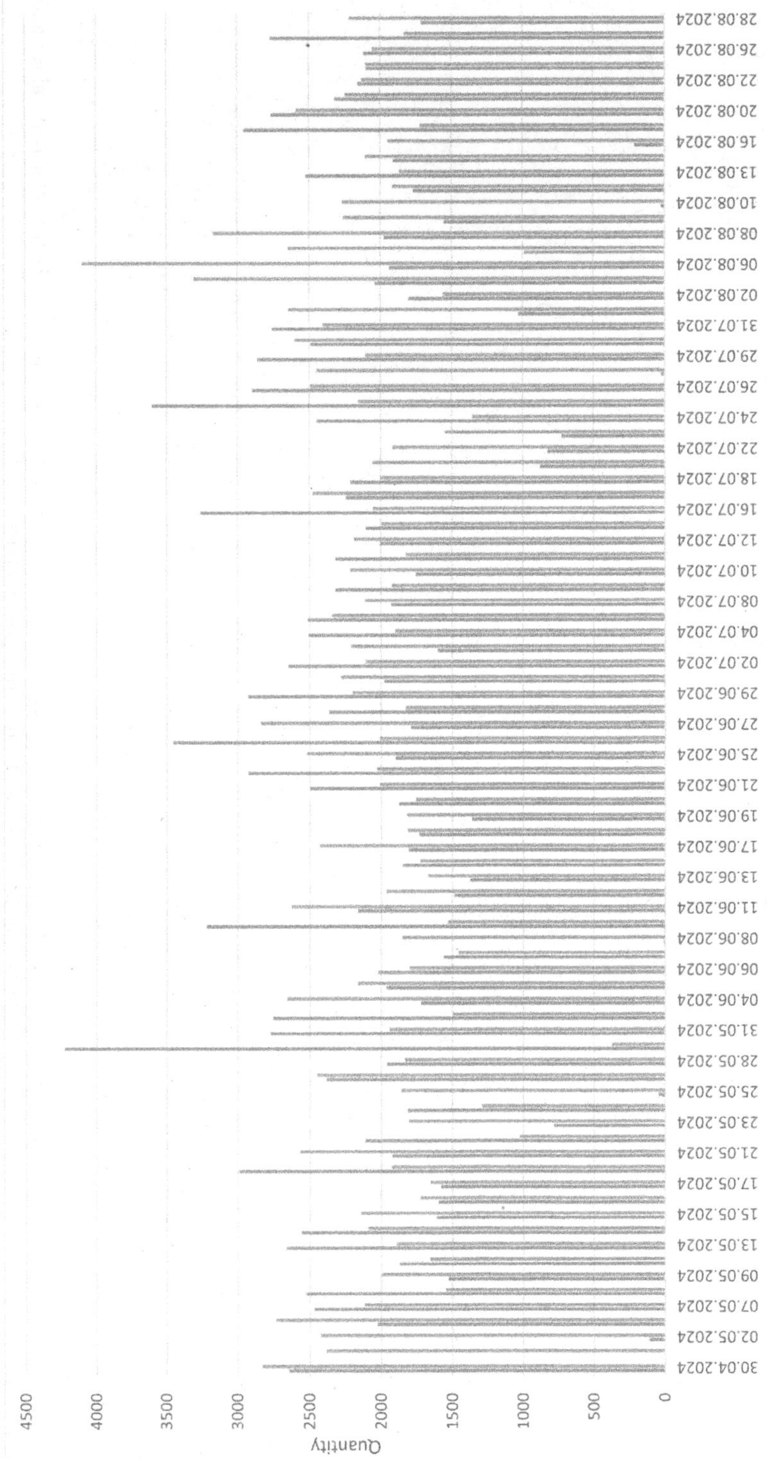

Figure 4.9 Outbound total pallets—GPT model forecasts accuracy (warehouse 1, left bar on the chart is the total real values and right bar on the chart is the total forecasted values per day).

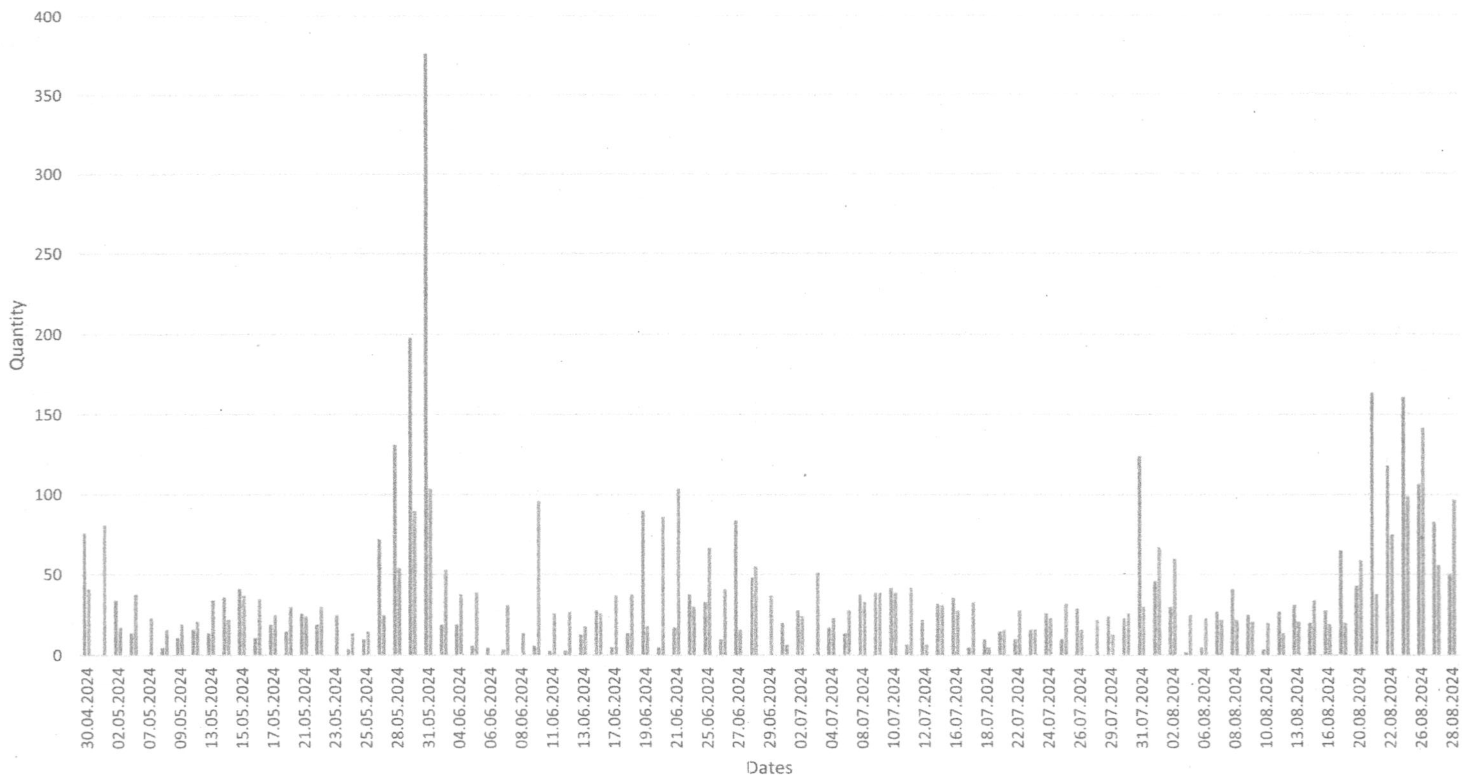

Figure 4.10 Outbound homogeneous pallets – GPT model forecasts accuracy (warehouse 1, left bar on the chart is the total real values and right bar on the chart is the total forecasted values per day).

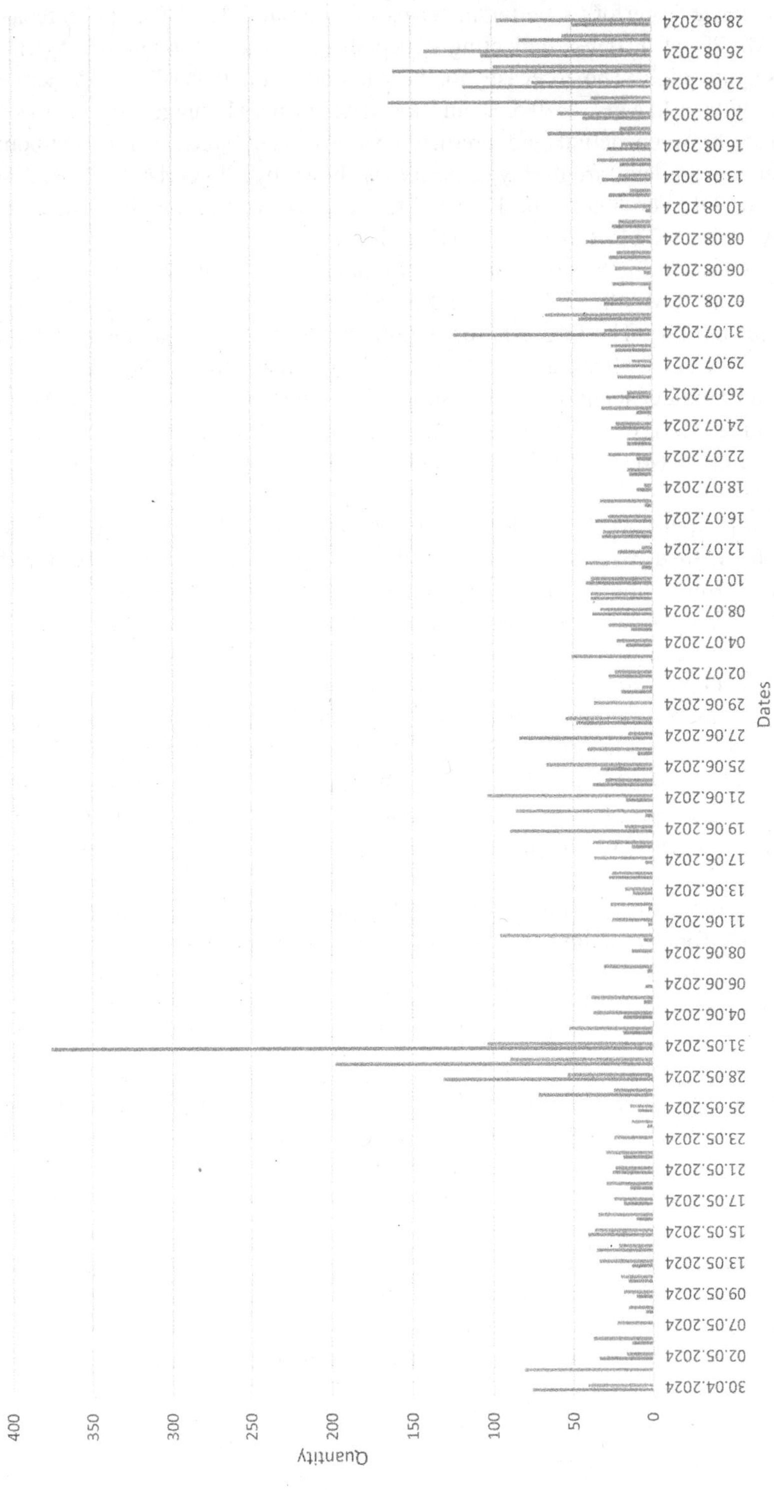

Figure 4.11 Outbound parcels – GPT model forecasts accuracy (warehouse 1, left bar on the chart is the total real values and right bar on the chart is the total forecasted values per day).

Warehouse 2 performs better in terms of "Inbound Total Pallets" forecasts, with a MAPE of 17.05%, indicating acceptable accuracy, though the MAE of 2,930 is quite high. The forecasts for "Outbound Total Pallets" are moderately accurate, with a MAPE of 20.52% and an MAE of 6,973, suggesting significant differences between actual and predicted values. The forecasts for "Outbound Homogeneous Pallets" are highly accurate, as shown by a low MAPE (9.01%) and an MAE of 990. For "Outbound Parcels," the forecasts exhibit moderate accuracy, with a MAPE of 27.44% and an MAE of 1,166.

In warehouse 3, the forecasts for "Inbound Total Pallets" show moderate accuracy, with a MAPE of 35.10% and an MAE of 4,650, suggesting substantial differences in units. The forecasts for "Outbound Total Pallets" are also moderate, with a MAPE of 27.16% and an MAE of 7,795. In contrast, the forecasts for "Outbound Homogeneous Pallets" demonstrate high accuracy, with a MAPE of 8.46% and an MAE of 427. However, forecasts for "Outbound Parcels" have a high percentage error (MAPE of 50.91%) and an MAE of 817, indicating significant forecast errors.

For warehouse 4, the forecasts for "Inbound Total Pallets" are relatively inaccurate, with a MAPE of 43.53% and an MAE of 1,340. The forecasts for "Outbound Total Pallets" have a high error level, with a MAPE of 52.38% and an MAE of 5,343, indicating substantial differences between forecasted and actual values. The forecasts for "Outbound Homogeneous Pallets" are also imprecise (MAPE of 43.28% and MAE of 1,293). However, the forecasts for "Outbound Parcels" are more accurate, with a MAPE of 15.99% and an MAE of 1,452.

Warehouse 5 presents significant problems with forecast accuracy. For "Inbound Total Pallets," the MAPE is 61.24%, and the MAE is 2,384, suggesting substantial differences between forecasts and reality. For "Outbound Total Pallets," the MAPE reaches 104.38%, indicating extremely poor accuracy, with an MAE of 6,012 further confirming large errors. The forecasts for "Outbound Homogeneous Pallets" are moderate, with a MAPE of 38.29% and an MAE of 1,142. However, the forecasts for "Outbound Parcels" are highly accurate, with a low MAPE of 4.85% and an MAE of 1,051.

Warehouse 6 shows high forecast accuracy for "Inbound Total Pallets," with a MAPE of 7.93%, though the MAE of 3,128 indicates moderate differences in units. However, the forecasts for "Outbound Total Pallets" are highly imprecise, with an extremely high MAPE of 81.71% and an MAE of 1,009,834, suggesting substantial discrepancies between forecasts and actual values. The forecasts for "Outbound Homogeneous Pallets" are moderately accurate, with a MAPE of 12.24% and an MAE of 2,061. In the case of "Outbound Parcels," the forecasts are highly accurate, as reflected by a MAPE of 4.99% and an MAE of 2,306.

Forecast accuracy varies significantly depending on the warehouse and data type. Some forecasts, especially for parcels (Outbound Parcels) in warehouses 5 and 6, are highly accurate, while others, such as "Outbound Total Pallets" in warehouses 5 and 6, show significant errors, indicating the need for further optimization of the forecasting model.

4.5.3 Comparison of Forecasts Accuracy

Comparing the forecast results generated by the ARIMA model supported by ML and the ChatGPT-based model, certain similarities and differences in accuracy for individual warehouses can be observed. For both models, the forecasts for warehouse 1 in the "Inbound Total Pallets" category are relatively inaccurate, with MAPE values of 49.68% for ARIMA and 48.79% for ChatGPT, indicating significant discrepancies between actual and predicted values. In both cases, forecasts for "Outbound Total Pallets" are more precise, with low MAPE (6.65% for ARIMA and 6.62% for ChatGPT), although the MAE values are similar.

For warehouse 2, both models generate similar results for "Inbound Total Pallets," with an acceptable MAPE of around 17%. The forecasts for "Outbound Homogeneous Pallets" are very accurate in both models, as confirmed by the low MAPE (9.02% for ARIMA and 9.01% for ChatGPT). Meanwhile, forecasts for "Outbound Total Pallets" have moderate accuracy in both models, with MAPE around 20–21%.

Warehouse 3 shows very similar results for both models. In both cases, "Inbound Total Pallets" displays moderate accuracy, with MAPE around 35–36%, while "Outbound Homogeneous Pallets" is highly accurate, with a low MAPE of 8.46%. However, forecasts for "Outbound Parcels" are less accurate in both models, with MAPE exceeding 50%.

For warehouse 4, the forecast results are also comparable. In both models, "Inbound Total Pallets" has a MAPE of over 43%, indicating low forecast accuracy. Forecasts for "Outbound Total Pallets" and "Outbound Homogeneous Pallets" show high error levels in both models, suggesting challenges in predicting these categories. In both cases, forecasts for parcels ("Outbound Parcels") are more accurate, with MAPE around 16%.

The most significant problems arise in warehouse 5, where both models show extremely high MAPE for "Inbound Total Pallets" and "Outbound Total Pallets," particularly for "Outbound Total Pallets" (over 100%). However, forecasts for parcels (Outbound Parcels) are highly accurate in both models, with a low MAPE of 4.85%.

In warehouse 6, the forecasts for "Inbound Total Pallets" have very similar results in both models, with a low MAPE of around 7–8%. However, forecasts for "Outbound Total Pallets" are very inaccurate in both models, with MAPE exceeding 80%.

Both models generate very similar forecast results, suggesting that both ARIMA supported by ML and ChatGPT can be effective tools for forecasting. It should be noted that GPT could indeed utilize ARIMA and often did so, but it was also capable of selecting other models in a flexible manner, based on the analysis of input data. This approach is beneficial as it allows the model to adapt dynamically to the characteristics of the data, potentially improving forecast accuracy for data patterns that are not well-suited to traditional ARIMA modeling.

4.6 CONCLUSION AND FUTURE DIRECTIONS

The results obtained demonstrate that forecasting models based on ARIMA supported by machine learning (ML) elements, as well as models based on generative artificial intelligence (gen-AI), can effectively support the demand forecasting process in 3PL logistics companies. The findings indicate that these models can accurately predict demand in the "Outbound Homogeneous Pallets" category, while forecasts for "Inbound Total Pallets" and "Outbound Parcels" exhibit larger deviations from actual values, particularly in some warehouses (e.g., warehouses 5 and 6). An analysis of forecast errors (MAPE and MAE) identified areas where the algorithms require further optimization, especially for complex data related to pallet flows. One unexpected result was the low accuracy of forecasts for the "Outbound Total Pallets" and "Inbound Total Pallets" categories in warehouses 5 and 6, where MAPE exceeded 100% for both ARIMA with ML and GPT models.

Some authors [28] show that the use of neural networks leads to significant improvements in forecast accuracy, suggesting that ML techniques may better capture data complexity than classical ARIMA models, which may struggle with nonlinearity and seasonality. However, the results also suggest that in certain situations, such as forecasts for "Inbound Total Pallets," ML models may be less effective. This is consistent with some other researcher's observations who point out the limitations of ARIMA models in more complex conditions, which can lead to underestimating demand in specific contexts [33]. In the context of demand forecasting across different industries, shows that integrating data from various sources, such as point-of-sale data, can significantly improve forecast accuracy [34]. This underscores the need for a holistic approach to forecasting that considers data diversity and methods, which may be key in light of our findings.

REFERENCES

[1] Singh, P. 2023. Digital transformation in supply chain management: artificial intelligence (AI) and machine learning (ML) as catalysts for value creation. International Journal of Supply Chain Management. 12(6): 57–63. doi: 10.59160/ijscm.v12i6.6216.

[2] Murphy, P.R. and D.F. Wood. 2011. Nowoczesna logistyka, Gliwice: Helion.

[3] Skowron-Grabowska, B. 2011. Wpływ funkcjonowania operatorów logistycznych na rozwój rynku usług w Polsce. Zeszyty Naukowe Uniwersytetu Szczecińskiego. (685): 225–234.

[4] Witkowski, J. and M. Kiba-Janik. 2012. Rozwój europejskich centrów i klastrów logistycznych na podstawie doświadczeń hiszpańskich. Zeszyty Naukowe Uniwersytetu Szczecińskiego. (719): 397–414.

[5] Hirt, R., N. Kuhl, Y. Peker and Y. Satzger. 2020. How to learn from others: transfer machine learning with additive regression models to improve sales forecasting. *In*: Proceeding 2020 IEEE 22nd Conference on Business Informatics.

[6] Ayiomamitou, N. 2016. Improving forecasting capabilities in the 3PL industry. Master Thesis, Logistics and Operations Management Section of Cardiff Business School.

[7] Grzelak, M., A. Borucka and Z. Buczyński. 2019. Forecasting the demand for transport services on the example of a selected logistic operator. Archives of Transport. 52(4): 81–93.

[8] van Aarde, M. 2017. Forecasting transportation service demand for fleet optimization: The case of a third-party logistics provider.

[9] Sirikulvadhana, S., N. Kreemaha, A. Thongthangthai and T. Rujirapaiboon. 2019. Last mile optimization for a young 3PL provider. *In*: Proceeding 2019 6th IEEE International Conference on Engineering Technologies and Applied Sciences (ICETAS).

[10] Rutkowski, K. 2015. Rekonfiguracja międzynarodowych łańcuchów dostaw jako narzędzie zapobiegania zagrożeniom kryzysowym. Prace Naukowe Uniwersytetu Ekonomicznego we Wrocławiu. 382: 92–104.

[11] Aertsen, F., I.I. Blanc, J. Rongen and L. Wouwe. 2016. Building a competitive demand planning organization. An Eyeon White Paper. 4–16.

[12] Ch. Pfhol, H. 1998. Systemy logistyczne, Poznań: Instytut Logistyki i Magazynowania.

[13] Brito, B. 2016. Centralization of supply chain management operations: The case of Unilever Ultralogistik, Universidade do Porto, Porto.

[14] Kristianto, Y., P. Helo, J. Jiao and M. Sandhu. 2012. Adaptive fuzzy vendor managed inventory control for mitigating the Bullwhip effect in supply chains. European Journal of Operational Research. 216(2): 346–355.

[15] Ageron, B., S. Benzidia, O. Benthar and J. Husson. 2018. Investigating automation and AGV in healthcare logistics: A case study-based approach. International Journal of Logistics Research and Applications.

[16] Kramarz, W. 2013. Modelowanie przepływów materiałowych w sieciowych łańcuchach dostaw. Warszawa: Difin.

[17] Cimini, C., A. Lagorio, D. Romero, S. Cavalieri and J. Stahre. 2020. Smart logistics and the logistics operator 4.0. IFAC PapersOnLine. 53(2): 10615–10620.

[18] Arshinder, K., A. Kanda and S.G. Deshmukh. 2008. Supply chain coordination: Perspectives, empirical studies and research directions. International Journal of Production Economics. 115: 316–335.

[19] Wang, Y. 2023. Overview of logistics demand forecasting methods. Frontiers in Business Economics and Management. 9(2): 251–255. doi: 10.54097/fbem.v9i2.9293.

[20] Wang, J., M.K. Lim, Y. Zhan and X. Wang. 2020. An intelligent logistics service system for enhancing dispatching operations in an IoT environment. Transportation Research Part E. 135: 101886.

[21] Lin, Y.H., Y. Wang, L.H. Lee and E.P. Chew. 2022. Omnichannel facility location and fulfillment optimization. Transportation Research Part B: Methodological. 163: 187–209.

[22] Kramarz, M. and M. Kmiecik. 2022. Quality of forecasts as the factor determining the coordination of logistics processes by logistic operator. Sustainability. 14(2): 1013. doi: 10.3390/su14021013.

[23] Kmiecik, M. 2025. Supply and demand prediction by 3PL for assortment planning. Management Science Letters. 15(2): 97–112. doi: 10.5267/j.msl.2024.5.001.

[24] Ping, H., T. Mei, X. Liu and W. Fan. 2016. A method for forecasting regional logistics demand based on BP neural network. Destech Transactions on Computer Science and Engineering. doi: 10.12783/dtcse/icte2016/4811.

[25] Gotzamani, K., P. Longinidis and F. Vouzas. 2010. The logistics services outsourcing dilemma: Quality management and financial performance perspectives. Supply Chain Management an International Journal. 15(6): 438–453. doi: 10.1108/13598541011080428.

[26] Singh, A. 2024. Prediction of intermittent demand occurrence using machine learning. EAI Endorsed Transactions on Internet of Things. 10. doi: 10.4108/eetiot.5381.

[27] Elufioye, O. 2024. AI-driven predictive analytics in agricultural supply chains: A review. Computer Science and IT Research Journal. 5(2): 473–497. doi: 10.51594/csitrj.v5i2.817.

[28] Silva, E.S., H. Hassani, S. Heravi and X. Huang. 2019. Forecasting tourism demand with denoised neural networks. Annals of Tourism Research. 74: 134–154. doi: 10.1016/j.annals.2018.11.006.

[29] Böse, J.-H., V. Flunkert, J. Gasthaus, T. Januschowski, D. Lange, D. Salinas, et al. 2017. Probabilistic demand forecasting at scale. *In*: Proceedings of the VLDB Endowment. 10(12): 1694–1705. doi: 10.14778/3137765.3137775.

[30] Seyedan, S. and Mafakheri, F. 2020. Predictive big data analytics for supply chain demand forecasting. Journal of Big Data. 7(1). doi: 10.1186/s40537-020-00329-2.

[31] Kuzlu, M., Ü. Cali, V. Sharma and Ö. Güler. 2020. Gaining insight into solar photovoltaic power generation forecasting utilizing explainable artificial intelligence tools. IEEE Access. 8: 187814–187823. doi: 10.1109/access.2020.3031477.

[32] Xu, H. 2024. Exploring the integration of a global AI model with traditional data assimilation in weather forecasting. doi: 10.21203/rs.3.rs-4756398/v1.

[33] Ducharme, C., B. Agard and M. Trépanier. 2024. Improving demand forecasting for customers with missing downstream data in intermittent demand supply chains with supervised multivariate clustering. Journal of Forecasting. 43(5): 1661–1681. doi: 10.1002/for.3095.

[34] Narayanan, A., F. Sahin and E. Robinson. 2019. Demand and order-fulfillment planning: the impact of point-of-sale data, retailer orders and distribution center orders on forecast accuracy. Journal of Operations Management. 65(5): 468–486. doi: 10.1002/joom.1026.

Chapter **5**

Demand Forecasting for Sustainable Supply Chain Management Leveraging AI

Izabela Rojek* and Dariusz Mikołajewski
Faculty of Computer Science,
Kazimierz Wielki University in Bydgoszcz, Poland

5.1 INTRODUCTION

The fourth industrial revolution (Industry 4.0), which began at the end of the 20th century and continues to this day, is characterised by the fusion of digital, physical, and biological technologies, blurring the boundaries between these spheres and marking the beginning of a new era of connectivity, automation, and intelligence. Figure 5.1 illustrates a timeline of the four phases of industrialisation along with the technological advances achieved during this time. Among the technologies driving Industry 4.0, artificial intelligence (AI) and machine learning (ML) are the basic foundations. AI and ML are currently serving as catalysts for innovation and productivity across industries. AI, which includes machine learning techniques, allows systems to learn from data, adapt, and make autonomous decisions, facilitating automation and resource optimisation. These technologies power intelligent systems that can handle massive amounts of data, extract valuable insights, and support predictive analytics [1]. From advanced manufacturing and healthcare to finance and transportation, the integration of AI and machine learning within Industry 4.0 is transforming workflows,

*For Correspondence: izabela.rojek@ukw.edu.pl

DOI: 10.1201/9781003541875-5

improving decision-making, and enabling unprecedented levels of connectivity and personalisation [2]. As Industry 4.0 evolves, AI and ML will remain key in driving transformation, shaping the future of global business and economies (Figure 5.1).

Supply chain management (SCM) has evolved significantly across the various industrial revolutions. During Industry 1.0, SCM was largely manual, relying on human labor and basic steam-powered mechanization, with limited ability to manage complex networks or respond to disruptions. Industry 2.0 introduced mass production via assembly lines and electricity, enabling greater efficiency and standardisation of supply chains, but still focused on linear, centralised control with minimal flexibility. With Industry 3.0, developments in automation, computers, and electronics enabled SCM to become more data-driven and efficient, incorporating early versions of enterprise resource planning (ERP) systems for better coordination and forecasting [3]. The introduction of the Internet and early digitization further improved communication and decision-making in supply chains. Industry 4.0 brought the integration of advanced technologies such as AI, the Internet of Things (IoT), and big data analytics, enabling real-time tracking, automation, and predictive analytics, significantly improving the agility, transparency, and resilience of global supply chains [4]. Today, the emerging Industry 5.0 focuses on human-machine collaboration, where technologies such as AI and robotics work with humans to create more personalised and sustainable supply chains. This era emphasises adaptability, environmental responsibility, and strengthening the role of humans in decision-making [5]. This is also depicted through Figure 5.2.

When describing the principles of sustainable SCM in Industry 4.0 and Industry 5.0, we should consider that sustainable supply chain management (SSCM) in Industry 4.0 focuses on the use of advanced technologies such as AI, IoT, and blockchain to increase transparency, efficiency, and environmental responsibility in supply chains. A key principle is the use of real-time data monitoring to track emissions, energy consumption, and resource use, ensuring that sustainable practices are followed throughout the manufacturing and logistics process. Automation and predictive analytics help optimise resource allocation, reduce waste, and minimise environmental impact by forecasting demand more accurately and avoiding overproduction [6]. Another principle is to implement the principles of a circular economy, encouraging recycling, reuse, and repurposing of materials through intelligent systems that facilitate product lifecycle tracking. SSCM also emphasises supplier collaboration and integration, where technology enables better communication and ensures that all partners adhere to sustainability standards. Blockchain can ensure ethical sourcing by providing transparent, immutable records of material origin and working practices [7].

In Industry 5.0, the principles of SSCM are shifting towards a more human-centred approach, with an emphasis on balancing advanced technologies and human decision-making expertise. One principle is personalised sustainability, using AI and robotics to adapt production while reducing the environmental footprint and meeting individual customer preferences. There is also a focus on human-robot collaboration to optimise sustainability, where humans drive strategic

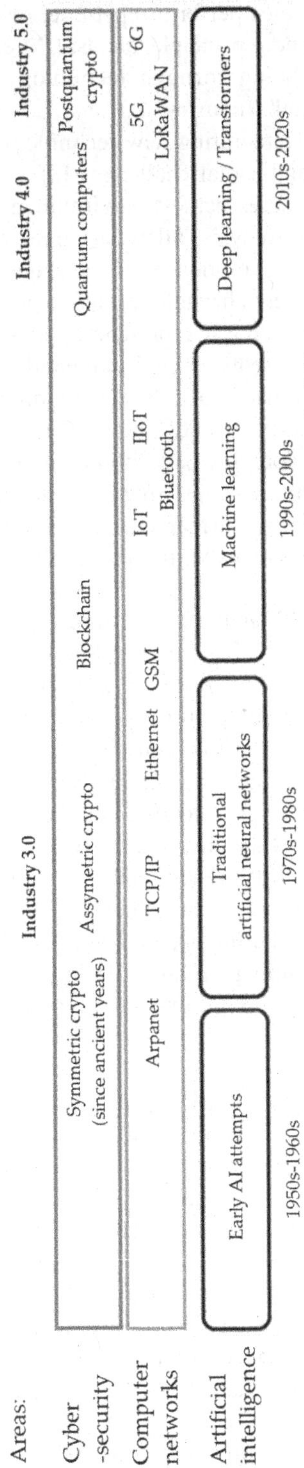

Figure 5.1 Industrial revolution development against the background of AI.

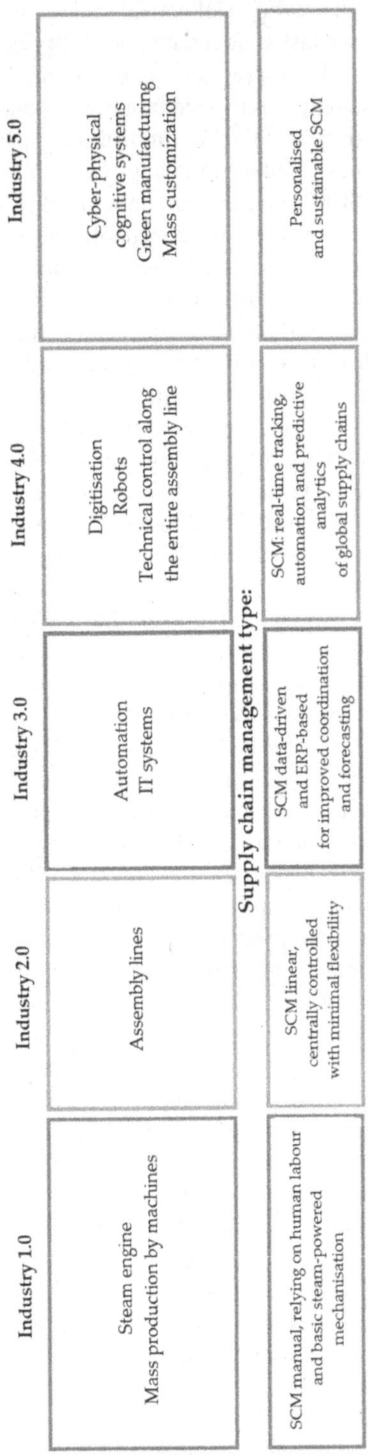

Figure 5.2 Steps of SCM evolution.

decisions and ethical considerations while machines perform repetitive, resource-intensive tasks. Social responsibility becomes a core principle, and SSCM ensures fair working practices and community well-being through technology-based transparency and accountability. Finally, in both Industry 4.0 and 5.0, SSCM prioritises sustainable innovation, continuously integrating new technologies and practices to adapt to changing environmental and social challenges [8].

SSCM using AI is changing the way companies achieve environmental and social responsibility. AI enables real-time data analysis, allowing companies to monitor energy use, emissions, and resource consumption at every stage of the supply chain, ensuring sustainability goals are met. Through predictive analytics, AI helps to forecast demand more accurately, reducing overproduction and waste, which in turn minimises resource depletion and reduces environmental impact. AI-based inventory management systems optimise stock levels by predicting future needs based on historical data and market trends, helping to prevent overstocking that leads to waste. By analyzing complex patterns in supply chain logistics, AI can also recommend more efficient transport routes, reducing fuel consumption and emissions. AI-based systems can further optimise production schedules to accommodate energy-efficient practices, minimizing the carbon footprint during production processes [9].

In the context of supplier management, AI enables companies to assess suppliers' sustainability performance by analyzing data related to their environmental impact, ethical working practices, and resource use. Blockchain integrated with AI ensures transparency and accountability by creating secure, traceable records of product origin, ensuring responsible sourcing of materials and adherence to ethical standards. AI also facilitates the automation of routine tasks such as demand forecasting and order processing, allowing human resources to focus on strategic sustainability initiatives. Furthermore, AI can enhance recycling and circular economy efforts by identifying optimal ways to reuse materials and products, reducing the need to extract raw materials. It plays a key role in product lifecycle management, predicting when components will need maintenance or replacement, thereby extending product life and reducing waste. AI helps companies stay compliant with environmental regulations by continuously monitoring and flagging any breaches, ensuring sustainable practices are maintained throughout the supply chain [10].

Furthermore, AI supports scenario planning and risk management, helping companies anticipate and mitigate environmental risks, such as supply chain disruptions caused by climate change or resource scarcity. With natural language processing (NLP) tools, AI can sift through vast amounts of regulatory data, identifying emerging trends and ensuring that companies stay ahead of new sustainability regulations. AI-based customer insights allow companies to understand consumer preferences for sustainable products, enabling more targeted production that meets demand without excessive waste. AI supports collaboration and communication within the supply chain, streamlining the exchange of data between stakeholders, ensuring that all partners are aligned with sustainability goals. With the ability to process large data sets, artificial intelligence helps companies achieve continuous improvement, using insights to improve sustainability practices over time. Ultimately, AI enables companies to make informed, real-time decisions that drive both environmental and economic sustainability throughout the supply chain [10].

Table 5.1 Summary of results of bibliographic analysis (WoS, Scopus)

Parameter/Feature	Value
Number of publications	WoS: 115 (2019–2024), Scopus: 95 (2019–2024)
Leading type of publication	Article (35.8%), Conference paper (18.9%), Review (16.8%), Book chapter (15.8%)
Leading area of science	Engineering (19.1%), Computer Science (15.6%), Business, Management and Accounting (13.6%), Decision Sciences (8.9%), Energy (7.8%), Environmental Science (7.4%)
Leading topic	Environmental Sciences Ecology (32.18%), Engineering (31.30%), Science Technology Other Topics (30.43%), Industrial: Business Economics (26.01%), Computer Science (14.78%), Operations Research Management Science (10.44%), Food Science Technology (4.34%), Materials Science (3.48%)
Leading countries	India, UK, France, USA, Australia, Italy, South Africa
Leading scientists	S.V. Akram, P.E. Dossou, A. Gehlot, R. Singh
Leading affiliation	Uttaranchal University, INRAE, Universite Gustave Eiffel
Leading funding (where information available)	National Natural Science Foundation of China, Ministry of Science and Technology of China, Tshwane University of Technology

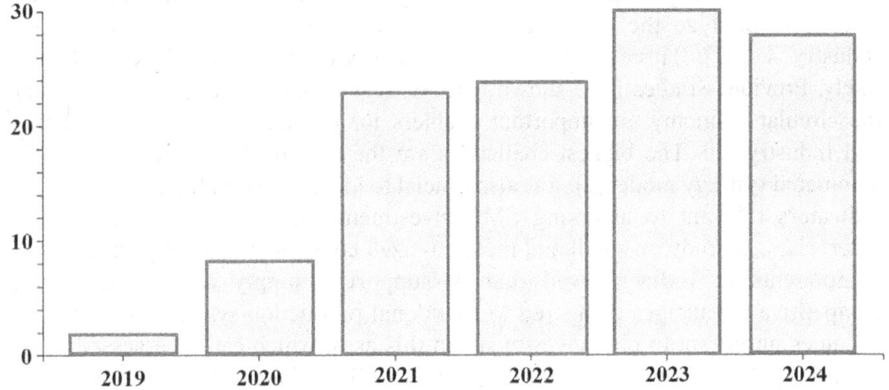

Figure 5.3 Number of publications in the review.

Two databases (Web of Science, Scopus) were searched using the keywords “artificial intelligence” or “machine learning”, “supply chain”, “sustainability”, “Industry 4.0” or “Industry 5.0”. The obtained publications were subjected to further selection (Table 5.1, Figure 5.3). Bibliometric research in the Web of Science (WoS) and Scopus databases was conducted to analyse scientific output, trends, and impact in the specific field of this article. Using keywords, researchers were able to systematically identify and assess patterns in the number of publications, citation networks, and collaborations between authors, institutions, or countries. The main objective was to gain insights into the structure and evolution of the field, enabling the identification of influential papers, new research areas, and knowledge gaps. Such analyses help strategic decision-making in academia, fund allocation, and policy development. In addition, bibliometric research enhances the understanding of the scientific landscape by providing a basis for comparing the reach and impact of research outputs within and across disciplines.

5.2 CURRENT AND FUTURE FUNCTIONS OF AI-SUPPORTED SUSTAINABLE SUPPLY CHAIN

5.2.1 Basic Solutions

Supply chain resilience (SCRes) and performance are becoming critical and can be improved through digitalization, integration, and globalization of the supply chain, including the use of advanced information processing techniques such as AI in planning, building, and maintaining SCRes. The concept of using AI in the supply chain was created in the organizational information processing theory (OIPT). AI has a direct impact on SCR in the short and long term, it is recommended to use longitudinal studies to investigate more aspects of this phenomenon [1]. To identify the link between the circular economy (CE) and Industry 4.0, principal component analysis—decision-making trial and evaluation laboratory (PCA-DEMATEL) is proposed. In this case, PCA is used to identify the linking factors between the circular economy and Industry 4.0, while DEMATEL is used to analyze the causes and effects between the circular economy and Industry 4.0 [1]. Three data sets are used: optimistic, pessimistic, and most likely. Previous studies have shown that AI, service and policy frameworks, and the circular economy are important enablers for connecting circular economies and Industry 4.0. The biggest challenges are the design of the interface and the automated synergy model [2]. It is also crucial to identify and validate performance indicators relevant to assessing SMS investments in small and medium-sized enterprises. A study on small and medium-sized companies producing automotive components in India showed that AI-supported supply chains offer more competitive advantages compared to traditional production systems. Therefore, it becomes important to plan investments in this area, which can be assessed in ten dimensions of performance: cost, quality, flexibility, time, integration, optimized productivity, real-time diagnostics and forecasting, computation, social and ecological sustainability. The aforementioned Smart Manufacturing Performance.

Measurement System (SMPMS) framework will allow for better targeting of decision-making in the area of increasing the digitalization of the supply chain [3]. Industry 5.0 can reduce the pressure on technology, as the progress in this phase is based on collaboration between humans and machines in the supply chain, but also in healthcare, industrial manufacturing, cloud manufacturing, etc. Key technologies in AI-supported supply chains in Industry 5.0 include big data analytics, IoT, collaborative robots, Blockchain, digital twins, and future 6G systems. Difficulties. but increasingly less, can cause the organization of collaboration between robots and humans on the assembly line and in the supply chain. This is especially true for the collaboration between smarter machines (cobots) and humans in terms of hyper-personalization and hyper-adaptive customer requirements using a combination of human originality and machine competence. It should be emphasized that robots are needed to manage the supply chain in standard procedures at high production volumes, with human specialists ensuring smooth end-to-end supply chain processes (e.g., selection of raw materials for personalization and customization for individual consumers). This helps to adapt the end-user experience and optimize workflows. The enhancement of the effect of utilizing human intelligence is realized through cognitive computing and intelligent automation capabilities [4].

Similarly, Agri-Food 4.0 is an analogy to the term Industry 4.0. Currently, all agricultural machines contain electronic controls and, in part, use data from sensors and drones to increase their current efficiency, taking into account weather, spatial geographic representation, animal and crop behavior, and the entire life cycle of the farm. However, this requires improving methods sometimes distant from Industry 4.0, hence, the concept of Industry 4.0 has evolved and adapted to Agriculture 4.0 and the analysis of behavior and performance in this specific domain. Agriculture 4.0 supports better decision-making in the supply chain, helping farmers save time to make effective decisions based on objective data, developing future paths of the agri-food domain in the AI-based supply chain [5]. This broadens the meaning of data management, manufacturing competitiveness, manufacturing processes, and efficiency to include phenomena such as droughts and floods in the supply chain [6]. There is still a need for the systematization of knowledge that not only shapes the production and operations of companies but also encompasses their broader concepts and complementary elements, such as lean production in Industry 4.0. The key elements here are considered to be the cyber-physical production system, big data and intelligent communication, safety and security, AI for sustainable development, circular economy in the digital environment, business intelligence and virtual reality, and environmental sustainability [7].

The industry sees increasing levels of digitalization and automation as elements of competition transforming many aspects of the operational aspects of manufacturing organizations. Higher levels of productivity and adaptation mean introducing innovations into the company's business and operational processes. The roadmaps developed by companies towards Industry 4.0 are not only complex and multi-faceted but also subject to dynamic changes (new generations of devices, support, etc.) and consider the transformation process as multi-stage, taking into account operational efficiency and focusing on sustainable development [11].

5.2.2 Global Phenomenon

It is a global phenomenon. One study surveyed 223 Vietnamese supply chain experts on the type and manner of digital technologies used, the expected level of future investment, and necessary preparations for opportunities to improve supply chain sustainability. Despite the low adoption of Industry 4.0 in Vietnamese supply chains, IoT is the most widespread (48%), but drones and big data analytics are also being used, which may provide a greater chance of achieving future sustainability outcomes [8]. Institutional pressure moderates green logistics practices to adopt CE and improve supply chain flexibility towards green logistics and CE practices [12]. Emerging Industry 4.0 technologies can be assessed in terms of capabilities that enable sensing, analyzing, collaborating, and executing. This allows for a more objective assessment of the impact of supply chain improvements on adding revenue, differentiating, reducing costs, optimizing risk, innovating, and transforming business models and processes [9]. In this way, cyber-physical production networks and IoT-based real-time production logistics using AI-based decision-making algorithms enable the further targeted development of sustainable, data-driven smart production [10]. It identifies seven key technologies transforming supply chains: big data analytics, digital twins, augmented reality, blockchain, 3D printing, AI, and IoT. These technologies can improve three subthemes of organizational social performance (employment practices, health and safety, and business practices) and three subthemes of community social performance (quality of life and social well-being, social governance, and economic well-being and growth). This suggests that organizational programs for Industry 4.0 and social responsibility can complement each other, for example, providing companies with a competitive advantage by helping them build back better. In the Industry 5.0 paradigm, people and communities are at the center of decisions about operations and supply chains, giving the organization responsibility for the social well-being of employees throughout the supply chain and the broader community in which they operate. This also applies to a long-term strategy for embedding social responsibility in operations and supply chains [13].

The hierarchical structure of the circular supply chain with big data (qualitative and quantitative information subject to trends) is also highlighted. The optimal hierarchical structure of the circular supply chain consists of a big data set. The combination of data-driven content analysis and clustering shows that Industry 4.0, digitalization, resource recovery implementation, and reverse supply chain practice are in the causal group, and the circular business strategy and life cycle sustainability assessment are in the effect group. In this case, the decisive criteria are AI, material efficiency, waste-to-energy, machine learning, e-waste, and plastic recycling [7]. For the above reasons, CE implementation is already a challenge for traditional linear business models, especially in the area of the need to manage geographically dispersed product life cycles and value chains [14]. Text mining allows for a semi-automatic summary of the current state of knowledge in the field of supply chain digitalization. This shows that the most important topics in digital transformation are still SSCM, circular economy, and industry 4.0 technologies. The most important technologies facilitating the transformation in this area are AI, ML, IoT, big data, data analytics, and blockchain. New trends concern Industry 4.0, digital transformation, SCM, decision-making, and sustainability [15]. In particular, fast analysis of large data sets and their availability in real time are game changers, increasing the accuracy of decision-making. They significantly affect the marketing results of companies dealing with digital production and digital services [16]. This is especially true for minimizing business disruptions in a world dominated by human-centric approaches. As the workforce increasingly interacts with new technologies, predictive maintenance processes and AI-based human-centric decision support frameworks for predictive maintenance in asset management, including supply chains, have become increasingly important.

The human-in-the-loop mechanism leverages tacit knowledge explained by subject matter experts to provide decision support. An accuracy rate of 82% was achieved in a real-world case study, indicating the potential of the aforementioned solution [17]. As the workforce adapts to advanced technologies, predictive maintenance processes supported by AI-based human-centric decision-making frameworks are becoming essential for effective asset management, including in supply chains. This framework improves reliability by using AI to predict maintenance needs while ensuring that human-informed decisions are made. The human-in-the-loop mechanism integrates tacit knowledge from domain experts, enabling AI systems to provide nuanced decision support tailored to the complexities of the real world. This approach optimises maintenance operations, reduces downtime, and provides a synergistic collaboration between human judgment and AI capabilities. Challenges include trade-offs between different sustainability metrics, life-cycle environmental impacts, technology maturity, and access inequality. The concept of focusing on the balance between sustainability metrics across the life-cycle, human-centric technology transformation, system integration and digital twin, semi-autonomous transport solutions, smart reverse logistics, rather than just screwing up a few selected metrics, is gaining importance [18]. New business models and practices are needed in line with industry dynamics. Currently, there are gaps in the integration of micro, meso, and macro levels to obtain the systemic benefits of CE implementation, and many CE frameworks described in the literature for implementation need to be empirically tested and obtain comparable performance results [19].

5.2.3 Sustainable Supply Chains

Several key factors are shaping the future of AI-powered sustainable supply chains. Key among them are advances in machine learning and predictive analytics that will increase demand forecasting accuracy, reducing overproduction and waste. The growing availability of big data will enable AI to make more informed decisions on resource and energy optimization. Stricter environmental regulations will force companies to adopt AI-powered solutions to achieve sustainability goals and reduce their carbon footprint. Consumer demand for transparency and ethical sourcing will drive the integration of AI with blockchain to provide supply chain visibility. Innovations in AI-powered automation, such as autonomous vehicles and drones, will improve logistics efficiency while reducing emissions [20]. The rise of circular economy models will encourage the use of AI to enable better waste management, recycling, and reuse in supply chains. The growing adoption of renewable energy sources will require AI to manage and optimize energy consumption throughout the supply chain [21]. AI-enabled collaboration across companies will become essential to achieving shared sustainability goals. AI-enabled advances in materials science will lead to the development of environmentally friendly materials and products. Global supply chain disruptions, such as those caused by climate change, will make AI essential for real-time risk management and adaptive decision-making [22].

Sustainable supply chains supported by AI are changing the way companies operate, optimizing processes for environmental and economic benefits. Today, AI is being used to improve demand forecasting, helping companies produce only what is needed, reducing waste and overproduction. AI-based predictive analytics are improving inventory management, enabling companies to maintain optimal stock levels and reduce excess materials. AI systems are also being used to optimise routes, which minimises fuel consumption by selecting the most efficient delivery paths, leading to a reduction in carbon emissions. By analyzing data from a variety of sources, AI helps companies track and reduce energy consumption in their supply chains. AI-based sensors and IoT technologies are now being used to monitor machine health and performance, promoting predictive maintenance that reduces downtime and energy waste [23]. Blockchain technology combined with AI increases supply chain transparency, enabling better tracking of product sustainability attributes such as carbon footprint and ethical sourcing. In purchasing, AI helps identify sustainable suppliers by analyzing environmental, social, and governance (ESG) indicators [24]. AI's role in waste management is significant, facilitating circular supply chains where materials can be reused or recycled.

In the future, AI is expected to further automate decision-making in supply chains, enabling real-time adjustments that increase sustainability. Advanced AI models are likely to optimize entire supply chain ecosystems, finding synergies between companies to share resources and reduce waste. AI could also lead to the development of more sustainable materials, using machine learning algorithms to discover and predict the environmental impact of new compounds [25].

Future AI technologies are likely to create circular supply chains, where waste from one process becomes input to another, minimizing environmental damage. As AI becomes increasingly integrated into smart cities and smart factories, it will enable a fully connected, data-driven approach to sustainability in supply chains. AI-powered autonomous transportation will further reduce emissions through efficient, energy-efficient logistics systems. In addition, AI will enable greater collaboration between companies by identifying mutually beneficial sustainability goals, supporting more responsible manufacturing practices. In short, AI is shaping today's sustainable supply chains and paving the way for a future where efficiency, waste reduction, and environmental responsibility are deeply intertwined.

Demand forecasting for SSCM using AI involves using advanced algorithms to predict future customer demand while taking into account sustainability goals. AI improves the accuracy of demand forecasts by analyzing huge datasets, including historical sales, market trends, and external factors such as economic indicators, weather patterns, and even social media trends. This level of precision helps companies avoid overproduction, which reduces waste, excess inventory, and unnecessary resource consumption. AI-based forecasting can also take into account environmental factors, enabling companies to align their operations with sustainability goals such as carbon footprint reduction and energy efficiency [26].

SSCM focuses on minimizing environmental impact and promoting ethical sourcing, which AI can facilitate by improving visibility across the supply chain. Real-time data processing allows AI to dynamically adjust forecasts, responding to disruptions such as supply shortages or sudden changes in demand. This flexibility helps companies optimise transport routes, reduce fuel consumption and lower emissions [16]. AI-based tools can simulate different scenarios, enabling companies to make decisions that balance cost efficiency with environmental sustainability [25].

Incorporating AI into demand forecasting allows for more collaborative planning between suppliers and manufacturers, promoting the use of sustainable materials and environmentally friendly practices [12]. By improving the accuracy of demand, AI minimises the risk of supply disruptions or overstocking, increasing supply chain resilience and reducing the burden on the environment. In addition, AI can monitor sustainability metrics and regulatory compliance, ensuring that green practices are followed throughout the supply chain [27]. This is also depicted in Figure 5.4.

In the longer term, the use of AI in demand forecasting supports the transition to a circular economy by promoting the reuse and recycling of materials based on accurate demand patterns. This approach helps companies meet consumer expectations for sustainable products while maintaining profitability. Integrating AI into SSCM is a critical advance toward achieving global sustainability goals, such as reducing greenhouse gas emissions and conserving natural resources.

5.3 RESULTING REQUIREMENTS TO FUTURE SUSTAINABLE AI-SUPPORTED SUPPLY CHAIN

Future AI-powered sustainable supply chains will require several key elements to thrive. Seamless integration of data across the supply chain will be essential to enable accurate AI-driven insights and real-time decision-making. Transparency and traceability must be a priority, with AI systems able to track every step of production, transportation, and sourcing to meet regulatory and consumer demands. The ethical use and management of data will be critical, ensuring that AI models are trained on accurate and unbiased data. Robust cybersecurity measures will be necessary to protect sensitive information shared between AI systems and supply chain partners [28]. Energy-efficient AI algorithms will be necessary to minimize the environmental impact of running advanced AI models. Scalable AI solutions will need to be developed to accommodate both small businesses and large global supply chains. Collaboration across industries will be key, requiring AI systems that can facilitate collaboration to achieve shared sustainability goals. Training and ongoing employee upskilling will become even more necessary as workers need to manage, interpret, and interact with AI tools [29].

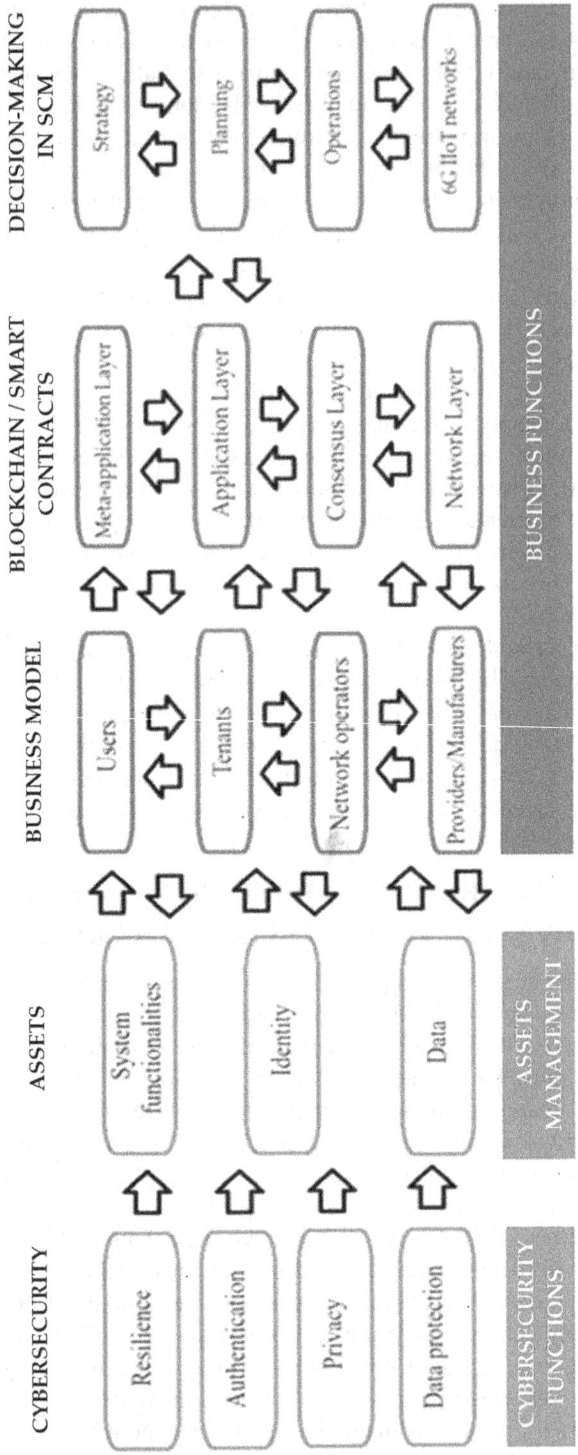

Figure 5.4 Processes improving AI-based supply chain.

Flexibility to adapt to changing environmental regulations and changing market demands will also be key. Companies will need to invest in AI systems that can promote circular economy practices, enabling efficient reuse and recycling throughout the supply chain [30].

The architecture of the future AI-powered sustainable supply chain will be a dynamic, connected ecosystem built on several key technology layers. At its core, data is the foundation, flowing over the 6G network from a variety of sources, including sensors, IoT devices, enterprise systems, and external stakeholders such as suppliers and customers (Figure 5.5). AI-based supply chains using 6G networks integrate cloud-based services to manage data-intensive tasks such as demand forecasting, inventory optimization, and real-time tracking with increased processing speed and scalability. The core network provides highly reliable, low-latency communication, seamlessly connecting different nodes such as satellites, balloons, and drones. Satellites and high-altitude platforms (such as balloons) provide extensive and uninterrupted connectivity for remote and global operations, while drones streamline last-stage deliveries and real-time inventory inspections. The overall IoT network connects the elements of the supply chain - vehicles, warehouses, and manufacturing facilities enabling artificial intelligence to optimise operations through advanced analytics, automation, and dynamic resource allocation. This real-time data will be processed via cloud-based platforms, providing scalability and seamless access to different parts of the supply chain. AI algorithms will be embedded throughout the chain, performing advanced analytics on this data to optimize processes such as demand forecasting, inventory management, and route planning. A key element of this architecture will be decentralized, blockchain-based (eventually quantum cryptography-based) systems for transparency and traceability. These systems will enable verification of each stage of the supply chain, from raw material extraction to product delivery,

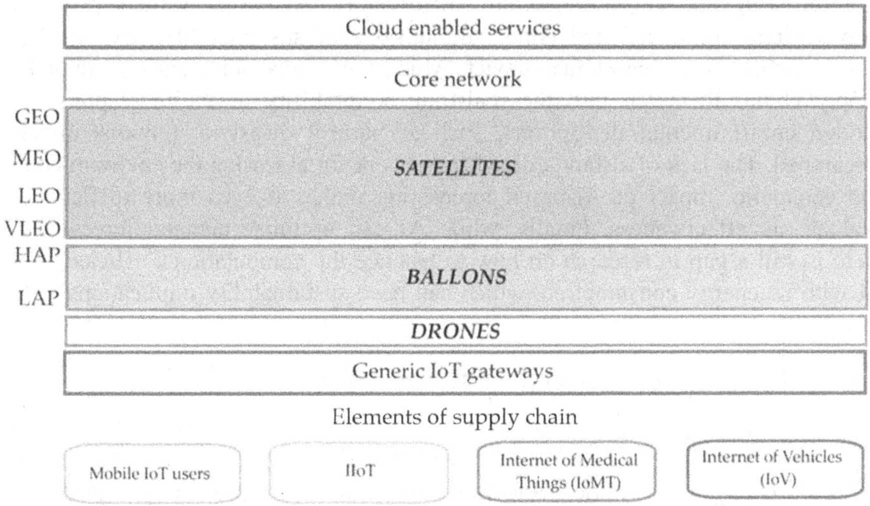

Figure 5.5 Elements of AI-based supply chain using 6G network (own version based on own concept showed in [27]).

for sustainable and ethical practices. Machine learning models will be used to detect inefficiencies and recommend improvements in energy use, emissions reduction, and waste management, continuously learning and adapting over time [29]. Autonomous vehicles and robots will provide a logistics layer managed by AI to optimize transportation routes and warehouse operations, minimizing carbon footprint and increasing delivery efficiency. The architecture will also integrate renewable energy sources, and AI systems will dynamically adjust operations based on real-time energy availability and costs (Figure 5.5).

5.4 DISCUSSION

5.4.1 Limitations of Current Studies

Current research into demand forecasting for SSCM using AI faces several limitations. Firstly, many AI models require huge amounts of high-quality data, which can be difficult to collect or unreliable, especially in less digitized supply chains. Second, sustainability indicators and environmental factors are often difficult to quantify and incorporate into traditional AI models, making it difficult to align AI-based forecasts with sustainability goals. Additionally, AI models are often focused on past data patterns, which limits their ability to predict future disruptions or changes related to environmental policy or market shifts toward sustainability. Furthermore, research often focuses on individual elements of the supply chain rather than providing an integrated view of how AI can drive sustainability across the supply chain ecosystem. Another limitation is that AI systems can be complex and expensive to implement, especially for smaller companies with limited resources, making widespread adoption difficult. Ethical concerns around AI transparency and data privacy further complicate its use in forecasting and decision-making. Furthermore, AI-based systems may not fully address the social and ethical dimensions of sustainability, such as fair labor practices and community impact, which are crucial for a truly sustainable supply chain. Research into the real-time adaptability of AI in response to sudden environmental disruptions, such as natural disasters, remains under-researched. The lack of a standardized framework for assessing the environmental and economic impact of AI-based forecasting makes it even more difficult to evaluate its effectiveness. Finally, while AI can optimise demand forecasting, there is still a gap in research on how to balance the computational efficiency of AI with its energy consumption, which can have sustainability implications [30].

5.4.2 Direction for Further Research

Further research into demand forecasting for SSCM using AI should focus on developing models that better integrate sustainability metrics, such as carbon footprint, energy consumption, and waste reduction in to forecasting algorithms. Increasing the availability and quality of real-time data across the supply chain, especially for smaller or less digitized companies, is key to improving AI

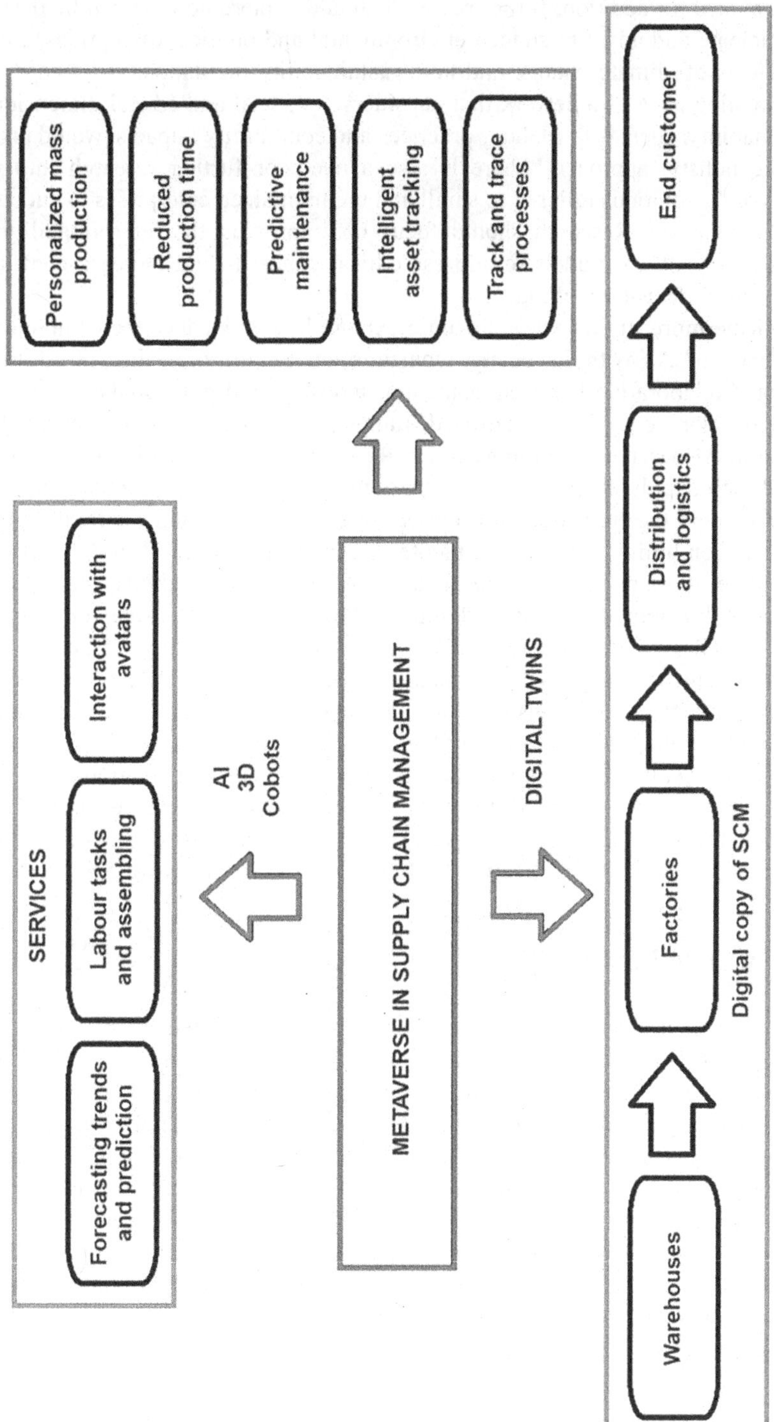

Figure 5.6 Metaverse in supply chain management (own version based on [30]).

performance. In addition, future research should explore how AI can be designed to anticipate and adapt to sudden environmental and political disruptions, such as the effects of climate change and new sustainability regulations.

Creating an AI framework that considers the social and ethical dimensions of sustainability, such as fair labour practices and community impacts, would provide a more holistic approach. There is also a need for further research into cost-effective AI solutions tailored to small and medium-sized enterprises to encourage greater adoption. Research should focus on improving the interpretability and transparency of AI models to address ethical concerns and increase confidence in AI-based decision-making.

Furthermore, future research could explore how to balance the computational efficiency of AI with its energy consumption to minimize its environmental impact. Collaboration between academia, industry, and policymakers could lead to the development of a standardised framework for measuring the sustainability impact of AI-based demand forecasting. Research into the role of AI in supporting closed-loop supply chains by predicting demand for recycled or reused materials could support the transition to a closed-loop economy. Finally, interdisciplinary research combining AI, environmental science, and SCM would likely yield innovative solutions to accelerate the achievement of sustainability goals. Various sectors within manufacturing and supply chains can benefit from reinforcement learning (RL). This includes robotic automation, welding processes, the semiconductor industry, injection molding, metalworking, milling processes, and energy production and consumption. The main factors hindering the adoption and implementation of RL technologies in industrial settings such as model complexity, availability of simulation environments, implementation constraints, safety, and model interpretability. The correctness of sample performance and bridging the simulation-to-reality gap would be an additional benefit, including such complex solutions as Metaverse [30], as depicted in Figure 5.6.

5.5 CONCLUSIONS

Supply chain problems observed earlier cannot be repeated, hence, automation and computerization of supply chains, asset tracking, simulation, and prediction of disruptions with AI are obvious solutions. Intelligent SCM within the Industry 4.0/5.0 paradigm will not only provide more fluidity of supply but also faster response to changes in market availability or prices, enabling finding and considering substitutes in the production process and its logistics supply within the framework of sustainable development. IIoT, ML, and 6G will provide the supply chain with unprecedented speed, connectivity, and efficiency, improving visibility, automation and collaboration, sustainable and safe operations. Manufacturers and service providers will be able to design, plan, and operate their supply chains with greater precision, flexibility, and responsiveness.

REFERENCES

[1] Belhadi, A., V. Mani, S.S. Kamble, S.A.R. Khan and S. Verma. 2024. Artificial intelligence-driven innovation for enhancingsupply chain resilience and performance under the effect ofsupply chain dynamism: An empirical investigation. Annals of Operations Research. 333(2–3): 627–652.

[2] Rajput, S. and S.P. Singh. 2019. Connecting circular economy and Industry 4.0. International Journal of Information Management. 49: 98–113.

[3] Kamble, S.S., A. Gunasekaran, A. Ghadge and R. Raut. 2020. A performance measurement system forindustry 4.0 enabled smart manufacturing system in SMMEs—A review and empirical investigation. International Journal of Production Economics. 229.

[4] Adel, A. 2022. Future of industry 5.0 in society: Human-centric solutions, challenges and prospective research areas. Journal of Cloud Computing—Advances Systems and Applications. 11(1).

[5] Lezoche, M., J.E. Hernandez, M.M.E.A. Dia, H. Panetto and J. Kacprzyk. 2020. Agri-food 4.0: A survey of the supply chains and technologies for the future agriculture. Computers in Industry. Vol. 117.

[6] Jamwal, A., R. Agrawal, M. Sharma and A. Giallanza. 2021. Industry 4.0 Technologies for ManufacturingSustainability: A Systematic Review and Future Research Directions. Applied Sciences. 11(12).

[7] Tseng, M.L., H.M. Ha, T.P.T. Tran, T.D. Bui, C.C. Chen and C.W. Lin. 2022. Building a data-driven circularsupply chain hierarchical structure: Resource recovery implementation drives circular business strategy. Business Strategy and the Environment. 31(5): 2082–2106.

[8] Akbari, M. and J.L. Hopkins. 2022. Digital technologies as enablers of supply chain sustainability in an emerging economy. Operations Management Research. 15(3–4): 689–710.

[9] Mithas, S., Z.L. Chen, T.J.V. Saldanha and A.D. Silveira. 2022. How willartificial intelligence and Industry 4.0 emerging technologies transform operations management? Production and Operations Management. 31(12): 4475–4487.

[10] Andronie, M., G. Lăzăroiu, R. Ştefănescu, C. Uţă and I. Dijmărescu. 2021. Sustainable, smart, and sensing technologies for cyber-physical manufacturing systems: A systematic literature review. Sustainability. 13(10).

[11] Hughes, L., Y.K. Dwivedi, H.M. Ha, T.D. Bui and V. Raghavan. 2022. Perspectives on the future of manufacturing within the Industry 4.0 era. Production Planning and Control. 33(2–3): 138–158.

[12] Sharma, M., S. Joshi and K. Govindan. 2023. Overcoming barriers to implement digital technologies to achieve sustainable production and consumption in the food sector: A circular economy perspective. Sustainable Production and Consumption. 39(20).

[13] Asokan, D.R., F.A. Huq, C.M. Smith and M. Stevenson. 2022. Socially responsible operations in theIndustry 4.0 era: post-COVID-19 technology adoption and perspectives on future research. International Journal of Operations and Production Management. 42(13): 185–217.

[14] Pham, T.T., T.C. Kuo, M.L. Tseng, R.R. Tan, K. Tan, D.S. Ika and C.J. Lin. 2019. Industry 4.0 to accelerate the circular economy: A case study of electric scooter sharing. Sustainability. 11: 6661.

[15] Tavana, M., A. Shaabani, I. Raeesi Vanani and R.A. Kumar Gangadhari. 2022. A review of digital transformation on supply chain process management using text mining. Processes. 10: 842.

[16] Gupta, S., T. Justy, S. Kamboy, A. Kuumar and E. Kristoffersen. 2021. Big data and firm marketing performance: Findings from knowledge-based view. Technological Forecasting and Social Change. 171: 120986.

[17] Chen, J., C.P. Lim, K.H. Tan, K. Govindan and A. Kumar. 2021. Artificial intelligence-based human-centric decision support framework: an application to predictive maintenance in asset management under pandemic environments. Annals of Operations Research. https://doi.org/10.1007/s10479-021-04373-w.

[18] Sun, X., H. Yu, W.D. Solvang, Y. Wang and K.S. Wang. 2022. The application ofIndustry 4.0 technologies in sustainable logistics: A systematic literature review (2012–2020) to explore future research opportunities. Environmental Science and Pollution Research. 29(7): 9560–9591.

[19] Khan, S.A.R., A.S.A. Shah, Z. Yu and M. Tanveer. 2022. A systematic literature review on circular economy practices: challenges, opportunities and future trends. Journal of Entrepreneurship in Emerging Economies. 14(5): 754–795.

[20] Kazancoglu, I., M. Ozbiltekin-Pala, S.K. Mangla, A. Kumar and Y. Kazancoglu. 2023. Using emerging technologies to improve thesustainability and resilience of supply chains in a fuzzy environment in the context of COVID-19. Annals of Operations Research. 322(1): 217–240.

[21] Santhi, A.R. and P. Muthuswamy. 2022. Pandemic, war, natural calamities and sustainability: Industry 4.0 technologies to overcome traditional and contemporary supply chain challenges. Logistics. 6(4).

[22] Marinagi, C., P. Reklitis, P. Trivellas and D. Sakas. 2023. The impact of Industry 4.0 technologies on key performance indicators for a Resilient Supply Chain 4.0. Sustainability. 15(6).

[23] Amjad, M.S., M.Z. Rafique, S. Hussain and M.A. Khan. 2020. A new vision of LARG Manufacturing—A trail towards Industry 4.0. CIRP Journal of Manufacturing Science and Technology. 31: 377–393.

[24] Jahani, N., A. Sepehri, H.R. Vandchali and E.B. Tirkolaee. 2021. Application of Industry 4.0 in the procurement processes of supply chains: A systematic literature review. Sustainability. 13: 14.

[25] Hassoun, A., J. Cropotova, H. Trollman, S. Jagtap, C. Parra-Lopez, G.G. Garcia, et al. 2023. Use of Industry 4.0 technologies to reduce and valorize seafood waste and by-products: A narrative review on current knowledge. Current Research in Food Science. 6.

[26] Chauhan, S., R. Singh, A. Gehlot, S.V. Akram, B. Twala and N. Priyadarshi. 2023. Digitalization of supply chain management with Industry 4.0 enabling technologies: A sustainable perspective. Processes. 11(1).

[27] Rojek, I., E. Dostatni, D. Mikołajewski, L. Pawłowski and K. Wegrzyn-Wolska. 2022. Modern approach to sustainable production in the context of Industry 4.0. Bulletin of the Polish Academy of Sciences: Technical Sciences. 70(6): e143828.

[28] Nievas, N., A. Pagès-Bernaus, F. Bonada, L. Echeverria and X. Domingo. 2024. Reinforcement Learning for Autonomous Process Control in Industry 4.0: Advantages and Challenges. Applied Artificial Intelligence. 38(1): e2383101.

[29] Rojek, I., D. Mikołajewski, E. Dostatni and J. Kopowski. 2023. Specificity of 3D printing and AI-based optimization of medical devices using the example of a group of exoskeletons. Applied Sciences. 13(2): 1060.

[30] Prabadevi, B., N. Deepa, N. Victor, T.G. Gadekallu, P.K.R. Maddikunta, G. Yenduri, et al. 2023. Metaverse for Industry 5.0 in NextG Communications: Potential applications and future challenges. arXiv:2308.02677.

Chapter 6

Demand Forecasting for AI in Supply Chain Management

Harika Rajashekaraiah, Noor Sakina, Ajith Pulinchuvattil Arun*, Praveen Kumar Gupta and Thippareddy

RV College of Engineering, Bengaluru, Karnataka, India

6.1 INTRODUCTION

Supply chain management is a strategically critical function of modern business, outside its roots in logistics, and has become a sophisticated system controlling and coordinating the movement and delivery of goods and services, and information across all networks of a supplier, manufacturer, and distributor. At its very core, SCM aims to create a seamless, cost-effective process that ensures timely delivery of products to end consumers while improving efficiency and reducing operational costs. No greater importance can be than that for SCM in today's volatile global, highly competitive markets—complexities mastered can bring an organization a sustainable competitive advantage and provide a better answer to changing customer expectations [1].

Demand forecasting is one of the cornerstones of an effective SCM. This allows companies more accurate predictions of their customer needs, enabling them to more precisely coordinate schedules for productions, inventory management and distribution, and resource allocation [2, 3]. Accurate predictions help in the avoidance of overstocking and stockouts since these two not only damage profitability but also affect customer trust. In contrast to conventional methods

*For Correspondence: ajithparun2020@gmail.com

DOI: 10.1201/9781003541875-6

that rely on historical data and statistical models, AI uses real-time data and learns continuously, adapting to changes more effectively. This advanced capability allows AI to uncover complex patterns and make highly accurate predictions, even in unpredictable environments [4]. As a result, AI strengthens demanding processes with greater precision, adaptability, and efficiency. AI-driven demand forecasting uses big datasets that can trace patterns through the behavior of consumers, market trends, and other external variables to produce predictions that are highly accurate and adaptable [5].

As AI continues to revolutionize SCM, it transforms not only how demand is anticipated but also enhances the decision-making capability of all elements of the entire supply chain. AI tools can analyze real-time data. This means that companies can dynamically respond to shifts in demand, streamline logistics, and facilitate greater cooperation among all the stakeholders involved in the supply chain. Ultimately, the supply chain becomes more resilient, agile, and efficient in navigating the dynamics of changing fast-paced markets. SCM will, therefore, enhance not only the operating performance of integrating AI but also lay down the next area where future innovations in supply chain optimization will be built which will be a way for organizations to maintain growth and competitiveness in an increasingly uncertain global environment [6, 7].

6.1.1 Understanding the Supply Chain Management

This major stage of supply chain management is how planning is done merely in the beginning of demand and supply strategizing, creating forecasts, and coordinating supply chain actions with the business goals with a specific focus on efficiently allocating resources so that they provide for customer demand.

- *Sourcing.* This involves the choice of suppliers and managing their relationships to get raw materials, goods, or services required for production, like managing contracts and performance evaluation of suppliers.
- *Production.* In this phase, raw materials are changed to finished goods through the manufacturing process. Here, in terms of efficiency and quality of the product, the activities involved are quality control, production planning and control, and controlling and monitoring.
- *Delivery.* Also known as the logistics stage. In this stage, the finished products are moved and delivered to the customers. This also includes warehousing and inventory management and transportation and freight management for timely delivery.
- *Return.* Return is the last process that deals with returns matters relating to return and exchange procedures involved in the product. The procedure involves complaints from consumers and faulty goods among others to ensure effective returns.

These five phases collectively control the flow of resources, information, and products starting from sourcing raw materials to the final delivery of finished products. Thus, at the end of this exercise, the entire supply chain increases efficiency in supplying and servicing goods.

6.1.2 Why is Supply Chain Management Important?

The SCM plays a crucial role in the delivery of products. As organizations increasingly operate in competitive markets, effective SCM becomes essential for establishing a sustainable advantage over rivals by minimizing costs and maximizing service quality [8].

Moreover, effective supply chain management enhances the ability to respond to the market in the overall success of businesses by assuring that products are delivered to customers efficiently and cost-effectively. Effective SCM optimizes every stage of the supply chain, from sourcing raw materials to manufacturing and distribution. It is through a comprehensive approach that the organization is able to cope with new developments and effectively offer its products, thus enhancing operations and increasing customer satisfaction. With real-time data analytics and improved communication across the supply chain, businesses can quickly adapt their operations to meet shifting demand patterns. This coordination is vital in today's fast-paced environment, where consumers expect rapid responses and companies must maintain a flexible approach to inventory management and logistics [9, 10].

6.2 CHALLENGES IN TRADITIONAL SUPPLY CHAIN MANAGEMENT

The major challenges faced in SCM are depicted in Figure 6.1 and elaborated as follows:

- *Transparency and Visibility:* It tracks every resource, from top to bottom of the very last supply chain with proper accountability. Therefore, communication and data availability is correct at all levels of the supply chain. This makes way for real-time decision-making in the stakeholders' hands.
- *Stock management:* Stock Control stock management should not result in shortages or oversupply of resources. Resource availability is optimal when a stock control ensures that stock is available when and wherever it is needed, wastages are avoided, and maximum storage is achieved.
- *Demand Forecasting:* In reality, demand forecasting is just the same problem as that of the kind of disaster; it improves the effectiveness of an organization to make the right decisions and to reach in time for resource arrangements to get prepared during emergency conditions to face massive upsurges.
- *Data Sharing and Interoperability:* Humanitarian work is always between various kinds of organizations and partnerships. The sharing of data and interoperability between the systems and stakeholders enhance coordination, reduce duplication of efforts, and thus enhance the overall responsiveness to the crisis.

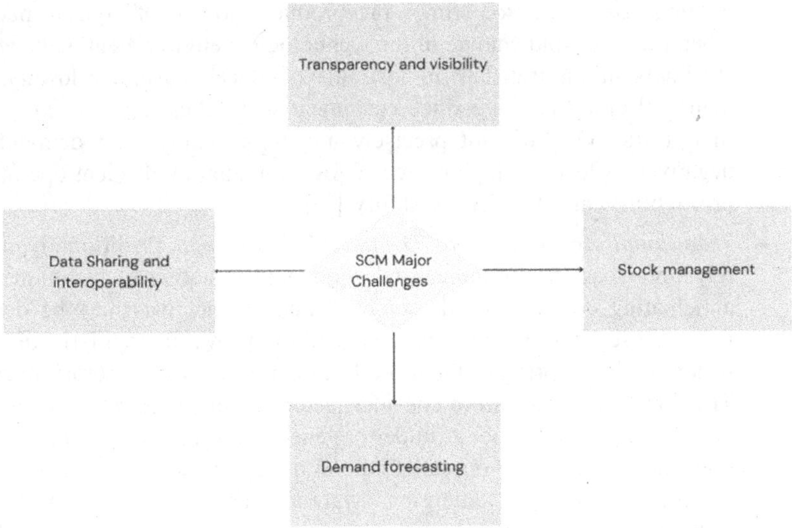

Figure 6.1 Major challenges in SCM.

The above problems would greatly contribute toward ensuring continuous improvements in the efficiency, responsiveness, and reliability of humanitarian supply chains.

6.2.1 Demand-Supply Mismatch

The scenario of demand-supply mismatch holds a great challenge when done traditionally under the supply chain management policy, mainly presented in terms of extreme inefficiencies, losses, and dissatisfaction from the customer end. This issue usually occurs when the quantity demanded by the consumers does not correspond to the amount supplied by the producers, thereby leading to scenarios such as overstocking and stockouts. This section shall detail the demand-supply mismatch with causes, impacts, and possible solutions where possible roles of technology can be taken into account [11].

- *Causes of Demand-Supply Mismatch:* Several factors contribute to the demand-supply mismatch in supply chains. Volatile consumer preferences can significantly affect demand, leading to inaccurate forecasting and production planning [12]. Seasonal fluctuations also play a crucial role. For instance, demand for seasonal products can drastically vary over time, making it challenging for suppliers to maintain appropriate inventory levels. Additionally, unexpected disruptions such as natural disasters, pandemics, or geopolitical events can alter supply capabilities, further complicating the balancing act of supply and demand.
- *Impacts on Supply Chain Operations:* The results of a demand-supply mismatch are severe as they most often bring about economic losses to the company. Overstock situations tie up the working capital, enhance

holding costs, and sometimes the products go out of style, especially when there is rapid change in the technological environment. Conversely, stockouts might translate to lost sales, reduced customer loyalty, and damaged brand prestige since customers seek other suppliers to quench their thirst. Overall, not precisely matching supply with demand can negatively affect a company's capability to maintain efficient operations, profitability, and long-run viability [13].

- *Traditional Approaches to Demand Forecasting:* Traditionally, firms rely upon past performance and rudimentary statistical techniques for anticipating demand. While some limited perspectives may be derived from these methods, by necessity they prove unsophisticated and inflexible in adapting to the more fluid nature of contemporary markets. These methods also fail to consider factors unrelated to business that are determined by consumer attitudes or general market circumstances. Thus, often there is reliance on outdated and usually inapplicable information. As such, there is an emerging awareness of using better forecasting techniques that contain the latest sources of data and analytics [14].
- *The Impact of Technology and AI on Demand Forecasting:* Advanced technologies, most notably artificial intelligence and machine learning, have totally redefined the landscape of demand forecasting. The AI algorithms take tons of data coming from social media trends, market reports, and even economic indicators as inputs and therefore their output is much closer to reality. Such systems empower firms to respond directly to shifted conditions at or very near the moment mismatches are observed, where expectations of unrealistic shifts in demand may be more effectively minimized [15].
- *Utilization of Data Analytics*: Data analytics plays a great role in managing demand-supply mismatch. Using predictive analytics, firms can identify certain patterns and trends in consumption that enable them to be more precise in predicting changes in consumer demand. In addition, by integrating data at various levels of the supply chain from the supplier's level down to the customer level companies can gain better visibility to harmonize their operations in line with true demand by attaining the proper alignment between supply and demand. This integration not only enhances accuracy in forecasting but also allows for collective planning among supply chain partners [16].

6.2.2 Logistic Disruptions and Risk Management in Supply Chain Management

Logistical disruption is one of the greatest threats to supply chain management. This event poses challenges for the most efficient, dependable, and customer-satisfied company. It may be caused by a natural calamity, pandemic, geopolitical crisis, or technological malfunction. The best course of action will then be to apply efficient risk management strategies to prevent the arising of logistical disruptions and to strengthen the supply chain resilience. This section covers the nature of logistic disruptions and, above all, their effects, but most importantly the crucial part risk management plays in reducing these difficulties [16].

- *Nature of Logistic Disruptions:* Logistic disruptions refer to any stoppages, the usual contributing factors in the flow of goods and services, which can occur in any part of the supply chain. Include natural threats such as earthquakes or floods, human-made challenges such as strikes or political unrest, and systemic issues such as transportation breakdowns [17]. Understanding the types of disruptions is essential for organizations to prepare and respond effectively. Natural disasters can lead to physical damage to infrastructure, affecting transportation networks and causing delays in delivery [18]. Similarly, geopolitical tensions can hinder trade routes and supply access, leading to scarcity of materials [19]. Additionally, global events, like the COVID-19 pandemic, have underscored vulnerabilities within supply chains, severely impacting logistics and operational capacities across various sectors.
- *Implications of Logistic Disruptions:* The implications of logistic disruptions are immense, including financial loss, damage to reputation, and customer dissatisfaction. The operating cost becomes higher because the organizations begin to seek alternative suppliers or logistics partners due to disruption. It can even cause shortages in terms of inventory, and companies may need to review their production schedules which also affects their market position later on. Beyond the ripple effect, disruption in a supply chain will affect the firm together with its suppliers and customers. For example, if one manufacturer is getting behind schedule with logistics it may bring halting production by the downstream partner complicating their subsequent operations, and jeopardizing contractual obligations, among many more. It really underlines the necessity for taking a holistic risk management approach that takes into consideration all parties within the supply chain [20].
- *Risk Management Strategies:* Good management of risks in logistics was accompanied by a risk identification process, where the impacts were analyzed and mitigated strategies were set in motion. Proper mapping of the supply chain is crucial in identifying dependencies as well as vulnerabilities. Partial supply chain mapping makes it easy for organizations to predict potential disruptions in advance and prepare contingency plans. Diversification practices are very crucial in SCM. A firm that relies on various suppliers and logistics partners is less vulnerable to the risks of single-point failure in comparison. In this regard, companies can also invest in more advanced technologies, such as AI and predictive analytics, to facilitate more insightful visibility and proactive decision-making during disruptions. Lastly, building collaborative relationships with suppliers can help these companies share necessary information and increase their response systems together to address a better response capability at times of crisis.

6.2.3 Cost Implications and Customer Satisfaction

The critical aspect of traditional supply chain management is the relationship between cost implications and customer satisfaction. Most challenges faced by organizations in the process of optimizing their supply chain procedures relate to both of these aspects: operational costs and the ability to achieve expectations in regard to customer requirements. Hence, it is fundamental to the business when it aims to be efficient enough while remaining at high levels of customer satisfaction. This section delves into cost implications that arise as a result of traditional supply chains and their effects on customer satisfaction.

- *Comprehension of Cost Consequences:* The supply chains that operate regularly incur many major costs at the operational level. These include overhead costs at the operational level, holding of inventory, and transportation costs. Such overheads are often manifested to affect the bottom line of these companies to a great extent. For example, the holding costs of excessive inventory may lead to a decrease in profit margins as well as waste if it constitutes perishable goods. Additionally, high transport costs may be attributed to poorly designed logistics processes [21]. Understanding these costs is important for organizations to ensure that they have strategies that reduce them without allowing service quality to be impaired.
- *The Trade-Off Between Cost and Quality:* A cost reduction usually comes with some deterioration of service quality expected by the customer. Cutbacks on employees or cheaper suppliers may mean a reduction in product quality or delayed deliveries, which decreases consumer satisfaction. However, expensive investment in top-quality materials and efficient logistics processes might ensure the delivery of services up to the customers' expectations. Companies should then balance out effectively the cost reductions with the quality enhancements to satisfy customers.
- *Customer Expectations and Satisfaction:* The ever-increasing needs of the consumer define today's customer satisfaction by speed, delivery reliability, or even the quality of the product. Traditional supply chains have to accommodate the growing demands of the consumer. Failure to deliver on promises or specifications reduces customers and takes away the business. An example is a poorly managed system of inventory that allows for stock-outs; it communicates unreliability to customers and drives them to seek other channels.
- *Cost Implications of Technology Adoption:* While there are costs to adopting technology in supply chain management, these investments are often long-term savers when successful; customers appreciate higher service levels while the cost to provide those levels is reduced. With automation, data analytics, and artificial intelligence comes managed inventory levels, better demand forecasting, and streamlined logistics.

Although there are significant upfront investments with these technologies, operational cost saves can be large and improve service, providing strong returns on investment over time. In addition, data analytics provides better customer insights that would lead to informed decisions hence high satisfaction rates.

6.2.4 Evolution of Supply Chain Management

Understanding the historical evolution in demand forecasting techniques will give an outline of how technological advancement along with a change in the business needs is expected to shape how organizations forecast the demand. From simple estimation techniques to sophisticated models based on AI, all techniques for demand forecasting have continuously evolved as marketplace conditions continued to change major milestones. From the historical overview of the available strategies of demand forecasting, there is an indication of a dynamic evolution that has adapted to changes in markets, technology, and consumer behavior. In the early stages, demand forecasting was considered to rely on simple quantitative techniques, including moving averages and naive forecasting. These methods gauged future demand only from historical sales data. Generally, these techniques lack accuracy in the prediction of the occurrence and frequency of patterns since they do not relate to seasonality, economic conditions, or market trends in any way. Over time, professionals came to realize these deficits so developed some more involved techniques.

This exponential smoothing model became more accepted in the middle of the 20th century, but it supposes that more current observations were given greater weights than less current ones which bettered accuracy more. Regression analysis later was the stronger framework for describing the relationship of demand with its principal influencing factors. It enabled more accurate forecasting. By the closing of the 20th century, it was possible to apply multivariate regression whereby several variables could be analyzed together and accuracy can be further refined. This new application of AI in demand forecasting represents a definite shift from the traditional methods applied. The organization can easily and rapidly adjust to changes in demand and consumer preferences in real time.

- *Early Estimation and Judgmental Forecasting (Pre-20th Century):* The early days of trade were marked by demand estimation through judgmental methods and not much else. Merchants and traders relied on personal experience, subjective judgment, and insights from customer interactions in estimating future demand. There was limited information and hardly any data, so such estimations were crude and imprecise.
- *Primary Statistical Techniques and Time Series Analysis (Early 1900s):* Statistical methods were emerging during the early 1900s, whereby businesses started applying quantitation techniques to forecast requirements. Basic statistical techniques of moving averages and trend analysis allowed for more structured forecasting using a historical pattern.

- *Introduction of Exponential Smoothing and ARIMA Models (Mid-20th Century):* The 1950's and 1960s saw the arrival of exponential smoothing models and ARIMA models, which were substantially more developed than what came before. These models possessed higher flexibility in handling seasonal variation in demand and improved the accuracy of forecasts. Exponential Smoothing: It accorded exponentially decreasing weights to older observations so that newer data was given more importance. It allowed for short-term changes to be captured and responded much better to changes in demand than averages.
- *Econometric Modeling (1970–1980):* In the 1970s and 1980s, econometric models existed in demand forecasting. It utilized techniques to model demand relationships with other economic indicators such as price income levels and marketing conditions.
- *Computer-Based Models and Early AI Approaches (1990s):* Along with increased computing power, improved sciences in computers made models related to demand forecasting much more sophisticated yet effective. There is considerable room for better computing capability by which large sets of data are analyzed to show a faster application of earlier AI in demand forecasting. During this time Monte Carlo Simulations and Neural Networks are used.
- *Machine Learning Models Emerge (2000s):* The techniques of ML are said to have begun the revolution in demand forecasting from around the 2000s. Traditional models could not treat large, complex data collections and recognize subtle patterns and relationships without explicit programming of the algorithms. Therefore, it became possible to be much more accurate with faster-changing markets.
- *Deep Learning and Neural Networks (2010s):* In the 2010s, deep learning models significantly improved the capacities of demand forecasting. Advanced neural networks, like RNNs and LSTM networks, were particularly successful with sequential time-series data in handling large datasets with nonlinear patterns and capturing seasonality, trends, and irregular fluctuations.
- *Current State-of-the-Art in AI-Based Forecasting for Streaming Data (2020s).* In the contemporary era, AI-driven demand forecasting can now combine real-time data sources and multiple AI techniques to produce adaptive, accurate, and highly responsive forecasts. The advancements in data science and IoT have further allowed companies to incorporate various sources of data, be it sensors, weather data, or social media—to demand forecasts.

6.3 AI TECHNIQUES IN SUPPLY CHAIN MANAGEMENT

6.3.1 Intelligent Supply Chains: Using NLP, ML, RL, and Deep Learning

6.3.1.1 Machine Learning (ML)

Supply Chain Management has emerged as the top discipline thanks to its integration with ML, thus enabling more rational decisions that accompany better performance of all the levels within the chain. These are some of the most important applications of ML in supply chain management

- *Demand Forecasting:* In this case, there would be a decomposition of historical data and patterns, while also looking at other factors such as cyclical variations and how certain macroeconomic factors affect future demand. It mitigates the problem of overstock and stockout situations.
- *Supplier Risk Assessment:* For any given supplier, ML can analyze its past performance records, help locate its geographical area and how long it would take to get there based on certain parameters, and even incorporate news about that supplier to highlight any risks in good time.
- *Supply Chain Visibility: C*apabilities of ML include analyzing the status of the shipment, controlling the environment as well as data analytics across the chain of operations so that the companies react to the disturbances in time.
- *Route Optimization and Transportation:* The ML models will also predict optimal routing in terms of speed and cost taking into account traffic, fuel pricing, weather, and other components.
- *Predictive Maintenance*: In relation to logistics, equipment and vehicle maintenance shall be predictive in a way that will lessen the downtime of such equipment and also shorten their wear and tear period.

6.3.1.2 Deep Learning

This is the workflow of a deep learning workflow in the supply chain but this time with an emphasis on using a Deep Q-Learning framework particularly for the optimization of other parts. Below are details illustrated in the Figure 6.2 below:

- *Input Data.* The supply chain begins with acquisition of raw data from different sources. The data could be sales data, inventory data, logistics data, suppliers' data. It should consist of ERP systems, inventory management systems, and even data from the IoT in the warehouses.
- *Data Cleaning.* Eliminates duplicate records, missing values, errors, checks on data consistency. Scaling data to comparative scales and encoding is done. It ensures data accuracy and completeness by scaling for meaningful analysis.

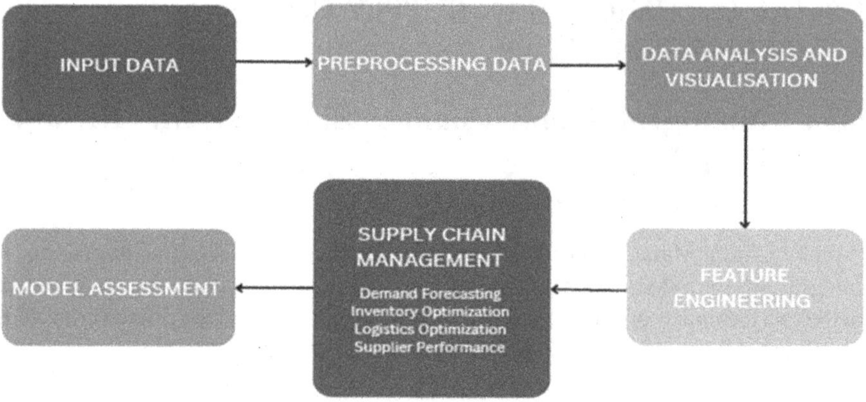

Figure 6.2 Workflow diagram for deep learning.

- *Data Analysis and Visualization.* The preprocessing techniques of supply chain management will, therefore, include the analysis and visualization of various trends and patterns to give actionable insights. These include tracking inventories over time to determine reorder points, logistics analysis in route determination, time, and cost, which helps point out the bottlenecks and inefficiencies, and supplier analysis in monitoring delivery times and defect rates.
- *Feature Engineering.* Feature engineering of supply chain management enables the development of new information that explains much more about the problem than what is in the data. For instance, a computation of the average lead time can be done as a feature to enhance the planning of the levels of inventories, a tracking of frequency of stockouts that will aid in the optimizing of the inventory, tracking of the trends in demand, including their seasonality or regional behavior, supplier reliability score assigned based on delivery performance and defect rates.
- *Supply Chain Management Optimization.* In the management of supply chains, data and engineered features play central roles in key functions, such as demand forecasting, inventory optimization, transport optimization, and supplier performance evaluation. This is a process of predicting future demands using historical data and seasonal trends as influencing factors to avoid overstocking as well as stockouts. Inventory optimization seeks to achieve the right amount at every point, not holding extra, which will surely lead to potential loss through stockout. Optimization in transportation includes seeking the best routes, consolidating shipments into fewer but larger lots, and saving cost while ensuring on-time delivery. Lead times are widely applied measures for supplier performance; the better suppliers receive higher rewards. Most of these optimizations are heavily dependent on statistical models, machine learning, or advanced analytics to support the decision-making process [22].
- *Model Evaluation.* Its efficiency is measured through key metrics that evaluate optimization in supply chain management. Some of the key

measures are the accuracy of demand forecasting, measuring how well actual demand matches forecasted demand; inventory turnover, indicating the stock's productivity; and on-time delivery rate, measuring the percentages of orders as delivered on or before schedule, of course, reflecting customer satisfaction. Additional critical metrics include cost savings which improves both logistics and inventory management on the optimal levels. Supplier reliability is monitored by tracking how consistent and good the suppliers are. These metrics together help in the assessment of how effectively the improvement has been done and areas that still require enhancement.

6.3.1.3 Reinforcement Learning

Reinforcement learning is one form of machine learning where it is possible to make dynamic and adaptive decisions for demand forecasting in the context of supply chain management. This is one branch of machine learning where the agent is trained to act upon the environment. This occurs by trial and error based on maximum long-term reward accumulation. Unlike traditional forecasting models, which rely on historical data to predict future demand, RL provides a framework where demand forecasts are continuously optimized based on real-time feedback. This adaptive learning approach allows supply chains to handle dynamic environments where demand and other influencing factors constantly fluctuate, making it especially beneficial for applications like inventory management, replenishment planning, and resource allocation [23].

- *How Reinforcement Learning Functions in Demand Forecasting:* A single autonomous agent, in this case, a forecasting model, acting upon an environment of supply chain data, would make action decisions like changing the forecast models or inventory quantities with which it gets positive reward or penalty feedback, through which it could learn better policies leading to rewarding consequences in the long-run from taking appropriate actions. For instance, in the stock level control in demand forecasting, RL might involve a system that adjusts stock levels depending on projected sales and the cost of supplies. Each decision is affected by customer order patterns, supplier lead time, and storage costs among others that change with time. The RL agent finds an optimal balance that leads to minimizing overstocking and stockouts.
- *Markov Decision Process (MDP) Framework:* The problem definition with the incorporation of RL into the framework of MDP will define states, actions, rewards, and transitions as shown in Figure 6.3. States describes present conditions in the supply chain, like current levels of inventory, forecasted demands for the following period, and lead times of the suppliers. Actions represent options available to the agent, which include increasing and decreasing levels of inventories, adjustments in the production schedules, and order quantity. Rewards represent feedback based on the closeness of an action to goal alignment (minimization of holding costs, preventing stockouts, maximization of service levels).

Transitions represent probabilistic change in state following some of the actions. Within this MDP-based framework for learning, the demand forecast model adjusts the policies over time as a consequence of changing supply chain scenarios and is therefore well suited to volatile markets where effective forecasting would be critical.

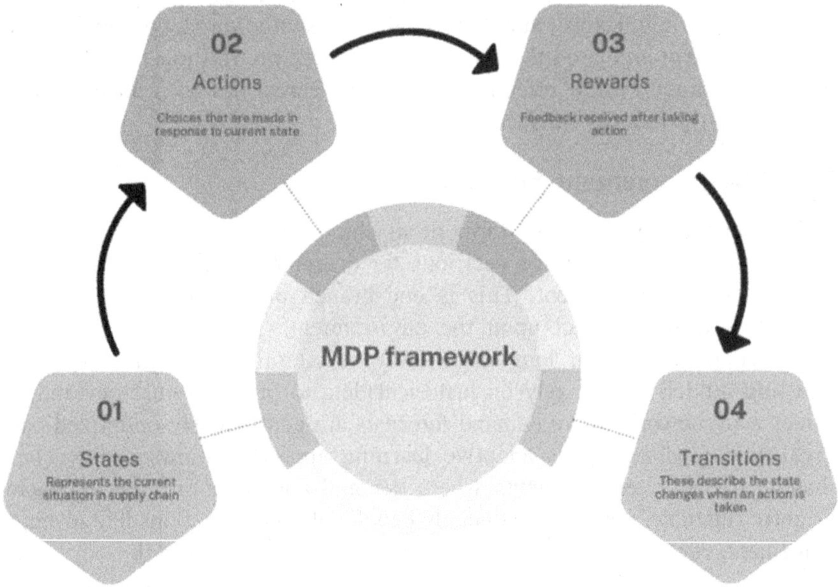

Figure 6.3 Markov Decision Process (MDP) framework.

6.3.1.4 Natural Language Processing (NLP)

NLP uniquely offers capabilities in the realm of demand forecasting for supply chain management by analyzing unstructured text data, such as social media, customer reviews, news, and market reports. NLP is a subfield of artificial intelligence that enables machines to understand, interpret, and generate human language, making it an invaluable tool for extracting insights from textual data that traditional structured data cannot capture. This analysis gives the supply chain manager another dimension to add to the process of forecasting, including anticipation of any change in demand because the customer is shifting preferences or because there is an up-and-coming trend emerging and improves the basis for the betterment of the forecasting related to real-time sentiment at the market. This paper will go further in how NLP helps in more efficient demand forecasting in supply chains and which approaches or applications contribute to this [24].

- **Demand Indicators Sentiment Analysis.** One of the core NLP techniques is sentiment analysis, which measures the tone and polarity of text data like customer reviews, social media posts, and news articles. With the quantification of customer sentiment, supply chain managers understand changes in consumer preferences and attitudes toward particular products or brands. Sentiment positivity about a product is normally associated with increasing demand, while negative sentiments indicate a waning interest in a product. This makes NLP-based sentiment analysis the ideal input for demand forecasts of supply chains to be prepared way ahead of a sudden shift in consumer behaviors.

Application Example: A retailer could use sentiment analysis over all social media channels where it monitors reviews on products it is selling. If its newly launched products for the period consistently feature a positive sentiment, it will alert the retailer of the likely high demand and thus stock adequately to prevent a stock-out situation.

- **Social Media and News Source Trend Analysis.** One would scan large amounts of text coming from social media, news sites, and forums which may reveal upcoming trends that will hit demand. By analyzing keywords, hashtags, and topics, an NLP model can be developed to recognize trends in consumer interest toward specific products or categories. Such analysis can alert the supply chain manager to early indicators of demand, thus allowing for proactive planning of inventories and production.

  Application Example: For example, a fashion brand that has a focus on NLP will monitor the social media streams to figure out currently prevailing colors, styles, or brands. This leads the brand to predict customer demands for these emerging trends through necessary adjustments to their available stocks and marketing channels, not becoming obsolete but remaining vibrant with the competitive edge that exists.
- **Using customer reviews to analyze signal demands.** Consumer preference and pain points revealed by customer reviews are sources of precious data to refine a demand forecast. NLP can parse thousands of reviews for recurring themes, whether customers are satisfied with specific features of the product or complaints about product limitations and praising specific attributes. Such information lets supply chain managers correctly estimate demand for products more highly valued by customers by ensuring their strategies are not misplaced compared to the actual demand of the market.

  Application Example: An electronics retailer uses NLP to analyze the best-selling products' customer reviews in order to identify the main drivers of demand, like battery life or ease of use. Equipped with such insights, the retailer is more focused on stocking attractive products, thereby enhancing the precision of demand forecasting.
- **Market Report and Economic Indicators via Text Summarization.** NLP text summarization techniques, whose workflow is shown in Figure 6.4, help supply chain managers process vast amounts of market reports and economic indicators, which would be too voluminous to consider for demand forecasting. By automatic summarization, NLP reduces long reports to key points, thus helping decision-makers stay updated about changes in the economy, policies, and other elements that might influence demand.

Application Example: A supply chain team at an automobile manufacturer may use NLP-based summarization to rapidly gather insights on raw material prices and consumer purchasing power from economic reports. These insights will drive demand for different models of cars, so inventory levels align with expectations of market conditions.

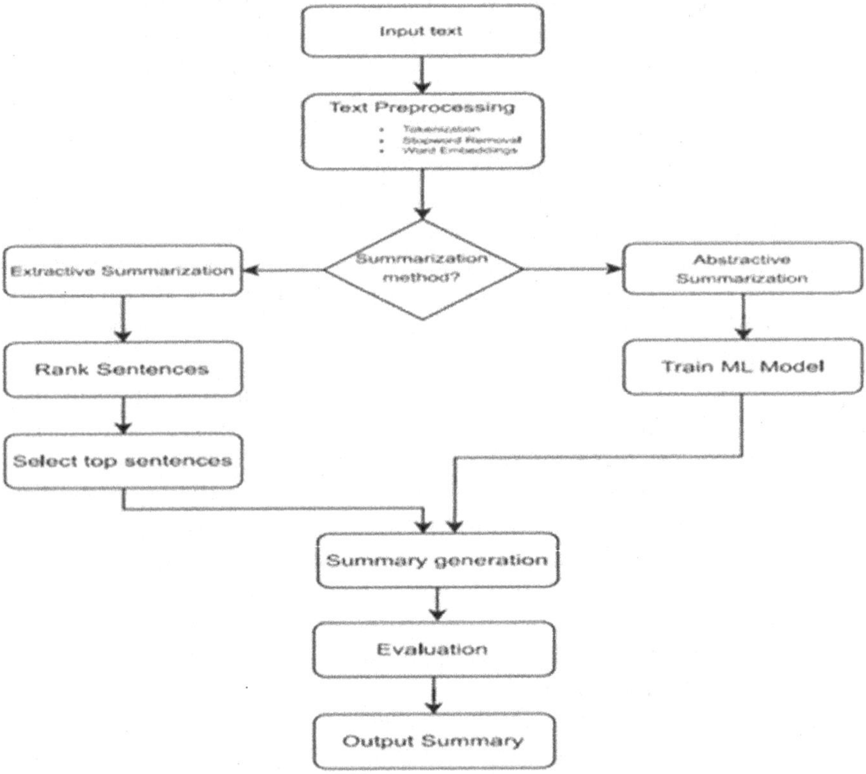

Figure 6.4 Workflow of NLP text summarization techniques.

6.3.2 Popular AI Algorithms in Demand Forecasting

6.3.2.1 Q-Learning

The main use is for demand forecasting in discrete action spaces. For each possible action in any state, a Q-learning algorithm associates a Q-value that tracks the expected cumulative reward earned after executing such an action. Gradually, in such cases, the learning agent realizes which specific action optimizes future returns; the developed framework also guides adaptive decisions in various aspects of policies related to the inventory and order.

6.3.2.2 Deep Q-Networks

Combining the Q-learning algorithm with the efficiency of deep neural networks, DQN will handle large and complex state spaces of a demand forecasting environment. Thus, in distributed supply chain planning, DQN can process multi-dimensional data like regional demand variations, supplier lead times, and seasonal changes in demand.

6.3.2.4 Policy Gradient Methods

The policy gradient algorithms directly optimize the agent's policy by changing the probability of selecting specific actions. This approach is beneficial in continuous action spaces, wherein demand forecasting and inventory adjustments can take a range of values rather than discrete steps. Policy gradient methods may be particularly useful in dynamic pricing and stock replenishment strategies.

6.3.2.4 Actor-Critic Methods

These techniques contain two parts: an actor (policy) that determines an action and a critic (value function) assessing the action. This structure enables more stable learning as the critic guides the actor toward better actions. In multi-product forecasting, actorcritic methods are beneficial since balancing demand forecasts of different products demands high-level decision-making.

6.4 ARTIFICIAL INTELLIGENCE IN INDUSTRY: CASE STUDIES AND APPLICATIONS

6.4.1 Case Studies

Artificial Intelligence (AI)-driven demand forecasting has changed retailing dramatically as far as accuracy and response to market dynamics are concerned. This section looks into four case studies that well identify notable examples of how retailers use AI-driven demand forecasting to manage their supply chains effectively, as summarized in Table 6.1.

Case Study 1: Walmart

Walmart has always been the first company to spearhead any innovation in the management of supply chains. Recently, it has adopted AI towards enhancing the precision of its demand forecasting. This was due to a huge driving force towards data analytics, machine learning, and real-time decision-making. In such scenarios, Walmart has always managed to dynamically respond to fluctuating consumer demands and ever-changing market conditions.

Implementing Machine Learning Algorithms

Walmart applies sophisticated algorithms of machine learning to analyze enormous data that carries information on past sales, customer purchase behaviors, seasonal patterns, and even extraneous factors such as weather conditions and local events. It is this kind of data-driven approach that will enable the company to uncover hidden patterns in aspects of consumer behavior that may not always be discernible with more conventional approaches to forecasting.

Table 6.1 AI techniques, algorithms, and applications in demand forecasting across leading retailers

Company	AI Techniques	Algorithms	Application Areas	Use Cases	Reference
Walmart	Predictive analytics, real-time data integration	Machine learning, time-series forecasting, neural networks	Inventory optimization, dynamic stock distribution, real-time demand prediction	Predicting demand for bottled water and nonperishable items during hurricane seasons; automated stock redirection based on weather events	[25]
Amazon	Deep learning, consumer behavior modeling	Neural networks, deep learning algorithms, reinforcement learning	Personalized demand forecasting, inventory management, seasonal trend prediction	Adjusting inventory based on browsing history, customer reviews and purchase trends; proactive stock replenishment during Black Friday and holiday seasons	[26]
Target	Machine learning, real-time analytics	Decision trees, regression models, anomaly detection	Pandemic-driven demand forecasting, inventory ledger management, customer behavior analysis	Adjusting stock for essentials (e.g., cleaning supplies, toilet paper) during COVID-19; implementing a real-time Inventory Ledger system	[27]
Kroger	Automated inventory control, collaborative demand planning	Machine learning, weather-based forecasting, demand sensing models	Supply chain waste reduction, personalized marketing, vendor collaboration	Forecasting summer demand shifts (e.g., grilling products during heatwaves); reducing food spoilage via AI-driven restocking	[28]

These algorithms will identify that the increased demand for bottled water, as well as nonperishable food products, will occur during the hurricane season. By using this Predictive analytics, Walmart, in advance, produces stocks of these necessities before the rush period.

This way it remains out of selling out since no products go out of stock.

Real-Time Integration in Data

Walmart's system of forecasting is further optimized by the integration of current data from digital and real sales channels. This has online shopping behaviors, point-of-sale transactions as well as social media sentiment analysis. This will allow Walmart to process and have real-time analyses, thus enabling timely and informed decisions regarding the adjustment of inventory and distribution. One such example is in the instance if there is some forecast that a certain weather condition would strike, Walmart redirects all its supplies to a certain region of stores, given the fact that the customer is to receive what he/she requires at exactly when it is required.

Stock Distribution Optimization

With the cutting-edge AI system used to manage the inventory of goods, Walmart is in the position to organize well stock distribution across a wide distribution network of thousands of outlets and fulfillment centers. The system uses complex algorithms to analyze the different levels of existing stock, the expected demand, and the logistics of deliveries. This is not only simplifying the supply chain, but also making it efficient by eliminating unnecessary levels of stocks and minimizing waste. For instance, with the ability to accurately make a forecast of demand, Walmart has significantly reduced carrying costs for inventory. Historically, such costs have been among the heaviest cost burdens which retailers incur at bottom lines.

Enhancing Customer Satisfaction

Walmart has taken initiatives on AI-driven demand forecasting and this has improved customer's satisfaction. Improved predictability in demand means high-velocity items are kept resh on the shelves to significantly minimize disappointment from inventory issues. Better visibility to these inventory levels can therefore promote better promotions and focus in marketing, thus significantly further driving sales. Consumers can enjoy a seamless purchase journey knowing that their expected merchandise is in stock.

Operational Efficiency and Profit Margins

Owing to the demand forecasting AI implementation, Walmart realizes substantial operational efficiency. Savings resulting from unsold products plus the inefficiencies of logistics make the supply chain very lean. Furthermore, as a consequence of these efficiency gains, profit margins get enhanced, enabling Walmart to preserve its competitive standing in the retail industry. The advanced system of managing inventory has reportedly made Walmart both save on expenses and raise the responsiveness level of the supply chain so that they can adapt accordingly to either fluctuations in the demand pattern or other environmental disturbances..

Case Study 2: Amazon

Amazon has become the benchmark for using AI in demand forecasting. The company uses high-level predictive analytics to track and predict consumer behavior in real-time. Being the pioneer in e-commerce, the company is constantly innovating new methods of forecasting, which has significantly enhanced operational efficiency and customer satisfaction with its wide range of products.

Predictive Analytics and Consumer Insights

It's underpinned by a powerful predictive analytics framework that utilizes intricate algorithms that sift through a mountain of data on consumer purchases, seasonal fluctuations, and actual customer insight captured at the point of interaction across all touchpoints like browsing history and product reviews. In this sense, this is a data-centric approach in which Amazon creates richer consumer profiles to improve the ability of the firm to better predict demand. For instance, if any particular item suddenly picks up interest based on marketing campaigns or because of seasonal events, the Amazon system identifies those patterns and adjusts the inventory on that basis.

Role of Deep Learning Algorithms

Demand forecasting system of Amazon has matured into a model so efficient that it adopts deep learning algorithms, where a vast dataset's complex patterns and relationships can be identified.

These algorithms can make multifaceted inputs work, such as previous data from sales, demographics from customers, and even such factors as economic conditions and activities of competitors. Amazon is able to give these detailed demand predictions that transcend the vast scope of all products, thus making optimal stock levels in response to the needs of consumers.

Proactive Inventory Management

This means that one of the notable key benefits of Amazon's AI-based forecasting system is the prediction of changes in demand before they occur. For instance, if a newly promoted product becomes trendy, it can predict when the surge in demand is going to be expected and, therefore, proactively adjusts the stock levels to prevent running out of stock. This proactive strategy of managing the inventory reduces the lost sales opportunities and boosts customer satisfaction because shoppers have a likelihood of finding their desired stock. During the super promotional seasons, especially Black Friday and Christmas, making quick changes in the inventory is a huge break or factor for performance in sales.

Learn from External Impacts

To enable the forecasting system to learn controlling demand factors completely outside of its control by internal data analysis, several external factors that influence it are also learned. Changes in patterns followed by consumers due to general economic shifts, social networking trends, or unexpected, unforeseen global events caused by natural disasters could be included.

For example, Amazon keeps on modifying its forecasting models to try and incorporate these variables continually, thereby enhancing its power to manage the inventory effectively by optimizing the operational costs. This flexibility makes the company strong against dynamic market and consumer demand.

Customer Satisfaction Improvement

The highest level of customer satisfaction is the end result of Amazon's superior abilities in demand forecasting. Since Amazon keeps its inventory ready for its customers, the company earns customer loyalty and enhances the chances of repeat sales. This smooth shopping facility is complemented by the good forecasts of Amazon as stockouts and backorders are a great hassle to the customers.

Case 3: Target

Target has dramatically enhanced demand forecasting with the help of artificial intelligence, given the uncertainty of the COVID-19 pandemic. The retail giant realized it needed an inventory management system that could adapt more rapidly and responsively to the sudden shifts in consumer behavior and demand patterns during this challenging period.

Leveraging Historical Data and Machine Learning

Target's AI-based demand forecasting at its core is the best utilization of historical sales data combined with advanced machine learning models. Target has developed its forecasting methods by studying past purchasing behaviors, seasonal trends, and emerging market patterns to predict spikes in consumer demand. The pandemic was unique in that there was an unprecedented surge in demand for household essentials, which required swift and strategic adjustments in inventory management. Target used machine learning algorithms to understand the rapid changes in consumer behavior and replenish inventory on time to avoid stockouts.

Improving Forecasting Accuracy

Target has focused on improving its forecasting capabilities, and it has achieved a very high level of improvement in forecast accuracy, which is said to be more than 30 percent. This improvement in forecast accuracy had a direct impact on the management of inventory by the company, as it ensured that the necessary products were always available to the customers. For example, had Target used its AI for prediction, when that large peak demand came out through huge increases in usage such as cleaning supplies and toilet paper, and, naturally personal care items plus most staple grocery products then used, it could actually increase inventory replenishment which prevented any out-of-stocks or at least decreased occurrences through their supply chain that saw peak uncertainty during such critical early months of this outbreak.

Inventory Ledger System Installation

One of the greatest changes Target underwent in inventory management is having its Inventory Ledger system introduced. It has allowed a previously undiscovered situation: out-of-stock, when issues could have been buried in older inventory management. Since the Inventory Ledger brings real-time stock visibility on its enormous networks of distribution centers and stores, the use of this allows Target to actually carry out effective replenishment procedures. It would not only optimize the productivity of the inventory but also serve as a way of reacting to shifting consumer demands at once.

Bettering Customer Satisfaction

Changes in demand forecasting followed by the alteration in managing the inventory led Target to achieve better customer satisfaction as the correct goods are sold at the proper time, hence making chances to find what a customer desires higher, leading to loyalty and chances for revisit. Such factors as the fact that during unpredictable times such as a pandemic, there will always be a balanced stock will always ensure a reliable image of Target for customers. Additionally, due to more products being on hand, customers are having less difficulty with shopping either inside the stores or online.

Case Study 4: Kroger

Kroger is one of the largest grocery chains in the United States and has adopted artificial intelligence (AI) to refine demand forecasting along several dimensions. As demand prediction is a critical function in a competitive retail environment, Kroger invested in advanced machine learning algorithms that enhance its inventory management and operational efficiency.

Advanced Algorithms in Machine Learning

The front liners of Kroger's demand forecast are complex machine learning algorithms used in analyzing large volumes of data. These algorithms take a historical sales database, seasonality, and other macro-environmental factors including weather conditions and market conditions to provide a highly precise forecast for all kinds of products. For example, if a heatwave was expected to influence consumer preference on some food items — such as summer grilling products — then the AI models will be able to predict that demand shift, and Kroger will get ahead of it by adjusting the inventory levels accordingly. This will ensure that at the point of sale, stores have the right products during the right times that are likely to increase customer satisfaction and reduce lost sales opportunities.

Inventory Management Automation

This brings numerous improvements regarding the inventory management in Kroger, by automating most of the operations such as restocking with a drastic reduction in cases of overstocking and stockout. Kroger was able to keep at an optimal stock level due to the accurate demand forecasts which prevented the losses associated with the spoiling of perishable goods otherwise. This mechanization also facilitates more effective operation processes and aids in a cleaner supply chain due to the minimization of waste. As such, Kroger is becoming more efficient with its inventory turnover. In the grocery business, this is quite crucial since anything old would not do much good.

Collaborative Demand Planning

Kroger does not stop with internal systems but closely engages with Consumer-Packaged Goods (CPG) manufacturers to enhance demand planning. This collaboration brings forth the more accurate forecasting as well as the right aligning of Kroger's strategies with its partners in Their respective supply chains. Through such data and insights shared among Kroger and CPG brands, it harmonizes the production and distribution to have enough products in reserve at all times and wait for the consumer's needs. Such an approach tends to build a robust ecosystem in the supply chain toward making Kroger more responsive and effective in reacting to a change in the market.

Minimization of Supply Chain Waste and Maximize Profitability

Kroger's AI-based demand forecasting project reduced supply chain wastes by a huge extent. The firm has the capacity to enhance the margins of profitability due to improved inventories and low incidences of spoilage. It is according to several sources that Kroger reduced various wastes resulting from the perishable products left in stores at the close of sales season. Such helped the firm in achieving relatively healthier profit margins because they promoted sustainability efforts. This would position Kroger at the top of grocery chains in terms of operation efficiency and customer satisfaction since it can balance supply and demand.

6.4.2 Industrial Uses of AI

AI is changing demand forecasting in manufacturing by optimizing the schedules of production and, therefore, improving resource allocation. This incorporates the use of machine learning algorithms to evaluate and analyze vast datasets comprising historical sales data, market trends, and consumer behavior patterns. This all-around analysis helps companies generate accurate forecasts regarding the future demand, thereby their productions coming according to actual need in the market. For example, automated systems based on AI can identify a seasonal pattern and a fluctuation in these patterns, which can be used by manufacturers to ramp up production before the peak demand periods, reducing lead times and minimizing idle resources.

AI-driven predictive analytics also enable the process of the supply chain to be more efficient with just-in-time inventory management. Manufacturers avoid too much excess cost and risks from stock outs due to accurate predictions in demand signals. For example, companies such as Siemens apply AI-driven demand forecasting to optimize production processes and ensure having the right amount of materials on hand, thus enhancing operational efficiency and waste elimination.

The integration of AI tools allows a manufacturer to push advanced analytics in real time, which will see to adapting manufacturing plans on the spot if market conditions change. Such environments are those facing changes in consumer preference or supply disruptions. Manufacturers can thus calibrate feedback through even more refined predictions that are always based on real-time data from IoT sensors and other sources, staying responsive to shifts in demand under continuous flexibility.

It all depends on machine learning algorithms for identifying defects and ensure quality control in the manufacturing process. By predicting possible failures, AI helps avoid production shutdowns due to equipment malfunction and align production capabilities better with demand forecasts. This proactive approach to resource management contributes to increased productivity and cost savings, turning the efficacy of manufacturing supply chains around.

6.5 METHODOLOGIES FOR AI-DRIVEN DEMAND FORECASTING

AI-Based Demand Forecasting

AI in demand forecasting has changed the dynamics of inventory management by providing companies with very accurate predictions of customer behavior. The methodologies include statistical modeling, machine learning, deep learning, ensemble methods, and hybrid approaches in analyzing data to produce forecasts.

Demand Forecasting with Machine Learning

This refers to the ability of a system to learn from data and thus optimize its performance without explicit programming. Machine learning may enable the accuracy of forecasting, especially if large amounts of diverse data are processed in regard to sales history, market trends, and customer behavior, and empower proactive decision-making [29].

Types of Machine Learning Techniques

- *Supervised Learning*: Implemented when the relationship between input and output is known. It employs labeled datasets. Major algorithms are linear regression, decision trees, random forests, and gradient boosting machines, which use historical data to make predictions regarding future demand.
- *Unsupervised Learning*: When labeled data is not available. It describes underlying structures by employing K-means and hierarchical clustering

techniques, thus allowing firms to categorize its customers or products to develop customized strategies [30].

- *Reinforcement Learning:* The agent learns to take actions in an environment to maximize rewards. Demand forecasting allows it to make adaptive forecasts with real-time feedback on optimizing inventory and waste.

Major Machine Learning Algorithms in Demand Forecasting

- *Linear Regression:* Relates input variables to demand with a linear model, providing the simplicity and interpretability of [31].
- *Decision Trees:* Manages both numeric and categorical variables, thus perfectly capturing nonlinear relations.
- *Random Forests:* Improves decision trees by averaging multiple models, thereby reducing overfitting and improving accuracy in complex datasets.
- *Gradient Boosting Machines:* Models are built sequentially by correcting errors from previous iterations, which makes them suitable for capturing complex demand patterns.
- *Neural Networks:* The more useful deep learning models for time series are RNNs that are better.

6.5.1 Model Training and Testing Procedures

In the context of demand forecasting approaches, supervised learning approaches for supply chain management depend significantly on robust procedures for training and testing models. Such procedures ensure proper construction of models which are to be learned and then tested. A good understanding of cross-validation, regularization, and performance metrics enables practitioners to improve the reliability and precision of predictive models.

- *Overview of Model Training and Testing:* Two of the fundamental processes of supervised machine learning are training and testing. These helps develop a model generalizing well to unseen data, which is an important aspect of dealing with the supply chain while practicing demand forecasting [32]. The process of training fits a model to a training dataset, whereas the process of testing evaluates the performance of the model on another dataset [33], detached and separate.
- *Dataset Splitting Methods:* Splitting the datasets is a key step taken in both the training and testing phases of model building. In most cases, an entire dataset is split into three parts - a training, testing, and validation set. Here, a training set is useful for model training, a validation set for validating the results, and a test for final evaluation. A typical split might comprise 70% of the data for training, 15% for validation, and 15% for testing [34].
- *Cross-Validation Methodologies:* Cross-validation is a technique employed to ascertain the robustness of a trained model. K-fold cross-validation is

popular, where the dataset is divided into subsets, and the model is trained times, each time using a different subset as the test set while the remaining subsets are utilized for training [35]. This method assures that every single data point has the opportunity to be part of both training and testing, yielding a more reliable performance metric.

- *Regularization Techniques:* Regularization methods are applied during model training to prevent overfitting, ensuring that the model does not learn noise from the training data. Techniques such as L1 (Lasso) and L2 (Ridge) regularization add a penalty term to the loss function, which constrains the magnitude of the coefficients [36]. This trade-off is critical in demand forecasting, where capturing the underlying trends without fitting noise is paramount.
- *Importance of Continuous Learning*: The landscape of demand forecasting in supply chain management is dynamic and influenced by changing market conditions. As such, models must be regularly updated and retrained on new data to maintain relevance and accuracy [37]. Continuous learning frameworks, where model performance is continuously monitored, allow businesses to adapt and forecast effectively in changing environments.

Hence the process of continuous learning empowers models to adjust to evolving market conditions which include modifications in consumer behavior patterns as well as supply chain interruptions along with numerous external influences such as economic status. The continuous process of retraining and updating the model allows businesses to maintain high forecasting accuracy which leads to cost savings while reducing waste and enhancing supply chain service levels.

6.6 IMPLEMENTATION OF AI-BASED DEMAND FORECASTING PLAN

6.6.1 Implementation of Recommendations

Strategic implementation of AI-based demand forecasting in supply chains is required in order to be efficient and sustainable. The best practices enumerated above constitute the full framework that the organization may adopt in order to enhance its capability to forecast using artificial intelligence [38].

6.1.1 Data Preprocessing Techniques

Data preprocessing is the backbone of good AI-based applications, especially in demand forecasting. These include all manipulations needed to be performed for cleaning, transformation, and structuring raw data into a format useful for analysis by machine learning algorithms.

- *Data Cleaning.* Data cleaning can therefore be defined as finding and correcting errors and inconsistencies within the data. In this regard, there is processing of missing values and duplicates and the inappropriate format with respect to data. For missing values, there are several methods utilizing statistical techniques like imputation. These include replacing a missing value with the mean or median of the variable in question, interpolation, or more complex predictive models. This was aimed at providing a relevant dataset for the scenarios under consideration, which would then culminate in better forecasting.
- *Data Transformation:* Data transformation techniques are used to transform data so that it can be helpful in improving the efficiency of a machine-learning algorithm. Normalization and standardization are the two main techniques adopted, which normalize the scale data attributes. Such normalization scale values in the range of 0 to 1 and standardization scale data to have zero mean with unit standard deviation. Other methods like one-hot encoding convert categorical variables into numerical formats. This enables the algorithms to process non-numerical data.
- *Feature Engineering:* Extricate, modify, or create new features from existing data that can provide more insight to the model using feature engineering. Some of the techniques applied include developing interaction terms between variables, extracting date components such as day, month, and season among others, or grouping similar categories to minimize noise. Good features tend to be the difference between mediocre and outstanding performance by a model since they directly influence how well a machine-learning model can learn from the data.
- *Outlier Detection.* An important function of data preprocessing is outlier detection. The presence of outliers in data can skew the output of statistical analysis and may also taint a prediction's accuracy. The statistics approaches can be z-scores or IQR, while the machine learning methods are based on clustering, which identifies data points that deviate significantly from the mean. Once the outliers are identified, organizations can choose to eliminate or modify or classify them as the case may be with a contextual understanding of the data.
- *Data Integration.* Data integration is the process of combining data from multiple sources into a complete dataset to be analyzed. For example, in supply chain management, extracting data could be from systems associated with sales, inventory, marketing, and suppliers. Proper data integration enhances the predictive power of the model by providing all relevant variables. That is why ETL the extraction, transformation, and loading processes-automate the process of data extraction, transformation, and loading that indeed delivers the data reliably as well as at scheduled times.

6.7 FUTURE OF SUPPLY CHAIN MANAGEMENT

6.7.1 Emergent Technologies

Emergent technologies are fundamentally repositioning supply chain management's approach to demand forecasting as these technologies enable the organization to better predict and enhance their in-house competencies and adjust pretty easily for changing market factors. However, AI as well as advanced analytics are just now entered into the earlier solutions of supply chains by autonomous vehicles, drones, and blockchain technology. But whereas earlier on it was just going to streamline logistics and increase visibility, hence highly optimizing better processes in making decisions, it even, accordingly, leads to an improvement of the customer's satisfaction levels and the achievement of a competitive advantage.

- *Autonomous Cars and Drones:* T Autonomous vehicles, such as self-driving cars and drones, will bring a revolution in logistics and transportation within supply chains, promising efficiency, speed, and reliability that never existed before. Delivery can be made with the minimum involvement of humans by an autonomous truck or drone through real-time data and algorithms that optimize delivery routes. To this end, firms like Waymo and Amazon plough money into autonomous vehicle technology where it is hoped that delivery times and costs will be reduced by cutting instances of human drivers in some scenarios.

  These inventions can help through faster reaction to changes in demand from customers, which are considerably affected by traffic congestion in most urban scenarios; thus, drones may bypass land traffic to deliver packages directly to the consumers' doorsteps, further enhancing the ease of logistics operations. In addition, IoT sensors with self-driving automobiles allow for the monitoring of supply chain assets in real-time, thus offering precious data for demand forecasting. More firms will then witness an improvement in operational efficiency, decreased delivery times, and increased customer satisfaction.
- *Blockchain for Transparency:* Perhaps blockchain technology is one innovation that helps in transparency and traceability in management processes for supply chains. Through this immutable ledger record from blockchain technology, all the transactions of the supply chain get accounted for to ensure that stakeholders are handed verified and accurate information. Transparency will be key in successful demand forecasting; hence, tracking an organization's product movement, verifying authenticity, and monitoring real-time inventory levels can be achieved.

For example, in the food and beverages sector, traceability from farm to table is enabled so that the stakeholders will enjoy safety compliance in conformity with the standards and regulations enacted. Companies like Walmart and De Beers are examples of businesses that applied blockchain solutions to track provenance for their products, thereby positively reinforcing consumer trust and satisfaction.

In addition, blockchain may simplify communication by various parties in the supply chain, which allows for shorter lead times and better responsiveness to demand trends. As organizations see more value in blockchain for a clearer and more reliable picture of their supply chains, its adoption will increase to more fully integrate demand forecasting with real-time data and insights.

6.7.2 The Future of Automated Decision-Making

The use of automatic decision-making will increasingly locate the supply chain at a central position where firms try to improve response and operational efficiency. The further development of machine learning and AI algorithms in processing enormous datasets in real time benefits companies by enabling timely, appropriate, and speedy decisions. For instance, the application of AI would come up with historical patterns in sales against market trends, weather patterns, and supply chain disruption with the aim of attempting to offer predictive insight that would guide related activities such as inventory management and production scheduling. The other benefits of computerized decision-making include minimizing human errors while at the same time increasing uniformity of operations. Traditional decision-making, therefore, is usually done through manual inputs and subjective judgments, with sometimes inefficiency and inaccuracies in determining things. AI systems make use of data-driven insights in optimizing processes such as demand forecasting and procurement planning and minimize costly errors in the supply chain while making them agile and responsive to the fluctuations of the market.

The sophistication of AI brings about the fact that what has, for all practical purposes, been so far the automation of straightforward tasks is going to be the automation also of much more complex strategic decisions. For example, AI can be employed to support a supply chain manager in selecting suppliers or assessing risks or even optimizing pricing strategy. Organizations implement AI-driven decision intelligence platforms that help them simulate different scenarios, derive actionable recommendations, and strengthen their strategic planning capabilities.

The sheer availability of cloud computing and IoT technologies also increases the ease with which companies can collect and share data in real time. We'll then find interconnectivity delivering collaborative, fact-based decision-making regarding supply chains. Overall, we can then expect a future where automated decision support pervades the information landscape of the supply chain, but what would be more interesting is the pervasive application for competitive advantage in the supply chain business.

6.7.3 Consumer Experience and Satisfaction Implications

The integrating impact of AI into supply chain management would essentially make a bridge between consumer experience and satisfaction. The better accurate availability of AI-enabled advanced demand forecasting, the greater will be the match between actual demands by consumers and product availability, enhancing shopping experiences. Predictive AI systems, based on purchasing trends and preferences, ensure the right product at the right time in stock, thereby reducing occurrences of out-of-stock items and thus enhancing customer satisfaction.

In the future, AI will personalize not only the interactions but also the recommendations that are put across to a customer. Analyzing the customer's behavior and preferences by the algorithms of AI, there can be provision of the most personalized marketing strategies or product suggestions and promotions for individual customers specifically. A targeted approach does not only enhance the possibilities of converting the sale but also anchors much greater custómer loyalty based on the overall shopping experience.

Another area where AI-powered chatbots and virtual assistants provide support to the customer service function of a business is in faster resolution of inquiries and complaints due to better communication and support operations that bridge the customer with the real information they require regarding their order, product availability, and other such transactions. This enhances a better experience for the customer and strengthens relationships for companies.

As AI increases in the supply chain, it also presents a challenge to be reckoned with in terms of the ethics of automated decision-making. AI processes should be transparent so that consumers understand how their data is being used and what parameters are influencing personalized recommendations. This will be the panacea that will ease consumers' concerns to create trust between consumers and businesses. Over time, it will have the effect of higher satisfaction and loyalty in an increasingly automated landscape.

6.8 CONCLUSION

AI forecasting for demand has revolutionized supply chains into most efficient, responsive, and customer-co-centric processes. The anterior enabling machine learning and predictive analytics using AI methodology has finally improved forecasting accuracy and allowed these organizations to better move through fluctuations in demand, optimize inventories, and ultimately, cost savings.

All the speeds allow making combined real-time decision making on data processing; hence markets can change speedily. Thirdly, with the use of its automation, robotics and driverless transport, artificial intelligence can minimize human error undertaking steps. It also has the potential to predict risks for supply chains, therefore allowing to preplan for them.

They also need to set up advanced AI technologies, integrate diverse sources of data, and collaborate among supply-chain partners to enhance the accuracy level of forecasts for effective inventory management. Besides, employee training and a sustainable orientation must feature so that AI adoption is carried out in the context of ethical and responsible business.

Future research will be directed toward new algorithmic developments in AI with a focus on big data and other resource-efficient systems, such as quantum computing and advanced neural networks, for propelling improvements in forecast accuracies. The future research will also look into the AI contribution for collaborative SCM, trade-offs in sustainability, and ethical considerations such as privacy of data and bias. Longitudinal studies will also have to be undertaken to measure the long-term effects of AI on the performance of the supply chain.

REFERENCES

[1] Mukhsin, M. and T. Suryanto. 2022. The effect of sustainable supply chain management on company performance mediated by competitive advantage. Sustainability. 14(2): 818. doi: 10.3390/su14020818.

[2] Babai, M.Z., J.E. Boylan and B. Rostami-Tabar. 2022. Demand forecasting in supply chains: a review of aggregation and hierarchical approaches. International Journal of Production Research. 60(1): 324–348. doi: 10.1080/00207543.2021.2005268.

[3] Feizabadi, J. 2022. Machine learning demand forecasting and supply chain performance. International Journal of Logistics Research and Applications. 25(2): 119–142. doi: 10.1080/13675567.2020.1803246.

[4] Goltsos, T.E., A.A. Syntetos, C.H. Glock and G. Ioannou. 2022. Inventory–forecasting: Mind the gap. European Journal of Operational Research. 299(2): 397–419. doi: 10.1016/j.ejor.2021.07.040.

[5] Prakash, S.M.B., P.P. Kumar, S. Devi, K.P. Reddy and M. Satish. 2023. Predicting Consumer Behaviour with Artificial Intelligence. *In*: 2023 IEEE 5th International Conference on Cybernetics, Cognition and Machine Learning Applications (ICCCMLA), IEEE. 698–703. doi: 10.1109/ICCCMLA58983.2023.10346660.

[6] Pournader, M., H. Ghaderi, A. Hassanzadegan and B. Fahimnia. 2021. Artificial intelligence applications in supply chain management. International Journal of Production Economic. 241: 108250. doi: 10.1016/j.ijpe.2021.108250.

[7] Hao, X. and E. Demir. 2024. Artificial intelligence in supply chain decision-making: an environmental, social and governance triggering and technological inhibiting protocol. Journal of Model Management. 19(2): 605–629. doi: 10.1108/JM2-01-2023-0009.

[8] Harsasi, M. and N.A. Minrohayati. 2017. The impact of supply chain management practices on competitive advantage. International Journal of Economic Policy in Emerging Economies. 10(3): 240. doi: 10.1504/IJEPEE.2017.086623.

[9] Sajja, G.S. 2021. Impact of Supply Chain Management Strategies on Business Performance. International Journal of Computer Applications. 183(38): 45–49. doi: 10.5120/ijca2021921790.

[10] Lee, R. 2021. The Effect of Supply Chain Management Strategy on Operational and Financial Performance. Sustainability. 13(9): 5138. doi: 10.3390/su13095138.

[11] Ali, I., A. Arslan, Z. Khan and S.Y. Tarba. 2024. The Role of Industry 4.0 Technologies in Mitigating Supply Chain Disruption: Empirical Evidence From the Australian Food Processing Industry. IEEE Transactions on Engineering Management. 71: 10600–10610. doi: 10.1109/TEM.2021.3088518.

[12] Boudouaia, M.A., S. Ouchani, S.M. Qaisar and A.T. Almaktoom. 2024. Supply Chain 5.0: Vision, Challenges and Perspectives. *In*: 2024 21st Learning and Technology Conference (L&T), IEEE. 203–208. doi: 10.1109/LT60077.2024.10469476.

[13] van Hoek, R. 2019. Unblocking the chain—Findings from an executive workshop on blockchain in the supply chain. Supply Chain Management: An International Journal. 25(2): 255–261. doi: 10.1108/SCM-11-2018-0383.

[14] Oztekin, A., R. Kizilaslan, S. Freund and A. Iseri. 2016. A data analytic approach to forecasting daily stock returns in an emerging market. European Journal of Operational Research. 253(3): 697–710. doi: 10.1016/j.ejor.2016.02.056.

[15] Khan, M.A., Shazia Saqib, Tahir Alyas, Anees Ur Rehman, Yousaf Saeed, Asim Zeb, et al. 2020. Effective demand forecasting model using business intelligence empowered with machine learning. IEEE Access. 8: 116013–116023. doi: 10.1109/ACCESS.2020.3003790.

[16] Barbosa, M.W., A. de la C. Vicente, M.B. Ladeira and M.P.V. de Oliveira. 2018. Managing supply chain resources with big data analytics: A systematic review. International Journal of Logistics Research and Applications. 21(3): 177–200.

[17] Parilla, E.S. and M.E. Abadilla. 2022. Impacts of Covid-19 on supply chain and business operations on enterprises in the province of Ilocos Norte. Logistics and Operation Management Research. 1(1): 34–46. doi: 10.31098/lomr.v1i1.927.

[18] Alfina, K.N. and R.M.C. Ratnayake. 2023. Upstream healthcare supply chain risk management in the implementation of circular economy at the primary care level. *In*: 2023 IEEE International Conference on Industrial Engineering and Engineering Management (IEEM), IEEE. 0813–0817. doi: 10.1109/IEEM58616.2023.10406400.

[19] Nagy, G. and S. Szentesi. 2024. Navigating uncharted waters: Black swan events and global supply chain resilience. Advanced Logistic Systems—Theory and Practice. 18(1): 41–54. doi: 10.32971/als.2024.005.

[20] Baghersad, M. and C.W. Zobel. 2021. Assessing the extended impacts of supply chain disruptions on firms: An empirical study. International Journal of Production Economics. 231: 107862. doi: 10.1016/j.ijpe.2020.107862.

[21] Wu, L., X. Yue, A. Jin and D.C. Yen. 2016. Smart supply chain management: a review and implications for future research. The International Journal of Logistics Management. 27(2): 395–417. doi: 10.1108/IJLM-02-2014-0035.

[22] Bu, S. 2021. Logistics engineering optimization based on machine learning and artificial intelligence technology. Journal of Intelligent and Fuzzy Systems. 40(2): 2505–2516. doi: 10.3233/JIFS-189244.

[23] Singh, S.P., J. Rawat, M. Mittal, I. Kumar and C. Bhatt. 2022. Application of AI in SCM or Supply Chain 4.0. 51–66. doi: 10.1007/978-3-030-85383-9_4.

[24] Yadav, A., R.K. Garg and A. Sachdeva. 2024. Artificial intelligence applications for information management in sustainable supply chain management: A systematic review and future research agenda. International Journal of Information Management Data Insights. 4(2): 100292. doi: 10.1016/j.jjimei.2024.100292.

[25] Humayun Kabir, M., A. Sobur, M. Ruhul Amin and G. student. 2023. Walmart Data Analysis Using Machine Learning. 11(7): 2320–2882. doi: 10.1729/Journal.37947.

[26] Anshu, K., S.K. Singh and R. Kumari. 2021. A machine learning model for effective consumer behaviour prediction. *In*: 2021 5th International Conference on Information Systems and Computer Networks (ISCON), IEEE. 1–5. doi: 10.1109/ISCON52037.2021.9702495.

[27] Reddy, J.G. and S. Porika. 2020. Anomaly detection using machine learning: A rule based classification and ordered regression tree with real time datasets.International Journal of Innovative Technology and Exploring Engineering. 9(7): 108–112. doi: 10.35940/ijitee.F4578.059720.

[28] Zhang, X., D. Meiser, Y. Liu, B. Bonner and L. Lin. 2014. Kroger uses simulation-optimization to improve pharmacy inventory management. Interfaces (Providence). 44(1): 70–84. doi: 10.1287/inte.2013.0724.

[29] Mediavilla, M.A., F. Dietrich and D. Palm. 2022. Review and analysis of artificial intelligence methods for demand forecasting in supply chain management. Procedia CIRP. 107: 1126–1131. doi: 10.1016/j.procir.2022.05.119.

[30] Aamer, A., L.P. Eka Yani and I.M. Alan Priyatna. 2020. Data analytics in the supply chain management: review of machine learning applications in demand forecasting. Operations and Supply Chain Management: An International Journal. 1–13. doi: 10.31387/oscm0440281.

[31] Carbonneau, R., R. Vahidov and K. Laframboise. 2007. Machine learning-based demand forecasting in supply chains. International Journal of Intelligent Information Technologies. 3(4): 40–57. doi: 10.4018/jiit.2007100103.

[32] Suthaharan, S. 2016. Supervised Learning Algorithms. 183–206. doi: 10.1007/978-1-4899-7641-3_8.

[33] Jiang, T., J.L. Gradus and A.J. Rosellini. 2020. Supervised machine learning: A brief primer. Behavior Therapy. 51(5): 675–687. doi: 10.1016/j.beth.2020.05.002.

[34] Uçar, M.K., M. Nour, H. Sindi and K. Polat. 2020. The Effect of training and testing process on machine learning in biomedical datasets. Mathematical Problems in Engineering. 1–17. doi: 10.1155/2020/2836236.

[35] Miyato, T., S.-I. Maeda, M. Koyama and S. Ishii. 2019. Virtual adversarial training: A regularization method for supervised and semi-supervised learning. IEEE Transactions on Pattern Analysis and Machine Intelligence. 41(8): 1979–1993. doi: 10.1109/TPAMI.2018.2858821.

[36] Caruana, R. and A. Niculescu-Mizil. 2006. An empirical comparison of supervised learning algorithms. *In*: Proceedings of the 23rd International Conference on Machine Learning—ICML '06, New York, New York, USA: ACM Press. 161–168. doi: 10.1145/1143844.1143865.

[37] Pargent, F., R. Schoedel and C. Stachl. 2023. Best practices in supervised machine learning: A tutorial for psychologists. Advances in Methods and Practices in Psychological Science. 6(3). doi: 10.1177/25152459231162559.

[38] Brandtner, P., S. Schober, R. Zimmermann and F. Staberhofer. 2023. Status-quo of IoT in supply chain management—Applications, potentials and challenges in Austria. *In*: Proceedings of the 2023 6th International Conference on Computers in Management and Business, New York, NY, USA: ACM. 133–138. doi: 10.1145/3584816.3584837.

Chapter 7

Artificial Intelligence Based Alternate Energy Demand Forecasting Incorporating Weather Data Analysis

Pratapa Raju Moola*, Gopi Krishna Pasam, Praveen N and Sami Al Ghnimi
University of Technology and Applied Sciences-Ibra, Oman

7.1 INTRODUCTION

RESs such as sunlight and wind, are naturally replenished at a rate that exceeds their consumption. In contrast, non-green energy sources like fossil fuels take millions of years to form. The burning of these conventional fuels releases toxic greenhouse gases, particularly carbon dioxide.

In comparison, RES produces far fewer emissions. Fighting the climate catastrophe requires a shift away from fossil fuels, which are a significant source of emissions, and toward renewable energy. Sustainable energy sources, which are enormous and constantly refilled by natural processes, put forward a vital solution to this urgent global challenge.

Climatic dependence makes the majority of RESs seem most unpredictable and changeable. For instance, it has been found that solar cells generate less power on overcast and wet days, while windmills are reliant on air intensity and wind speed, both of which are influenced by temperature variations. Weather-related changes can

*For Correspondence: pratapa.moola@utas.edu.om

DOI: 10.1201/9781003541875-7

also affect other types of RES, including hydro, biomass, geothermal, and ocean. The sections that follow provide a thorough explanation of the various RESs.

Predictive methods should be used to predict the availability of RESs because they are unpredictable. Forecasting the RESs for improved grid management is made possible by the most recent developments in AI and data analytics. Big Data, which is used to train and test AI algorithms, is the source of AI-based forecasting. However, before it can be utilized for this purpose, it must first be obtained. This chapter examines the various forecasting algorithm types with various case studies, delving thoroughly into the overall forecasting technique using various AI algorithms and intelligent data analytics.

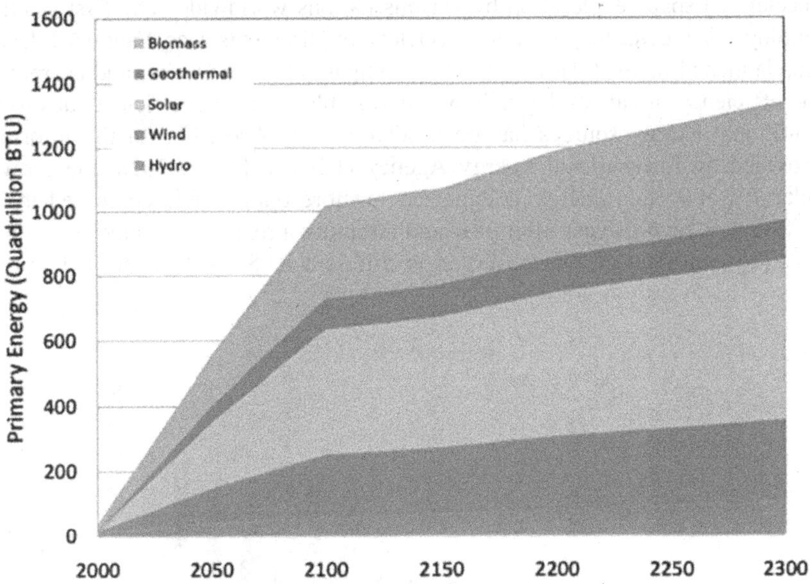

Figure 7.1 Renewable energy contribution [1].

Currently, 8% of the world's energy comes from renewable sources, primarily from hydroelectric energy collection and biomass production. An estimated 1,400 quads will need to be supplied by renewable sources by the year 2300, a significant increase of 3,780%, according to projected estimations. According to the data in [1], the contribution of RES to the world's energy demands is substantial, as seen in Figure 7.1.

7.2 EVOLUTION OF DIFFERENT RENEWABLE ENERGY SOURCES

Among the main renewable energy sources, solar, wind, biomass, and geothermal energy are particularly noteworthy. The historical development and contemporary situations of these sources are explored in detail in the section that follows.

7.2.1 Solar Energy

In the 1950s and 1960s, there was significant experimentation and development in the field of photovoltaic cells, which are devices that convert sunlight into electricity. One of the most notable events during this time was the development of the first practical photovoltaic (PV) cell at Bell Labs in 1954. Chemist Calvin Fuller, physicist Gerald Pearson, and Daryl Chapin have created a silicon solar cell that proved the feasibility of converting sunlight into electricity. Following Bell Labs' achievement, the first commercial solar cells appeared in the late 1950s and were primarily used to power satellites, navigational buoys, and remote telecommunications equipment. Technological developments in solar cells have accelerated space exploration by various nations worldwide. The first satellite to employ solar cells to power its electrical requirements was Vanguard 1, which was launched in 1958. However, when compared to more recent and current cells, the efficiency of early solar cells was noticeably lower. An efficient substitute for traditional energy sources has been solar panels. According to the information provided by International Energy Agency (IEA) in [2], by 2028, the growth of solar PV and wind energy is expected to more than double compared to 2022, setting new records year after year and attaining a remarkable total of around 710 GW [2], continual growth observed in different RESs is depicted in Figure 7.2.

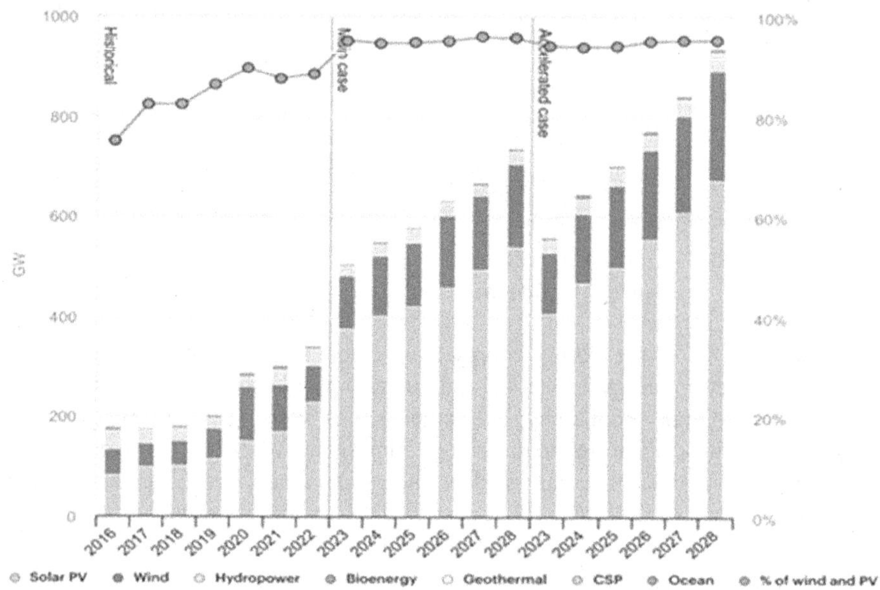

Figure 7.2 RES forecast for 2016–2028 as per [2].

Direct heating and electricity generation are both possible with solar energy. Improvements in solar conversion efficiency, possible increases in government incentives, and the growing affordability of installed solar systems are all helping solar power become a major contributor to the world's energy mix.

Given its universal accessibility, solar energy can lessen the dependence on costly distribution infrastructure, particularly in developing regions. Given its considerable growth prospects, it is expected that solar energy will expand at a rate that allows it to mitigate 40% of the annual deficit between global demand and nonrenewable supply. Ramos et al. has done modeling and simulation to perform analysis under various environmental conditions [3].

7.2.2 Wind Energy

Denmark is where wind energy harvesting was initially developed. Danes used a 23-meter-diameter wind turbine to generate power as early as 1890. Several hundred units with outputs ranging from 5 to 25 kW were in service in Denmark in 1910. Commercial wind-electric plants featuring two- and three-bladed propellers were introduced to the American market around 1925.

During this time, Wincharger and Jacobs were well-known brands with capacities ranging from 200 to 1200 W and 1.5 to 3 kW, respectively. On farms, these systems were used to power radios, lights, storage batteries, and small appliances with voltage ratings of 12, 32, or 110 volts. Various 32 V DC appliances were produced by the industry in response to the need. A major turning point in the broad use of wind power was the creation of the "Rural Electric Administration" (REA) by the Congress in 1936.

According to Figure 7.2, Solar PV is the most prominent energy source in the renewable energy capacity additions, consistently dominating the total share from 2016 to 2028. Its contribution has grown significantly over time, making it the primary driver of renewable energy expansion. Solar PV is growing at a fast and steady rate, surpassing other renewable energy sources including wind, hydropower, and biomass, with a compound annual growth rate (CAGR) of 11.6%. This trend highlights the increasing reliance on solar technology as a key solution for meeting global energy demands and accelerating the transition toward a sustainable energy future [2]. In [4], the modeling and simulation of wind turbine generators where the speed of rotation is the variable to be controlled and discusses the importance of controlling the rotational speed in wind turbine generators to optimize energy conversion and maintain stability under varying wind conditions.

7.2.3 Geothermal Energy

Geothermal energy is the term for heat energy found beneath the surface of the earth. The origin of this heat is intricately connected to the interior assembly of the planet and various physical processes taking place beneath its surface. Prince Piero Ginori Conti, in 1904, achieved a significant milestone by inventing the world's first plant of geothermal energy in Tuscany, Italy. Subsequently, John D. Grant drilled a well at Geysers to generate electricity. Despite the initial setback, Grant succeeded the following year at a different location across the valley. This achievement marks the establishment of the United States' initial geothermal power plant. With the installation of many wells, the system efficiently generates 250 kW, which is sufficient to adequately light the resort's streets and houses. He used the steam from the first well to build a second well. Regretfully, the plant struggles to compete with other electricity sources, which ultimately results in its closure [5].

Energy from geothermal technologies currently accounts for about two quads of the world's energy consumption. Geothermal energy's contribution to the world's energy supply is anticipated to increase due to anticipated increases in geothermal source growth, including the exploitation of hot dry rock reservoirs, improvements in alteration techniques, and the cost-effective extraction of lower-quality reservoirs [1].

7.2.4 Biomass Energy

Indeed, the history of biomass precedes our own, and there is strong evidence to support the claim that people have been using biomass as a source of energy for a very long time—between 230,000 and 1.5 million years ago. In fact, bioenergy comes from using biomass, which is effectively the best chemical storage battery available. The fact that bioenergy is a renewable resource must be emphasized.

Plant components that have gone through the photosynthesis process are the main source of biomass. Currently, burning renewable biomass produces around 53% of the world's non-conventional energy. But in the long run, a sustainable balance between crops cultivated for food and those grown for fuel needs to be struck. It is assumed that 30% of the difference between traditional supply and demand for energy will be filled by biomass energy [1].

7.3 RENEWABLE ENERGY SOURCES MODELLING

Prior to gathering data from RESs, it is crucial to examine their mathematical modeling. Though the data taken into consideration from mathematical modeling does not yield reliable outcomes on forecasts, this data is eventually employed for analysis and prediction reasons. The mathematical modeling of windmills and solar power is explained in the section that follows.

7.3.1 Solar Cell (Photovoltaic Cell) Modelling

The solar cell plays a pivotal role in a photovoltaic module, serving to convert sunlight or photons into electrical power. The PN junction, which has electrical properties like those of a diode, is a frequently used solar cell. The optimum model for a solar cell can be conceptualized as the anti-parallel connection of a diode and a current source, as shown in Figure 7.3. As explained in the sections that follow, improving the photovoltaic (PV) cell model requires considering the effects of shunt and series resistance. Solving equations (1) and (2) is the process of modeling solar cells [3].

$$I = IL - ID \tag{1}$$

$$I = I_L - I_o \cdot \left(e^{\frac{(V+IR_s)}{akT_{ck}}} - 1 \right) \tag{2}$$

where I_D is the dark current in Amps, I_o is saturation current of a diode in A, V_C is the cell's voltage (V), q is the charge of an electron, a is the ideality constant of a diode, k: Boltzan's constant (1.38×10^{-23} J/K), T_{cK} is the cell's temperature.

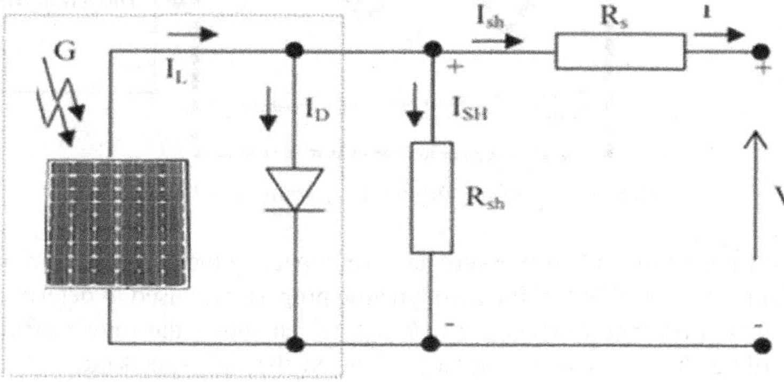

Figure 7.3 Analogous circuit for optimal solar cells [3].

7.3.2 Wind Turbine Modelling

The main goal is to replicate the characteristics of a wind turbine. This method entails creating an effective, mechanically simple model that accurately captures a wind turbine's electrical properties. Non-dimensional curves of the power coefficient (Cp) with respect to the tip speed ratio (λ) and blade pitch angle θ are used to show important points. The linear speed at the blade tip divided by the wind speed is known as the tip speed ratio. The kinetic energy of flowing air, or wind, is transformed into mechanical energy at the turbine shaft and then electrical energy by a wind turbine. The process of converting wind energy into mechanical and ultimately electrical power is shown in Figure 7.4. Even though the turbine and wind interact in a complex way, modeling the aerodynamic torque or power can provide a very simplistic approximation [4].

Torque and power (Aerodynamic) are given by equations (3) and (4).

$$T_{rot} = \frac{P_{aero}}{W_{rot}} = \frac{1}{2\lambda} \rho \pi R^3 C_p(\lambda, \theta_{pitch}) \tag{3}$$

where P_{aero} is the Aerodynamic power of the main shaft developed by the turbine, with 'R' radius, with 'u_{eq}' wind speed and ρ air density.

$$P_{aero} = \frac{1}{2} \rho \pi R^2 u_{eq}^3 C_p(\lambda, \theta_{pitch}) \tag{4}$$

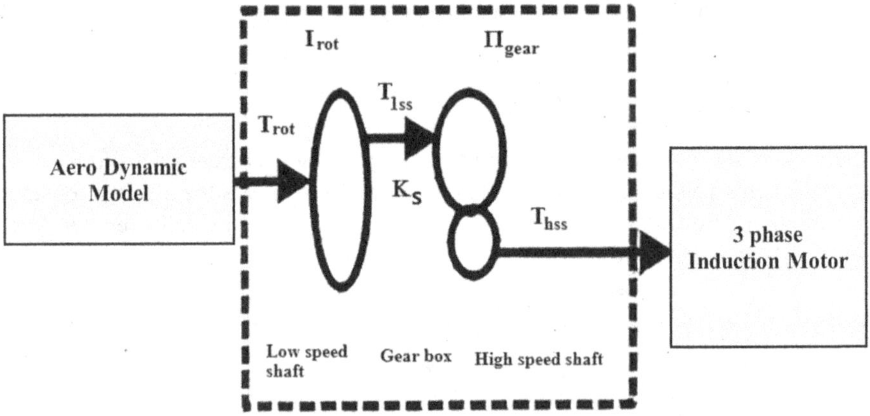

Figure 7.4 Wind turbine drive train model [4].

Both temperature and air pressure have an impact on the density of air, or ρ. A lookup table with specific turbine aerodynamic properties is used to determine the dimensionless power coefficient $C_p(\lambda, \theta_{pitch})$, which shows the rotor's efficiency.

Regarding the coefficient, it is dependent on the tip's speed ratio, $\lambda = W_{rot}$. W_{rot} indicates the rotor speed, together with R/u_{eq} and the blade angle θ_{pitch}. This coefficient decreases when wind speed (λ small) increases in the case of a turbine operating at a constant speed [4].

7.3.3 Geothermal Energy-based Generator Modelling

One of the three renowned outcomes in thermodynamics is the general principle of mass conservation, as articulated in equation (5).

$$\frac{d}{dt}\int_{S_i}\rho dv = \sum_{i}\left(\int_{S_i}\rho v_n ds\right) - \sum_{O}\left(\int_{S_o}\rho v_n ds\right) \tag{5}$$

The control volume's internal density is denoted by ρ, i and o indicate the input and output states, S_i, S_o indicate inlet and outlet surfaces respectively, the volume by v. In I/O states, v_n is the fluid velocity normal to the surface S.

The equation (6) defines the general energy conservation concept.

$$\frac{d}{dt}\int_{V} e\rho\, dv = \dot{Q} + \dot{W} + \sum_{i}\left(\int_{S_i} e\rho v_n\, ds\right) - \sum_{o}\left(\int_{S_o} e\rho v_n\, ds\right) \tag{6}$$

In this case, $\dot{Q}$ and W stand for the general power of the control volume and the general heat flow over time, respectively. The total energy generated can be given as:

$$e = h + \frac{v^2}{2} + gZ \tag{7}$$

where, h and e stand for precise enthalpy and energy interactions, respectively. The letters g and Z in equation (7) stand for normal Earth's gravity and height, respectively.

7.4 RENEWABLE ENERGY SOURCE MONITORING AND INTELLIGENT DATA ANALYSIS

In the past decade, monitoring of RES and Intelligent Data Analysis (IDA) has emerged as critical areas of focus. Effective data collection and monitoring are essential for the successful implementation of IDA in any application, making these processes closely interrelated. This section offers a thorough analysis of RES monitoring and IDA, providing a detailed overview for the reader's comprehension.

The field of IDA provides a platform for examining problems related to the study and use of AI methods in data analysis across a range of fields. For the IDA approach to be implemented effectively, certain processes and stages must be followed. The initial phase of data collection, acquisition, and storage is crucial to the entire IDA process.

As a matter of fact, the accuracy of IDA and future estimation derived from the same depends on the data collected. Hardware devices, and embedded software considered along with database management techniques/tools are pivotal in step 1. Step 2 is about defining and implementing IDA methods/algorithms to achieve the set objective. In this step, the algorithms that basically accommodate the intended IDA are trained, tested, and the data is cleaned and visualized. As the final phase of the technique, the next step focuses on implementing analytics, where the outcomes and consequences of the IDA are examined. The following Figure 7.5 shows the three phases of IDA implementation.

DAQ systems/devices are the key role players in stages 1 and 2, the data collected from the RES sensor network is acquired and processed in DAQ systems. Subsequently, the data acquired is sent to store in the server (in stage 2), which also enables data monitoring. SCADA system is key in data monitoring and control for all types of industrial requirements. The detailed discussion concerning SCADA systems and other advanced systems for monitoring the RES is presented in the section below, and case studies about the same are presented towards the end of this chapter.

7.4.1 Stage 1 and Stage 2: Real-time Systems for Data Monitoring and Acquisition

Significant improvements in real-time monitoring techniques have been noted because of recent developments in information and communication technologies (ICT). The recommended technology for RES monitoring and control, however, is SCADA systems. Different types of SCADA systems are available for monitoring renewable energy, each of which is made to address a particular aspect of monitoring and managing renewable energy sources. RESs prefer the following kinds of SCADA systems, IoT-based monitoring, and IDA systems.

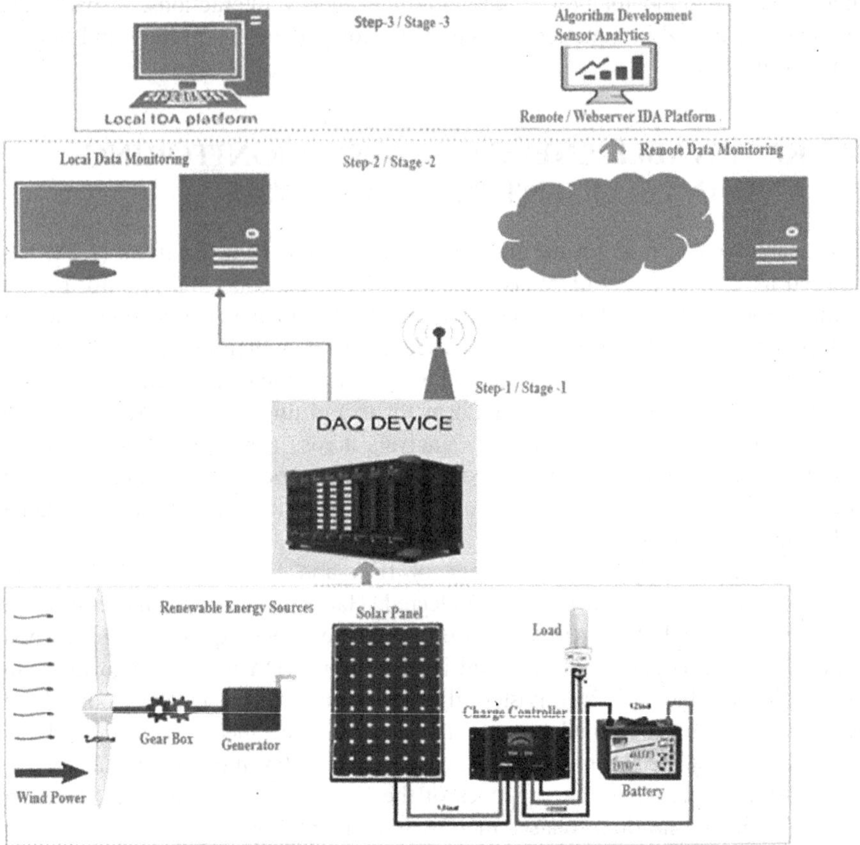

Figure 7.5 IDA implementation phases.

1. SCADA Systems for Solar
2. SCADA Systems for Wind
3. SCADA Systems for Geothermal
4. SCADA Systems for Hydropower.
5. Wireless Monitoring based on IoT

The efficient and dependable development of renewable energy sources depends on these SCADA systems, which offer real-time data, control capabilities, and analytics for efficient optimization and decision-making.

7.4.2 SCADA Systems for Solar Power Plant

In a solar photovoltaic (PV) plant, Solar SCADA makes use of the regular recurrence of data points. The goal of this affordable hardware solution is to establish globally applicable standards for all PV sites by creating a standardized commodity.

The monitoring of RES through SCADA heavily relies on sensors. These sensors play a pivotal role in solar power generation systems, providing essential data for assessing environmental conditions, system efficiency, and overall health.

Diverse sensor types are utilized to monitor and optimize the performance of solar power generation. Figure 7.6 shown below illustrates the detailed architecture of the solar SCADA system [6].

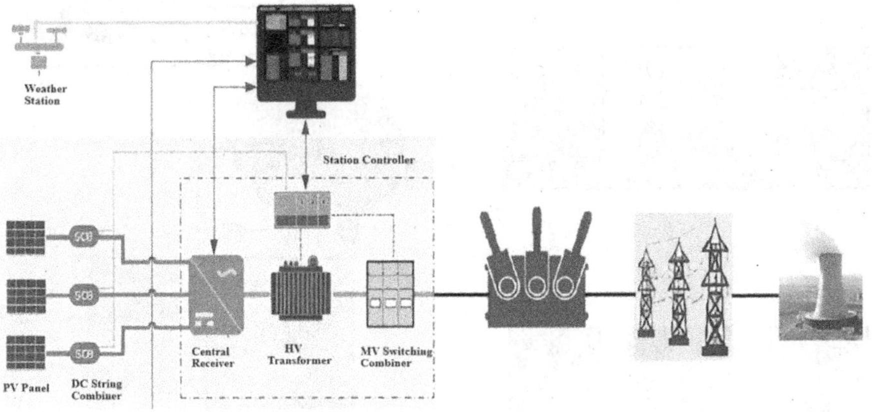

Figure 7.6 Solar SCADA systems.

For power distribution, the solar power system uses PV arrays and a battery system. To prevent instability and failure due to a lack of monitoring and control, a SCADA (Supervisory Control and Data Acquisition) system is implemented. This system oversees operations, collects data for analysis, and detects potential errors in the solar power system. The SCADA system monitors power, voltage, and current, as well as the status of the battery systems. Similar system is simulated in MATLAB Simulink to obtain necessary data for the SCADA system [6–8].

7.4.3 SCADA Systems for Wind Power Plant

Monitoring and coordinating different measurements within the Wind Turbine Generators (WTGs) is a critical function of SCADA (Supervisory Control and Data Acquisition) in the wind turbine generation system. SCADA is integrated with turbines and acts as the main interface between the wind farm's equipment and the operator of the wind power facility. Architecture of SCADA system used for wind power plants is shown in Figure 7.7. It simplifies the gathering of data about substations, weather masts, and WTGs into a single control point. SCADA makes it easier for the plant operator to send control signals to the wind turbine controller while also capturing and storing operational data and alarm signals from the WTGs.

Every wind turbine has a control box that contains input/output (I/O) components, a power adapter, control panels, and a PLC or Remote Terminal Unit (RTU). Wind speed, wind direction, and shaft rotation are among the sensor data collected and sent to the PLC. This data can be used by the SCADA control system to identify changes in wind direction and improve turbine alignment for maximum power generation. All RTUs or PLCs associated with the turbines are interconnected via a local area network (LAN) using Ethernet connections.

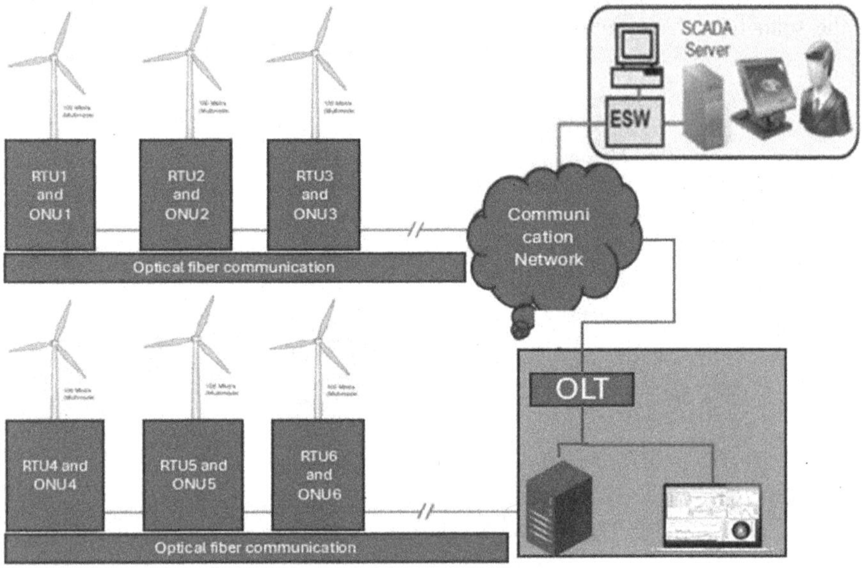

Figure 7.7 SCADA system for wind.

The communication structure in the SCADA system is depicted in Figure 7.8, with data consolidated and transmitted over a communication link, such as optical-fiber cables, to the master station (control center). In the Wind Power Plant's SCADA system, the SCADA server functions as the master, while RTUs act as slaves. Occasionally, one RTU may function as a master, gathering information from another slave RTU. The total efficiency and dependability of the wind turbine generation system are enhanced by this SCADA system, which guarantees efficient monitoring, control, and coordination of the system [9–11].

7.4.4 SCADA Systems for Geothermal

A Programmable Logic Controller (PLC) serves as the primary controller in the Geothermal Power Plant (GPP) SCADA system design, which is seen in Figure 7.8. It has a redundant CPU and power supply. Data collection and processing from a variety of sources, including field instruments (sensors-actuators), the Generator Control Panel (GCP), Motor Control Center (MCC) 1, and MCC 2, are made possible in large part by this PLC. Hardwired connections are used in the communication infrastructure, which uses 4–20 mA current for analog transmissions and 24 VDC for digital signals.

The SCADA system uses a single computer as the workstation for operator control, connecting to the PLC via the OMRON Ethernet (OMETH) protocol.

Through the Modbus Transmission Control Protocol/Internet Protocol (TCP/IP) protocol, this computer communicates with a number of devices, such as a digital excitation control system, load-sharing, relay protection, power monitoring, and speed controller. Modbus-TCP/IP converters are used to translate Modbus serial signals into the TCP/IP protocol to guarantee smooth communication [12]. By improving the Geothermal Power Plant's monitoring and control capabilities, this architecture raises the plant's operational dependability and efficiency.

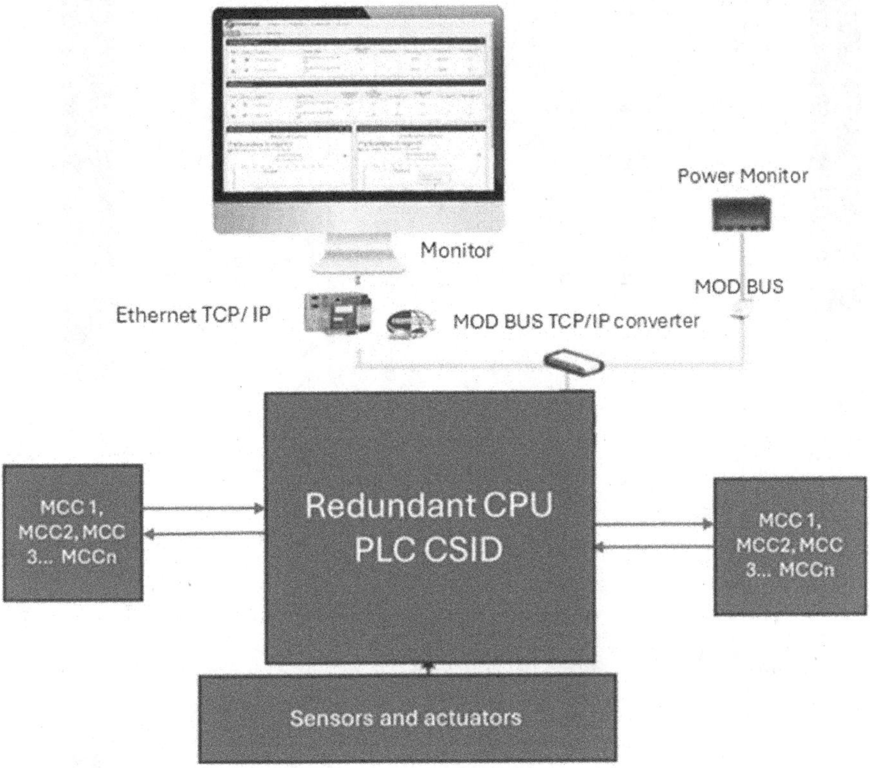

Figure 7.8 SCADA system for GPP.

7.4.5 SCADA Systems for Hydropower

Figure 7.9 shows the architecture of the SCADA system that was installed in a hydroelectric power plant unit. In addition to PLCs and a PLC network that facilitates the interfacing of input and output signals, this unit incorporates transducers, actuators, and Remote Terminal Units (RTUs) such as temperature supervision blocks, power measurement devices, and level measurement blocks. The process server, which functions as a PC with data logger capabilities and is connected to the PLC network, is essential for monitoring and managing the loop process.

Numerous measurements are processed at the local control level, including vibrations, levels, flow, temperature, electrical, and mechanical. They include

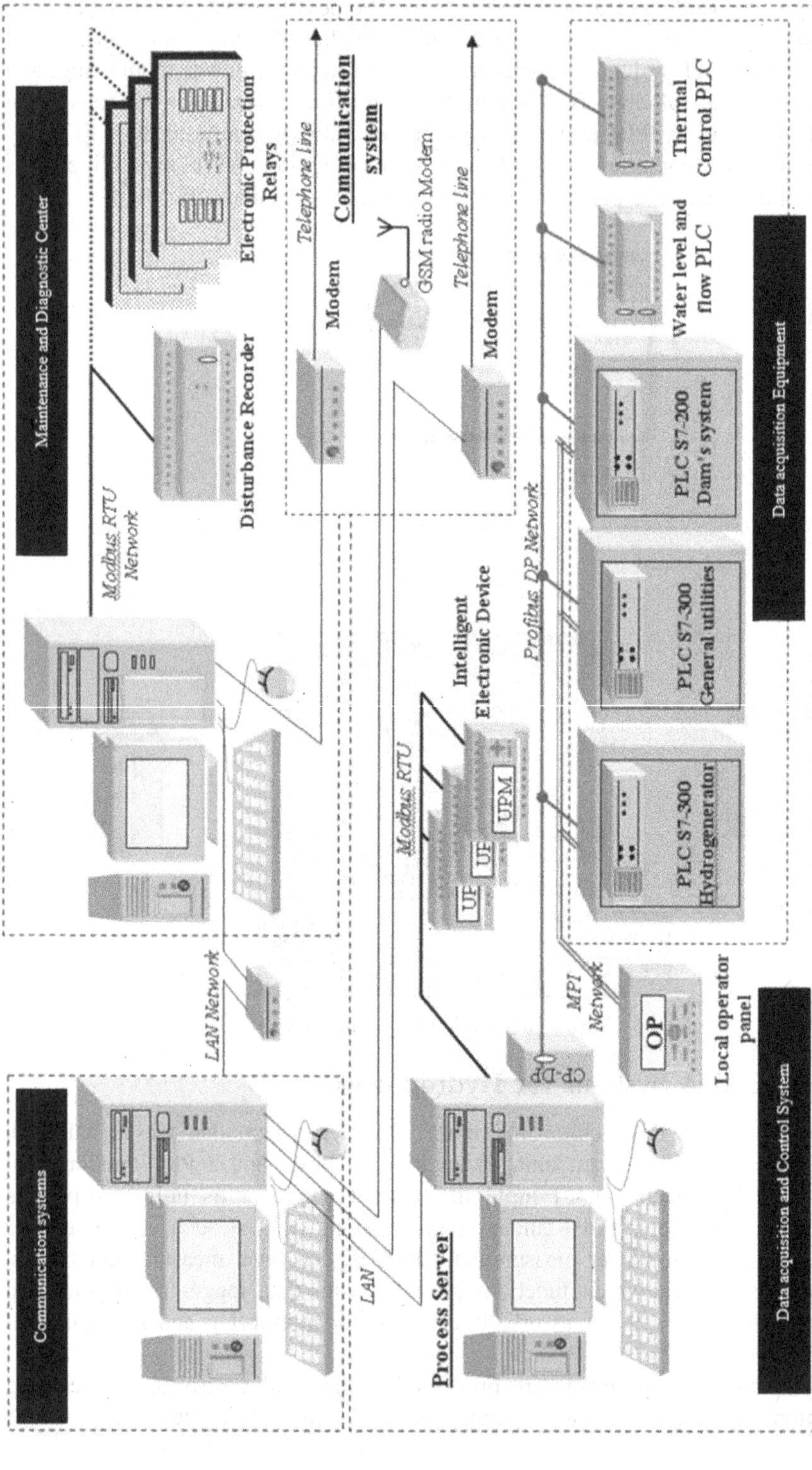

Figure 7.9 Hydro SCADA system.

both digital and analog signals obtained from the electrical machinery of the hydroelectric power plant. While analog signals cover electric parameters including voltage, currents, power factor, frequency, and energy parameters (active, reactive, and apparent power and energies), digital input signals communicate the function status of switching equipment and the status of the protection loop in real-time. The control and data acquisition systems are made up of these parts.

The process server station acts as the Human Machine Interface (HMI) and handles tasks such as data logging, event recording, and plotting of process parameters. Multiple responsibilities are delegated among hydraulic engines, electric generators, particular power and voltage controller units, connecting devices, control loops, and utilities to control the power plant [13]. The hydroelectric power plant unit's monitoring and control capabilities are improved by this extensive SCADA system architecture, guaranteeing dependable and effective operation.

7.5 MAJOR COMPONENTS IN SOLAR SCADA SYSTEM

Several key parts cooperate to monitor, regulate, and maximize solar power generation in a solar SCADA (Supervisory Control and Data Acquisition) system. These are the essential components: sensors, Dedicated Remote Telemetry Units (RTU)/ Programmable Logic Controllers (PLC), Dedicated SCADA Master, and Communication networks.

7.5.1 Sensors

This section lists the main sensors used to collect data from geothermal, wind, and solar sources.

7.5.1.1 Solar Sensors

A handful of the many sensors used to monitor solar energy are crucial and are the subject of debate.

(a) Solar Irradiance Sensors
(b) Sun Trackers
(c) Solar Radiometers
(d) Temperature Sensors
(e) Panel Orientation Sensors
(f) Dust and Dirt Sensors
(g) Cloud Cover Sensors

7.5.1.2 Wind Turbine Sensors

There are several sensors used in the industry for monitoring power generation from wind DG, these sensors pivotal in data acquisition. Wind power monitoring employs various sensors to measure wind speed, direction, and other parameters crucial for assessing wind turbine performance.

(a) Anemometers
(b) Sonic Anemometers
(c) Wind Profilers
(d) Windsock or Wind Vane Flags
(e) Temperature Sensors
(f) Geothermal energy system sensors

7.5.2 Remote Telemetry Units (RTU)

SACDA systems use RTUs to process the gathered sensory input. Signal conditioning units, or RTUs, are used to analyze or condition the collected data.

The following elements make up Remote Terminal Units (RTUs), as seen in Figure 7.10.

(i) **Mother RTU Unit Micro Computer:** In the next scan, this unit communicates the results of its operations to the master unit. It comes with add-ons such as typewriter, console, and Cathode Ray Tube (CRT).
(ii) **Programmable Logic Controller (PLC) Driver:** This specialized controller contains logic circuits and memory.
(iii) **Modems:** These features empower the Remote Terminal Units (RTUs) to receive messages from the master unit, acknowledge the reception of messages, and confirm the successful execution of the desired operation.
(iv) **Relays:** Situated within the RTUs, these components either open or close specific control circuits in response to commands from the master unit. The relays can indicate changes in the status of lines and breakers, indicating whether they are open or closed, and the RTU can communicate back to the master unit after an operation is finished.
(v) **PLCs:** They run the relays, which manage the switches and other components, using the modem signal as fuel.
(vi) **Transducers:** To convert values like current, voltage, watts, and vars, RTUs use transducers. Transducers are installed to enable data transfer between RTUs and the master unit, and vice versa, and analog-to-digital (A/D) converters are utilized for this purpose.
(vii) The newest are the Modern Remote Terminal Units (RTUs), which are equipped with microcomputers with memory and logic capabilities. Intelligent remotes, Sub-masters, or Smart RTUs (SRTUs) are RTUs equipped with these microcomputers and logic capabilities. Modern Remote Terminal Units (RTUs) are the newest and are equipped with microcomputers with memory and logic capabilities. These SRTUs can perform specific tasks on their own. Intelligent remotes, Sub-masters, or Smart RTUs (SRTUs) are RTUs equipped with these microcomputers and logic capabilities. These SRTUs can perform specific tasks on their own without the master unit's guidance. Nevertheless, in the next scan, the master unit must be informed of every action carried out locally by SRTUs.

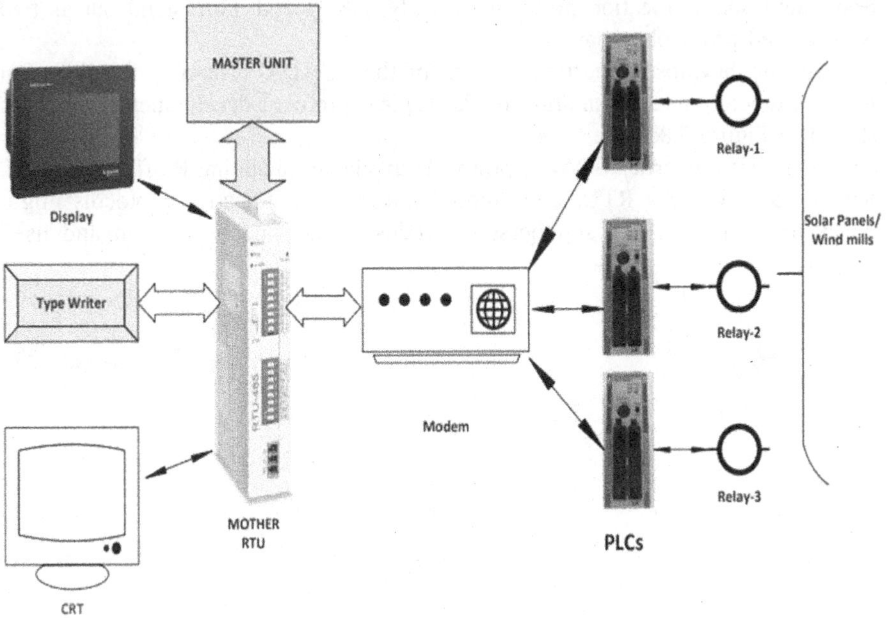

Figure 7.10 RTU connection diagram.

7.5.3 SCADA Master

The master unit, which is the main component of the supervisory system, usually has two identical digital computers and the necessary communication equipment to communicate with Remote Terminal Units (RTUs). For efficient communication with RTUs, this communication equipment comprises a modem that transforms digital pulses into a transmittable format. In conjunction with the computers, the master unit incorporates peripheral devices such as relays and energy meters as depicted in Figure 7.11.

Graphic display programs are designed to generate a one-line diagram on a CRT color monitor screen as shown in Figure 7.10. This visual representation employs different colors to distinguish between voltage levels, and color changes serve to indicate variations in equipment states.

A flash indicator is also used to notify states or signify changes in device statuses. An auditory alarm is included to improve situational awareness. It acts as a warning system to inform the operator of anomalous conditions in the system.

7.5.4 Communication Networks

7.5.4.1 Wired Communication

SCADA system has three functional components: Master Station, Remote Terminal (RTU/PLC), and the infrastructure supports communicating/ connecting these components. Effective communication between these elements relies on a designated communication protocol. Notably, DNP3 and T101 stand out as two widely used protocols today.

One of the most important choices in the SCADA system's overall design is the protocol. A representation of the typical protocol development process is shown in Figure 7.8.

There are numerous SCADA protocols available, including Profibus, Conitel, RP-570, and Modbus RTU. Even though these communication protocols might be exclusive to SCADA suppliers, the industry has widely adopted and used them [14].

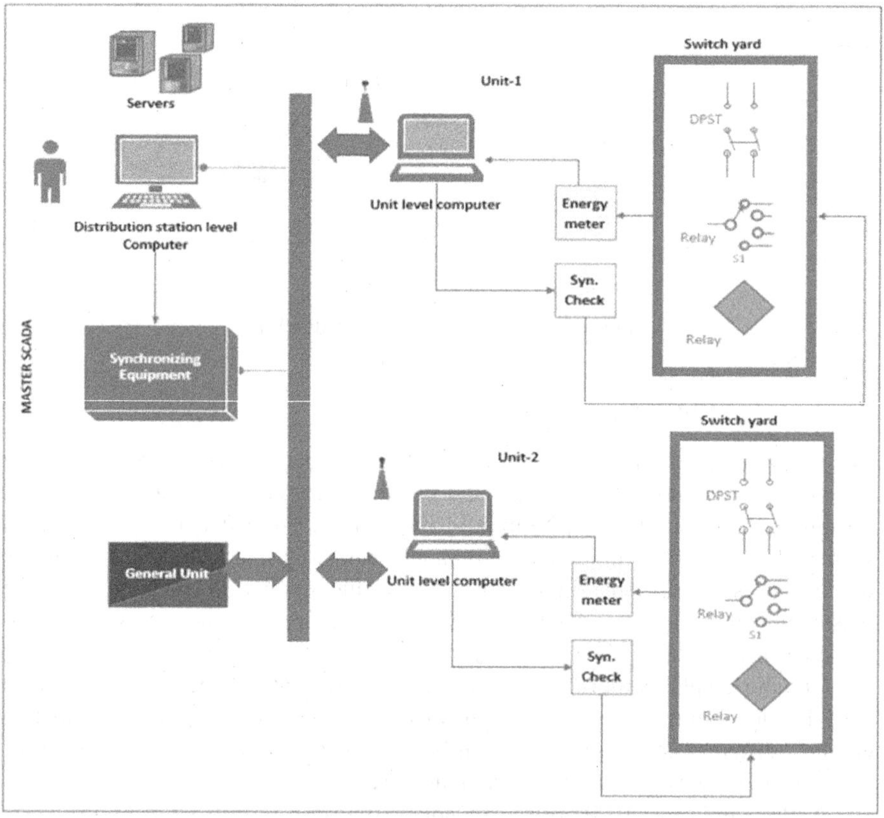

Figure 7.11 Master SCADA.

7.5.4.2 IEC 60870-5 Protocol

This protocol, which is a set of standards created by the International Electrotechnical Commission (IEC), is an open standard for the transfer of SCADA telemetry control and data [15]. IEC 60870-5's primary goal is to provide a thorough functional description for telecontrol devices and systems—with a special emphasis on SCADA systems—that are intended to manage operations that are spread out across several locations. This standard contains data objects designed especially for use in the electrical industry or related fields. The IEC

60870-5 protocol is mostly used in the electrical industries of European nations, even though it can be applied to general SCADA applications across other industries [16, 17].

7.5.4.3 DNP3 Protocol

Process automation systems make extensive use of the Distributed Network Protocol (DNP3) set of communication protocols [17, 18]. Although it is theoretically adaptable for deployment in many utility contexts, its principal application is in utilities, specifically in industries like water and electric companies. DNP3 is an essential component of SCADA (Supervisory Control and Data Acquisition) systems, which are specifically made to enhance communication between various data collection and control systems.

Intelligent Electronic Devices (IEDs), Remote Terminal Units (RTUs), and SCADA Master Stations or Control Centers all use DNP3 in SCADA systems. Its main function is to establish communication between a master station and IEDs or RTUs. DNP3 supports multiple-slave, peer-to-peer, and multiple-master communications. It also accommodates operational modes of polled and quiescent operation, with the latter also known as reporting by exception. In general, DNP3 improves the communication efficiency and dependability of SCADA systems, especially in utility sectors such as electricity and water [17, 18].

A key component of SCADA systems, which are mainly made up of a master station (M), remote terminal units (RTUs), and the communication lines that connect them, is communication. these systems. SCADA systems use a variety of communication channels that allow information to be exchanged constantly throughout the day at regular intervals with adequate signal-to-noise ratios at predetermined rates. This section describes a few of the crucial communication circuits.

- Two-wire circuits
- Coaxial Cables
- Microwave channels
- Optical fibers
- Satellite Communication Links etc.

To ensure efficient and dependable SCADA operations, each of these communication techniques has unique benefits and can be chosen depending on variables like distance, data transmission needs, and environmental considerations.

7.5.4.4 Wireless Communications

SCADA systems comprise four fundamental components: the master station or central controller, PLC/RTU (deployed in remote stations), fieldbus, and sensors. In the architecture of the SCADA system, the traditional fieldbus is replaced with wireless communication, and the system is extended to include the Internet. This configuration forms a private network, ensuring exclusive access for the central controller to remote assets. Additionally, the central controller features an extension that acts as a web server, enabling SCADA users and customers to access data through the SCADA provider's website [19]. Ethernet and TCP/IP-based protocols are gradually supplanting older proprietary standards in SCADA systems. While certain features of frame-based network communication technology, such as determinism, synchronization, protocol selection, and environment suitability, have limited the adoption of Ethernet in specific applications, most markets have embraced Ethernet networks for HMI/SCADA.

7.6 IoT-BASED MONITORING

7.6.1 IoT System Architecture

An IoT system primarily consists of four levels, which are described in the paragraph below.

- The sensing and act device layer and the intelligent device layer are two examples of IoT hardware devices.
- The information of things layers includes IoT Basic Service Layer, Service Middle Layer, Physical Information Layer, and Logical Information Layer
- Application Layer.

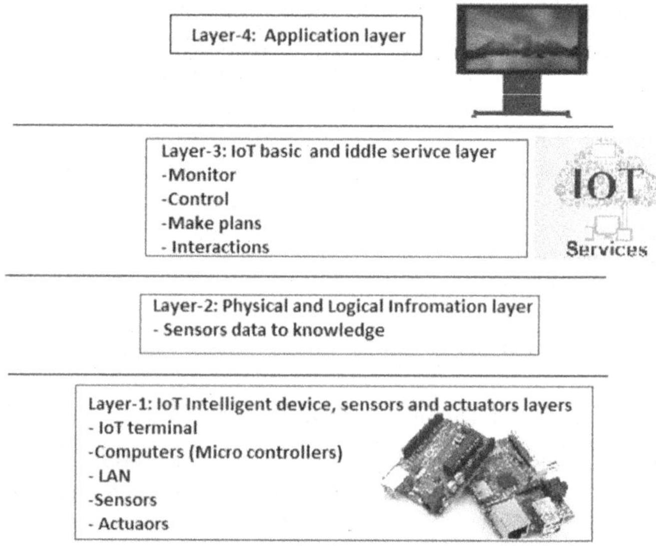

Figure 7.12 Architecture of an IoT systems.

The convergence of automation, control systems, wireless sensor networks, and embedded systems is known as the Internet of Things (IoT). While Figure 7.13 shows a block diagram of a typical IoT system, Figure 7.12 shows the architecture of the IoT system. This technology facilitates the creation of connected industrial manufacturing factories, intelligent retail environments, advanced healthcare solutions, smart homes and cities, wearable devices, and monitoring systems for renewable energy. IoT technologies empower businesses to undergo transformative changes by harnessing data-driven insights, refining operational processes, establishing new business lines, and optimizing material utilization. With the rise of multiple service providers, a wide range of platforms, and millions of new devices every year, the world of IoT technology is rapidly growing. In recent years, the Internet of Things (IoT) has played a significant role in smart grids, especially in the monitoring, control, and forecasting of renewable energy through data analytics. The study described in [20] explores solar power monitoring through the Internet of Things, illuminating its potential and extent. Furthermore, the analysis done on data collected from a solar plant over a 12-month period is described in the work published in [21].

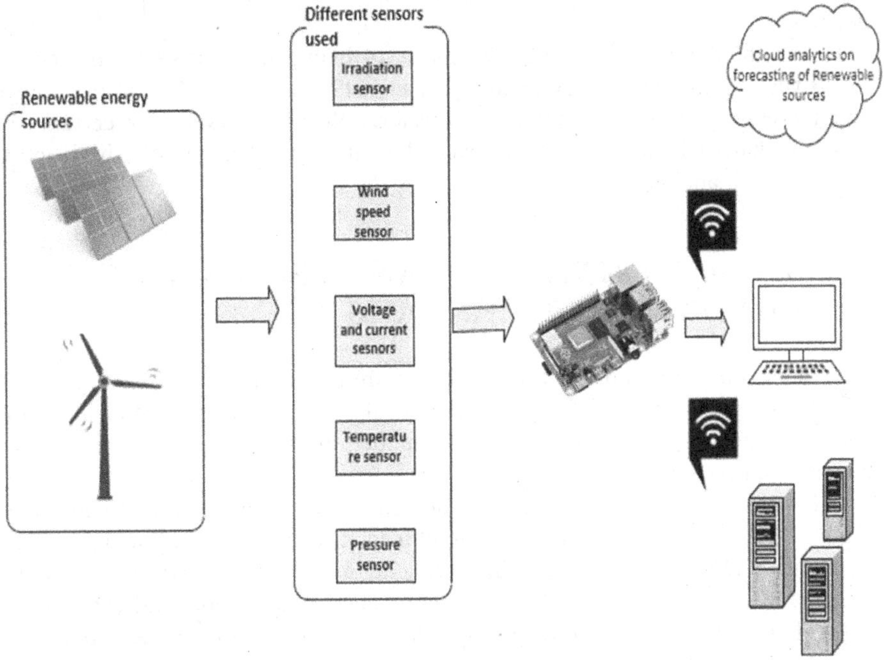

Figure 7.13 IoT based real time monitoring with analytics: Block diagram.

7.6.2 IoT Protocols

The choice of IoT protocols, which specify how devices connect and interact, is an important factor in IoT technology planning. Devices in the IoT technology stack link to one another via integrated functionality or gateways. Commonly used protocols like WiFi, MQTT, CoAP, or HTTP make it easier to send data to the cloud or a central server.

7.6.3 Wi-Fi (Wireless Fidelity)

Wi-Fi, short for Wireless Fidelity, is among the most widely adopted IoT communication protocols for Wireless Local Area Networks (WLAN). It operates based on the IEEE 802.11 standard and utilizes both the 2.4 GHz UHF and 5 GHz ISM frequencies.

Wi-Fi functions as a wireless network technology primarily designed for internet connectivity. Wi-Fi gives consumers the freedom to easily connect devices to the internet by operating between the 2.4 GHz and 5 GHz frequency ranges. With a maximum data rate of up to 600 Mbps, depending on the number of antennas and channel frequency in use, it provides internet access for devices that are within 50 to 100 meters of the source.

Espressif's ESP series controllers, especially the ESP32 and ESP8266, are well-liked options for creating Internet of Things (IoT) applications in the embedded systems space. Many embedded applications make use of these Wi-Fi devices.

Even though Wi-Fi has the advantages of being inexpensive for devices or infrastructure and being easy to set up, it's vital to be aware of its limited range and increased power consumption. Therefore, Wi-Fi shows fit for certain use cases, including home automation, even though it might not be the best option for every IoT application.

7.7 STAGE 3: INTELLIGENT ANALYSIS USING DIFFERENT AI TECHNIQUES

The final step is the most crucial in this entire approach, as seen in Figure 7.5. It is the stage of IDA tools, methods, and algorithms that are implied for the data sets that have been collected. A number of these algorithms have been documented recently.

IDA algorithms cover a broad range of instruments, techniques, and algorithms; Figure 7.14 provides a full classification of them. The most popular Intelligent Data Analytics (IDA) tools and techniques include ARMA and ARIMA time series models, ML, deep learning (DL) algorithms, data visualization, and data mining tools. This section goes into length and discusses these tools and techniques.

7.7.1 Machine Learning Algorithms

As mentioned earlier, the efficiency of the predictive algorithms employed for future learning is crucial to the success of integrating Distributed Generation (DG).

Nineteen ML techniques for temperature and power consumption prediction are examined in this study. These ML methods can be broadly divided into three categories: reinforcement learning, supervised learning, and unsupervised learning.

7.7.1.1 Supervised Learning

With this method, a set of predictors (independent variables) are used to forecast a target or outcome variable. These variables are used to create a function that maps inputs to desired outputs.

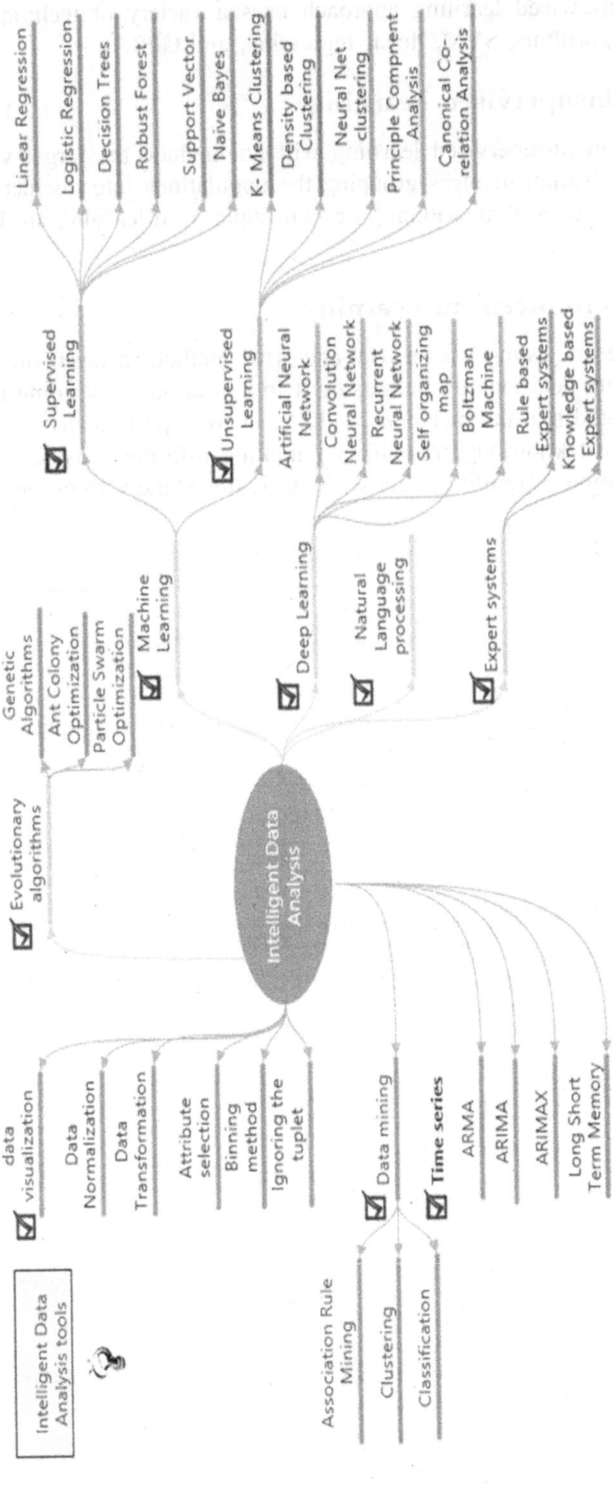

Figure 7.14 Classification of different IDA methods/tools.

This supervised learning approach uses a variety of techniques, such as ensemble algorithms, SVM, linear regression, and GPR.

7.7.1.2 Unsupervised Learning

Predictions in unsupervised learning will not include the target variable. This method's derivation involves grouping the populations into distinct groups. The two key categories of algorithms in this unsupervised learning are K-Means and Apriori.

7.7.1.3 Reinforcement Learning

Reinforcement learning uses a trial-and-error method to teach the computer to make accurate decisions by immersing it in a continuous learning environment. It is anticipated that the machine would learn from past experiences in order to obtain the best knowledge possible for making informed business decisions. A good illustration of reinforcement learning is the Markov Decision Process.

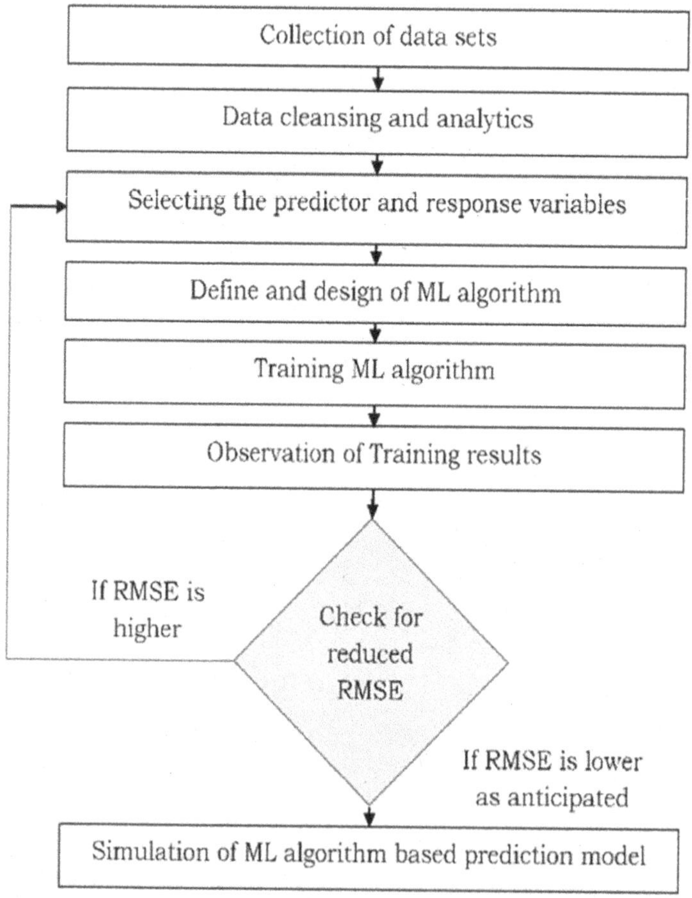

Figure 7.15 AI algorithm implementation stages.

Various steps involved in the construction of prediction models using ML algorithms are illustrated in Figure 7.15. The flowchart outlines the ML model development process. It starts with data collection, cleansing, and selecting relevant predictors and response variables.

The next steps involve designing and training the ML algorithm, followed by analyzing training outcomes. RMSE (Root Mean Square Error) is evaluated to assess model performance. If RMSE is within an acceptable range, the model is finalized for prediction simulation; otherwise, it is refined further.

7.7.2 Regression based on ML Algorithms

For forecasting and determining cause-and-effect relationships between variables, regression is a popular ML technique that makes predictions about a target value based on independent predictors. The application of four regression techniques is the main goal of this study. Linear Regression (LR) is the initial supervised ML algorithm utilized for modeling and regression, examining relationships between dependent and independent variables [22]. Multi-Variable LR (MVLR) extends this to establish relationships between multiple independent variables and one dependent variable, as described by Equation (8).

$$y = k_1 x_1 + k_1 x_1 + k_2 x_2 + k_4 x_4 \ldots k_n x_n + b \tag{8}$$

The study makes use of the Robust LR (RLR) model to reduce the effect of outliers and include a maximum number of data points in regression models. In order to reduce the impact of outliers, this model uses repeatedly re-weighted least squares, modifying weights according to the inverse proportion of residual size. By adopting Interactional LR (ILR), which incorporates interactional variables for combinations of categorical variables, interactional effects between variables are also taken into consideration.

Furthermore, Step Wise LR (SWLR), which combines the Forward Selection (FS) and Backward Elimination (BE) techniques, is used. These algorithms guarantee that the residual sum of squares decreases with each additional variable by stopping when no more can be added.

7.7.3 Support Vector Machines

Although it is mostly used for classification problems, the Support Vector Machine (SVM) is a supervised ML technique that may be applied to both classification and regression situations. This approach uses points in an n-dimensional space to represent data objects, where 'n' is the number of features, and the value of each feature is a coordinate.

By locating a hyperplane that successfully divides the two classes, classification is accomplished. Chen et al. first proposed Support Vector Regression (SVR) for regression issues in 2001 [23], while Smola et al. later provided a thorough tutorial on SVR in 2004 [24]. Through a survey on time series prediction using SVM, Sapankevych et al. expanded the use of SVR in 2009 [25].

Five distinct SVM ML techniques are trained using different kernel functions in order to predict temperature and PT: Quadratic SVM (QSVM), Cubic SVM (CSVM), Fine Gaussian SVM (FGSVM), Medium SVM (MSVM), and Coarse Gaussian SVM (CGSVM).

7.7.4 Ensemble Algorithms

Ensemble algorithms, utilized in classification and regression problems, combine multiple models for making predictions. Classification involves assigning discrete categories, while regression deals with continuous decisions. Ensemble forecasting includes competitive and cooperative approaches. Notably, Soares et al.'s survey stresses the usefulness of ensemble MLs in addressing problems associated with regression [26]. In 2015, Ren et al. presented EM and the latest updates in that, specifically focusing on predicting renewable energy sources based on solar and wind [27]. Two methods have emerged in ensemble algorithms. The first is bagging, a popular subsampling technique that creates models by generating training sets with replacement at random. This contributes to the effectiveness of bagging as described by Breiman and Domingos [28] by allowing some occurrences to show more than once, while others may not appear at all. Boosting, a noteworthy family of ensemble subsampling techniques, is the second approach [29]. One of the most often used boosting algorithms is AdaBoost (Adaptive Boosting), which was first presented by Freund et al. based on Schapire's work [30, 31]. Applications of ensemble ML methods for load forecasting problems include bagging and boosting (subsampling-based) algorithms.

7.7.5 Gaussian Process Regress Algorithm

A least-square approach, called linear regression, can be used to fit a straight line when the underlying function $f(x)$ is predicted to be linear and some input data assumptions are satisfied. Several options can be investigated using model selection principles if $f(x)$ is suspected of being quadratic, cubic, or even polynomial in nature. For even higher accuracy, a more sophisticated method called GPR is used. A Gaussian process strictly and indirectly depicts $f(x)$ rather than assuming a particular model (e.g., $f(x) = mx + c$), which gives the data a more distinct voice. While still a type of supervised learning, GPR makes more sophisticated use of training data [32].

In difficult nonlinear situations with large dimensions and few samples, GPR exhibits outstanding adaptability and robust generality. GPR is simple to use, self-adaptive for better parameter estimation, and adaptable enough for nonparametric conclusions when compared to neural networks and SVM.

Different kernel functions, such as "squared exponential," "Matern52," "exponential," and "rational quadratic," are used in the development and application of four different ML algorithms: Squared Exponential GPR (SE-GPR), Matern52 GPR (MG-PR), Exponential GPR (EG-PR), and Rational Quadratic GPR (RQ-GPR).

7.7.6 Feed Forward Artificial Neural Networks

The processing pattern of the human brain serves as the inspiration for ANNs. Instead of using explicit programming, they learn from data patterns and correlations through experience. Artificial neurons arranged in layers with weighted connections make up ANNs. Every neuron generates an output, has inputs, and a transfer function. The architecture, learning rules, and transfer functions all affect how the network behaves. To reduce prediction mistakes, connections are improved during training.

New input data can be predicted by trained networks. Even though there are many kinds of neural networks, they all have something in common, like learning rules, connection formulae that control their neurons, and transfer functions [33, 34]. As shown in Figure 7.16, there are essentially two types of ANNs: single-layered ANNs and multi-layered ANNs. The former have a set of inputs and outputs with hidden layers.

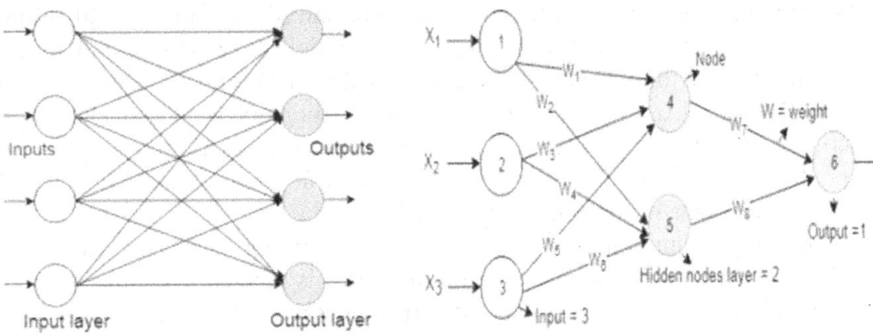

Figure 7.16 Single-layered ANN and multi-layered ANN [34].

7.7.7 Deep Neural Networks

Deep Neural Networks (DNN) are widely used in many different fields and are essential to ML. DNN sequentially processes information from the retina to the visual center, taking inspiration from the layered nature of the mammalian visual system. Abstract notions are created by this sequential processing, which includes the extraction of features like edges, components, and shapes. The alignment with biological visual processing enhances DNN's effectiveness in capturing hierarchical representations, making it well-suited for handling complex learning tasks [35]. DNNs are equal and greater than to 4 Multilayer Perceptron ANN (MLP ANN). An example is the Multilayer Perceptron (MLP) with more than one hidden layer, forming a Deep Neural Network (DNN) framework. To identify distributed expressions in data, DNN extracts features layer by layer and combines low-level features to build high-level features. DNN has better feature expressions and a higher ability to model complex mappings than shallow Neural Networks (NN) [36]. Figure 7.17 provides a clear explanation of the DNN with an activation function. The figure shows a basic artificial neuron where inputs x_1 to x_4 are multiplied by corresponding weights w_1 to w_4. The weighted sum is computed and passed through a Rectified Linear Unit (ReLU) activation function. The result is the neuron's output used in further layers or prediction.

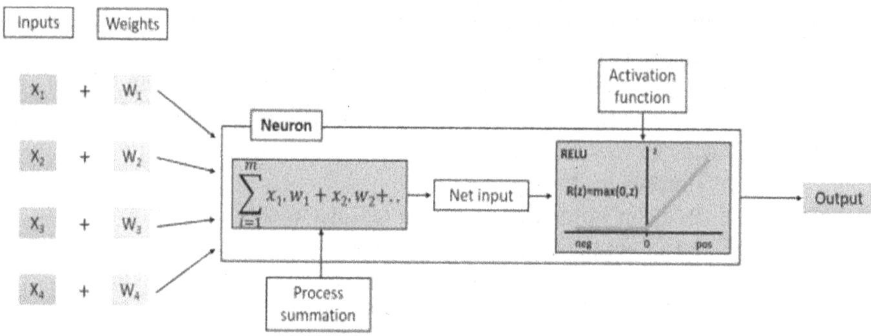

Figure 7.17 DNN description.

Determining the kind of problem that has to be solved—clustering, regression, classification, prediction, optimization, or applications like sensor and motor controls in robotics and vision—is the first stage in building a Deep Neural Network (DNN). For example, interpreting a chest radiograph is a vision challenge, predicting mortality is a classification problem, and projecting a future occurrence is a prediction problem. Every kind of difficulty necessitates a Deep Neural Network (DNN) that is specially constructed.

Another important consideration is the type of training data that is available. Supervised learning is used when the training data is labeled, meaning that the outcome (such as mortality in a binary classification issue) is known. Unsupervised techniques like clustering or dimensionality reduction are required when the output label is uncertain. A third category, semi-supervised learning, uses labeled datasets to enhance unsupervised learning outcomes [37].

7.7.8 Time Series Models

A time series is an ordered collection of historical data that represents observations or groups of data continuously gathered over time. The collected data can be formatted at various intervals, such as daily, weekly, monthly, quarterly, or yearly, depending on appropriateness. Time series data typically consists of four components: trend, seasonal effect, cyclical patterns, and irregular effects [38].

Autoregressive Moving Average (ARMA) and Autoregressive Integrated Moving Average (ARIMA) are two popular forecasting methods that dominate time series models. These methods are used to identify trends and patterns in renewable energy [39].

7.7.9 Long Short-Term Memory

One specialized architecture in the field of Recurrent Neural Networks (RNNs) is Long Short-Term Memory (LSTM). It is made especially to address the vanishing gradient issue, which conventional RNNs face. Tasks requiring the efficient handling of sequences, time series data, and long-term dependencies are well suited for LSTMs. Three gates are used by LSTMs to control the information flow. The input gate controls the flow of fresh data into the cell. Second, the Forget Gate controls whether data is kept in the cell or deleted. Finally, the output gate controls how information is released from the cell to the output [40]. As seen in Figure 7.18, an LSTM network consists of four layers.

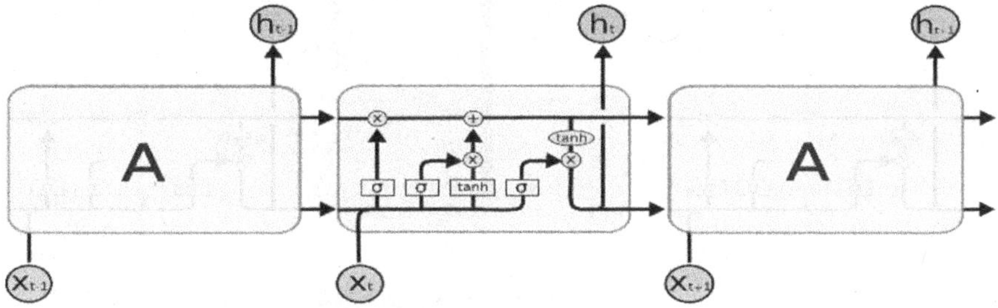

Figure 7.18 LSTM layers.

7.7.10 Naïve Bayes ML Algorithms

Bayesian classifiers use an example's feature vector to determine which class it is most likely to belong to. Equation (9), which assumes that features are independent of class, simplifies the learning process for these classifiers.

$$P(X \mid C) = \prod_{i=1}^{n} P(X \mid C) \tag{9}$$

where, X: feature vector ($X_i = X_1, X_2 \ldots X_n$), and C: Class.

Despite the unrealistic assumption of feature independence, the resulting classifier, known as naive Bayes, proves remarkably successful in practice. It often competes with more sophisticated techniques and has demonstrated effectiveness in practical applications such as text classification, medical diagnosis, and systems performance management.

7.8 REAL TIME MONITORING OF RES

7.8.1 Case Study 1: RES Monitoring

A case study of a specific real-time monitoring platform designed for the operational DERs is shown in this section. This platform incorporates necessary data security measures and operates as a wireless bidirectional communication system.

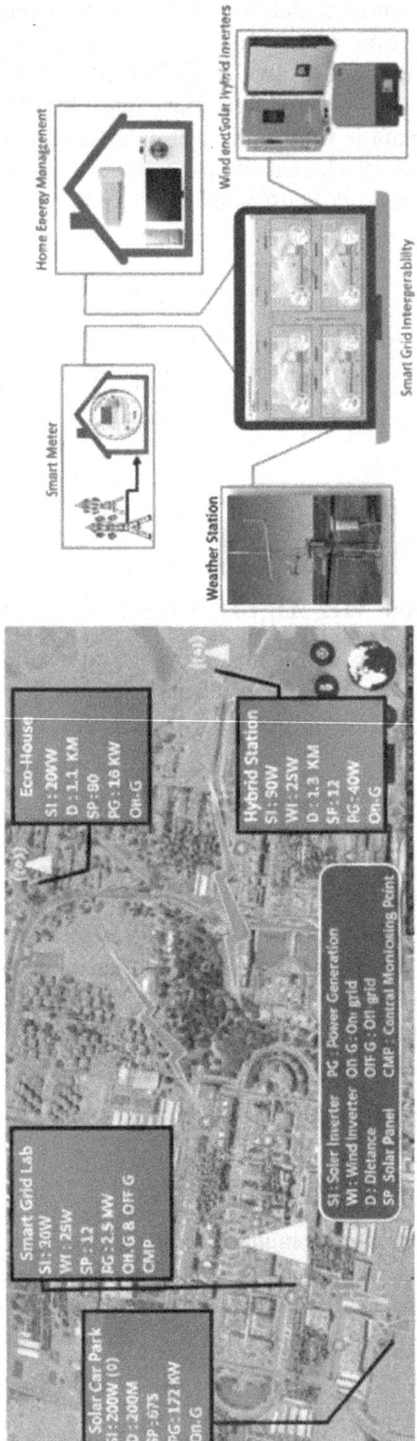

Figure 7.19 Wireless system for RES monitoring.

7.8.1.1 System Architecture

Four separate renewable energy systems on the Sultan Qaboos University campus in the Sultanate of Oman are the subject of the study, which focuses on small-scale DERs. There are four RESs, specifically:

(a) Smart Grid Lab
(b) Solar Car Park
(c) Eco-House
(d) Hybrid Station

These are placed strategically within a few kilometers of one another, as seen in Figure 7.19. By using solar panels and wind turbines, each RES actively contributes to the production of electrical energy [41].

The collective power output from all Renewable Energy Sources (RESs) reaches its peak at approximately 50 kW. A high-speed IEEE 802.11n wireless link establishes seamless connectivity among the Renewable Energy Sources (RESs), facilitating efficient data transfer to a central server dedicated to storage, analysis, and visualization.

Figure 7.20, which depicts the overall architecture of a real-time monitoring system within a building, shows that each RES is outfitted with a separate monitoring system. Ensuring the monitoring system's interoperability so it can receive data from several devices is the main goal. Solar panels, wind turbines, storage batteries, one or more inverters, smart meters, and an optional weather station are among the system's components [41].

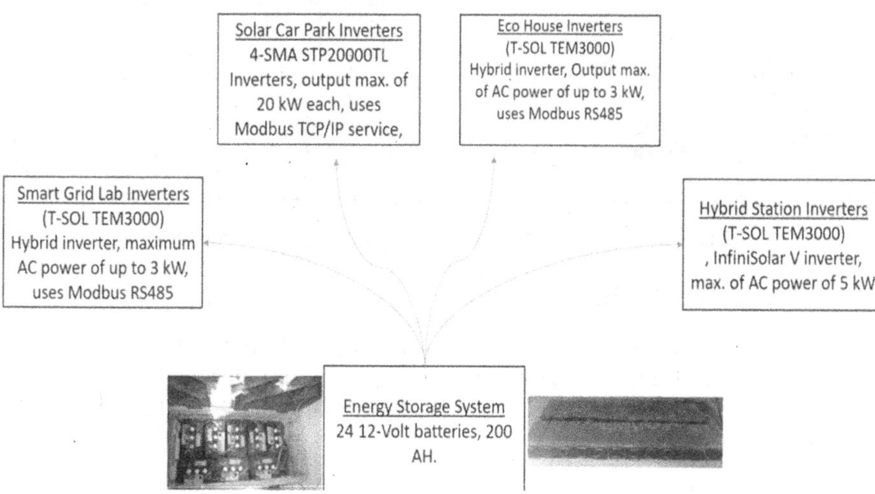

Figure 7.20 Different inverters connected in the system.

7.8.2 Wireless Communication System

The system is set up with a central access point that is linked to the primary server and several wireless clients that connect distant stations to it. Unhindered line of sight (LOS) connectivity is ensured by the strategic placement of all wireless devices on Distributed Energy Resources' (DERs') rooftops. By using the 5 GHz spectrum, possible interference with the current 2.4 GHz wireless network is reduced.

A smart energy monitoring and control system integrating a Smart Grid Lab and a Solar Car Park is presented in [41]. In the lab, PV and wind inverters transmit power data via registers and communication interfaces like WattNode and IFD9507, with data acquisition managed by LabVIEW and stored in a MySQL database. The Solar Car Park comprises four PV arrays, each connected to inverters with registers, managed by a SAM cluster controller over TCP/IP. Both sites communicate wirelessly, enabling remote data exchange and control. This setup supports real-time monitoring, distributed energy resource (DER) integration, and efficient smart grid management. The layout of the real-time monitoring system is as shown in Figure 7.21.

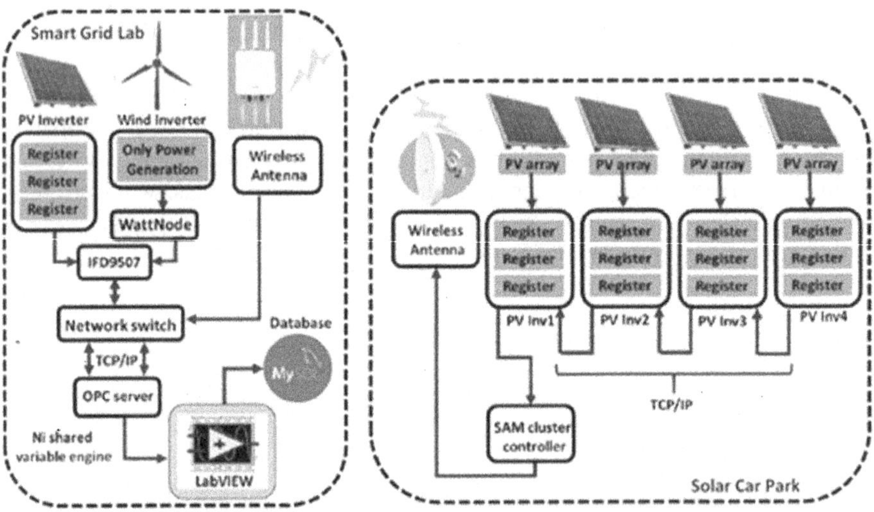

Figure 7.21 Layout of the real time monitoring system.

7.8.3 Software Architecture

Open Platform Communications (OPC) is the preferred software for this installation since it enables real-time plant data transmission across equipment made by different manufacturers. Three essential parts make up the software:

(i) Open server
(ii) LabVIEW Core
(iii) MySQL Database Management System

Figure 7.22 illustrates the interaction between an inverter and the aforementioned software components.

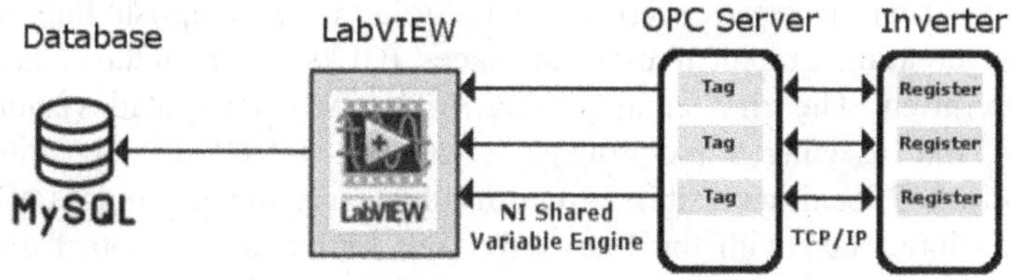

Figure 7.22 OPC components [41].

7.8.3.1 NI OPC Server

An industry-standard, high-performance server with a reputation for real-time data monitoring across many communication protocols is the National Instruments (NI) OPC server. Its flawless integration with the Modbus protocol is noteworthy because it facilitates seamless communication between devices and the LabVIEW environment. Through assigned IP addresses, the server effectively locates Modbus-TCP/IP-compliant devices on the local network, increasing its adaptability in managing data from a variety of devices for successful real-time monitoring applications.

7.8.3.2 LabVIEW Core

Numerous industrial communication protocols are supported by the flexible software program LabVIEW. For activities like data visualization and instrumentation control, its graphical programming interface enables the development of graphical user interfaces (GUI). LabVIEW makes it easier to connect to well-known database platforms like MySQL thanks to its extensive library of modules, which includes a database storage module. The Data Logging and Supervisory Control (DSC) module must be installed for LabVIEW and OPC Server to communicate software. This module expands LabVIEW's functionality, especially in tasks involving supervisory control and data logging, making it an effective tool for a range of industrial applications.

7.8.3.3 MySQL Database

MySQL is an open-source relational database management system known for efficiently storing large volumes of data locally. It utilizes the SQL programming language, allowing for querying, storage, deletion, and modification of data. In the context of server configuration and management, XAMPP is installed for database-related tasks.

An ODBC (Open Database Connectivity) driver must be installed on the server in order to connect MySQL to LabVIEW. With the required parameters set, this driver creates a smooth connection to the MySQL database. This configuration makes it easier for LabVIEW and MySQL to communicate and manage data effectively.

7.8.3.4 Data Visualization

Making a graphical user interface that is both informative and easy to use is essential, particularly when displaying a lot of parameters. Due to the difficulty of this work, two strategies were used in order to accomplish the intended goal. When creating graphical user interfaces (GUIs), two methods are taken into consideration. The first entails using LabVIEW's integrated visualization capabilities, like as gauges and graphs, to create the GUI directly within the program. Limited local accessibility is a disadvantage, though, unless a custom web page is integrated with the LabVIEW web server or a remote front panel server is built.

By using the open-source Grafana platform to develop the GUI, the second method overcomes this constraint. Grafana displays parameters in a variety of visual representations and establishes connections with databases. This technique gets over LabVIEW's local accessibility limitations by enabling clients to view results via a dashboard from any web browser. The next subsections cover the specifics of each approach's implementation, and Figure 7.23 shows the GUIs for Grafana and LabVIEW, respectively.

7.8.4 Case Study 2: IoT-based Wind Turbine Data Monitoring and ML-based Analysis

The most important thing in a smart micro-grid setting is tracking and predicting the renewable energy sources. Accurately forecasting renewable energy sources is crucial in the present environment of AI-enabled Distributed Generation (DG) based networks. The case study uses ML techniques to demonstrate analytics and monitoring in an Internet of Things context. Several ML algorithms, such as Feed Forward ANN (FF-ANN), are used to assess wind power availability in Oman.

The effectiveness of the monitoring and forecasting of renewable energy sources is illustrated by the data pertaining to ANN. An alternative to conventional/offline forecasting is the creative method of combining AI and IoT to provide online monitoring and forecasting. Using an Arduino Uno and additional sensors for data collection, a prototype for the aforementioned AI and IoT monitoring and forecasting is created. ML algorithms are then trained on the cloud platform thingspeak.com, and the outcomes are shown on the cloud for efficient gird operations.

By improving the precision and responsiveness of renewable energy projections, this all-encompassing strategy seeks to improve energy management in intelligent microgrid settings. An innovative approach to guaranteeing a sustainable and dependable energy supply is the integration of ML algorithms, IoT, and online forecasting. A student project experiment conducted in March 2021 at the University of Technology and Applied Sciences Ibra in Ibra, Oman, is the subject of the case study that is being presented.

7.8.4.1 Methodology

Figure 7.24 shows the comprehensive block diagram for the AI and IoT-based monitoring system that is intended for wind power forecasting and monitoring.

The several sensors used, the Arduino MEGA, and the Wi-Fi module are shown in Figure 7.26. This block diagram, which shows how the flow starts from

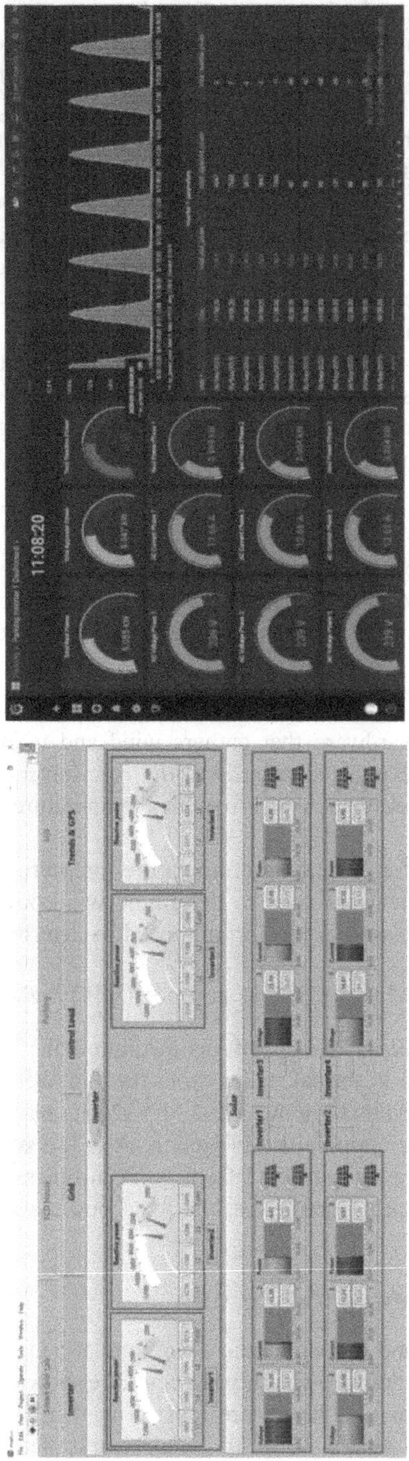

Figure 7.23 GUI on LabVIEW and open-source Grafana platform.

the windmill connected to both current and voltage sensors, serves as the basis for the hardware design. After that, the Arduino MEGA receives the signals. Sensor data is gathered, processed by the Arduino MEGA, and sent to the cloud through the Wi-Fi module. The cloud—more especially, Thingspeak—oversees displaying and storing the data in various fields during this process. Wind power data is then connected and analyzed using an integrated MATLAB analysis tool on the cloud. Real-time forecasting and analysis of renewable energy sources is made possible by this all-encompassing technique. Current and voltage sensors help with wind power acquisition, and other sensors including LDR, DHT11, pressure, and wind speed are used to collect weather data.

An Arduino that has been configured to collect data at 15-second intervals receives the collected sensor data. An LCD display is another element of the system that gives users real-time visibility into wind power data. All things considered, the configuration guarantees regular cloud storage, a steady flow of data, and on-site monitoring via the LCD panel.

7.8.4.2 Systematic Flow Chart

The methodology adapted in this project to forecasting solar and wind power using cloud computing abilities on Thingspeak cloud has eights stages. Generalized methodology for solar and wind power is presented in Figure 7.25.

7.8.4.3 Hardware Setup for Data Acquisition

Figure 7.26 shows the hardware that gathers wind and weather data, logs it to the cloud, and sends the updated records to the cloud every 15 seconds. Figure 7.27 displays the collected data, which includes temperature, humidity, pressure, and wind speed.

Weather characteristics including temperature, pressure, air intensity, sweep area, and power coefficient are used to determine wind power, which is shown in Figure 7.28. The following is the formula used to determine wind power.

$$Pw = 0.5 * p * A * Cp * V_3 \text{ and } p = (MW) * P/(R * T) \tag{10}$$

Where, MW is Molecular weight of gas in gram/mole: $MW = 29$ gram/mole (assumed), P is Pressure in Pascal' taken from the Big Weather Data, R is Ideal gas Constant = 8314.5 Joules/Mole K, $A = 3.14 * r2$ (the blade radius "r" is taken to be 4 meters), T is the temperature in Kelvin, A is the sweep area in m^2, and $Cp = 0.4$ (the average power extracted from wind turbines is 59%). Thus, using the uploaded meteorological parameters, the wind power value is computed and updated on the cloud.

7.8.4.4 Implementation and Results

An FF-ANN is created and trained on the cloud in relation to the analytics carried out to anticipate the wind power, and the outcomes are shown in the section below. The input, hidden, and output layers are most crucial in ANN implementation. Figure 7.29 represents a feedforward Artificial Neural Network (ANN) with an

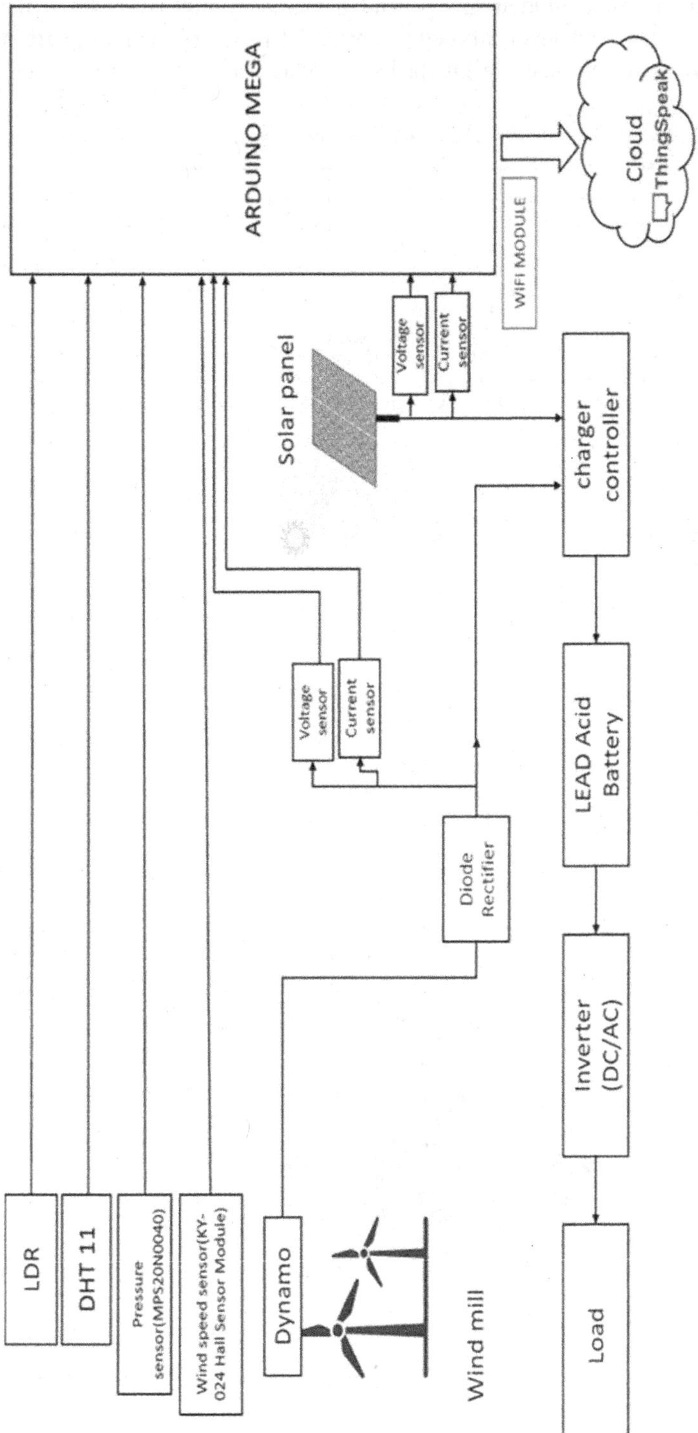

Figure 7.24 AI and IOT based monitoring and forecasting.

input layer, multiple hidden layers, and a single output layer. Each neuron is connected to the next layer, allowing the model to learn complex patterns. This architecture is widely used in DL tasks like classification and regression.

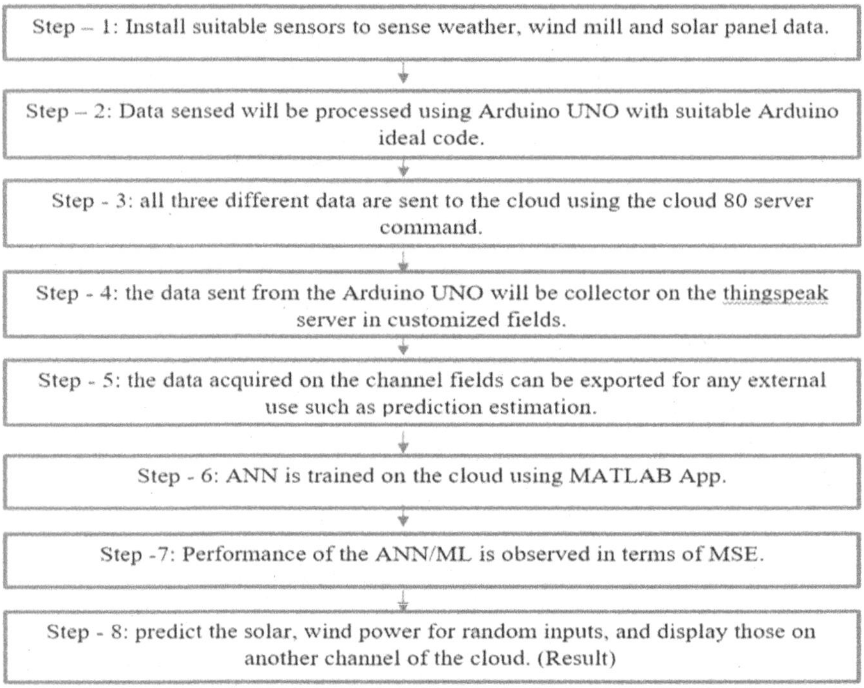

Figure 7.25 Methodology: Data acquisition, monitoring and implementation of ML/ANN.

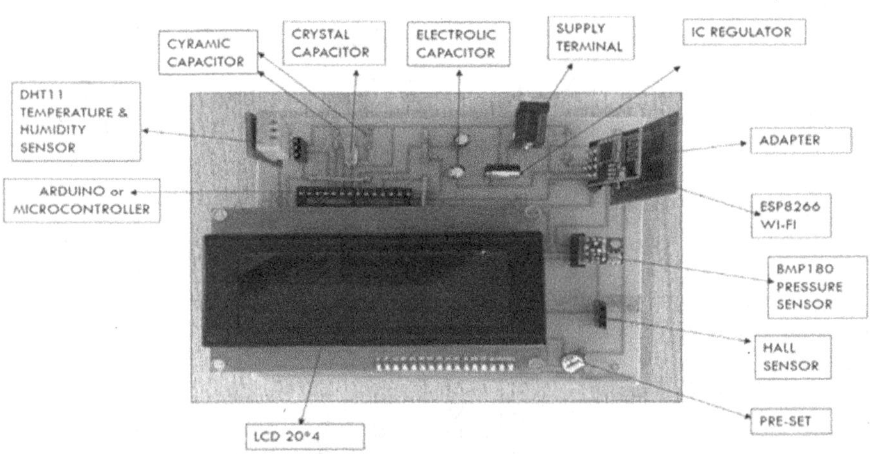

Figure 7.26 Hardware setup for data acquisition.

Figure 7.27 Data acquired on the cloud.

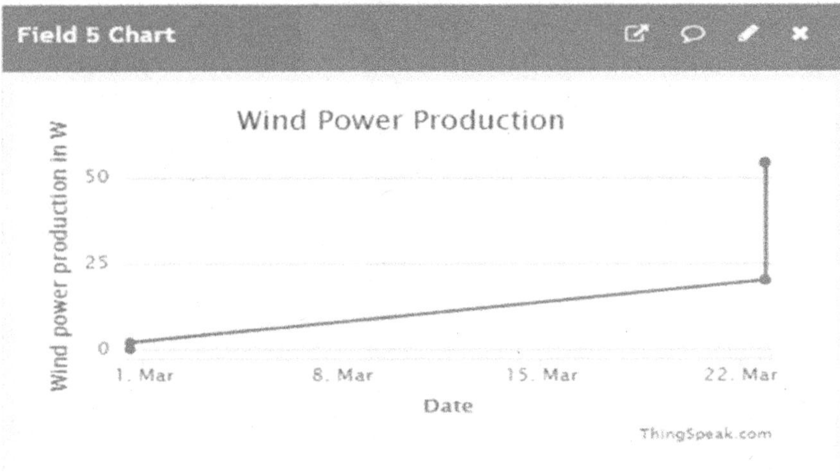

Figure 7.28 Data acquired on the cloud.

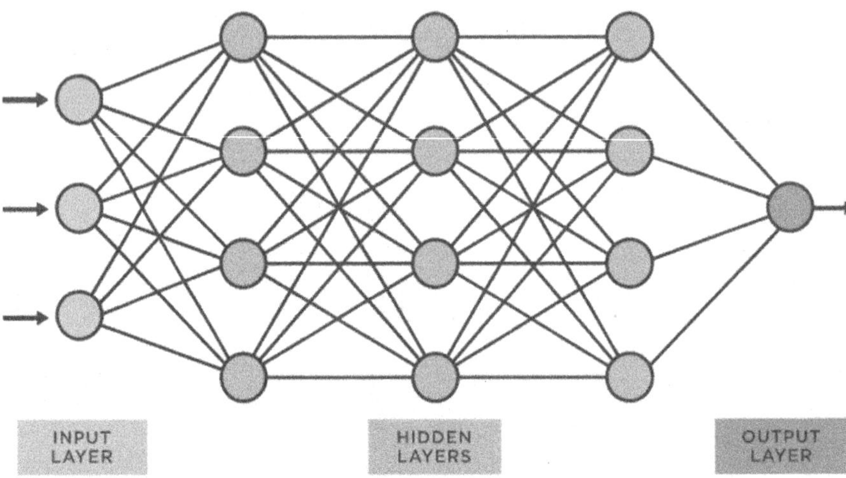

Figure 7.29 FF-ANN.

Figure 7.30(a) illustrates the implementation of cloud-based MATLAB code. The inputs for the net are temperature, humidity, pressure, and wind speed. Goals for the Net: Wind power, with ten layers. Approximately 100 samples are considered when training ML algorithms. Figure 7.30(b) displays the anticipated wind power using FF-ANN.

Likewise, the same amount of input and target variables are used to train several ML algorithms, and Table 7.1 displays the implementation's outcomes. Among the outcomes are Mean Square Error (MSE), Mean Average Error (MAE), R-Squared, and Root Mean Square Error (RMSE). GPR is the most accurate and has the least amount of error among all the ML algorithms.

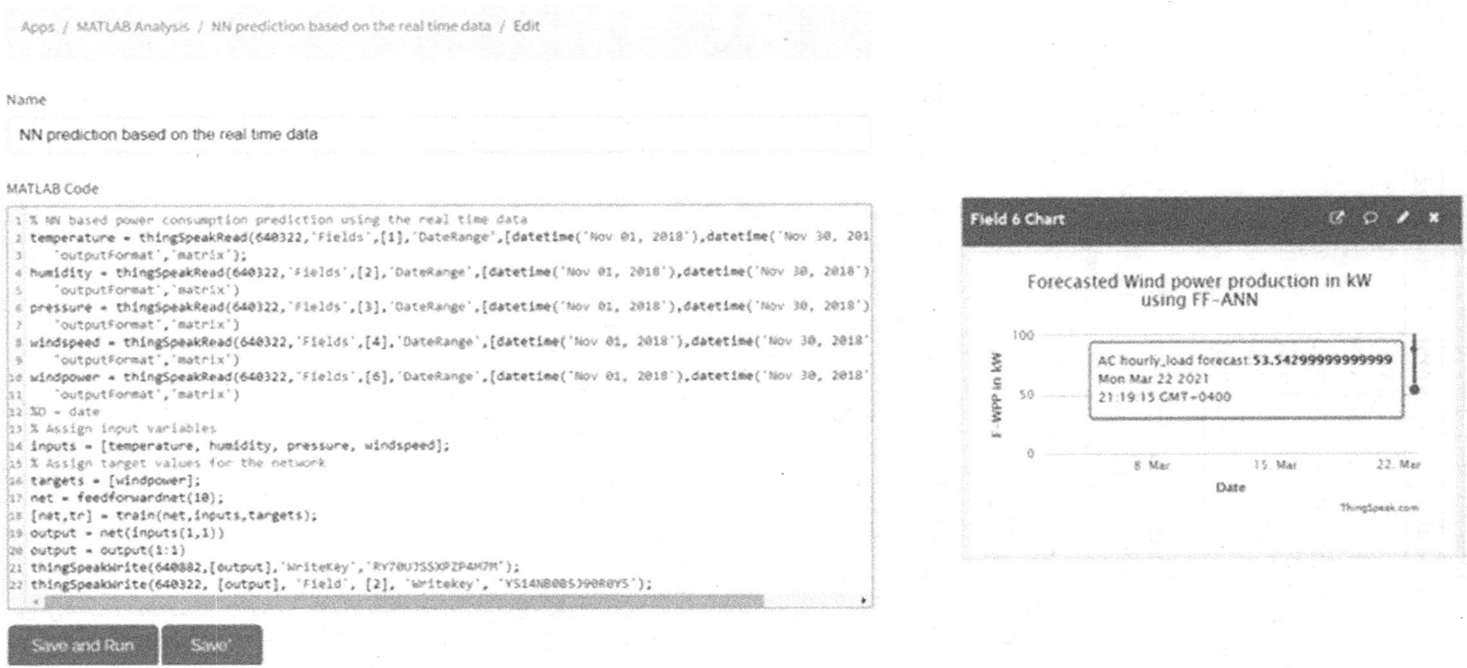

Figure 7.30(a, b) MATLAB code on the cloud for ANN and forecasted output.

Table 7.1 Outcomes of various ML algorithms

Name of the ML Algorithm	RMSE	R-Squared	MSE	MAE
LR	2.1938	0.11	4.8127	0.7134
SVM	2.3336	–0.01	5.4457	0.28573
Ensemble Boosted Trees (EBoT)	1.9513	0.29	3.8076	0.34928
Ensemble Bagged Trees (EBaT)	1.9728	0.28	3.8919	0.33194
GPR	1.768	0.41	3.8761	0.3213
Neural Network (NN)	1.9591	0.29	3.38	0.32776

The case study presents the feasibility study implementing IoT based online monitory and AI based analytics on cloud. Different ML algorithms can also be trained and implemented to enhance the accuracy of the implementation.

7.9 CONCLUSION

This chapter demonstrates that effective forecasting and monitoring of renewable energy sources (RES) are essential for overcoming the challenges posed by their inherent variability, largely influenced by weather conditions. By leveraging intelligent data interpretation techniques, including ML and DL, it becomes possible to not only improve forecasting accuracy but also to enhance the overall efficiency and stability of renewable energy systems. The integration of Supervisory Control and Data Acquisition (SCADA) systems, IoT platforms, and cloud-based solutions provides a robust infrastructure for real-time data acquisition, surveillance, and remote management of DERs.

The chapter further illustrates the design and implementation of advanced frameworks for both real-time monitoring and predictive forecasting of RES, using platforms such as Thingspeak.com and a suite of ML algorithms including DT, SVM, EBoT, EBaT, GPR, and ANN. These methodologies enable the transformation of raw data into actionable insights, allowing for more adaptive and data-driven energy management strategies. Ultimately, this multi-faceted approach fosters greater resilience, reliability, and sustainability in energy systems, supporting the global transition toward cleaner and smarter energy infrastructure.

REFERENCES

[1] Fronk, B.M., Neal, R. and Garimella, S. 2010. Evolution of the transition to a world driven by renewable energy. Journal of Energy Resources Technology. 132(2): 021009. doi:10.1115/1.4001574.

[2] IEA. 2024. Renewable electricity capacity additions by technology and segment. 2016–2028. IEA, Paris. https://www.iea.org/data-and-statistics/charts/renewable-electricity-capacity-additions-by-technology-and-segment-2016-2028, Licence: CC BY 4.0.

[3] Ramos Hernanz, J.A., J.J. Campayo Martín, I. Zamora Belver, J. Larrañaga Lesaca, E. Zulueta and E. Puelles Pérez. 2010. Modelling of Photovoltaic Module.

International Conference on Renewable Energies and Power Quality (ICREPQ'10) Granada (Spain).

[4] IEEE Transactions on Industry Applications. 2004. Wind Turbine Generator Modeling and Simulation Where Rotational Speed is the Controlled Variable Lucian Mihet-Popa, Frede Blaabjerg, Fellow, IEEE, and Ion Boldea, Fellow, IEEE. 40(1).

[5] Sanchez, E., C.F. Torres, P. Guillenc and G. Larrazabal. 2013. Modeling and simulation of the production process of electrical energy in a geothermal power plant. Mathematical and Computer Modelling. 57(9–10): 2140–2148.

[6] Wiencek, R., S. Ghosh, M.C. Laurent-Rice, E. Black, T. Mujahid, S. Kalyan, et al. 2023. Simulation of the 5G Communication Link Between Solar Micro-Inverters and SCADA System. 5th Global Power, Energy and Communication Conference (IEEE GPECOM2023). Cappadocia/Turkey.

[7] Sayed, K. and H.A. Gabbar. 2018. Building energy management systems (BEMS). *In*: Energy conservation in residential, commercial, and industrial facilities. 15–81.

[8] Sayed, K. and H.A. Gabbar. 2017. SCADA and smart energy grid control automation. *In*: Smart Energy Grid Engineering. 481–514.

[9] Ahmed, M.A., A.M. Eltamaly, M.A. Alotaibi, A.I. Alolah and Y.-C. Kim. 2020. Wireless network architecture for cyber physical wind energy system. IEEE Access 8: 40180–40197.

[10] Eltamaly, A.M., M.S. Al-Saud and A.G. Abo-Khalil. 2020. Dynamic control of a DFIG wind power generation system to mitigate unbalanced grid voltage. IEEE Access. 8: 39091–3910.

[11] Sayed, K., A.G. Abo-Khalil, and A.M. Eltamaly. 2021. Wind power plants control systems based on SCADA system. *In*: Eltamaly, A.M., A.Y. Abdelaziz and A.G. Abo-Khalil. (Eds). Control and Operation of Grid-Connected Wind Energy Systems. Green Energy and Technology. Springer, Cham. https://doi.org/10.1007/978-3-030-64336-2_6.

[12] Prihantoro, J., H. Taufiqurrohman, Suyanto, Cahyadi, A. Larasati and A. Nurrohim. 2022. Implementation SCADA web client for monitoring geothermal power plant 3 MW Kamojang—Indonesia. 2022 2nd International Conference on Electronic and Electrical Engineering and Intelligent System (ICE3IS), Yogyakarta, Indonesia. 270–275. doi: 10.1109/ICE3IS56585.2022.10010311.

[13] Ioan, S., E. Stâncel, D. Câpâtînâ, O. Ghiran, I. Kovacs and T. Sanislav. 2007. SCADA on hydro power plant cascade—Case study. IFAC Proceedings Volumes. 40(8): 38–43. ISSN 1474-6670, ISBN 9783902661388, https://doi.org/10.3182/20070709-3-RO-4910.00006

[14] Choi, M. 2013. Wireless communications for SCADA systems utilizing mobile nodes. International Journal of Smart Home. 7(5): 1–8.

[15] Robles, R.J., M.-k. Choi and T.-h. Kim. 2010. The Taxonomy of SCADA communication protocols. *In*: Proceedings of the 8th KIIT IT based Convergence Service Workshop and Summer Conference, Mokpo Maritime University (Mokpo, Korea). 23. ISSN 2005-7334.

[16] Clarke, C., D. Reynders and E. Wright. 2004. Practical modern SCADA protocols: DNP3, 60870.5 and Related Systems.

[17] Station Automation COM600 3.4 IEC 60870-5-101 Master (OPC) User's Manual 2004.

[18] DNP Users Group. 2011. Overview of the DNP3 Protocol. (2011), http://www.dnp.org/About/Default.aspx

[19] Robles, R.J., K.-T. Seo and T.-h. Kim. 2010. Communication security solution for internet SCADA. Korean Institute of Information Technology 2010 IT Convergence Technology—Summer workshops and Conference Proceedings. 461–463.

[20] Bhau, G.V., R.G. Deshmukh, T.R. Kumar, S. Chowdhury, Y. Sesharao and Y. Abilmazhinov. 2023. IoT based solar energy monitoring system. Materials Today: ProceedingsVolume 80, Part 3. 3697–3701, ISSN 2214-7853, https://doi.org/10.1016/j.matpr. 2021.07.364.

[21] Ledmaoui, Y., A. El Maghraoui, M. El Aroussi, R. Saadane, A. Chebak and A. Chehri. 2023. Forecasting solar energy production: A comparative study of machine learning algorithms. Energy Reports. 10: 1004–1012. ISSN 2352-4847, https://doi.org/10.1016/j.egyr.2023.07.042.

[22] Moghram, I. and S. Rahman. 1989. Analysis and evaluation of five short-term load forecasting techniques. IEEE Transactions on Power Systems. 4(4): 1484–1491.

[23] Chen, B.J., M.W. Chang and C.J. Lin. 2004. Load forecasting using support vector machines: A study on EUNITE competition 2001. IEEE Transactions on Power Systems. 19(4): 1821–1830.

[24] Smola, A.J. and B. Schölkopf. 2004. A tutorial on support vector regression. Statistics and Computing. 14(3): 199–222.

[25] Sapankevych, N.I. and R. Sankar. 2009. Time series prediction using support vector machines: A survey. IEEE Computational Intelligence Magazine. 4(2): 24–38.

[26] Mendes-Moreira, J., C. Soares, A.M. Jorge and J.F. de Sousa. 2012. Ensemble approaches for regression: A survey. ACM Computing Surveys. 45(1): 1–10.

[27] Ren, Y., P.N. Suganthan and N. Srikanth. 2015. Ensemble methods for wind and solar power forecasting: A state-of the-art review. Renewable and Sustainable Energy Reviews. 82–91.

[28] Breiman, L. 1996. Bagging predictors. Machine Learning. 26: 123–140.

[29] Domingos, P. 1997. Why does bagging work? A Bayesian account and its implications. In the Proceedings of third International Conference on Knowledge Discovery and Data Mining. 155–158.

[30] Schapire, R. 1990. The strength of weak learnability. Machine Learning. 5: 197–227.

[31] Freund, Y. and Schapire, R. 1996. Experiments with a new boosting algorithm. Proceedings of the International Conference on Machine Learning, Murray Hill, N.J. 148–156.

[32] Hu, J. and J. Wang. 2015. Short-term wind speed prediction using empirical wavelet transform and Gaussian process regression. Energy. 93(2): 1456–1466.

[33] Jain, A.K., J. Mao and K.M. Mohiuddin. 1996. Artificial neural networks: A tutorial. Computer. 29(3): 31–44.

[34] Abiodun, O.I., A. Jantan, A.E. Omolara, K.V. Dada, A.M. Umar, O.U. Linus, et al. 2019. Comprehensive review of artificial neural network applications to pattern recognition. IEEE Access. Vol. 7. Digital Object Identifier 10.1109/ACCESS.2019.2945545.

[35] Serre, T., G. Kreiman, M. Kouh, C. Cadieu, U. Knoblich and T. Poggio. 2007. A quantitative theory of immediate visual recognition. Progress in Brain Research. 165: 33–56.

[36] Bengio, Y. and O. Delalleau. 2011. On the expressive power of deep architectures. *In*: Proceedings of the 14th International Conference on Discovery Science. Berlin: Springer-Verlag. 18–36.

[37] Mamoshina, P., A. Vieira, E. Putin and A. Zhavoronkov. 2016. Applications of deep learning in biomedicine. Molecular Pharmaceutics. 13: 1445–1454.

[38] Bowerman, B.L., R.T.O. Connell and A.B. Koehler. 2005. Forecasting, time series, and regression: An applied approach, 4th ed. The United States of America: Thomson Brooks.

[39] Chujai, P., N. Kerdprasop and K. Kerdprasop. 2013. Time series analysis of household electric consumption with ARIMA and ARMA models. Proceedings of the International Multiconference of Engineers and Computer Scientists. Vol. 1. Hong Kong: IAENG.

[40] De, V., T.T. Teo, W.L. Woo and T. Logenthiran. 2018. Photovoltaic power forecasting using LSTM on limited dataset. 2018 IEEE Innovative Smart Grid Technologies—Asia (ISGT Asia). Singapore. 710–715. doi: 10.1109/ISGT-Asia.2018.8467934.

[41] Hosseinzadeh, N., A. Al Maashri, N. Tarhuni, A. Elhaffar and A. Al-Hinai. 2021. A real-time monitoring platform for distributed energy resources in a microgrid—Pilot study in Oman. Electronics. 10(15): 1803. https://doi.org/10.3390/electronics10151803

Chapter **8**

Electricity Demand Forecasting during Special Events Using AI

Oscar Trull*[1], J. Carlos García-Díaz[1] and A. Peiró-Signes[2]

[1]Department of Applied Statistics, Operational Research and Quality, Universitat Politècnica de València, Spain

[2]Department of Business Management, Universitat Politècnica de València, Spain

8.1 INTRODUCTION

The partial or total liberalization of electricity markets in most countries has led to a radical change in how electricity markets are managed. The market has been divided into producers, transmitters, distributors, or sellers, all participating in an electricity pool where production and distribution are assigned and energy prices are established. A pool is a transaction market where producers make sales offers, and consumers make purchase offers, which help determine the cost of electricity. The electricity market system in the leading Western countries is described in detail in [1]. It is a system where decision-making is a challenge for participants. For pricing, bids are placed in the pool, and the price is set at the country's discretion. Generally, prices are set on a day-ahead basis, which may be revised occasionally throughout the day. Still, there are markets, such as some in the US and Australia, where pricing is set in real-time and updated every 5–15 minutes [2].

Within the market, transmission system operators (TSO) and distribution system operators (DSO) play a fundamental role, as the entire market depends

*For Correspondence: otrull@eio.upv.es

DOI: 10.1201/9781003541875-8

on the operators' forecasts of future demand. The (EU) 2019/944 shows the differences between TSO and DSO. Furthermore, the interconnection between different systems brings greater complexity to the functionality of TSOs. In Europe, the incorporation of the European Network for Transmission System Operators (ENTSO-e) allows access to data provided by European TSOs associated with the network [3].

The forecasts provided by TSOs are based on the use of very complex models with a large number of parameters. These models are continuously updated and require enormous computational capacity. However, one of the major problems remains the forecasts in special events, where the models encounter demands that are not regular. The models' main situations to be worked on are those produced by the calendar effect, such as holidays and long weekends.

This chapter addresses this problem from the point of view of a forecaster using artificial intelligence models to model special events. To improve forecasting in special event situations, new models are introduced that include discrete moving interval seasonality (DIMS) to improve forecasts.

The rest of the chapter is organized as follows. Section 8.2 reviews the literature related to the work. Section 8.3 describes the methods used, and Section 8.4 describes the results obtained. Finally, Section 8.5 summarises the conclusions reached.

8.2 RELATED LITERATURE

The electricity systems plan their activity based on demand forecasts made by the TSOs in the area of influence, whether at the national or regional level. Producers, DSOs, and resellers use the demand forecasts provided officially by the TSO to enter the electricity pool [4]. The system operator will establish production and consumption allocations in the pool at the price set by the marginal price system.

Introducing distributed production in homes and renewable energies increases the system's complexity and forecasts, introducing metaheuristic models for planning optimization [5]. Moreover, the trend is evolving toward DSOs increasingly taking on more responsibility for data acquisition and forecast management for regional nodes, coordinating with TSOs, and increasing the system's complexity [6]. The importance acquired by the need to make accurate forecasts has led to several competitions between academics in search of models that provide the best possible results, where TSOs have significantly been involved and have offered open data for their realization [7].

Electricity demand forecasting has generally been oriented towards statistical models, and recently, artificial intelligence models have been strongly introduced [8]. Although statistical models continue to offer excellent results today, machine learning models are gaining more and more influence among academics, and a wide variety of models are proposed based on neural networks, support vector machines, and trees [9].

However, advances in artificial intelligence are achieving more than remarkable results with forecasts. An interesting review and comparison of statistical and machine learning models is conducted in [10], comparing the accuracy results of the models using the mean average percentage error (MAPE). This work highlights how the calendar effect is influential in the results obtained and how, of the 164 articles analyzed, 66% of them use machine learning (ML) for forecasts. The commonly used ML models are K-nearest Neighbors (KNN), Random Forest (RF), Gaussian Process Regression (GPR), and Support Vector Machines (SVR), with accuracies up to 87.5% using SVR [11]. Developed SVM-based models emphasizing regional holidays are developed in [12], where an SVM model with optimization using the GWO (Gray Wolf Optimization) algorithm is proposed.

Demand forecasting on special days or events with ML uses different strategies. A continuous 24-hour demand variable staggered by one year and four binary variables have been used to determine the type of event involved [13]. This technique is common in statistical methods, where typical models include binary variables to determine these situations [14, 15].

Another approach uses an algorithm to select days similar to the holiday using Euclidean distances and calculate the average of the last three occurrences to make the forecasts [16]. This information is fed into an ANN, which includes binary variables indicating the day of the week. The forecasts are made with a 1 to 6-hour forecast and an accuracy of between 1% and 3%.

The use of reinforcement networks to improve these methodologies is shown in [17]. The working basis is that LTSM networks obtain similar MAPE but with daily forecasts, not hourly. In contrast, [18] indicates that Random Forest and XGBoost techniques offer better results. Holidays are classified in [19] according to 40 variables, including national and regional holidays and those with special causes, such as daylight-saving time. The automatic process for selecting the type of special day allows these days to be classified without the need for prior knowledge of the nature of the event [20].

A new approach of introducing holidays as a new discrete seasonality is proposed in [21], which is included at the level of input variables for both statistical and ML models.

8.3 METHODS AND MATERIALS

8.3.1 Artificial Neural Network

Artificial neural networks (ANN) are a tool commonly used in forecasting. It is based on the creation of a network of nodes, called neurons, organised in layers, which are capable of, once trained, being able to offer excellent forecasts. The concept of a neuron is based on an alleged similarity between the node and the functioning of human neurons. In reality, it is a node that receives information through weighted inputs, and the output is obtained through a function (called an activation function). This is shown in Figure 8.1.

Each neuron is connected to previous information ($I_{i,1 \ldots n}$), which can come from the original working variables or other neurons. This information in numerical format is weighted by the factor $W_{i,1 \ldots n}$ and added. This operation can also include a bias b_i, to correct displacements within the information. This aggregated set goes through an activation function (f), which determines the importance of this obtained information. With this, an output O_i is generated and used in the network. The operations performed by the neuron can be summarised in the equation (1).

$$O_i = f(\Sigma w^T I + b_i) \tag{1}$$

The importance of activation function is vital because it helps to determine within the network which neurons acquire more significant importance than others. There are different types of activation functions, but the most common are the sigmoid, tanh, and *ReLu* functions.

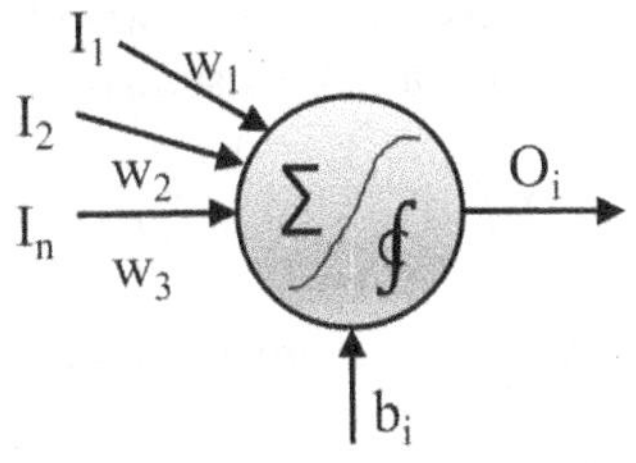

Figure 8.1 ANN neuron schema.

The arrangement and quantity of neurons determine how the network works. Thus, some neurons are placed at the beginning of the network and receive information from the variables. These are known as the input layer (see Figure 8.2). At the end of the network, there is a layer of neurons that collect the information and whose outputs are the response variable being sought. This layer is called the output layer.

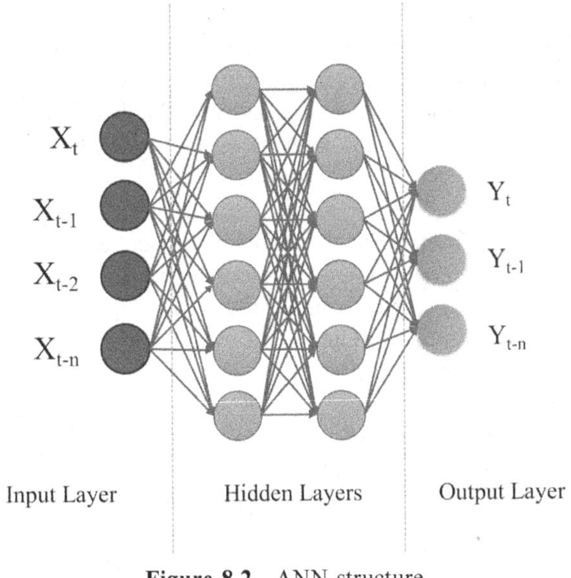

Figure 8.2 ANN structure.

Finally, there is an intermediate zone where neurons are interconnected, receiving information from other neurons and sending their processed output to other neurons. This is the hidden layer of the network. Understanding the inner workings of this layer to fit the problem is too complex, which is why we call neural networks black box models. The network shown in Figure 8.5 is a shallow network with two hidden layers. The typology, activation functions, layers, etc., are characteristics of the network that personalise the results obtained for each case. This is why they are commonly called hyperparameters and must be adjusted for each case.

For the network to be functional, it is necessary to set the values of the weights and biases so that the network produces adjusted forecasts. To do this, the network is trained to minimise the error committed, measured by a metric, usually the Mean Squared Error (MSE), as shown in (2).

$$MSE = \frac{1}{n}\sum_{t=1}^{n}(y_t - \hat{y}_t)^2 \tag{2}$$

Where y_t are the observed values, $\hat{y}_t$ are the predicted values by the network and n is the total number of observations.

The main problem with using networks is determining which variables to introduce into the system and how to do so. The information provided is essential to achieving good results.

8.3.2 Long Short-Term Memory Networks

In recent years, there has been a boom in applications of LSTM networks. These networks originate in recurrent neural networks (RNN), whose recurrence gives them short-term memory. This is shown in Figure 8.3a. Unlike the previous neural network, this network adds to the outputs y_t from the inputs x_t a hidden state vector a_t (called a recurrent unit), which allows it to work in different time steps, which is why it is said to offer it with memory. The hidden state vector is updated at each new time step and is used as feedback for the network. The mathematical representation of the network is shown in (3).

$$a_t = f(w_a^T a_{t-1} + w_x^T x_t + b) \tag{3}$$

where w_a is the weight matrix for the connections between a_t and a_{t-1}, and w_x is the weight matrix for the connections between inputs and hidden states at time t.

This memory is only short-term. LSTM networks can solve this problem. Figure 8.3b shows the structure of an LSTM unit. First, a memory section called a memory cell c_t is added, with a series of gates that perform different functions: the forget gate, which allows elements to be removed from the memory cell; the update gate, which adds new elements to the memory cell; and finally, the output cell, which updates the state of the hidden state vector (a_t). Each of these gates comprises neural networks that allow the flow of information to pass through according to the purpose for which they are included. Sigmoid functions allow the "opening" and "closing" of the gates. The data flow proceeds as shown in Figure 8.4.

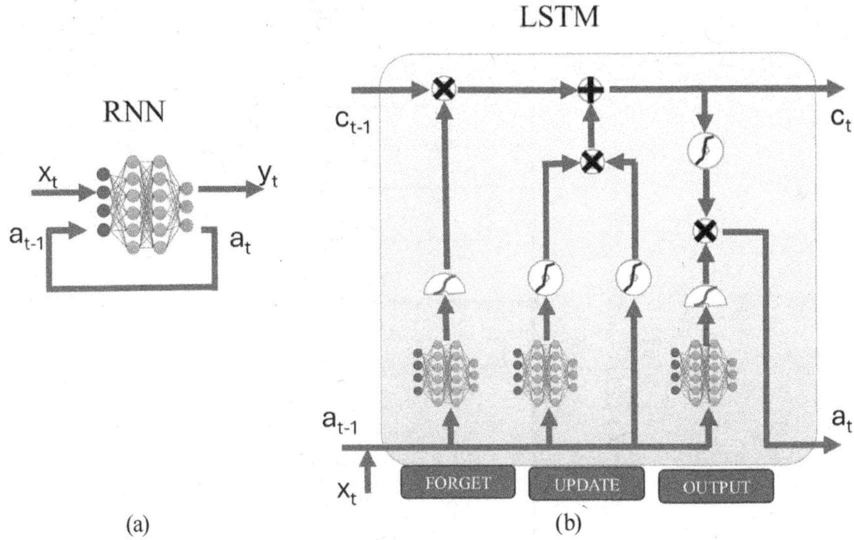

(a) (b)

Figure 8.3 RNN and LSTM network architecture.

Data is added sequentially; forecasts are obtained while the hidden state vector and the memory cell are updated. This is a basic structure. There are then numerous specific typologies for this type of network. The networks are trained and work similarly, minimising the forecast error.

8.3.3 Ensemble Bagging Trees

The use of ensemble models in machine learning is becoming increasingly common. The philosophy behind this methodology is based on combining forecasts made by simple models, which become highly accurate. Three main ensemble learning methods exist: bagging, boosting, and gradient boosting. This work focuses on bagging trees (BT), which have been used to generate forecasts.

The essential operation of decision trees is based on randomly dividing the training data into two parts and fitting a decision tree to both halves. Bootstrap aggregation or bagging is a general-purpose procedure applied to decision trees that allows for reducing the variance of a statistical learning method. The process consists of building different subsets from a data set to bootstrap (B), and producing forecasts $\widehat{f^i}(B_i)$ for each subset B_i, as shown in (4). The diagram in Figure 8.5 reflects the workflow.

$$\widehat{f}^1(B_1), \widehat{f}^2(B_2), \widehat{f}^3(B_3), \ldots, \widehat{f}^B(B_B) \tag{4}$$

Once the forecasts for each subset have been made, the average is obtained and used as the final forecast (5).

$$\hat{y}_t = \widehat{f}(B) = \frac{1}{B}\sum_{i=1}^{B} f^i(B_i) \tag{5}$$

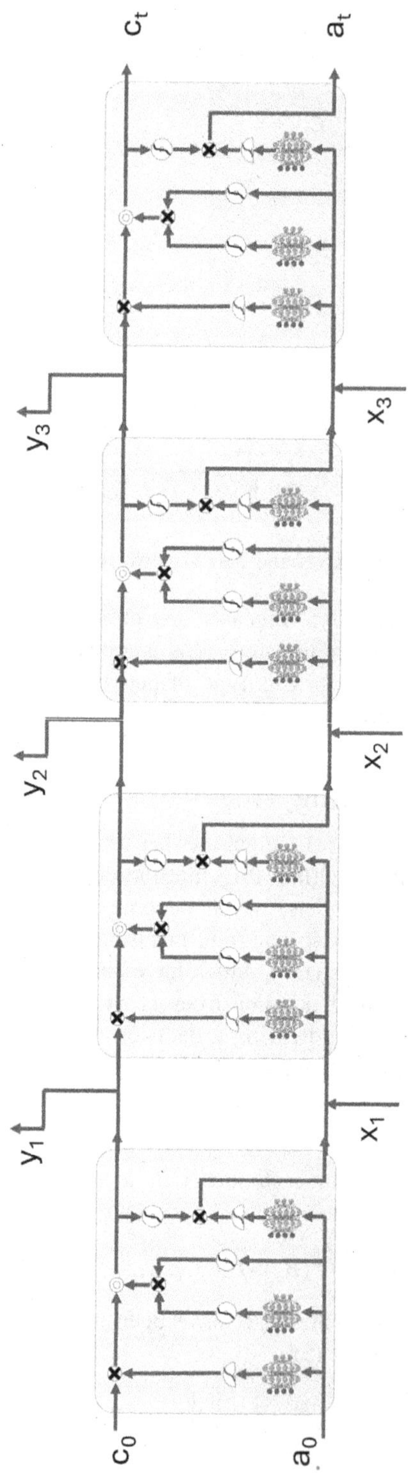

Figure 8.4 Data flow in LSTM cells.

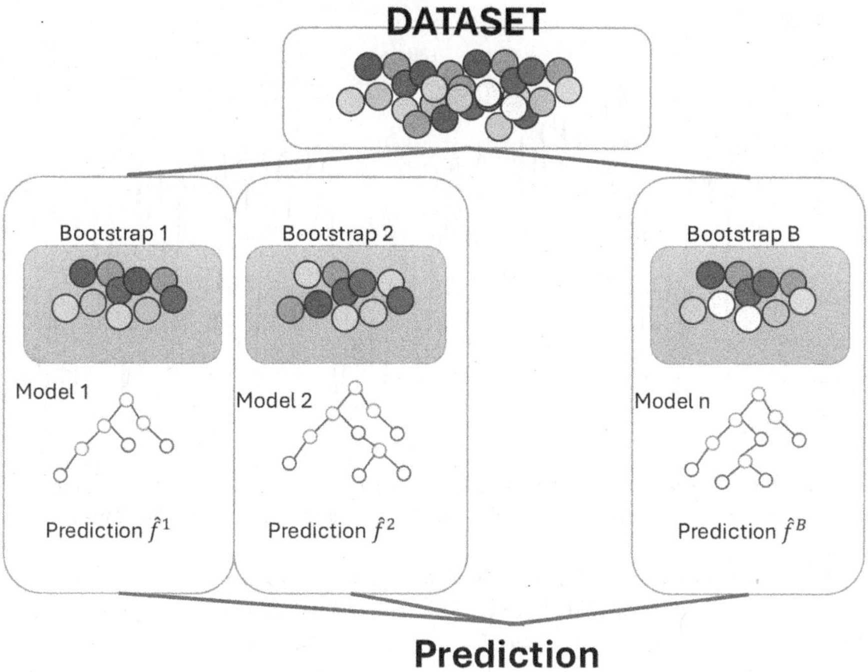

Figure 8.5 Workflow with ensemble bagged tree.

The training process consists of the following steps: First, *B* bootstrap samples are obtained from the training data. These samples allow the creation of many data subsets that meet the following conditions: they follow the same distribution, although they are slightly different. Next, for each sample obtained, an unpruned regression tree is trained. Finally, the individual forecasts of each tree are averaged to create an overall average predicted value. Cross-validation techniques are used to avoid overfitting.

8.3.4 Dataset

A diverse dataset has been chosen, and different circumstances are presented. On the one hand, from Red Eléctrica de España (REE), the Spanish TSO, the peninsular electricity demand in Spain has been used. These hourly data are accessible through its website, www.ree.es. On the other hand, the hourly demand series in France managed by Réseau de Transport d'Electricité français (RTE), the French TSO operator, has also been used. These have been obtained from the ENTSO-e platform. They are available directly from RTE, but using data directly from the European platform was considered appropriate. Finally, the average hourly demand data for England and Wales, provided by National Grid UK, the DSO (or distribution network operator) for this area, was also used.

Figure 8.6 shows the electricity demand in Spain from April 2017 to 2018. 2017 Easter took place on April 16, while in 2018, it took place on April 1.

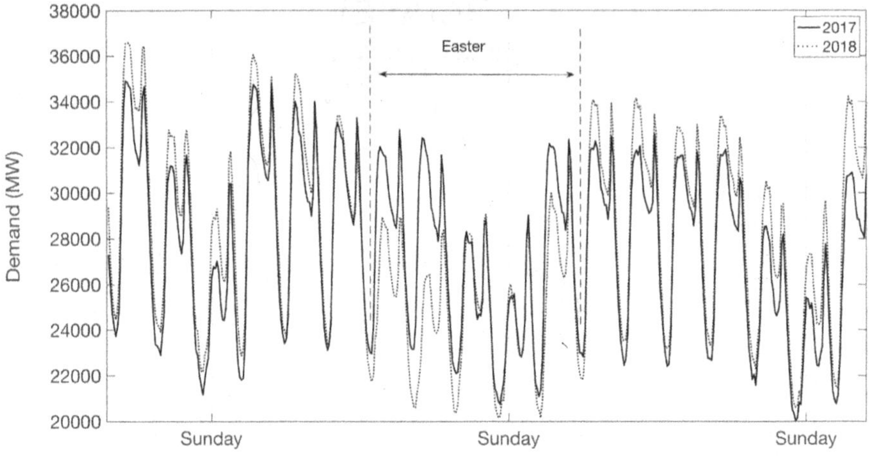

Figure 8.6 Representation of two weeks of Spanish' hourly electricity demand. It compares the electricity demand between 2017 and 2018 (Easter holidays).

The effect produced by Easter can be seen in the comparison, which influences approximately five days (120 hours). This special event occurs differently each year since, depending on the year, Easter Monday and/or Easter Thursday may or may not be a holiday. Similarly, Figure 8.7 shows another situation within the French hourly demand. It is presented in May 2017 and 2018. On these dates, the days of May 8 (Victory Day) and Ascension Thursday (May 10) occur. These situations are marked with an h in the graph.

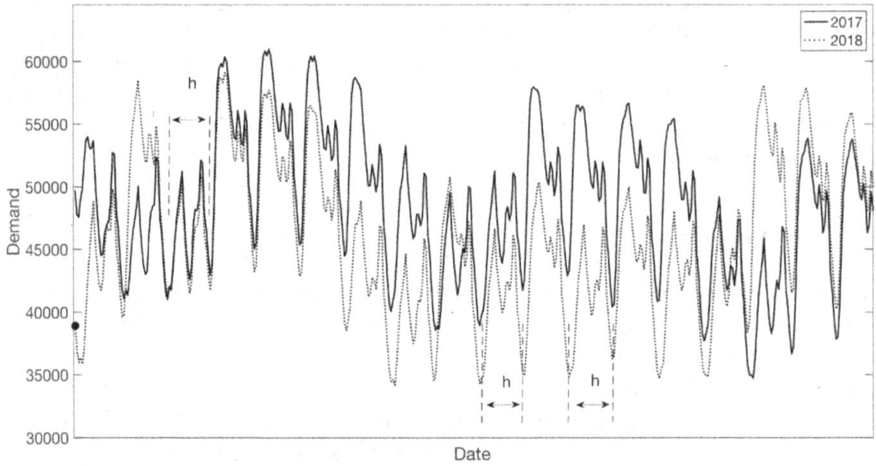

Figure 8.7 Representation of France's hourly electricity demand in May 2017 and 2018. Holidays are marked with *h*.

This time, it is less obvious to see the effect because the average consumption in that week and the previous one in 2017 was higher than in 2018. However, it can be observed how on the days marked with an h, which are holidays, the behaviour of the series becomes irregular, with a decrease in consumption sometimes comparable to that of a Sunday. This moment has been chosen because the effect of two holidays in the same week can be observed. Although it is not the subject of this work, it can be seen how the demand that week is lower than that of the previous year. This drop in consumption is clearly an effect produced by the long weekends or even the whole week.

Figure 8.8 shows electricity demand for England and Wales in Easter week in 2018. This time around, Easter falls only on Monday, 2 April.

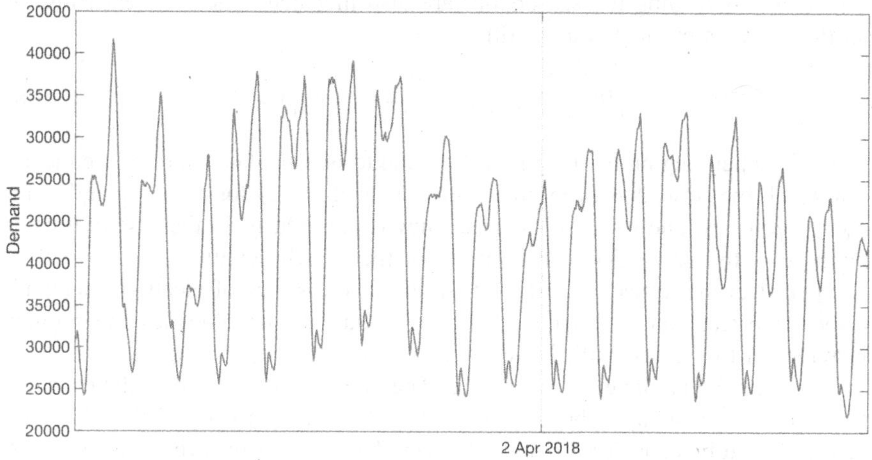

Figure 8.8 Electricity demand in England and Wales at Easter 2018.

Easter Monday is in similar demand to the previous Sunday. This justifies why, on many occasions, public holidays are simply substituted as Sundays for forecasts.

8.3.5 Strategies for Electricity Demand Forecasting with Special Events

This work uses different artificial intelligence models to forecast electrical demand, emphasising special events. A fundamental aspect of electricity demand forecast is the selection of variables to train the model. It can be found in the literature that climatological variables play an essential role. This can be explained if an air temperature value or other representative climatological variables are found. For short-term forecasts, it is not interesting or is not productive in many cases. As indicated in [22], the seasonality already includes this daily temperature variation when making short-term forecasts. In the case of a special situation, it should be considered a special event. We have, therefore, decided not to use climatological variables. This will not affect the forecasts' results.

All electricity demand series generally have more than one seasonality, reflected by intra-day and intra-weekly seasonality. This implies the need to include a variable that indicates the day of the week on which consumption occurs and when it takes place. To include the seasonal effect in the model, it is expected to include lagged variables as in (6–7).

$$y_{intraday} = L^{24}(y_t), y_{intraweek} = L^{168}(y_t), \quad \text{for hourly data} \tag{6}$$

$$y_{intraday} = L^{48}(y_t), y_{intraweek} = L^{336}(y_t), \quad \text{for half-hourly data} \tag{7}$$

To include possible long-term variation (trend), moving average variables immediately preceding the seasonality are also included, where for each instant t in the series is calculated as in (8).

$$y_t^{ma,s} = \frac{1}{s}(y_{t-s-1} + y_{t-s} + \cdots + y_{t-1}) \tag{8}$$

Here, depending on the length of the trend to be calculated and the frequency with which the series has been obtained, it is used $s = 24$ for a daily length with hourly frequency, and $s = 48$ if the frequency is half hourly. In the case of greater lengths, $s = 168$ or $s = 336$ can be used for the weekly length.

Special events cause irregular situations in the series of electrical demand. A special effect can be attributed to any situation that modifies the regular behaviour of the series. Still, in general, the interest in their study is focused on those that can be predicted in the future. They are usually related to the calendar effect, such as a holiday, but it does not have to be limited to that. A strike situation could be considered a special event. The World Cup's final match or the Super Bowl can be a special event. For this work, only those special events related to the calendar effect have been considered; thus, holidays and long weekends have been considered.

There are a wide variety of methods for including special events in models. However, the most widespread way is, without a doubt, the use of binary variables that allow the original model to be modified and the necessary variations to be introduced to adapt to the demand of that situation. Another variant is to consider the holiday a similar Sunday and make forecasts as if it were that Sunday. The results are usually entirely accurate given the stability that generally characterises this series type.

To improve the accuracy of the forecasts, a new methodology, in which the effect on demand for the special event is included as part of the model through discrete seasonalities (DIMS), was introduced. By introducing this new seasonality, the model receives more information about the behaviour of the series during special events and will be able to predict demand in these situations with greater accuracy.

DIMS are obtained by the decomposition of multiple seasonal trends by Loess (MSTL) with DIMS, as indicated in [23]. Three special events have been established: holidays, long weekends, and, in the case of Spanish demand, Easter. If they coincide on a weekend, it has not been considered. It may be that by state decision, a holiday that falls on a weekend is moved to a Monday or Friday. This case is considered if this change is national and affects the series.

The incorporation of the DIMS is carried out by including two continuous variables (3 in the case of Spanish demand) with the effects produced in the series by the DIMS. When there is no event, this effect is considered null. Additionally, and to help the algorithm better adjust the data, a qualitative variable is added to indicate the type of special event.

8.4 RESULTS

This section presents the results obtained after implementing three ML methods: Artificial Neural Networks (ANN), Long Short-Term Memory Networks (LSTM), and Bagging Trees (BT). To evaluate the effectiveness of these methods, the dataset was divided into two subsets: one used for training and in-sample testing, and another reserved for out-of-sample validation. This way ensures a robust evaluation of the models, guaranteeing that the results obtained are representative and generalisable to unseen situations during training. The MSE was used to train the models. Hyperparameter tuning was performed by evaluating the efficiency of the forecasts on the in-sample validation subset. Subsequently, the best-performing model for each methodology was selected to compare their forecasts on the out-of-sample data, which were made 24 hours ahead, day by day, and compared with the actual values using the MAPE.

The analysis was carried out using the three demand series included in the dataset. For the Spanish demand series, the data were taken from July 2, 2007, to December 31, 2018, to carry out training and validation within the sample and in 2018 to perform the analysis outside the sample. The French demand series included the data from January 1, 2006, to July 2, 2018, for training and validation and from November 1, 2018 to October 31, 2019, for the analysis outside the sample. The demand series for England and Wales used data from January 1, 2005, to December 31, 2018, for training and validation and from January 1, 2019, to December 31, 2019, for the analysis outside the sample. A summary of the events considered in each subset can be seen in Table 8.1.

Table 8.1 Summary of the special events considered in the analysis. Headers show the year 20' ('08 means 2008)

	'08	'09	'10	'11	'12	'13	'14	'15	'16	'17	'18	'19
Spain												
Holidays	5	6	6	6	7	6	5	6	7	8	7	6
Long Week	3	4	3	5	5	2	3	4	4	3	5	2
Easter	1	1	1	1	1	1	1	1	1	1	1	1
France												
Holidays	8	8	6	6	7	9	9	8	7	8	8	6
Long Week	5	4	2	3	5	3	6	4	3	2	5	2
UK												
Holidays	6	6	6	6	6	6	6	6	6	6	6	6
Long Week	2	3	2	0	2	3	2	3	0	0	2	3

The complexity of forecasting for public holidays can be seen in the table. There are 6 public holidays per year in Spain and the UK and 7.5 in France, compared to 250 working days. The complexity increases with public holidays, with an average of 4 for Spain and France and 2 for the UK. Only one has been considered when two or more holidays coincide.

The first comparison between models is made in the forecasts without contemplating using the DIMS as a base of the analysis to understand better how the algorithm increases precision. To compare, the MAPE is used as indicated in (9). This metric is the most common for forecast comparisons in demand for electricity—a 24-hour sliding window made t.

$$MAPE(h) = \frac{1}{h}\sum_{t=1}^{h}\left|\frac{\hat{y}_t - y_t}{y_t}\right| \tag{9}$$

Table 8.2 shows the means of the MAPE of the forecasts of each country. This is the average of the MAPE 24 hours of the forecasts during the entire period outside the sample.

Table 8.2 MAPE comparison for forecasts without using DIMS

	WITH NO DIMS			WITH DIMS		
	LSTM	**ANN**	**BT**	**LSTM**	**ANN**	**BT**
Spain	4.00	2.27	2.28	3.66	2.13	2.20
France	5.85	3.52	3.51	5.51	3.48	3.59
England and Wales	7.34	3.87	4.94	6.88	3.84	4.05

It can be observed that the introduction of DIMS has improved the forecasts. The improvement is not proportional in all cases. For example, the most remarkable improvement occurred in the Spanish case in the ANN models. In the case of England and Wales, the most significant improvement occurs in the BT models. In the French case, the BT models have worsened. LSTM networks have not been able to improve the ANN and BT regression models. This corroborates the conclusions made by Hong. Ultimately, the demand series are very stable, and accurate forecasts can be made with relatively simple models.

To check the performance of the improvements, some examples chosen from all the holidays and long weekends are shown. Figure 8.9 shows the forecasts made by the ANN models with and without DIMS for May 1, 2019, in France. These models were the ones that made the best forecasts on this day.

It can be seen that, since it is a public holiday, demand falls considerably. When including the DIMS, the model predicts a drop in demand that the regular model could not predict. This public holiday occurred on a Wednesday, which should not have significantly influenced the rest of the days of that week. However, as can be seen, for some reason not analysed by the model, demand fell more than expected that week.

Another situation in which DIMS helps improve forecasts is Easter. Figure 8.10 shows the comparison for demand at Easter 2019 in Spain. This situation affects Holy Thursday, Good Friday, and Easter Monday.

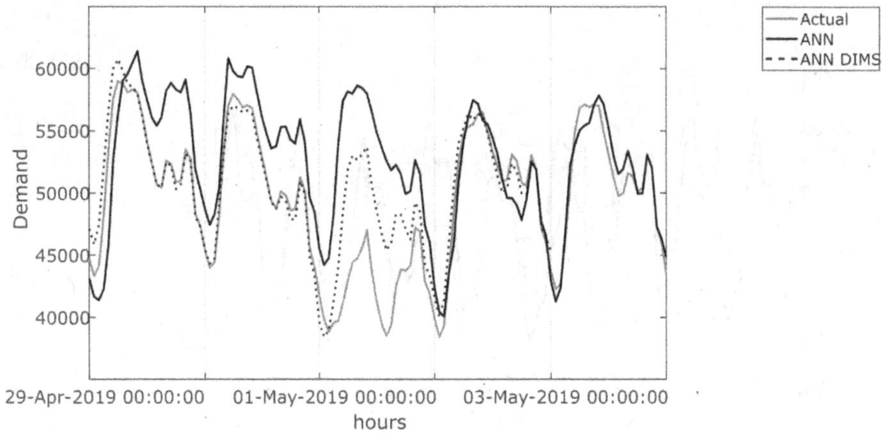

Figure 8.9 Comparison of forecasted demand for 1st May 2019 in France.

It can be seen how ANN models with DIMS adjust the forecasts much better than ANNs. Holy Thursday is still complex to forecast. This situation is due to the fact that, as previously mentioned, Thursday is not a holiday throughout Spain, and it is not always a holiday in the same regions. However, Friday and Monday are forecast with great accuracy.

Finally, Christmas week in England and Wales (Figure 8.11) were compared. This week is very complex for forecasts. Several consecutive days of public holidays that move throughout the week and with long weekends in between make the forecasts less accurate. In particular, Christmas Eve is a real challenge for the model.

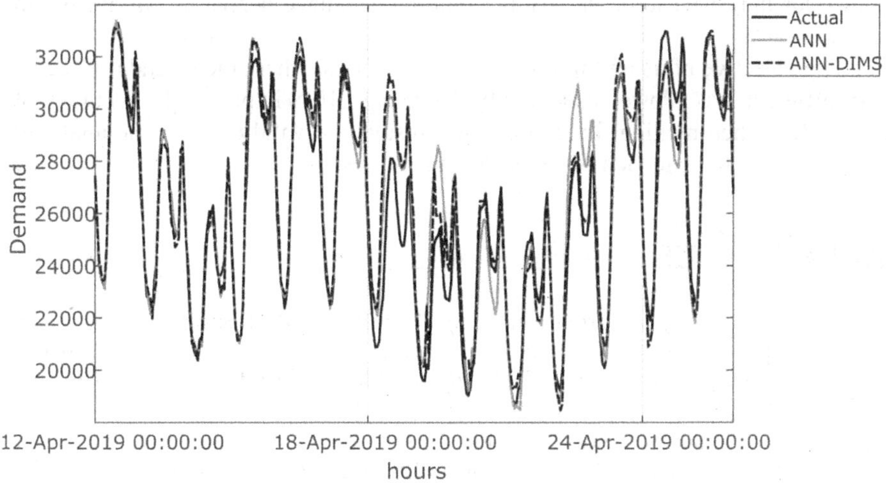

Figure 8.10 Comparison of forecasted demand in Easter 2019 in Spain.

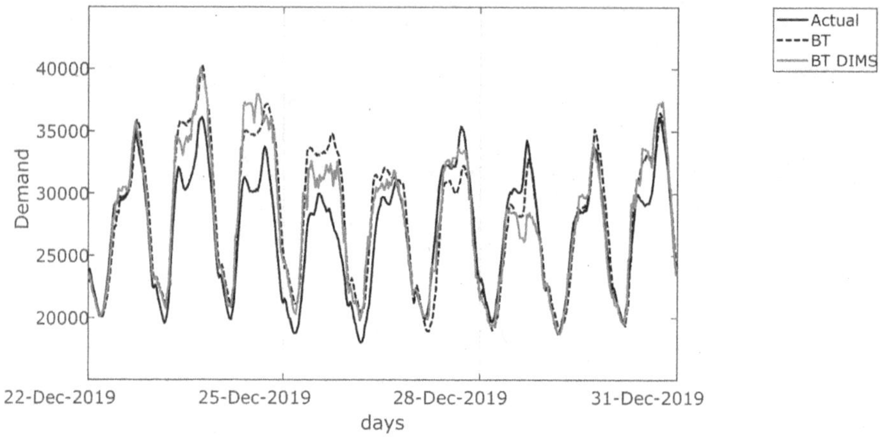

Figure 8.11 Comparison of forecasted demand for Christmas in England and Wales.

8.5 CONCLUSIONS

Artificial intelligence models offer a plausible alternative for short-term electricity demand forecast. The models developed here are based on LSTM networks, artificial neural networks, and Bagged Tree ensemble models, which have been applied to three electricity demand series from three countries, two TSOs, and one DSO. The models were analysed with forecasts for one day ahead and generated forecasts below 5% of MAPE.

To improve forecasts on days when an event occurs, the use of discrete moving interval seasonality (DIMS) has been included in the models, which allows for improved forecasts. Thus, some models have decreased MAPE by up to 1%.

The objective of using three very different series, where the calendar effect is very different, has allowed us to verify that using DIMS improves the accuracy of the models when making forecasts. These results are valid only for the analysed series but can be extended to other demand series.

REFERENCES

[1] Conejo, A.J., M. Carrión and J.M. Morales. 2010. Decision making under uncertainty in electricity markets. *In*: International Series in Operations Research and Management Science. Vol. 153. Boston, MA: Springer US. doi: 10.1007/978-1-4419-7421-1.

[2] Mayer, K. and S. Trück. 2018. Electricity markets around the world. Journal of Commodity Markets. 9: 77–100. doi: 10.1016/j.jcomm.2018.02.001.

[3] ENTSO-E Market Committee. 2024. ENTSO-E. Accessed: Sep. 01, 2024. [Online]. Available: https://www.entsoe.eu/

[4] Sioshansi, F. 2011. Competitive Electricity Markets: Design, Implementation, Performance. Elsevier.

[5] Jordehi, A.R. 2015. Optimisation of electric distribution systems: A review. Renewable and Sustainable Energy Reviews. 51: 1088-1100. doi: 10.1016/j.rser.2015.07.004.

[6] Küfeoğlu, S., M. Pollitt and K. Anaya. 2018. Electric Power Distribution in the World: Today and Tomorrow. [Online]. Available: https://about.jstor.org/terms

[7] Hong, T., J. Xie and J. Black. 2019. Global energy forecasting competition 2017: Hierarchical probabilistic load forecasting. International Journal of Forecast. 35(4): 1389–1399. doi: 10.1016/j.ijforecast.2019.02.006.

[8] Weron, R. 2006. Modeling and Forecasting Electricity Loads and Prices: A Statistical Approach. Chichester, England: John Wiley & Sons, Ltd.

[9] Hong, T. and P. Wang. 2022. Artificial intelligence for load forecasting: history, illusions and opportunities. IEEE Power and Energy Magazine. 20(3): 14–23. doi: 10.1109/MPE.2022.3150808.

[10] Vivas, E., H. Allende-Cid and R. Salas. 2020. A systematic review of statistical and machine learning methods for electrical power forecasting with reported MAPE score. Entropy. 22(12): 1412. doi: 10.3390/e22121412.

[11] Gonzalez-Briones, A., G. Hernandez, J.M. Corchado, S. Omatu and M.S. Mohamad. 2019. Machine learning models for electricity consumption forecasting: A review. *In*: ICCAIS 2019: 2nd International Conference on Computer Applications and Information Security: 01–03 May, 2019. Riyadh (Kingdom of Saudi Arabia): Institute of Electrical and Electronics Engineers.1–6.

[12] Barman, M. and N.B. Dev Choudhury. 2020. A similarity based hybrid GWO-SVM method of power system load forecasting for regional special event days in anomalous load situations in Assam, India. Sustainable Cities and Society. 61: 102311. doi: 10.1016/j.scs.2020.102311.

[13] Kim, K.-H., H.-S. Youn and Y.-C. Kang. 2000. Short-term load forecasting for special days in anomalous load conditions using neural networks and fuzzy inference method. IEEE Transactions on Power Systems. 15(2): 559–565. doi: 10.1109/59.867141.

[14] Lamedica, R. and A. Prudenzi. 1996. A neural network based technique for short-term forecasting of anomalous load periods. IEEE Transactions on Power Systems. 11(4): 1749–1756. doi: 10.1109/59.544638.

[15] Kim, M.S. 2013. Modeling special-day effects for forecasting intraday electricity demand. European Journal of Operational Research. 230(1): 170–180. doi: 10.1016/j.ejor.2013.03.039.

[16] Mandal, P., T. Senjyu, N. Urasaki and T. Funabashi. 2006. A neural network based several-hour-ahead electric load forecasting using similar days approach. International Journal of Electrical Power and Energy Systems. 28(6): 367–373. doi: 10.1016/j.ijepes.2005.12.007.

[17] Park, R.-J., K.-B. Song and B.-S. Kwon. 2020. Short-term load forecasting algorithm using a similar day selection method based on reinforcement learning. Energies. 13(10): 2640. doi: 10.3390/en13102640.

[18] Vantuch, T., A.G. Vidal, A.P. Ramallo-González, A.F. Skarmeta and S. Misák. 2018. Machine learning based electric load forecasting for short and long-term period. *In*: 2018 IEEE 4th World Forum on Internet of Things (WF-IoT). 511–516. doi: 10.1109/WF-IoT.2018.8355123.

[19] López, M., C. Sans, S. Valero and C. Senabre 2019. Classification of special days in short-term load forecasting: The spanish case study. Energies. 12(7): 1253. doi: 10.3390/en12071253.

[20] López, M., C. Sans and S. Valero. 2022. Automatic classification of special days for short-term load forecasting. Electric Power Systems Research. Vol. 202: 107533. doi: 10.1016/j.epsr.2021.107533.

[21] Trull, O., J.C. García-Díaz and A. Peiró-Signes. 2024. MSF, a forecasting library to predict short-term electricity demand based on multiple seasonal time series. Journal of Computer Science. 78: 102280. doi: 10.1016/j.jocs.2024.102280.

[22] Taylor, J.W., L.M. de Menezes and P.E. McSharry. 2006. A comparison of univariate methods for forecasting electricity demand up to a day ahead. International Journal of Forecast. 22(1): 1–16. doi: 10.1016/j.ijforecast.2005.06.006.

[23] Trull, O., J.C. García-Díaz and A. Peiró-Signes. 2022. Multiple seasonal STL decomposition with discrete-interval moving seasonalities. Applied Mathematics and Computation. 433: 127398. doi: 10.1016/j.amc.2022.127398.

Chapter 9

Predicting Peak Energy Demand Using Machine Learning Techniques for Efficient Electricity Supply Management

Imrus Salehin*[1, 2], Nazmul Huda Badhon[1]
Md. Tomal Ahmed Sajib[1], Md Sakibul Hassan Rifat[3]
and Nazmun Nessa Moon[1]

[1]Department of Computer Science and Engineering,
Daffodil International University, Dhaka, Bangladesh

[2]Information Convergence Engineering,
Pusan National University, Busan, Republic of Korea

[3]Department of Computer Science and Engineering,
Bangladesh University of Business & Technology, Dhaka, Bangladesh

9.1 INTRODUCTION

In this era, we cannot even think of our life without electricity as it has become the primary energy source. Electrical energy systems have become indispensable as it has a huge impact on human life. The primary objective of developing national systems for electric energy is to reliably and sustainably meet the energy

*For Correspondence: salehin@pusan.ac.kr

DOI: 10.1201/9781003541875-9

demand and annual peak load [1]. Forecasting the energy demand and annual peak load is the first step in developing a reliable and secure electric power system. Inaccurate forecasts can cause misestimation of national energy needs, leading to loaded losses or unnecessary investments.

This chapter focuses on long-term energy demand forecasting and yearly peak load for large-scale energy systems expansion and refurbishment. Predicting annual peak load, the highest yearly load curve value is challenging due to long-term uncertainty. We have applied machine learning and deep learning techniques to enhance prediction accuracy. We have used the BanE-16 [2] dataset for this study.

We have used historical load data (2018–2023) meteorological factors (wind, temperature, pressure, humidity), and other variables to train deep learning models for peak demand forecasting. Real-time updates ensure accuracy, creating a robust system for precise energy management and infrastructure planning.

The main contributions of our study are:

- Using new electrical grid data to forecast peak energy demand.
- Employing Machine Learning models (Random Forest, Multiple Linear Regression) and a Deep Learning model (ANN) for robust forecasting.

Our findings show that machine learning, particularly the Random Forest model, achieved better accuracy in energy demand forecasting, contributing to improved planning and reliability of energy systems. Accurate load forecasting allows better resource allocation, reduces overload risks, and enhances the sustainability and resilience of power networks.

9.2 LITERATURE REVIEW

The energy crisis is a major threat to national economies, inflicting extensive economic damage that affects growth. A critical challenge is the negative impact on industrial development and output due to insufficient and unstable electricity supply. With power shortages disrupting industrial operations, production levels struggle to be maintained. This leads to a decrease in available goods and a sharp rise in the cost of everyday items. The resulting inflation intensifies the economic strain on the country, making it increasingly difficult to pursue sustainable and long-term progress [3, 4].

A novel method for accurate and reliable electric device consumption and peak demand forecasting was developed using advanced methods like CLARA clustering, SVM, and ANN. Utilizing smart meter data from 995 houses, the effectiveness of integrating R programming language for clustering and Matlab for preprocessing and forecasting emphasizes the potential of machine learning techniques in enhancing energy demand management [5]. Pooling-based Deep Recurrent Neural Network (PDRNN) for household short-term load forecasting (STLF), effectively addressing overfitting by pooling load profiles before processing them through a Deep RNN. Their method outperforms traditional models like ARIMA, SVR, and classical Deep RNNs, demonstrating significant improvements in forecasting accuracy and potential applications in smart grid energy management [6].

A Long Short-Term Memory (LSTM) based model for forecasting monthly residential electricity demand, integrating social and weather-related variables utilizes 22 years of data from South Korea, the model demonstrates exceptional forecasting performance across six metrics, significantly outperforming four benchmark models [7]. The proposed LSTM model offers a powerful tool for enhancing decision-making in power-system planning, ensuring more accurate predictions of residential electricity demand, and contributing to the efficient utilization of energy resources. Regression-based machine learning techniques to forecast short-term electrical load for the Jajpur grid, with Rational Quadratic Gaussian Process Regression (GPR) achieving the lowest RMSE of 2.0466, making it the most accurate model. However, GPR's complexity resulted in the highest computation time among all models. Support Vector Machine (SVM) was the second-best algorithm with an RMSE of 2.0871 and significantly faster computation time, offering a practical trade-off between accuracy and efficiency. The study suggests that expanding the dataset and incorporating additional predictive variables could further enhance the model's performance, with potential improvements also achievable through hyperparameter tuning [8].

9.3 DATA PROCESSING

Data processing plays a crucial role in this chapter, particularly in the application of machine learning. Proper data preparation is essential, as issues such as missing values, outliers, and noisy data can negatively impact prediction accuracy. Therefore, significant effort should be dedicated to data collection and preprocessing. Effective data preparation involves several key steps, including data cleaning, integration, transformation, and reduction, all of which contribute to improving the overall quality and reliability of the dataset. Figure 9.1 illustrates the process of splitting the data for use.

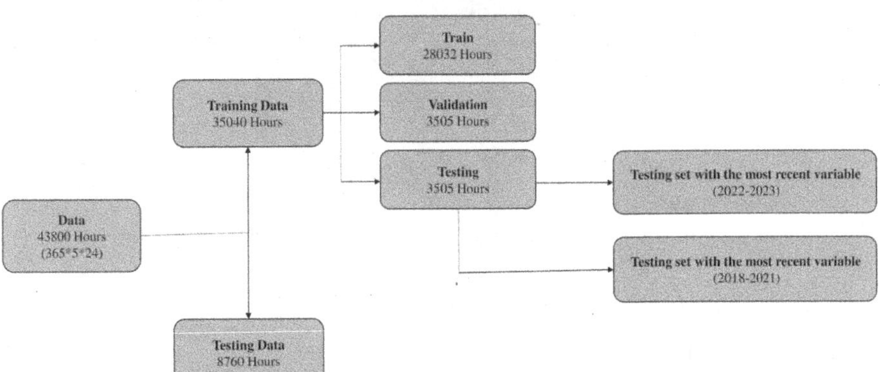

Figure 9.1 The original dataset [2] is split into testing and training data. The remaining training data followed the typical division: 80% for training, 10% for validation, and 10% for testing.

9.3.1 Data Collection

The Bangladesh Power Development Board (BPDB) is the source of the dataset that encompasses data from seven zones, spanning the period from January 2018 to April 2023. The primary variable under study is peak energy consumption, which is influenced by weather factors such as temperature, wind speed, humidity, cloud cover, and rainfall. Data collection is conducted using BPDB's daily records to maintain consistency and reliability. The objective of this chapter is to examine the significance of weather conditions on the demand for energy in Bangladesh.

9.3.2 Data Preprocessing

Figure 9.2 depicts the correlation analysis of the primary data variables, including rainfall, wind speed, humidity, temperature (average, maximum, and minimum), peak energy consumption, and cloud cover. This analysis reveals the relationships

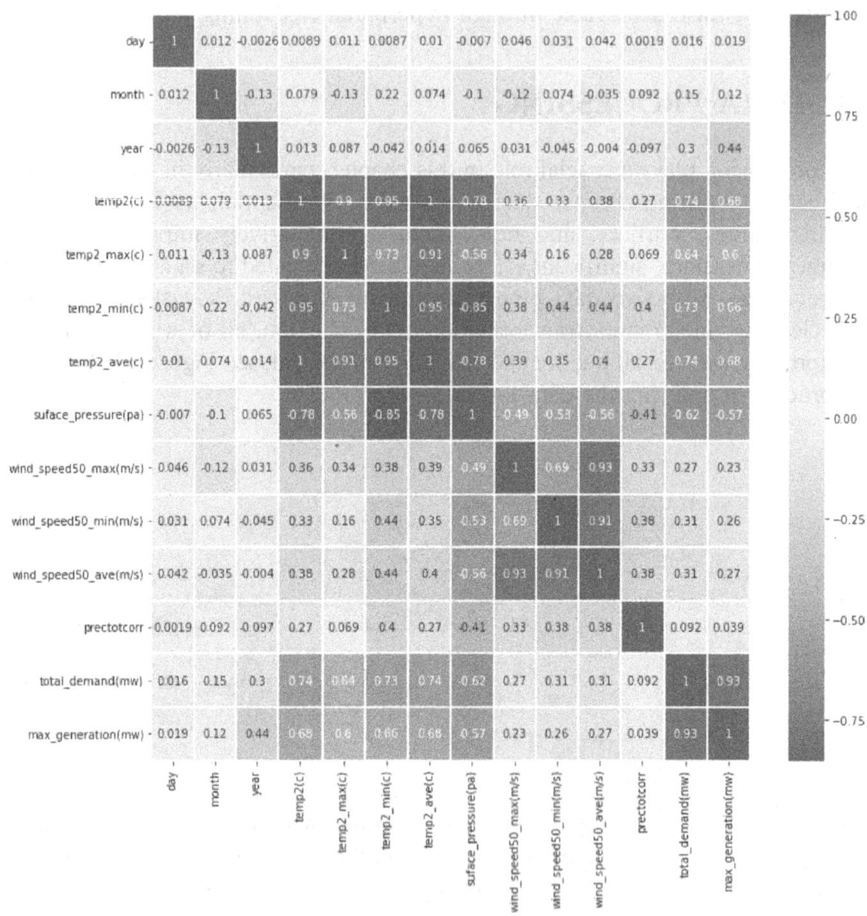

Figure 9.2 Correlations heatmap between data.

between these variables, providing insights into how weather affects peak energy consumption in Bangladesh.

The missing data in peak energy consumption and generation statistics, underscoring the need to identify gaps despite their small proportion, is highlighted in Figure 9.3.

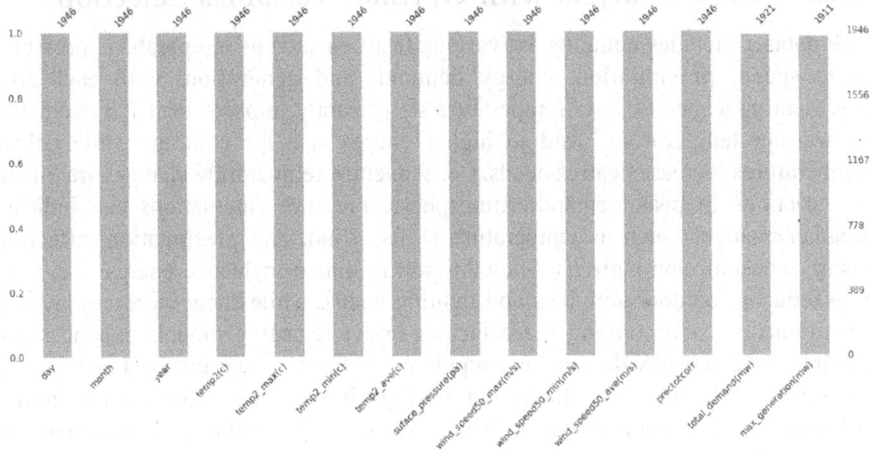

Figure 9.3 Missing values of demand and generation.

The results of data preprocessing, as shown in Figure 9.4, focus on the imputation of missing values and indicate that preprocessing effectively addressed the missing data issue, making the dataset ready for analysis and modeling.

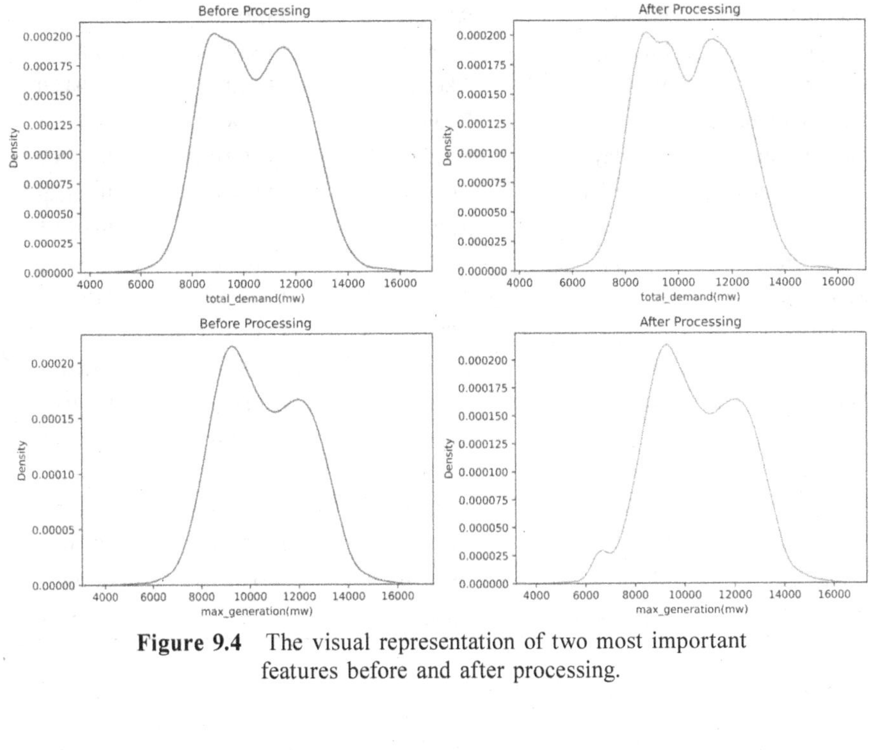

Figure 9.4 The visual representation of two most important features before and after processing.

Additionally, log transformation was applied to the target column to reduce skewness and stabilize variance, improving model performance for skewed or exponentially distributed features.

9.3.3 Data Analysis with Optimal Variables Selection

The dataset includes columns for various features such as temperature, pressure, wind speed, precipitation, energy demand, and generation, with each row representing a specific day. Temperature significantly impacts electricity demand, as warmer temperatures lead to higher energy use for cooling, while colder temperatures increase heating needs. Consequently, temperature changes are linked to variations in peak demand. Atmospheric pressure fluctuations can indicate weather changes, such as temperature shifts, wind, and precipitation, affecting energy consumption patterns. Snowfall and rain also influence energy use, with rain reducing outdoor activities and lighting needs, while snow increases heating requirements. Incorporating these factors into forecasting models enhances the accuracy of electricity demand and supply predictions, as summarized in Table 9.1 by season and day and illustrated in Figure 9.5 with seasonal minimum, maximum, and average values, which is vital for grid stability, cost management, and optimizing energy production.

Table 9.1 Demand statistics by season and day

Season	Day	Minimum Demand (mw)	Maximum Demand (mw)	Average Demand (mw)
Autumn	Friday	9,500.0	13,702.0	11,375.2
Autumn	Monday	10,000.0	13,828.0	11,876.3
Autumn	Wednesday	8,800.0	13,990.0	11,945.0
Late Autumn	Friday	7,234.0	12,698.0	9,592.4
Late Autumn	Monday	5,372.0	13,360.0	10,428.7
Late Autumn	Wednesday	8,000.0	12,878.0	10,525.9
Monsoon	Friday	9,302.0	12,800.0	10,934.5
Monsoon	Monday	9,378.0	13,674.0	11,578.5
Monsoon	Wednesday	9,000.0	13,450.0	11,589.2
Spring	Friday	7,066.0	12,067.0	8,964.2
Spring	Monday	8,154.0	12,888.0	9,830.8
Spring	Wednesday	8,276.0	12,860.0	10,005.4
Summer	Friday	6,850.0	14,461.0	10,430.1
Summer	Monday	8,129.0	15,386.0	11,193.3
Summer	Wednesday	6,108.0	15,370.0	10,885.1
Winter	Friday	7,039.0	10,425.3	7,910.0
Winter	Monday	7,800.0	10,425.3	8,796.6
Winter	Wednesday	6,500.0	9,797.0	8,653.8

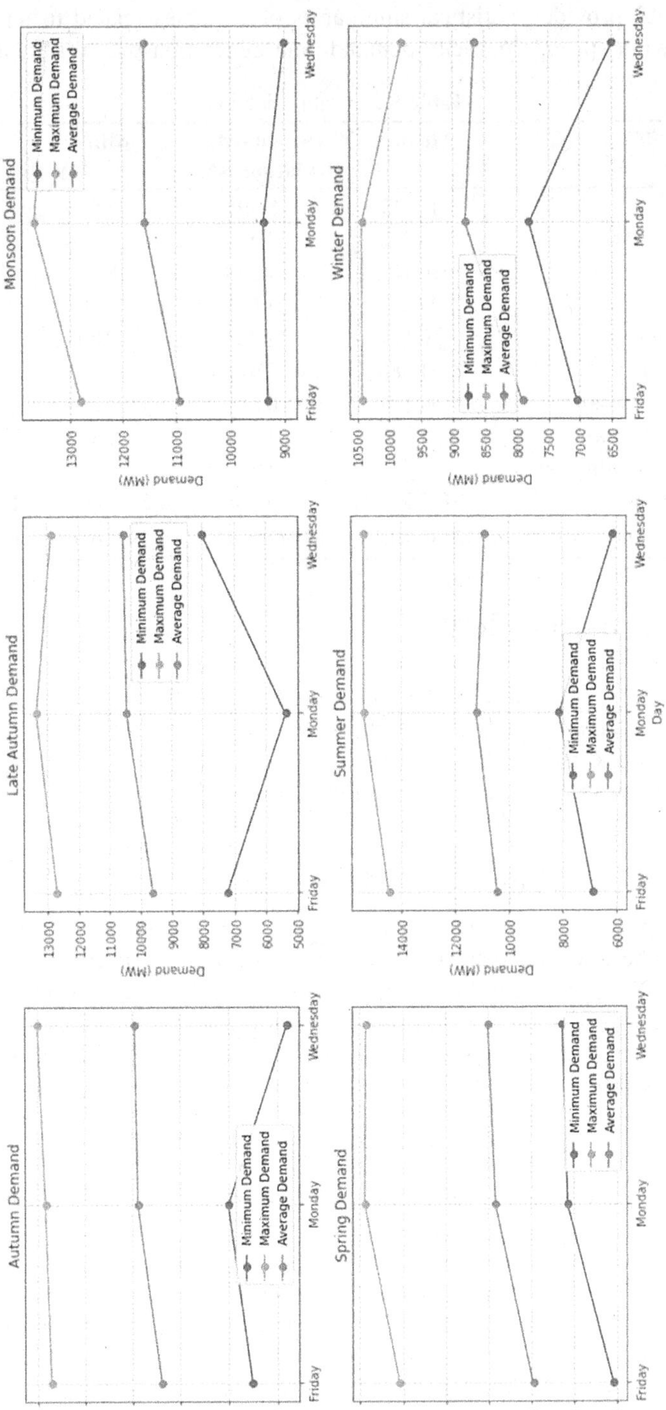

Figure 9.5 Seasonal minimum, maximum, and average demand.

Table 9.2 provides statistical summaries of variables related to temperature, pressure, wind speed, electricity demand, and generation over different periods.

Table 9.2 Data selection

Variable	Mean	Standard Deviation (std)	Min	Max
day	15.715	8.795	1.000	31.000
month	6.275	3.490	1.000	12.000
year	2020.185	1.548	2018.000	2023.000
temp2(c)	25.342	4.659	12.800	34.880
temp2_max(c)	30.155	4.263	17.800	43.550
temp2_min(c)	21.088	5.618	6.430	27.940
suface_pressure(pa)	100.723	0.566	99.030	101.860
wind_speed50_max(m/s)	5.801	1.966	1.470	21.300
wind_speed50_min(m/s)	2.323	1.682	0.020	10.610
total_demand(mw)	10425.376	1675.156	5372.000	15500.000
max_generation(mw)	10539.200	1742.789	4855.000	15648.000

9.4 METHODOLOGY

In this section, we discuss the methodology of our work along with the corresponding illustrations and diagrams. Multiple Linear Regression, Artificial Neural Network (ANN) and Random Forest algorithms are discussed and summarized in Section 9.4.1, 9.4.2 and 9.4.3 respectively.

9.4.1 Multiple Linear Regression

In this chapter, Multiple Linear Regression (MLR) is applied to simulate the relationship between a dependent variable and two or more independent variables, rather than Simple Linear Regression as the dataset contains many predictors [9, 10]. Unlike Simple Linear Regression, which involves only one predictor, MLR accounts for multiple variables simultaneously. The general equation of MLR is expressed as follows:

$$\hat{Y} = \beta_0 + \beta_1 X_1 + \beta_2 X_2 + \cdots + \beta_n X_n \quad (1)$$

In this equation, $\hat{Y}$ represents the predicted value of the dependent variable, $X_1, X_2, \ldots, X_n$ are n distinct independent variables, β_0 is the value of intercept, and $\beta_1, \beta_2, \ldots, \beta_n$ are the estimated regression coefficients.

However, MLR assumes a linear relationship between variables, which may limit its ability to model complex, non-linear patterns [11]. The model aims to minimize the total sum of squares, which quantifies the overall variability in the dependent variable [12]. This is calculated by summing the squared differences between the observed values and their mean, as shown in Equation 2.

$$\sum_{k=1}^{n}(y_k - \bar{y})^2 = \sum_{k=1}^{n}(y_k - \hat{y}_k)^2 + \sum_{k=1}^{n}(\hat{y}_k - \bar{\hat{y}}_k)^2 \tag{2}$$

where y_k represents the actual value of the dependent variable for observation k, $\bar{y}$ is the mean value of all observations, and y_k is the predicted value obtained from the regression model. By minimizing these errors, the model improves predictive accuracy and explains the variation in the dependent variable.

9.4.2 Artificial Neural Network

The concept of the Artificial Neural Network model is taken from the biological structures and operation of the human brain [13]. Artificial neurons are connected and arranged in layers (input layer, hidden layer, and output layer) to form ANNs. Fundamentally, the purpose of artificial neurons is to process inputs, apply transformations, and produce outputs to solve complex tasks such as classification, regression, and pattern recognition [14]. The ANN has hidden layers that can produce nonlinear output functions and is capable of adding more layers and nodes to handle complex tasks [15]. Sometimes, imbalanced or too many layers cause overfitting which has to be balanced through generalization [16, 17]. The architecture of an ANN is depicted in Figure 9.6 and consists of an interconnected input layer, hidden layer, and output layer.

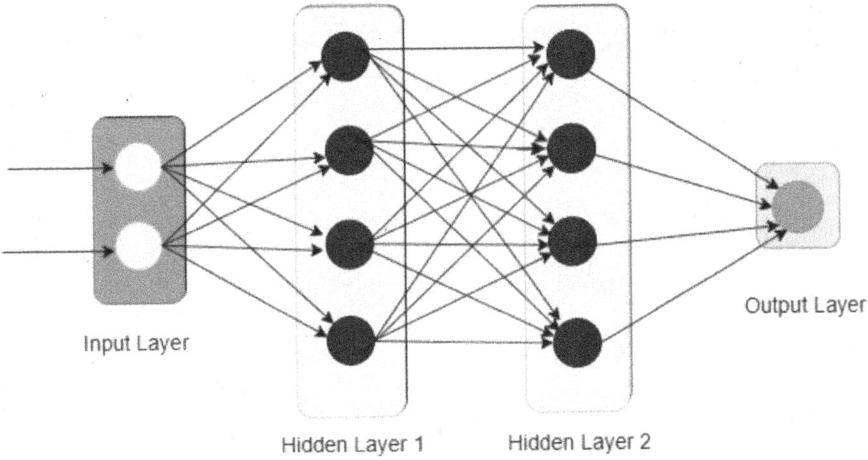

Figure 9.6 Artificial Neural Network (ANN) architecture.

9.4.3 Random Forest Algorithm

The Random Forest (RF) model is widely used in classification and regression in decision tree learning for its efficiency and higher regression accuracy [18].

As shown in Figure 9.7, the Random Forest workflow consists of three key steps. First, the procedure starts by selecting the number of trees (n) and their features (m) to split at each node into consideration. Each tree is built using a

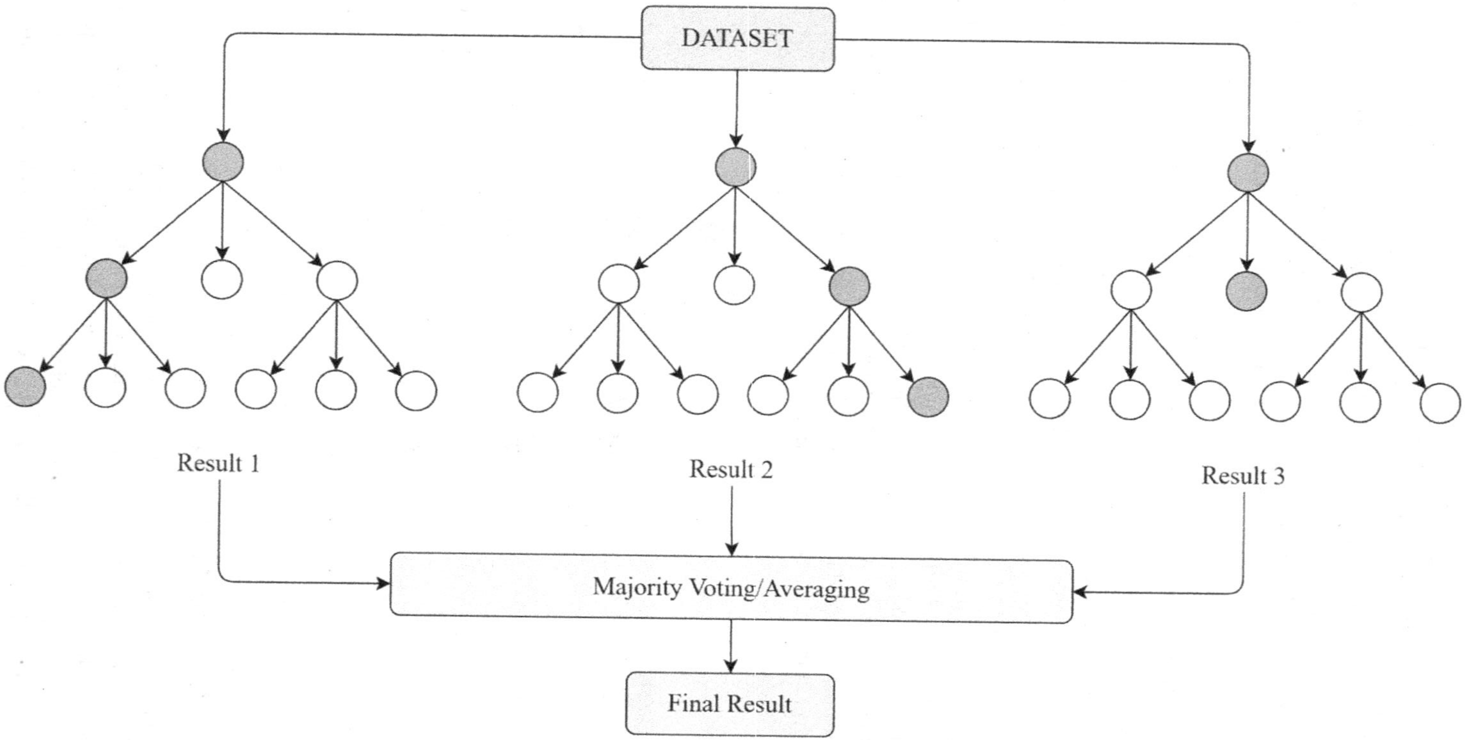

Figure 9.7 Random forest algorithm structure.

bootstrap sample of the training data during the training phase. The m features are randomly chosen at each node, and the best feature is used for splitting. This continues until a predefined stopping condition is met. In the prediction phase, each tree generates an output for new data, and the final forecast is derived by combining all of the individual predictions. Averaging is used for regression, and majority voting is used for classification problems. By combining multiple decision trees, this approach improves predictive accuracy and mitigates overfitting [19, 20].

9.5 RESULT AND ANALYSIS

This chapter shows the comparison between three machine learning techniques, Multiple Linear Regression, Random Forest, and Artificial Neural Network for forecasting Peak Energy Demand in the Electricity Energy Supply. We've used some metrics, Mean Squared Error (MSE), Root Mean Squared Error (RMSE), Mean Absolute Error (MAE), and accuracy.

The metrics for Multiple Linear Regression are MSE (0.003), RMSE (0.242), MAE (0.039), and accuracy (87.19%), where a minimum metrics MSE of 0.002, RMSE of 0.046, MAE of 0.025, and accuracy of 92.41% are provided by Random Forest. ANN achieves metrics of 0.002, 0.054, 0.035 and accuracy 88.33%. Among these three models, we can see in Figure 9.8 that with 92.41% accuracy, Random Forest shows how well it is in instance classification. Now, it can be seen that Random Forest can give the most possible accuracy among other machine learning models we have used so far.

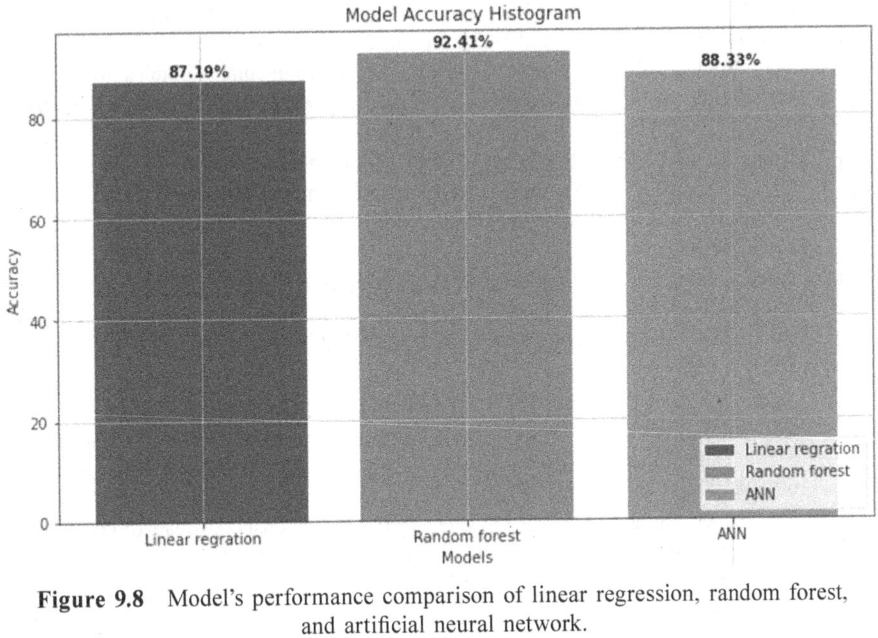

Figure 9.8 Model's performance comparison of linear regression, random forest, and artificial neural network.

9.6 CONCLUSION

In conclusion, we know that electricity has become more technologically advanced with the application of machine learning techniques being essential for long-term forecasting. The main challenge of developing nations is to fulfill electricity demand with affordable and efficient energy solutions for national grid management. Non-renewable gas, coal, and fossil fuels are limited and expensive, future electricity supply and economic growth can be affected if energy generation is mismanaged. This chapter uses the Random Forest (RF) model to improve yearly electricity demand forecasting by including daily weather and five years of power data. The method performed best during peak load demand, resolving future energy challenges by predicting and reducing potential energy crises.

ACKNOWLEDGMENTS

The authors extend their gratitude to the members of the Daffodil International University Multidisciplinary Action Lab and the anonymous reviewers for their insightful feedback on earlier versions of this chapter. Special appreciation goes to Prof. Moon for their valuable contributions in refining the manuscript.

REFERENCES:

[1] Tang, L., X. Wang, X. Wang, C. Shao, S. Liu and S. Tian. 2019. Long-term electricity consumption forecasting based on expert prediction and fuzzy Bayesian theory. Energy. 167: 1144–1154. doi: https://doi.org/10.1016/j.energy.2018.10.073.

[2] Salehin, I., S.M. Noman and M.M. Hasan. 2024. Electricity energy dataset 'BanE-16': Analysis of peak energy demand with environmental variables for machine learning forecasting. Data in Brief. 52: 109967–109967. doi: https://doi.org/10.1016/j.dib.2023.109967.

[3] Islam, A., M.T. Ahmed, M.A.H. Mondal, Md. R. Awual, M.U. Monir and K. Islam. 2021. A snapshot of coal-fired power generation in Bangladesh : A demand–supply outlook. Natural Resources Forum. 45(2): 157–182. doi: https://doi.org/10.1111/1477-8947.12221..

[4] Islam, A., Md. B. Hossai, Md. A.H. Monda, Md. T. Ahmed, Md. A. Hossain, M.U. Monir, et al. 2021. Energy challenges for a clean environment: Bangladesh's experience. Energy Reports. 7: 3373–3389. doi: https://doi.org/10.1016/j.egyr.2021.05.066.

[5] Abera, F.Z. and V. Khedkar. 2020. Machine Learning Approach Electric Appliance Consumption and Peak Demand Forecasting of Residential Customers Using Smart Meter Data. Wireless Personal Communications. 111(1): 65–82. doi: https://doi.org/10.1007/s11277-019-06845-6.

[6] Shi, H., M. Xu and R. Li. 2018. Deep learning for household load forecasting—A novel pooling deep RNN. IEEE Transactions on Smart Grid. 9(5): 5271–5280. doi: https://doi.org/10.1109/tsg.2017.2686012.

[7] Son, H. and C. Kim. 2020. A deep learning approach to forecasting monthly demand for residential–sector electricity. Sustainability. 12(8): 3103. doi: https://doi.org/10.3390/su12083103.

[8] Kumar, M. and N. Pal. 2023. Machine learning-based electric load forecasting for peak demand control in smart grid. Computers, Materials and Continua. 0(0): 1–15. doi: https://doi.org/10.32604/cmc.2022.032971.

[9] Dhaval, B. and A. Deshpande. 2020. Short-term load forecasting with using multiple linear regression. International Journal of Electrical and Computer Engineering (IJECE). 10(4): 3911–3917. doi: https://doi.org/10.11591/ijece.v10i4.

[10] Schmidt, A.F. and C. Finan. 2018. Linear regression and the normality assumption. Journal of Clinical Epidemiology. 98: 146–151. doi: https://doi.org/10.1016/j.jclinepi.2017.12.006.

[11] Ferreira, Â.P., J.G. Ramos and P.O. Fernandes. 2019. A linear regression pattern for electricity price forecasting in the Iberian electricity market. Revista Facultad de Ingeniería Universidad de Antioquia. (93): 117–127. doi: https://doi.org/10.17533/udea.redin.20190522.

[12] Kim, M.K., Y.-S. Kim and J. Srebric. 2020. Predictions of electricity consumption in a campus building using occupant rates and weather elements with sensitivity analysis: Artificial neural network vs. linear regression. Sustainable Cities and Society. 62: 102385. doi: https://doi.org/10.1016/j.scs.2020.102385.

[13] Li, G. and J. Shi. 2010. On comparing three artificial neural networks for wind speed forecasting. Applied Energy. 87(7): 2313–2320. doi: https://doi.org/10.1016/j.apenergy.2009.12.013.

[14] Karabiber, O. and G. Xydis. 2019. Electricity price forecasting in the Danish day-ahead market using the TBATS, ANN and ARIMA methods. Energies. 12(5): 928. doi: https://doi.org/10.3390/en12050928.

[15] Ofori-Ntow Jnr, E., Y.Y. Ziggah and S. Relvas. 2021. Hybrid ensemble intelligent model based on wavelet transform, swarm intelligence and artificial neural network for electricity demand forecasting. Sustainable Cities and Society. 66: 102679. doi: https://doi.org/10.1016/j.scs.2020.102679.

[16] Pourdaryaei, A., H. Mokhlis, H.A. Illias, S. Hr. Aghay Kaboli, S. Ahmad and S.P. Ang. 2019. Hybrid ANN and artificial cooperative search algorithm to forecast short-term electricity price in deregulated electricity market. IEEE Access. 7: 125369–125386. doi: https://doi.org/10.1109/access.2019.2938842.

[17] Saritas, M.M. 2019. Performance analysis of ANN and naive Bayes classification algorithm for data classification. International Journal of Intelligent Systems and Applications in Engineering. 7(2): 88–91. doi: https://doi.org/10.18201/ijisae.2019252786.

[18] Fan, G.-F., M. Yu, S.-Q. Dong, Y.-H. Yeh and W.-C. Hong. 2021. Forecasting short-term electricity load using hybrid support vector regression with grey catastrophe and random forest modeling. Utilities Policy. 73: 101294. doi: https://doi.org/10.1016/j.jup.2021.101294.

[19] Srivastava, R., A.N. Tiwari and V.K. Giri. 2019. Solar radiation forecasting using MARS, CART, M5 and random forest model: A case study for India. Heliyon. 5(10): e02692. doi: https://doi.org/10.1016/j.heliyon.2019.e02692.

[20] Xuan, Y., W. Si, J. Zhu, Z. Sun, J. Zhao, M. Xu, et al. 2021. Multi-model fusion short-term load forecasting based on random forest feature selection and hybrid neural network. IEEE Access. 1–1. doi: https://doi.org/10.1109/access.2021.3051337.

Chapter **10**

AI-based Electrical Load Forecasting for Residential Sector Using Smart Meter Data

Barkha Parkash[1], Tek Tjing Lie*[1],
Weihua Li[1] and Shafiqur Rahman Tito[2]

[1]Department of Electrical and Electronic Engineering,
Auckland University of Technology, Auckland, New Zealand

[2]Department of Engineering,
Waikato Institute of Technology, Hamilton, New Zealand

10.1 INTRODUCTION

Electrical load forecasting is a significant challenge for power system operators because it plays a major role in scheduling generation, transmission, distribution, and integrated resource planning [1]. This indicates that load forecasting is critically important and plays a vital role in the efficient and economic operation of a power system. Various computational techniques and methodologies have been implemented in the electricity market for accurate load forecasting. However, due to the emergence of different energy storage systems, such as electric vehicles, batteries, and customer-owned generation, it has become extremely difficult to develop models that produce accurate forecasting results. Designing a forecast model is particularly challenging, as real-world systems are complex and comprise many variables that are difficult to capture fully. Additionally, most of the existing

*For Correspondence: tek.lie@aut.ac.nz

DOI: 10.1201/9781003541875-10

forecast models are highly dependent on data, and any kind of inconsistency in the data affects the performance and accuracy of a model [2].

Moreover, electricity usage in the residential sector differs greatly across households based on socio-demographic factors such as income, household size, residents' age, and geographic location. Such features determine the consumption behavior of every household. These factors contribute to the complexity of accurately determining electricity demand. However, it is crucial for power system operators to precisely assess the demand they must meet to ensure the efficient operation of the power plant [1]. Current forecast models primarily focus on predicting load at either an individual household level or by aggregating multiple households. However, this approach has several limitations, which are detailed below:

- The residential consumption is extremely volatile, i.e., a model that is trained on one household may not work for another.
- Most of these models require a vast volume of data specific to the households to generate accurate forecasts, which is a tedious task from a practical implementation point of view.

On one hand, these limitations are evident, while on the other, there is a growing need for models that can forecast load consumption across the entire residential sector, rather than concentrating solely on individual households or specific household groups. This chapter introduces a novel methodology for developing a hierarchical load forecasting model that delivers forecasts at multiple levels within the hierarchy. The proposed approach leverages smart meter consumption data to identify common consumption patterns, which are then used to structure and cluster households with similar behaviours, enabling a hierarchical view of the residential sector. A key feature of this methodology is the identification of unique input variables that capture relationships across different levels of the hierarchy. This ensures consistency and compatibility between clusters and allows a single forecasting model to perform effectively at all levels, including aggregate and cluster-specific forecasts. By relying solely on smart meter data, the approach minimizes the need for house-specific inputs such as the physical characteristics of homes or the number of electrical appliances, which are often difficult to obtain.

10.2 HIERARCHICAL FORECASTING APPROACHES

The hierarchical load structure-based forecast is a family-oriented forecasting method that meets the diverse information needed. By offering insights at various levels of the hierarchy, it supports decision-making for a wide range of users [3]. Designing a forecast model for hierarchical load structure is possible by following either of the three approaches: bottom-up, top-down, and middle-up approach.

10.2.1 Bottom-Up Approach

In a bottom-up (BU) approach, forecasting is conducted for each series at the lowest level of the hierarchy, and then these forecasts are aggregated up to the top level. One advantage of this method is that it preserves all the details by forecasting at the most granular level, ensuring no information is lost due to aggregation. However, the data at the bottom level can be quite noisy, making it more difficult to model and forecast accurately [4, 5]. Additionally, acquiring detailed data for each series at the lower level is a very laborious task.

10.2.2 Top-Down Approach

In contrast, the top-down (TD) approach involves forecasting at the highest level of the hierarchy and then distributing those forecasts to lower levels based on distribution ratios derived from the relationships between historical load consumption and other load-dependent factors [4]. A key advantage of this approach is its simplicity, as it only requires modeling and generating forecasts for the most aggregated top-level series. This method generally produces reliable forecasts for aggregate levels and is particularly useful when dealing with low-count data. However, a downside is the loss of information due to aggregation. Additionally, the historical proportions used for disaggregation do not account for potential changes in those proportions over time [4, 5].

10.2.3 Middle-Out Approach

Middle-out approach is a midway option between top-down and bottom-up in which the lowest levels are grouped based on certain similarities such as geographical region, functionality, etc., and then an individual forecast model is created for every sub-group which is summed up to get a reasonable estimate at the aggregated level. Initially, a middle level is chosen, and forecasts are generated for all series at this level. For series above this level, the bottom-up approach is used to aggregate the middle-level forecasts, ensuring coherence. Meanwhile, for series below the middle level, the top-down approach is applied, disaggregating the forecasts accordingly. [4, 5].

Among the three approaches, the BU method is the most widely used, though it comes with certain disadvantages. This approach requires a separate model for each series at the lower levels, which increases computational complexity and makes it challenging to implement in practical scenarios [5]. On the other hand, the TD approach is simpler to implement and holds significant potential by effectively utilizing smart meter consumption data for modelling. Before building the forecast model, the first step is to establish the hierarchy. For the residential sector, there are different methods to create hierarchy, explained below.

- **Based on geographical location:** In this method, houses in a location having the same postal code can be grouped as one.
- **Based on socio-demographics:** In this method, houses with similar social demographical features are placed together.

- **Consumption patterns:** This is based on identifying similar consumption patterns from the load profiles and placing them together in one group.

This can be achieved by utilising clustering algorithms that group data points based on the chosen criterion. Figure 10.1 shows a basic hierarchical structure for the residential sector. At the highest level, all houses are aggregated, while the subsequent level consists of different groups, each containing a varying number of households.

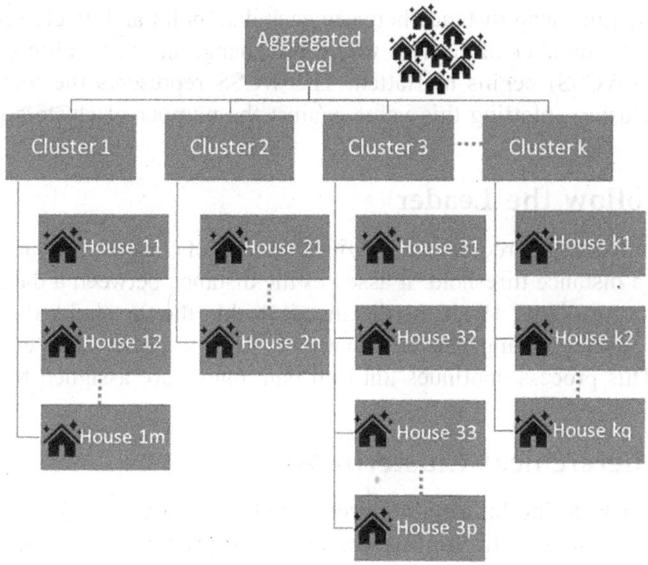

Figure 10.1 Hierarchical structure.

10.3 OVERVIEW OF CLUSTERING ALGORITHMS–INPUT AND EVALUATION METRICS

Clustering is defined as the task of segmenting data points into groups such that data points in one group are most like each other as compared to the data points in other groups. There are various clustering algorithms available, some of which are based on theories of statistics and some use principles of artificial intelligence [6]. Some of the most widely used algorithms for clustering [7] are explained as below.

10.3.1 K-means Clustering Algorithm

K-means clustering is among the most used unsupervised learning techniques for data clustering. It is a repetitive clustering method that partitions a dataset into similar groups by measuring the distance to their central points. The central point, or centroid, is determined as either the mean or median of all data points within the cluster, depending on the dataset's characteristics [8]. It works by assigning data points to clusters based on their distance from the centroid, typically using the Euclidean distance. The goal is to minimize the sum of these distances, with data points being grouped into the cluster whose centroid they are closest to. A higher number of clusters (K) leads to smaller, more detailed clusters, while a lower K value produces larger, less detailed clusters [8, 9]. This approach necessitates selecting the optimal number of clusters before implementation. Several techniques exist for determining the ideal cluster count, with the "Knee method" being one of the most widely used [10]. It is a visual technique, that calculates the Euclidean distance between each data point and its cluster centroid, then selects the number of clusters where the change in the "within-cluster sum of squares" (WCSS) begins to flatten. The WCSS represents the total variance within the clusters, plotting this value against the number of clusters [8, 10].

10.3.2 Follow the Leader

This algorithm does not require a predefined number of clusters. Instead, clustering is based on a distance threshold. It assesses the distance between a data point and the cluster's centroid [7, 11]. If the distance is within the threshold, the data point is assigned to the existing cluster; otherwise, it forms a new cluster, becoming its leader. This process continues until all data points are assigned to clusters.

10.3.3 Hierarchical Clustering

Hierarchical Clustering builds a hierarchy of clusters, where each cluster groups together data points with similar characteristics within a system [12]. This approach involves constructing an $M \times M$ similarity matrix using Euclidean normalized distance, where M represents the total number of data points. The M samples are then clustered based on linkage criteria derived from the similarity matrix. The linkage criterion measures the similarity between clusters at each level. Some common linkage criteria include minimum, maximum, ward and average distance. The process is repeated until all clusters are merged into one big cluster at the highest level [13].

These clustering algorithms employ various approaches to determine the optimal number of clusters. However, one essential criterion is that the number of clusters must be fewer than the total data points. Beyond this, there is no strict upper limit; the optimal number of clusters is typically identified based on factors such as computational feasibility, interpretability, and the data's inherent structure.

10.3.4 Input Features for Clustering Algorithm

All clustering algorithms require data, either numerical or categorical, depending on the algorithm applied. Examples of numerical input features include income or temperature, while categorical features might include gender or product type. It's important to ensure that all input features undergo scaling or normalization so that they are treated equally during the clustering process [8].

To perform clustering based on load consumption, appropriate input features that represent a household's load consumption must be identified. For residential customers, smart meter data is available, which can be used to derive both direct and indirect features. Although smart meter data is typically in the time domain, it is also possible to extract features from the frequency domain for clustering purposes [14, 15]. These features capture the load curves of the customers. The most straightforward approach to feature extraction is to normalize the load measurements of customers in the time domain and then utilize either all or a portion of the normalized power measurements. This method requires no additional post-processing, allowing the extracted features to be directly applied for clustering. The features that represent the customers' load patterns are defined by equation (1) [14].

$$C = \{c^{(m)}, m = 1, \ldots., M\}$$

$$c^{(m)} = [c_1^{(m)}, \ldots., c_1^{(H)}]^T \tag{1}$$

where M denotes the number of customers, and the value of H can be selected arbitrarily but it should not exceed the resolution of meter. The simplest approach to feature extraction involves normalizing customers' load measurements in the time domain and using either all or part of the normalized data. This method requires no further post-processing, and the extracted features can be directly applied for clustering, as shown in equation (2) [15].

$$\text{Average} = \frac{\sum \text{daily load profile}}{d} \tag{2}$$

where d refers to the number of days that belong to the representative cluster.

$$\text{RLP} = \frac{\text{Average}}{P_{\max}} \tag{3}$$

Indirect shape features can be extracted for clustering customers by dividing a single day into smaller periods, such as consumption during daylight hours (8 am to 6 pm), lunchtime (12 pm to 2 pm), and night-time (10 pm to 6 am). These features are then normalized to fall within the range {0, 1}. These indirect features can also be used for clustering [15]. The main objective is to generate a RLP for all the houses involved using one of the methods. The RLPs can be then utilized as input features by any clustering algorithm, enabling the clustering process.

10.3.5 Cluster Validation

It is important to evaluate the quality of clusters which is achieved by using some of the accuracy metrics available. One of the accuracy indicators commonly used Davies-Bouldin Index (DBI) evaluates the overlapping of clusters is given in equation (4). It is determined by calculating average intra-cluster distance, represented by *diam* (C_i) and comparing it for all pairs of clusters. Smaller values of DBI indicate that the clustering algorithm has separated the data well [16].

$$DBI = \frac{1}{K}\sum_{i=1}^{K}\left(\max_{j\neq i}\frac{\text{diam}(C_i)+\text{diam}(C_j)}{d(C_i,C_j)}\right) \tag{4}$$

Another available metrics that calculates the goodness of created clusters is given by Index of Agreement (IA) [17]. IA is a dimensionless quantity represented by equation (5). The closer the IA value is to 1, the better the clustering performance.

$$IA = 1 - \frac{\sum_{i=1}^{n}\left((P_i - O_i)^2\right)}{\sum_{i=1}^{n}(|P_i^{\sim}| - |O_i^{\sim}|)^2}$$

$$P_i^{\sim} = P_i - O' \qquad O_i^{\sim} = O_i - O' \tag{5}$$

where P_i represents the predicted variable at time i, O_i denotes the observed variable, n is the total number of observations, and O' is the average of the observed variables over n observations [14]. The closer the value of IA is to 1, better the clustering is. IA has proven to be an effective evaluation metric for clustering the residential sector based on load consumption patterns [14].

10.4 RELATED WORK ON AI BASED FORECAST MODELS

Once a hierarchy is established, the next step is to design and develop a forecasting model tailored to this hierarchy. For hierarchical load forecasting, models utilizing AI techniques tend to outperform traditional statistical methods. This section explores various AI-based forecasting models.

Traditional statistical models establish a direct relationship between forecasted values and historical data, predicting future load by creating a mathematical model that reflects causal relationships. Time series methods, for example, use curve fitting and parameter estimation on historical load data to develop these models [18]. While straightforward, these models often overlook other load-dependent factors, resulting in lower accuracy. In contrast, AI-based models can capture hidden relationships within the data because of its advanced learning capabilities. AI-based models are generally divided into two categories: machine learning models and deep learning models. Machine learning models include techniques like neural networks and statistical approaches. Deep learning models, on the other hand, consist of more advanced neural networks such as Long Short-Term Memory (LSTM) and Recurrent Neural Networks (RNNs). While deep learning approaches offer enhanced learning capabilities, models like Artificial Neural Networks (ANN) also show significant potential [18].

Accurate load forecasting plays a critical role in reducing uncertainty in power system operations. This is the key reason for striving to improve forecasting performance, ensuring the power system operates reliably. In [19], the authors developed a forecasting model using the Levenberg-Marquardt Backpropagation algorithm based on ANN to predict the hourly day-ahead load for two states in the North Eastern Region of India. They compared the results with a statistical model using Vector Auto-Regressive (VAR) techniques, finding that the AI-based model achieved higher forecasting accuracy. Furthermore, the model was tested with two different datasets: one derived from smart energy meters and the other from supervisory control and data acquisition (SCADA) data. The results revealed that data from energy meters yielded more reliable outcomes.

In [20], the authors propose a hybrid model that combines LSTM with statistical techniques to enhance short-term forecasting accuracy, particularly in the presence of renewable energy sources. The model integrates data from multiple sources, including smart meters, to not only improve forecasting precision but also provide deeper insights into load patterns. Numerous researchers have developed models to boost forecasting accuracy, and while artificial intelligence techniques are key, the choice of data sources is equally important. Studies have shown that smart meter consumption data holds great potential for both improving forecasting performance and offering valuable insights into load behaviour.

Hierarchical load forecasting (HLF) is crucial for effective demand response and the implementation of load management strategies. In [21], the authors present a methodology that forecasts load at different levels of the hierarchy, such as national, regional, and local. This model employs an AI-based approach, specifically Temporal Convolutional Networks (TCN), to capture temporal dependencies in time series data, significantly improving forecasting accuracy. Additionally, the paper introduces an optimal valley filling-based demand response strategy, which encourages households to shift energy consumption from peak to off-peak periods, reducing peak load and balancing the grid.

There is ongoing research in this field aimed at leveraging AI-based approaches to enhance forecasting accuracy and facilitate the implementation of demand-side management strategies. The reliance on purely statistical models has declined, with hybrid methodologies offering greater potential for optimal results across various applications. In the power sector, it is essential to make optimal use of smart meter consumption data for analysis, operational improvements, and overall performance enhancement.

The total consumption in the power sector comprises of various sectors, including commercial, industrial, residential and transportation. The consumption patterns in the residential sector are more volatile compared to those in the industrial and commercial sectors, making load forecasting models more challenging to develop. Despite this, the residential sector holds significant potential for adopting demand-side management (DSM) techniques, which makes accurate forecasts, particularly hierarchical forecasts, important. Hierarchical forecasts for the residential sector facilitate the identification of different household groups, allowing for targeted implementation of energy conservation strategies and DSM initiatives. The TD approach in HLF is particularly significant due to its simplicity and ease of practical implementation. The following section introduces a novel methodology tailored to the residential sector, utilizing a TD hierarchical forecasting model based on neural networks and optimal use of smart meter consumption data.

10.5 TOP-DOWN FORECAST MODEL

In a traditional TD approach, a forecast model is built for the highest hierarchical level and then proportionally distributed across lower levels using ratios derived from historical data. In this method, the forecasting model can be based on any methodology that best meets the requirements. For example, it could be a statistical model or even a more advanced machine learning approach. However, in the case of TD approach, the distribution ratios are calculated using historical data [4, 5]. Traditionally, mathematical ratios are calculated based on historical trends, either as the mean of past proportions or as a fraction of the historical average. These mathematical ratios help in forecasting aggregated levels, including monthly peak demand, daily energy usage, and weekly sales figures. However, this methodology is less effective for predicting hourly load consumption, as it relies on historical proportions that do not account for potential changes over time, leading to less accurate forecasts at lower hierarchical levels [5].

Figure 10.2 illustrates the importance of designing a forecast model based on TD approach. In contrast to other approaches, it directly provides a forecast at the aggregated level which is beneficial for the utility operators. On the other hand, this methodology will enable the identification of different customer groups that exist in the residential sector along with their corresponding demand, thereby, helping retailers in deciding tariff rates for different customer groups.

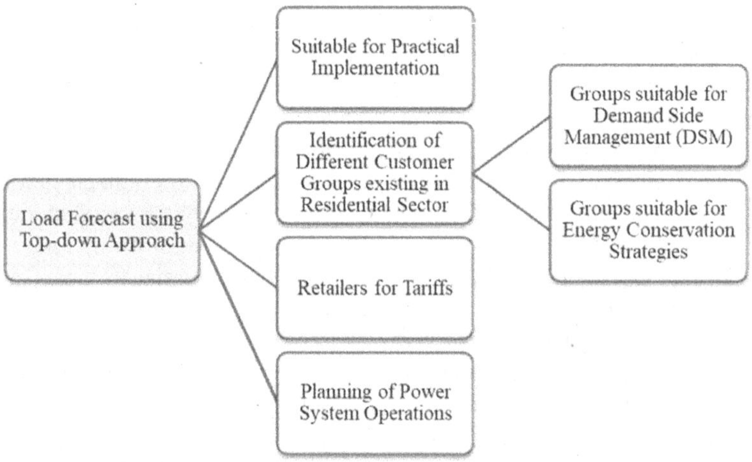

Figure 10.2 Importance of top-down load forecast model

This section below discusses the proposed methodology in [14] that explores the creation of a hierarchical load forecasting model that extends traditional TD principles, moving beyond solely relying on mathematical ratios for lower-level forecasts. The model focuses on improving forecast accuracy at all hierarchical levels by effectively leveraging smart meter consumption data and integrating cross-learning between different levels using artificial intelligence-based forecasting techniques [22].

10.5.1 Two Stage Approach

A forecasting model is required to predict energy consumption at different levels of a hierarchy. In a traditional TD hierarchical load forecasting approach, forecasting is conducted at the highest level of the hierarchy and then subsequently allocated to lower levels using mathematical distribution ratios derived from historical data [14]. This involves designing a single forecast model for the aggregated level, which generates predictions for the highest hierarchical level. These forecasts are then scaled down to lower levels based on the pre-determined distribution ratios. While this method is straightforward to implement, its accuracy is limited. This is because forecasts for the lower levels are heavily dependent on static distribution ratios, which may not adapt well to dynamic changes in load patterns. In contrast, the proposed approach enhances the hierarchical forecasting methodology by introducing a two-stage model that incorporates neural networks, ensuring a more dynamic and accurate representation of hierarchical relationships. The first neural forecast model predicts load at the aggregated level, like the traditional approach. However, instead of relying solely on distribution ratios, the second forecast model takes the aggregated-level forecast from the first model as an input, along with additional input features representing characteristics of the lower levels, to generate forecasts for the secondary level of the hierarchy. This methodology aligns with hierarchical principles by maintaining a clear relationship between the levels while addressing the limitations of traditional approaches. By dynamically linking forecasts across levels and leveraging neural network models, the proposed approach ensures that the hierarchical structure is preserved, while improving accuracy through data-driven learning at each level of the hierarchy.

The methodology, as shown in Figure 10.3, starts with data pre-processing and is followed by clustering, which structures households into a hierarchical arrangement. The input features for clustering are derived from consumption data. A RLP is created for each household using hourly consumption data. Since consumption patterns vary seasonally, a RLP is created for each season for all households. These seasonal RLPs serve as the input features for the clustering process.

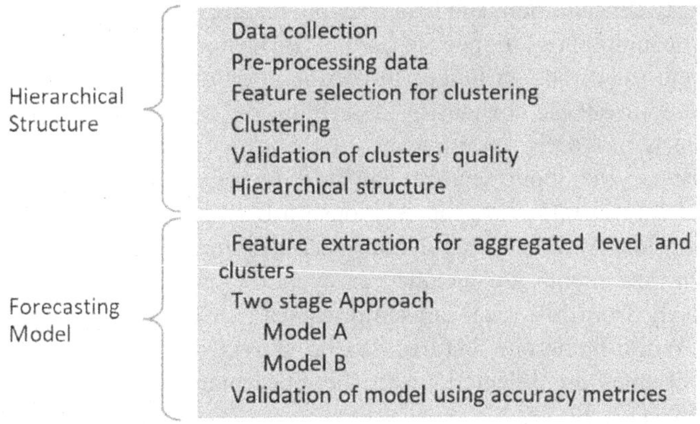

Figure 10.3 Methodology for building hierarchical load forecast model.

The second phase focuses on building a forecasting model for this structure using two models based on neural network. Model A predicts load consumption at the aggregated level, using input variables selected based on their correlation with load consumption, identified through the Spearman coefficient [23–25]. The key features include previous hour consumption, the average of the past three and six hours, and consumption at the same time the previous day. Model B forecasts load consumption for the clusters, with Model A's output serving as one of the inputs. This model estimates cluster-level consumption based on cluster-specific features and the aggregated load data from Model A. The two-stage approach involves separately training two neural network models. Model A focuses on aggregated load prediction, while Model B predicts cluster-level consumption, leveraging both cluster features and Model A's output [14].

10.5.2 End-to-End Learning Model

The two-stage approach involves training two independent models for each cluster forecast, following the principles of the TD approach. However, it does not account for the specific input features of the clusters or the relationships between the highest and lower hierarchical levels. Addressing these limitations, a new methodology was proposed in [22] that integrates TD principles with a cross-learning approach, introducing an end-to-end (E2E) model for forecasting load at any node by incorporating both aggregated and cluster-level input features. This approach employs a unified E2E model that incorporates input features from both hierarchical levels, along with an additional variable representing their relationship. This structure streamlines implementation while integrating the benefits of the top-down method with cross-learning capabilities.

10.5.3 Input Features for Forecast Model

The model's input features are extracted from past consumption data and calendar variables. At the aggregated level, these inputs include lag features, averages of previous hourly consumption, and load tracking features (LTFs) [26]. In time-series data, load consumption at a specific hour is influenced not only by past values but also by the trends and variations in consumption over time. LTFs, introduced in [22, 26], capture these changes by describing the rate of consumption change based on hourly and daily variations.

For clusters, the input features include averages of previous hours, lag features, and a ratio reflecting the relationship between aggregated and cluster-level consumption. Additionally, calendar variables including hour of the day, day of the month, and month are included as cyclic features. All input features are extracted solely from historical consumption data, with no exogenous variables considered. While numerous features can be extracted from historical data, the most relevant ones are selected using the Spearman coefficient to minimize dimensionality [22, 27, 28].

10.5.4 Evaluation Metrics

The effectiveness of any forecasting model must be assessed, usually by employing the Mean Absolute Percentage Error (MAPE) and the Mean Absolute Scaled Error (MASE) metrics [22, 29, 30]. MAPE assesses the precision of a forecasting technique, while MASE compares the model's effectiveness against a naïve forecasting approach. The naïve approach predicts the value at any given time as equal to the observed value at the previous time step. MASE is calculated as the ratio of the model's Mean Absolute Error (MAE) to the MAE of the naïve forecast. A MASE value of 1 indicates that the model performs similarly to the naïve forecast, while lower values suggest higher accuracy of the proposed model.

10.6 INSIGHTS FROM PRIOR PUBLICATION

The discussed two methodologies; two-stage approach and E2E learning approach were tested on a real-world dataset from the Dataport of PECAN Street, consisting of nine years of half-hourly electricity consumption data for 50 houses in the USA [31]. After pre-processing the data, a hierarchical clustering model was applied, grouping the houses into 10 distinct clusters based on their seasonal load profiles. The proposed E2E forecasting methodology was then evaluated and compared with other models, including SARIMA, SVR, and a two-stage approach [22]. The following section are taken from the published work in [22].

10.6.1 Comparison of Forecast Models Based on MAPE

To assess the effectiveness of the proposed E2E model with cross-learning features, it is compared against the previously discussed two-stage methodology [32] and traditional forecasting models, including SARIMA and SVR [33, 34]. The two-stage model follows a TD hierarchical forecasting approach, incorporating two models.

Among the benchmark models, SARIMA is an extension of the ARIMA model that accounts for seasonality. It is characterized by three parameters: p, d, and q for the non-seasonal component and P, D, and Q for the seasonal component, with m representing the seasonal period. These parameter values, (p, d, q) (P, D, Q, m), are identified by examining the autocorrelation function (ACF) and partial autocorrelation function (PACF) plots. [14, 35].

The SVR model, another comparison model, is a supervised regression-based approach that identifies an optimal hyperplane to best fit the data [34]. It utilizes a kernel function to transform data into a higher-dimensional space, with commonly used kernel functions including linear, polynomial, and radial basis function (RBF). A crucial parameter in SVR is C, the regularization parameter, which balances model complexity and training error. A higher C value improves model fit but risks overfitting, while a lower C value enhances generalization but may reduce accuracy. The kernel function and C value are optimized to enhance performance.

Since input features play a critical role in model accuracy, data pre-processing is conducted before evaluation, with features selected as per Table 10.1. All models are trained on the same dataset and evaluated using MAPE. The results, summarized in Table 10.2, present MAPE values across all 10 hierarchical clusters for the four forecasting approaches. The findings indicate that SARIMA has the highest mean MAPE among all clusters, followed by SVR, the two-stage model, and the proposed E2E model, which achieves the lowest mean MAPE.

Table 10.1 Input features

Level	Input Features	Description
Aggregated Level	L_{avg_3h}, $L_{avg\_t\_d}$	"Average of load consumption in the previous 3 h and average load consumption of the same 2 days of the week at the same time"
	L_{t-24}, L_{t_d}, L_{t-1}, L_{t-2}, L_{t-3}, L_{t-21}, L_{t-22}, L_{t-23}, L_{t-24}	"Load consumption at the same time as the previous day, load consumption on the same day of the week at the same time"
	LTF_1, LTF_2, LTF_3, LTF_4, LTF_5	"Load tracking features" [22, 26]
Cluster Level	L_{c,avg_t_d}	"Average load consumption of the whole day"
	$L_{c,t-24}$, $L_{c,t-1}$	"Load consumption at the same time as the previous day and previous hour"
	R_c	"Ratio between aggregated and cluster-level consumption"
Calendar Features	h_{sine}, h_{cos}, d_{sine}, d_{cos}, m_{sine}, m_{cos}, H	"Hour of the day, day of the week, and month of the year expressed as the cyclic feature"

Source: Adapted from [22]

Table 10.2 Comparison of all results using MAPE

Cluster	MAPE (%)			
	SARIMA	SVR	Two-Stage	E2E Model
C0	"19.41"	"23.7"	"6.19"	"3.4"
C1	"12.7"	"13.6"	"1.5"	"1.12"
C2	"16.22"	"16.7"	"6.35"	"5.4"
C3	"32.87"	"34.6"	"7.73"	"3.49"
C4	"14.41"	"13.8"	"5.02"	"2.6"
C5	"25.9"	"21.6"	"1.22"	"1.37"
C6	"34.7"	"26"	"3.1"	"2.07"
C7	"29.82"	"13.9"	"0.69"	"0.88"
C8	"34.9"	"28.5"	"3.32"	"1.71"
C9	"34.8"	"11.6"	"3.75"	"0.71"

Source: Adapted from [22]

The performance of SARIMA and SVR is noticeably weak, primarily because these models are well-suited for datasets with a linear structure, whereas residential load consumption is inherently non-linear due to multiple influencing factors. Both models struggle with capturing these complexities. SVR, in particular, assumes a deterministic relationship between input and output variables, which does not hold true for residential load data due to its randomness. Additionally, SVR's efficiency declines with large datasets due to the high computational cost and requires careful kernel selection. Similarly, SARIMA faces challenges in modelling the non-linear dependencies between input and output variables.

While improvements to these models are possible, they come at the cost of increased computational demands and memory requirements, making practical implementation challenging. Furthermore, enhancing their accuracy would require additional feature engineering steps, adding to the complexity.

In contrast, the MAPE for both the two-stage and E2E learning models is relatively low, reinforcing the effectiveness of basing the forecast model on the TD approach. The selected hyperparameters for the proposed model are optimized to perform well across the entire hierarchy while keeping MAPE within acceptable limits. The results demonstrate that the E2E model outperforms all other models, maintaining a percentage error below 6% across all clusters. Notably, the two-stage approach achieves a slightly lower MAPE for clusters 5 and 7; however, in both cases, the MAPE remains under 2% for both models. For all other clusters, the E2E model delivers superior accuracy. The highest MAPE recorded for the two-stage model is 7.73% for cluster 3, whereas the E2E model's highest MAPE is 5.4% for cluster 2. Overall, the MAPE for 9 out of 10 clusters using the E2E model remains below 5%, with only one cluster reaching close to 5%. These results highlight variations in MAPE across different clusters, reflecting differences in forecasting accuracy. However, these variations are considered acceptable due to the overall low error rates achieved throughout the forecasting process.

10.6.2 Comparison between E2E Model and BU Approach

The proposed E2E learning forecasting model is built using fundamentals of the TD approach, whereas a commonly used alternative is the BU approach, which requires separate local models for each group. This section compares the E2E learning model with the conventional BU approach. Unlike the E2E model, the BU approach relies on independent forecast models for each cluster, utilizing only the features relevant to that specific cluster. Features are carefully selected to capture the unique characteristics of each cluster, along with calendar variables. Since the BU approach focuses on localized forecasting, using aggregated-level features is considered inappropriate as it contradicts the core concept of the approach.

The individual models employed in the BU approach are also based on neural networks, incorporating cluster-specific features and calendar variables. These cluster features align with those used in the E2E learning model. The final forecast at the aggregated level is obtained by summing the results of the individual models. A comparison of the results from both approaches is presented in Table 10.3, revealing that the MAPE for the BU approach is significantly higher than that of the proposed model with cross-learning features.

Table 10.3 Comparison between E2E and BU approach

Cluster	MAPE (%)	
	E2E Model	**BU**
C0	“3.4”	“15.22”
C1	“1.12”	1“0.21”
C2	“5.4”	“14.7”
C3	“3.49”	“14.28”
C4	“2.6”	“11.19”
C5	“1.37”	“14.5”
C6	“2.07”	“13.97”
C7	“0.88”	“10.51”
C8	“1.71”	“14.78”
C9	“0.71”	“8.76”

Source: Adapted from [22]

Existing literature suggests that the BU approach performs better than the TD approach when forecasting load at sub-levels within a hierarchy. However, this advantage comes at the cost of requiring extensive additional data to maintain accuracy. In residential consumption forecasting, BU models typically incorporate physics-based models and behaviour related input features. The physics-based model considers factors such as appliance specifications, energy consumption, operating hours, and residents’ usage patterns to predict consumption [35]. However, in practical scenarios, obtaining such detailed data is often challenging, limiting the potential improvements in BU model performance.

On the other hand, smart meters provide valuable insights into consumption patterns and are recognized as essential tools for improving forecasting accuracy. The proposed E2E model capitalizes on historical consumption data to extract meaningful features and leverages cross-learning from different levels of the hierarchy to enhance overall forecasting accuracy.

The proposed model demonstrates resilience across various clusters, showcasing its ability to adapt to different consumption patterns. However, it is important to recognize that while the model’s structure and features remain consistent, retraining is necessary to optimize performance for each cluster. This need arises due to the inherent differences among clusters, where unique attributes and consumption patterns exist. Despite the requirement for retraining, the model consistently achieves high accuracy across diverse clusters, reinforcing its effectiveness and adaptability. This validates the concept that the proposed model, with its cross-learning capabilities, has significant potential for application in residential settings across different countries.

The experimental results published in [22] clearly indicate that the E2E model demonstrated superior performance, consistently achieving lower MAPE and MASE values compared to the other models. SARIMA and SVR performed poorly due to their inability to handle non-linear, dynamic data like residential load consumption. The E2E model excelled in forecasting accuracy, particularly at the aggregated level, benefiting from its cross-learning feature, which effectively captures relationships between hierarchical levels. The MAPE for most clusters remained below 5%, confirming the model's precision. Additionally, the results demonstrate that hierarchical forecasting models utilizing AI techniques are better equipped to handle complex, non-linear real-world scenarios.

The results also compared the E2E model to the BU approach, which requires separate models for each cluster and additional data inputs. The E2E model outperformed the BU approach, which struggled to maintain accuracy, particularly at the aggregated level. The findings suggest that the proposed E2E model is adaptable, accurate, and capable of effectively forecasting load consumption across different clusters, making it a promising tool for residential energy forecasting. The key findings using this methodology include:

- **Performance:** The E2E model based on neural networks achieved a MAPE of less than 6% across all clusters, outperforming traditional statistical methods like SARIMA and SVR, which did not achieve similar accuracy without extensive hyperparameter tuning.
- **Advantages:** The model handles all clusters effectively without requiring individual hyperparameter adjustments and performs well using only historical load data. It significantly improves forecasting accuracy compared to SARIMA, SVR, and BU-based models, with improvements of 91%, 85.8%, and 82.24%, respectively.
- **Strengths:** The model's adaptability allows it to accurately forecast for different clusters without altering its architecture or hyperparameters. It captures diverse load patterns through cross-learning features.
- **Limitations:** The accuracy may decline with sudden extreme data changes, and effective training requires a substantial amount of historical data, which can be challenging for smaller utilities.

Overall, the study demonstrates that the E2E learning model with cross-learning features provides robust and accurate load forecasting for hierarchical structures, offering improvements over traditional methods and reducing computational complexity.

10.7 EXPLORING CLUSTERING: EXTENSION OF PUBLISHED RESEARCH

This section is an extension of the authors' published work [22], and it discusses in depth about each of the created clusters and its unique attributes. Figure 10.4 illustrates the 24 hr load profiles for these 10 clusters represent the average energy consumption across all houses within each cluster. Each cluster demonstrates a unique consumption pattern, varying in both temporal distribution and magnitude.

Cluster 0 maintains relatively stable energy usage with minor fluctuations. In contrast, clusters 1, 3, and 8 show significant increases in consumption at specific times. Cluster 1 experience peak usage in the morning around 8 a.m., followed by a secondary peak in the evening around 6 p.m. Similarly, cluster 3 has two distinct peaks—one in the early morning between 4 and 5 a.m. and another in the evening near 8 p.m. Cluster 8 maintains a steady consumption level throughout the day, with a peak occurring around 8 p.m. Clusters 2, 4, and 6 display relatively lower variability in consumption. Cluster 2 has a notable peak in the late morning, between 11 a.m. and 12 p.m., while cluster 6 exhibits consistently low night-time consumption, followed by a gradual increase at 8 a.m., maintaining a higher but stable magnitude afterward. Clusters 7 and 9 maintain consistently low energy consumption throughout the day, with only minor increases at certain times.

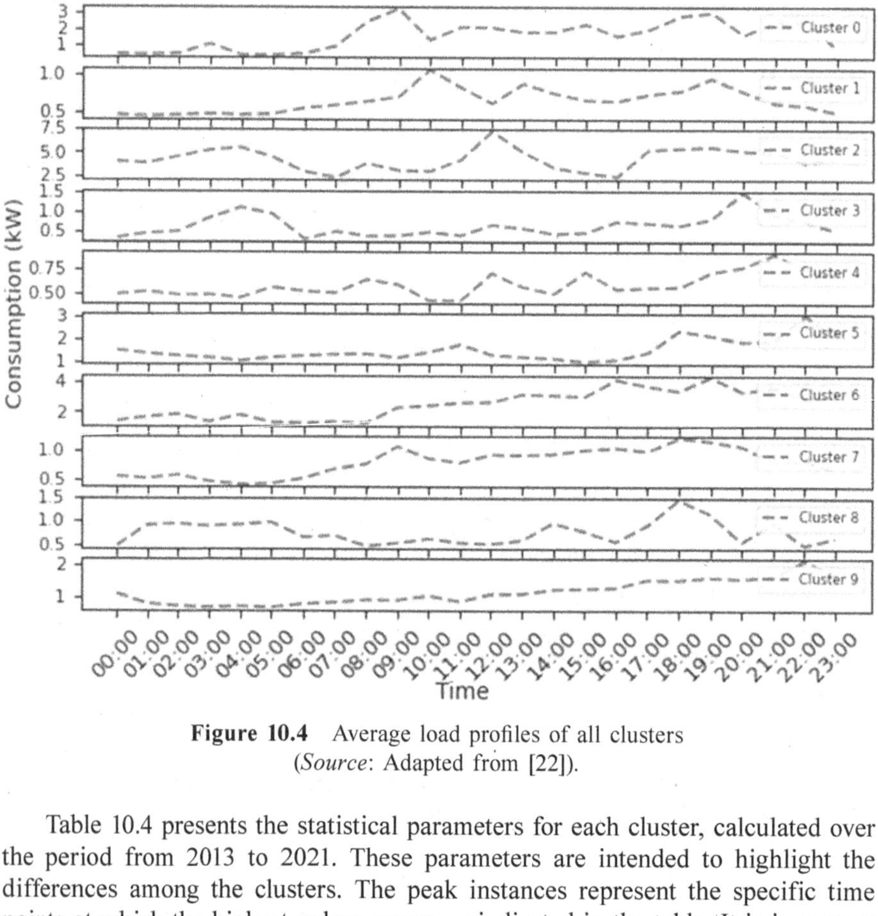

Figure 10.4 Average load profiles of all clusters (*Source*: Adapted from [22]).

Table 10.4 presents the statistical parameters for each cluster, calculated over the period from 2013 to 2021. These parameters are intended to highlight the differences among the clusters. The peak instances represent the specific time points at which the highest values occur, as indicated in the table. It is important to note that these peak instances differ from those shown in the accompanying figure, which illustrates the average behaviour of each cluster. Instead, the peak instances in the table are derived from actual cluster data over the years. Notably, for cluster 3, there is a 3 hr difference in the timing of peak occurrences. Similarly, clusters 1 and 8 exhibit comparable peak occurrence times, yet their mean values differ. These variations emphasize the unique characteristics of each cluster, reinforcing the validity and effectiveness of the clustering process.

Table 10.4 Statistical parameters of clusters

Cluster	Mean	Peak Value	Standard Deviation	Peak Instant
C0	"2.11"	"14.70"	"1.52"	"13:00"
C1	"5.12"	"25.41"	"3.80"	"17:00"
C2	"3.96"	"17.56"	"2.04"	"18:00"
C3	"2.46"	"12.52"	"1.46"	"21:00"
C4	"7.48"	"31.6"	"4.65"	"19:00"
C5	"3.88"	"17.23"	"2.60"	"18:00"
C6	"2.14"	"10.8"	"1.39"	"18:00"
C7	"15.08"	"58.56"	"9.61"	"17:00
C8	"3.69"	"27.45"	"2.53"	"16:00"
C9	"19.07"	"63.67"	"11.11"	"18:00"

Source: Adapted from [22]

10.8 RELATION BETWEEN SOCIO-DEMOGRAPHICAL FEATURES AND DIFFERENT CLUSTERS IN THE HIERARCHY

The residential sector is unique because consumers have varying habits and schedules, which influence their electricity consumption. These may include the unique characteristics of the dwelling type and the behaviour and demographic traits of the residents. This section explores the key factors that may significantly impact electricity usage among residential consumers and considers whether incorporating them can improve forecasting accuracy.

Social demographics refer to the social and demographic characteristics of a population, categorized based on specific criteria such as age, family size, income, and more. In the context of residential households, each household is classified by the demographics of its occupants such as age, gender, education, and income, as well as by characteristics of the house itself, like location and floor size [37]. These factors are pivotal in the energy sector, as they significantly influence how electricity is consumed. For example, a household where all members are employed may exhibit lower electricity usage during the day, with consumption peaks occurring in the early morning and evening. In contrast, a household with children or adults at home throughout the day may have more consistent electricity consumption.

Extensive research has been conducted to understand the various factors that impact electricity consumption. One study found that social and demographic characteristics, including personal attributes, socio-economic status, and socio-demographic factors, are directly related to electricity consumption [37]. Table 10.5 represents the different socio-demographic features that have been studied in various literature including the ones pose a significant impact on consumption [37, 38].

Table 10.5 Demographical features

Demographical Feature	Description
Family size	Family size plays a significant role in influencing household energy consumption. Therefore, the size of a household has a notable impact on overall energy use.
Age of the occupants	Household electricity consumption is closely linked to the age of its occupants, with a notable increase in the presence of teenagers who frequently use modern electronic devices. Furthermore, the presence of retirees also affects consumption, as they typically spend more time at home, leading to higher energy usage.
Income	Electricity consumption rises with income, as higher-income families tend to own more modern appliances, contributing to increased usage. Additionally, wealthier households often have larger homes equipped with more advanced lighting systems and centralized temperature control, further driving up energy consumption.
Education background	In general, individuals with higher educational backgrounds tend to have higher incomes, which leads to increased electricity consumption. However, some families with strong educational backgrounds are also more likely to use energy-efficient appliances.
Dwelling Type	There is a correlation between electricity consumption and dwelling type. Dwelling types refer to various categories of houses, such as detached, semi-detached, terraced houses, or apartments. Each type typically has a different floor size, and dwellings with larger floor areas tend to consume more electricity.
Floor size of the house	Larger floor sizes tend to have higher electricity consumption because they require more lighting and are more likely to use centralized heating systems.
No. of electrical appliances	Increase in the number of appliances has a direct impact on electricity consumption.

Among the factors studied, income status proved to be the strongest indirect predictor of the number of electrical appliances owned, highlighting its strong link to increased electricity consumption. Other factors that showed positive and significant correlations include educational level, gender, and employment status [37, 38].

To assess the impact of socio-demographic characteristics, the considered 50 houses were evaluated based on their maximum consumption values and compared against their unique features to identify correlations. The socio-demographic factors considered include income, family size, house floor area, and ownership of Electric Vehicles (EVs) or Photovoltaics (PVs). For each house, income range and floor area in square meters were provided. It is preferable to categorize income and floor area categorically rather than the absolute values, as shown in Table 10.6.

Table 10.6 Categorical input features of demographics

Income ($)	Categories	Floor Size (m^2)	Categories
< $50k	Low income	< 900	Small house
$50k–$74, 9k		900 – 1499	
$75k–$99k	Medium income	1500 – 1999	Medium house
$100k–$149k		2000 – 2499	
$150k–$300k	High income	2500 – 2999	Big house
> $30k		>3000	

To better understand maximum consumption, the specific time at which it occurs is also considered. For most houses, the peak consumption happens during the day, which is why the period from 11:00 AM to 11:00 PM is divided into four quarters: 11:00 AM to 2:00 PM, 2:00 PM to 5:00 PM, 5:00 PM to 8:00 PM, and 8:00 PM to 11:00 PM. As previously mentioned, the 50 houses were organized into 10 clusters. The demographic features of each house within these clusters were analyzed, and the distinct demographic characteristics of each cluster are detailed below.

- Cluster 0 consists of a single house, with its maximum consumption exceeding that of houses in other clusters, attributed to its larger size and higher income.
- All the houses in Cluster 1 have similar maximum consumption values, all occurring in the third quarter of the day between 5:00 PM and 8:00 PM.
- Cluster 2 features smaller houses with higher income levels, which significantly contribute to the maximum consumption value of 17 kW.
- Cluster 3 consists of houses with varying sizes. Two of them have the same number of occupants and income, yet one has a much higher maximum consumption due to its larger size. The third house, despite having only one occupant and a smaller floor size, reaches a higher maximum due to its high income. This indicates that income and floor size have a greater impact on consumption than the number of occupants. In cases where one demographic factor (income or floor size) is significantly larger, it influences consumption the most.
- Cluster 4 has similar maximum consumption values for all the houses involved.
- Cluster 5 houses share identical demographics: the same family size, large homes, and high income, leading to similar peak consumption values.
- Cluster 6 has a maximum consumption value between clusters 0 and 2. Though this cluster consists of just one house, the difference arises from the fact that its income and floor size are both moderate, unlike cluster 0 with its large floor size and cluster 2 with its higher income.
- Cluster 7 consists of houses with EVs, leading to higher maximum consumption values. These families have either medium or high income and most of them have medium sized houses. Houses without EVs tend to have lower maximum consumption, even if their income is high or medium.

- Cluster 8 exhibits a range of maximum consumption values. One house, inhabited by a family of five, demonstrates the highest maximum consumption due to its high income, large size, and ownership of an EV. Conversely, another house in this cluster, which also has a high income and a large floor area, shows lower maximum consumption because its family size is significantly smaller.
- Cluster 9 reaches the highest maximum consumption in this group, driven by very high income.

While significant work has been done to explore the relationship between electricity consumption and socio-demographic attributes, there has been comparatively less focus on using these features to predict consumption patterns. Therefore, the following section discusses the impact of demographics on electricity consumption and how these factors influence the accuracy of load forecasting.

10.8.1 Impact of Socio-Demographical Features on the Forecasting Accuracy

For the evaluation, all 50 houses with their demographical features were chosen. The most important identified features include family size, income, floor size. However, the considered houses have differences in ethnicity as well, so all four socio-demographic features have been considered.

The E2E learning model has been shown to outperform all other considered approaches. In the residential sector, energy consumption is heavily influenced by the social and demographic status of the consumers. Therefore, the impact of these factors on forecasting accuracy was also assessed. For the analysis, these demographic features were aggregated for each house and then converted into cluster-level percentages indicating the proportion of houses in each cluster corresponding to each demographic feature. The results are presented in Table 10.7.

Table 10.7 Comparison between forecasting accuracy with and without demographical features

Cluster No.	MAPE (%)	
	Without socio-demographics	Including socio-demographics
C0	3.4	2.67
C1	1.12	1.25
C2	5.4	2.26
C3	3.49	1.72
C4	2.6	0.96
C5	1.37	1.41
C6	2.07	1.72
C7	0.88	2.44
C8	1.71	1.99
C9	0.71	2.52

When comparing forecasting accuracy with and without demographic data, an important insight emerges: if a cluster has low variability in its demographic features, incorporating demographics as input features in the forecasting model enhances accuracy. Conversely, if the demographic variability within a cluster is high, as observed in clusters 7 and 9, the accuracy may decline, i.e., not all houses within a cluster share the same demographic characteristics. The clustering of these houses was solely based on load consumption, without considering socio-demographic features. If clustering had been conducted using demographic characteristics, there would have been no demographic variability within each cluster, which would have positively influenced the accuracy of the forecasts.

10.9 CONCLUSIONS AND FUTURE WORK

The transformation of the power sector from a regulated to a deregulated environment has highlighted the need for flexible solutions to manage these rapid changes. Among the key challenges is the accurate estimation of demand, making the development of robust load-forecasting models crucial. Extensive research has been conducted in this field, ranging from traditional statistical models based on mathematical regression to advanced AI-driven models.

As the energy sector transitions and integrates non-linearities like EVs, renewable energy sources, and battery systems, regression-based models struggle to perform optimally and accurately. This signifies the need for increased research in AI-based forecasting models. Unlike traditional models, AI models excel at learning patterns and capturing non-linear relationships, which are essential for handling the complexities of modern energy systems.

This chapter explores the various approaches in the literature where researchers are developing AI-based forecasting models for diverse applications. It specifically presents a methodology for generating accurate forecasts for the residential sector using a top-down hierarchical approach. The construction of this framework involves analysing half-hourly data obtained from residential smart meters and creating seasonal load profiles for individual households. The E2E learning model is rooted in the principles of the top-down hierarchical method, leveraging features from different hierarchy levels, and integrating cross-learning information to significantly improve forecast accuracy [22]. A key strength of this model is its ability to forecast load at any level of the hierarchy, utilizing input from both aggregated data and specific nodes.

To evaluate the effectiveness of the E2E model, it was compared against the two-stage approach and other conventional methods. Results showed the E2E model achieved a MAPE of 2.27%, outperforming other methods. A comparison with the BU approach further demonstrated the superiority of the E2E model, as the BU approach yielded a mean MAPE of 12.81% across all clusters [22]. This stark difference highlights the accuracy and efficiency of the E2E model. Its versatility, covering the entire hierarchy, is especially valuable for stakeholders in the power sector, providing accurate forecasts at every hierarchical level and supporting well-informed choices and efficient resource management.

This chapter also delves deeply into the insights gained from the clustering process, emphasizing the diversity and uniqueness of the generated clusters. These insights illuminate the varied consumption patterns in the residential sector and the challenges of building precise forecasting models for such a complex domain. In addition, a case study evaluates the role of socio-demographic factors in residential energy consumption. By exploring the inclusion of simple demographic features, the chapter assesses their potential to enhance forecasting accuracy and identifies scenarios where such features might significantly improve model performance. This comprehensive analysis offers valuable guidance for tailoring forecasting models to better address the complexities of residential energy consumption.

REFERENCES

[1] Guan, W., K. Chung, K.W. Cheung, X. Sun, P.B. Luh, L.D. Michel, et al. 2013. Advanced load forecast with hierarchical forecasting capability. *In*: 2013 IEEE Power and Energy Society General Meeting. 1–5. IEEE.

[2] Langtry, M., V. Wichitwechkarn, R. Ward, C. Zhuang, M.J. Kreitmair, N., et al. 2024. Impact of data usage for forecasting on performance of model predictive control in buildings with smart energy storage. arXiv preprint arXiv:2402.12539.

[3] Fliedner, G. 2001. Hierarchical forecasting: issues and use guidelines. Industrial Management and Data Systems. 101(1): 5–12.

[4] Brégère, M. and M. Huard. 2022. Online hierarchical forecasting for power consumption data. International Journal of Forecast. 38: 339–351.

[5] Hyndman, R.J., R.A. Ahmed, G. Athanasopoulos, and H.L. Shang. 2011. Optimal combination forecasts for hierarchical time series. Computational Statistics and Data Analysis. 55(9): 2579–2589.

[6] Chicco, G., R. Napoli, F. Piglione, P. Postolache, M. Scutariu and C. Toader. 2005. Emergent electricity customer classification. IEE Proceedings-Generation, Transmission and Distribution, 152(2): 164–172.

[7] Bidoki, S.M., N. Mahmoudi-Kohan, M.H. Sadreddini, M.Z. Jahromi and M.P. Moghaddam. 2010. Evaluating different clustering techniques for electricity customer classification. *In*: IEEE PES T&D. 1–5. IEEE.

[8] Kavlakoglu, E. and V. Winland. 2024. What is k-means clustering? https://www.ibm.com/topics/k-means-clustering.

[9] Tureczek, A., P.S. Nielsen and H. Madsen. 2018. Electricity consumption clustering using smart meter data. Energies. 11(4): 859.

[10] Tsekouras, G.J., N.D. Hatziargyriou and E.N. Dialynas. 2007. Two-stage pattern recognition of load curves for classification of electricity customers. IEEE Transactions on Power Systems. 22(3): 1120–1128.

[11] Wu, Q., X. Qi, E. Fuller and C.Q. Zhang. 2013. Follow the leader: A centrality guided clustering and its application to social network analysis. The Scientific World Journal. 2013(1): 368568.

[12] Shahid, N. 2023. Comparison of hierarchical clustering and neural network clustering: an analysis on precision dominance. Scientific Reports 13(1): 5661.

[13] Chicco, G., R. Napoli and F. Piglione. 2006. Comparisons among clustering techniques for electricity customer classification. IEEE Transactions on Power Systems. 21(2): 933–940.

[14] Parkash, B., T.T. Lie, W. Li and S.R. Tito. 2022. Hierarchical structure based energy consumption forecasting in top-down approach. *In*: 2022 7th Asia Conference on Power and Electrical Engineering (ACPEE). 1732–1737. IEEE.

[15] Chicco, G. 2012. Overview and performance assessment of the clustering methods for electrical load pattern grouping. Energy. 42(1): 68–80.

[16] Karo, I.M.K., K. MaulanaAdhinugraha and A.F. Huda. 2017. A cluster validity for spatial clustering based on Davies Bouldin index and Polygon Dissimilarity function. *In*: 2017 second international conference on informatics and computing (ICIC). 1–6. IEEE.

[17] Räsänen, T. and M. Kolehmainen. 2009. Feature-based clustering for electricity use time series data. *In*: Adaptive and Natural Computing Algorithms: 9th International Conference, ICANNGA 2009, Kuopio, Finland, April 23–25, 2009, Revised Selected Papers 9. 401–412. Springer Berlin Heidelberg.

[18] Hou, H., C. Liu, Q. Wang, X. Wu, J. Tang, Y. Shi, et al. 2022. Review of load forecasting based on artificial intelligence methodologies, models and challenges. Electric Power Systems Research. 210: 108067.

[19] Roy, N., P. Tripathy, S.C. De, S. Shadruddin, B. Swargiary, S. Kumar, et al. 2021. Load forecast using ANN & VAR techniques for Northeastern Regional (NER) grid of India. *In*: 2021 9th IEEE International Conference on Power Systems (ICPS). 1–5. IEEE.

[20] Wen, X., J. Liao, Q. Niu, N. Shen and Y. Bao. 2024. Deep learning-driven hybrid model for short-term load forecasting and smart grid information management. Scientific Reports. 14(1): 13720.

[21] Türkoğlu, A.S., B. Erkmen, Y. Eren, O. Erdinç and İ. Küçükdemiral. 2024. Integrated approaches in resilient hierarchical load forecasting via TCN and optimal valley filling based demand response application. Applied Energy. 360: 122722.

[22] Parkash, B., T.T. Lie, W. Li and S.R. Tito. 2024. End-to-end top-down load forecasting model for residential consumers. Energies. 17(11): 2550.

[23] McLoughlin, F., A uffy and M. Conlon. 2012. Characterising domestic electricity consumption patterns by dwelling and occupant socio-economic variables: An Irish case study. Energy and Buildings. 48: 240–248.

[24] Schober, P., C. Boer and L.A. Schwarte. 2018. Correlation coefficients: appropriate use and interpretation. Anesthesia and Analgesia. 126(5): 1763–1768.

[25] Wang, Z., J. Li, S. Zhu, J. Zhao, S. Deng, S. Zhong, et al. 2019. A review of load forecasting of the distributed energy system. *In*: IOP Conference Series: Earth and Environmental Science. 237(4): 042019. IOP Publishing.

[26] Rafati, A., M. Joorabian and E. Mashhour. 2020. An efficient hour-ahead electrical load forecasting method based on innovative features. Energy. 201: 117511.

[27] Schober, P., C. Boer, and L.A. Schwarte. 2018. Correlation coefficients: appropriate use and interpretation. Anesthesia and Analgesia. 126(5): 1763–1768.

[28] Kim, M.J. 2018. Characteristics and determinants by electricity consumption level of households in Korea. Energy Reports. 4: 70–76.

[29] Ahmad, N., Y. Ghadi, M. Adnan and M. Ali. 2022. Load forecasting techniques for power system: Research challenges and survey. IEEE Access. 10: 71054–71090.

[30] Franses, P.H. 2016. A note on the mean absolute scaled error. International Journal of Forecasting. 32(1): 20–22.

[31] Dataport. P.S. [Online]. Available: https://dataport.pecanstreet.org/

[32] Qiuyu, L., C.A.I. Qiuna, L.I.U. Sijie, Y.A.N.G. Yun, Y. Binjie, W. Yang, et al. 2017. Short-term load forecasting based on load decomposition and numerical weather forecast. *In*: 2017 IEEE Conference on Energy Internet and Energy System Integration (EI2). 1–5. IEEE.

[33] Nepal, B., M. Yamaha, A. Yokoe and T. Yamaji. 2020. Electricity load forecasting using clustering and ARIMA model for energy management in buildings. Japan Architectural Review. 3(1): 62–76.

[34] Dai, Y. and P. Zhao. 2020. A hybrid load forecasting model based on support vector machine with intelligent methods for feature selection and parameter optimization. Applied Energy. 279: 115332.

[35] Blázquez-García, A., A. Conde, A. Milo, R. Sánchez and T. Barrio. 2020. Short-term office building elevator energy consumption forecast using SARIMA. Journal of Building Performance Simulation. 13(1): 69–78.

[36] Kang, Z., Jin, M. and Spanos, C.J. 2014. Modeling of end-use energy profile: An appliance-data-driven stochastic approach. *In*: IECON 2014-40th Annual Conference of the IEEE Industrial Electronics Society. 5382–5388. IEEE.

[37] Supapo, K.R.M., L. Lozano, I.D.F. Tabañag and E.M. Querikiol. 2022. Untangling the impact of socio-demographic factors on energy consumption: Why is energy access difficult to achieve in off-grid island communities? Energy for Sustainable Development. 70: 32–44.

[38] Huebner, G., D. Shipworth, I. Hamilton, Z. Chalabi and T. Oreszczyn. 2016. Understanding electricity consumption: A comparative contribution of building factors, socio-demographics, appliances, behaviours and attitudes. Applied Energy. 177: 692–702.

Chapter **11**

Prosumer Electricity Demand Forecasting Using Artificial Intelligence-based Algorithms Incorporating Meteorological Data

Gülizar Gizem Tolun*[1], Ömer Can Tolun[2] and Kasım Zor[2]

[1]Department of Energy Systems Engineering, Osmaniye Korkut Ata University, Osmaniye, Türkiye

[2]Department of Electrical and Electronic Engineering, Adana Alparslan Türkeş Science and Technology University, Adana, Türkiye

11.1 INTRODUCTION

In recent times, traditional electrical energy systems have been substituted by cutting–edge advancements, including smart grids, microgrids, and the internet of energy. These systems utilize locally produced electricity with minimal cost and maximum efficiency, all with the aim of achieving environmental sustainability. Modern distributed energy systems are impacted by the intrinsically sporadic characteristics of renewable energy sources as they are integrated into the power grids [1]. Consequently, accurate forecasting of electricity demand has become essential to ensuring equilibrium between power generation and consumption.

*For Correspondence: gulizargizemunaldi@osmaniye.edu.tr

DOI: 10.1201/9781003541875-11

Typically, household consumers use the power system unidirectionally to use the supplied electricity. By integrating renewable energy sources, users can alter their electricity consumption habits, leading to the regeneration of the established energy pattern [2]. In the context of intermittent renewable energy sources, the introduction of the term prosumer brings more complexity to the sustainability of the equilibrium between generated and required power [3]. Within this specific context, accurate forecasting of electricity demand one quarter of an hour in advance becomes progressively crucial as a subject of research. The accuracy of these forecasts streamlines the task for generators to strategize their electricity usage, to improve the efficiency of distributed generation systems, and to participate in peer-to-peer energy trading networks. The significant role of consumers in load shifting and demand control is widely recognized as an essential component for modern electric power networks.

The concept of PEDF, which is illustrated in Figure 11.1, is increasingly recognized as a critical component of modern energy systems, particularly in the context of the global shift toward decentralized and renewable energy sources. PEDF is a sophisticated predictive method that specifically targets the prediction of energy consumption and production patterns of prosumers, who are entities that engage in both electricity consumption and generation, often using renewable sources such as solar panels or wind turbines. Contrary to conventional load forecasting, which only considers consumption, prosumer forecasting demands the consideration of the bidirectional energy flow, thereby increasing its complexity. Accurate forecasts in the integration of renewable energy need the use of advanced AI models and real-time data analytics due to the substantial unpredictability introduced [4, 5].

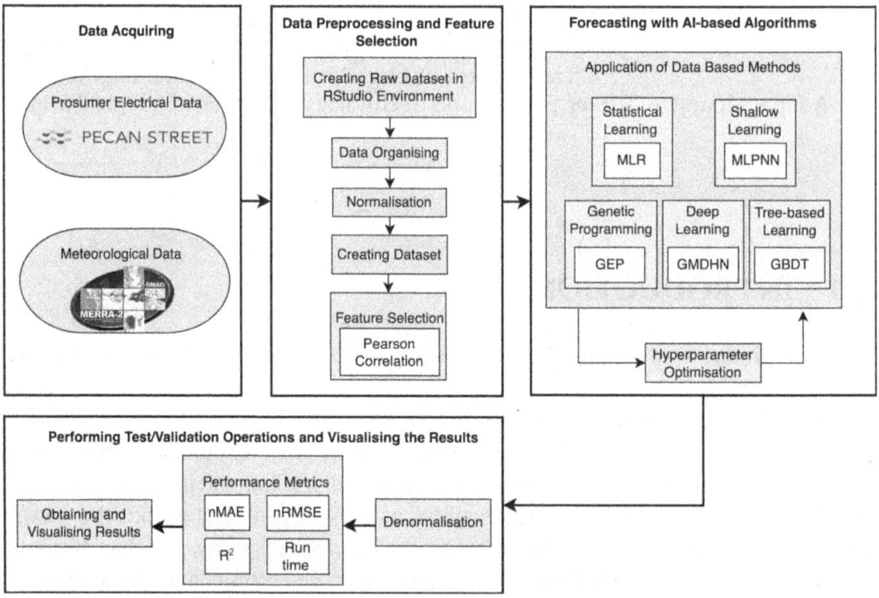

Figure 11.1 An illustration of PEDF concept.

Accurate forecasting of prosumer power use or generation is crucial for grid management as it allows operators to effectively balance supply and demand. Strategic forecasting is crucial in energy trading since it enables prosumers to make well-informed choices about when to sell surplus energy back to the grid, therefore maximizing their financial gains [6]. Precision load forecasting in microgrids is crucial for ensuring stable and efficient operation, especially in isolated or self-sustaining electricity networks. Furthermore, governments and utilities employ forecasting data to inform policy and planning, directing expenditures in infrastructure and formulating plans to enhance the integration of renewable energy sources [7]. By means of these applications, the predictions of prosumer load not only improve the stability of the power grid but also contribute to the wider objectives of sustainability and economic efficiency in the energy industry. In addition, through the use of sophisticated data analytics, AI, and real-time data, PEDF both develops the predictability of the power grid and also fosters economic effectiveness and environmental sustainability. Nevertheless, it also poses distinctive obstacles, namely in the management of the fluctuating nature of renewable energy generation and the intricacy of data [8].

Lately, the implementation of AI in data forecasting has undergone a significant transformation. Traditional forecasting methods were largely reliant on statistical models and historical data analysis, which often limited their predictive capabilities. However, AI algorithms have revolutionized this process by enabling the analysis of vast datasets and uncovering complex relationships within the data. For instance, machine learning algorithms can effectively identify patterns, thereby enhancing the accuracy of time series forecasts and predicting future trends across various domains, including meteorology, financial markets, and energy consumption [9]. The efficacy of AI in data forecasting is attributed not only to its ability to process large volumes of data but also to its capacity for continuous performance improvement. Deep learning techniques, particularly neural networks, facilitate the extraction of intricate relationships from datasets, which is essential for refining prediction accuracy over time. These algorithms excel at distinguishing between noise and significant anomalies in the data, ensuring reliable outcomes, especially in sensitive forecasting scenarios like electricity demand forecasting [10–12]. Furthermore, AI plays a crucial role in interpreting prediction results and integrating them into decision support systems, thereby enhancing operational efficiency and strategic planning.

A real-time PEDF analysis is carried out, employing comprehensive electrical, historical, and meteorological data for an average household residing in New York, USA. The key contributions of this study are outlined below:

- This study used electrical, historical, and meteorological data to conduct PEDF analysis for an average household in New York, USA, with the involvement of statistical and AI techniques, including MLR, MLPNN, GEP, GMDHN, and GBDT.
- Existing studies on PEDF are lacking, particularly in terms of comprehensive real-time applications. This study aims to address this gap and enhance the current body of literature.

- The employed data exhibits nonlinear properties, resulting in the impact of several phenomena on the PEDF. This scenario is the conclusion of an intricate assessment aimed at achieving PEDF, dependent upon the successful implementation of statistical and AI algorithms.

This chapter offers a comprehensive examination of the implementation of MLR, MLPNN, GEP, GMDHN, and GBDT for the PEDF in a residential household located in New York, USA. After the introduction section, which provides an in-depth overview of the subject, the chapter employs the following structure: Section 11.2 provides an exhaustive evaluation of the literature along with the title of the related work. A detailed explanation of the dataset and the fundamental concepts of MLR, MLPNN, GEP, GMDHN, and GBDT can be found in Section 11.3. Section 11.4 offers brief descriptions of performance metrics and summarizes the results of the forecasting algorithms. The results presented in Section 11.5 specifically address future perspectives.

11.2 RELATED WORK

A considerable amount of research has been published in the literature to provide insight into the subject of the PEDF and the summary of the literature in the research area of PEDF is shown in Table 11.1. Pinto et al. proposed a novel methodology for modelling and forecasting multi-period flexibility from residential prosumers, which considers uncertainty in net-load and PV forecasts and incorporates physical and operating constraints of distributed energy resources and customer preferences. The results showed that combined evolutionary particle swarm optimisation (EPSO) and support vector data description (SVDD) can efficiently model and forecast multi-period flexibility from home energy management system uncertainty in net-load and PV forecasts, and incorporating physical and operating constraints of distributed energy resources and customer preferences [13]. Bruno et al. aim to optimize the energy sources in residential prosumers with a control architecture that incorporates PV generation, battery storage, and interruptible loads. The approach employs a predictive optimal control problem and a closed-loop local controller. By considering prediction errors and the presence of appropriate technology and gadgets to facilitate consumers' active performance, the suggested control architecture can efficiently optimize energy resources for home prosumers [14]. Petrican et al. presented a comprehensive evaluation of various statistical and machine learning algorithms for household energy consumption prediction, involving seasonal auto-regressive integrated moving average (SARIMA), MLPNN, support vector regression (SVR), long short-term memory (LSTM), and ensemble models, to aid the integration of households with smart grids. The outcomes demonstrated that the ensemble model gives the highest accuracy [15].

Ruiz-Abellón et al. proposed a methodology to improve the accuracy of short-term forecasting of renewable energy generation and demand and applies Aggregators can effectively control the anticipated flexibility of demand by implementing demand response systems. The results indicated that the suggested approach could assist aggregators in effectively managing the demand flexibility on the aggregator side and balancing errors through a closed control loop that influences the net demand of prosumers [16]. Grimaldo and Novak presented a semi-automatic system combining explainable machine learning and visual analytics to forecast short-term energy demand, aiding utility analysts in understanding and managing energy supply and demand. The system provided forecasts of electricity demand based on the average of the five most similar days identified by the k-nearest neighbour (KNN) algorithm, with interactive visualizations to help users understand the results [17]. Faraji et al. introduced an innovative day-ahead operational and scheduling framework for prosumers employing a corrective two-level load forecasting technique which improves the optimal utilisation of renewable energy sources and battery energy storage systems. The findings indicated that the suggested strategy reduces both operational expenses and life loss costs associated with the battery energy storage system while also providing satisfactory load forecasting accuracy [18]. Panapakidis et al. presented a formulation and solution of profit maximization problem for a prosumer using price forecasting, PV power forecasting, and load forecasting to estimate future revenues and bill savings in a deregulated electricity market. The results show that the Elman neural networks (ENN) outperform the feed-forward neural networks (FFNN) in load forecasting, price forecasting, and PV generation forecasting [19].

Zhao et al. mainly focused on short-term load forecasting at the building level using AI and machine learning, specifically comparing support vector machines (SVM) and LSTM models for day-ahead and hour-ahead load forecasting. The results of the study showed that LSTM outperforms SVM models in hour-ahead, day-ahead, and peak hour prediction but at the cost of longer training time [20]. Zhou et al. suggested a multi-energy net load forecasting framework, utilizing deep learning technology to estimate the electrical, thermal, and gas net load of integrated local energy systems with heterogeneous prosumers simultaneously. The proposed approach is thoroughly and completely validated using actual data from prosumers at the household level. The results clearly demonstrate the superiority and high accuracy of the proposed methodology for forecasting [21]. Antal et al. suggested a hybrid deep neural network model for multi-step energy forecasting of prosumers. This model combines clustering and MLPNN classification models with MLPNN regression models. It also includes new features derived from raw energy data. The findings shown that the model provides high prediction accuracy for prosumers operating at small and medium scales, even when dealing with energy data streams [22].

Jiang et al. proposed a novel deep learning technique named Deep-Autoformer for short-term load forecasting. Experiments conducted on a microgrid system in Austin, Texas, demonstrate that the proposed model yields higher predictive outcomes relative to existing methodologies and that multilayer sensor configurations are effective for deep feature extraction. Long-term historical data can adversely affect model performance and pose a risk of overfitting [23]. Yazdani et al. presented a systematic framework for real-time trading in prosumer communities using a data-driven robust optimization model that deals with uncertainty and

Table 11.1 Literature Review for the PEDF

Reference	Year	PEDF Method	Optimisation Method	Methodology
[13]	2017	EPSO and SVDD	–	Combined EPSO and SVDD for forecasting.
[14]	2017	Model Predictive Control	Predictive Optimal Control	Proposed a two-stage control architecture targeting the optimization of energy resources for residential prosumers.
[15]	2018	SARIMA, MLPNN, LSTM, SVR, and Ensemble	–	Used five different forecasting models.
[16]	2019	Stochastic Gradient Boosting	–	The methodology comprises three sequential stages: (1) short-term energy consumption forecasting and generation of renewable sources; (2) categorization of the analysis of the daily renewable generation statistics using dynamic time warping; and (3) implementation of demand response strategies using load models based on physical processes.
[17]	2020	KNN	–	Used KNN algorithm to identify the most similar days in historical data based on user-defined weather parameters.
[18]	2020	MLPNN	–	Used a two-level load forecasting approach, where the first level uses an MLPNN for time-series forecasting, and the second level uses a feed-forward ANN for corrective load forecasting.
[19]	2021	ENN and FFNN	–	Used machine learning algorithms, specifically FFNN and ENN, to forecast future prices, PV power, and load.
[20]	2021	SVM and LSTM	–	Used data processing, feature selection using extreme gradient boosting (XGBoost) and auto-correlation, and model training using SVM and LSTM models.
[21]	2021	Hierarchical Clustering and DBN	–	Consists of two main components: a hierarchical clustering framework to aggregate heterogeneous prosumers and a deep belief network (DBN)-based forecasting method to extract the hidden features in multi-energy time series.

[22]	2022	K-means and MLPNN	Genetic Algorithm	Combined clustering and MLPNN models in order to identify the different categories of energy profiles. Additionally, used to MLPNN models to optimize the predicted energy values, taking into account the energy data streams.
[23]	2022	Deep-autoformer	–	Designed to optimize forecast performance by learning long-term dependencies and local variations. Particular focus is on automated feature extraction on time series data and improving forecast accuracy.
[24]	2023	K-means, Aggregative Hierarchical Clustering, and Gaussian Mixture Model, and Tree-Based Ensemble Learning	Alternating Direction Method of Multipliers	Used machine learning techniques, such as clustering and pattern recognition, to determine the cluster to which the recently observed net-load data belongs, and a hybrid of tree-based ensemble learning models to forecast power requirements.
[25]	2023	Ensemble Learning	P2P Energy Trading	Designed a P2P energy trading scenario with PV systems and an ensemble method is proposed to evaluate the effects of the accuracy of power generation and load forecasts.
[26]	2024	Propnet, LSTM, SARIMA, Smoothing Holt-Winter, and Empirical Regression-based	–	Used a comparative analysis of several variations of deep-learning-based machine learning models, including Facebook's Prophet and LSTM models, SARIMA and smoothing Holt-Winters models, and empirical regression-based models that utilize domain knowledge.

incorporates machine learning techniques for high-quality forecasts. The results demonstrated that the proposed framework could provide high-quality power and flexibility forecasts, reduce the overall cost of the system, and assist prosumers in trading their power and flexibility in a decentralized fashion [24]. Zhang et al. introduced an ensemble method integrating power generation and load forecasting with peer-to-peer (P2P) energy trading to optimize costs and enhance accuracy in community microgrids. The proposed method effectively reduced the total cost of power trading within the community microgrid by approximately 20% compared to direct purchases and sales with the grid. The estimation error derived from the combination of forecasts method is the lowest among all methods tested [25]. Kychkin and Chasparis reviewed and tested various AI-powered short-term load forecasting methodologies for prosumer communities, including Facebook's Prophet and LSTM models, SARIMA and smoothing Holt-Winters models, and empirical regression-based models that utilize domain knowledge. The findings indicated that the LSTM model effectively catches the highest levels of consumption, while the Prophet model accurately generates smooth forecast profiles [26].

11.3 MATERIAL AND METHODS

In the following part, the data collection and techniques that were utilized for forecasting methodologies that were specifically selected for PEDF are presented.

11.3.1 Material

The dataset utilized in this research is constructed to contain 15 minutes of load data for a residential household located in New York, USA. It has a total of 19 features which include electricity, meteorological, and calendar predictors. The dataset is obtained from the Pecan Street database for electricity predictions and the MERRA-2 database of NASA for meteorological forecasts [27, 28]. The provided information allows for the examination of the relationship between meteorological conditions and residential electrical consumption or generation, while also presenting a 15-minute temporal resolution. The details of input variables can be observed in Table 11.2. Furthermore, Figure 11.2 describes a systematic analysis in which predictors are classified into three categories: electrical, meteorological, and calendar.

The study contains three distinct scenarios, with the inputs to be included in each scenario outlined in Figure 11.2.

The selection of inputs for the scenario is based on the correlation map provided in Figure 11.3. The Pearson correlation coefficient is denoted by the parameter P in both Figure 11.2 and Figure 11.3. The first scenario utilized all inputs in the forecasting process, while the second scenario selected only 7 predictors with a P value greater than 0.1 and less than –0.1 as inputs. The third scenario involved selecting 6 predictors as input based on their P coefficients, which ranged between 0.4 and –0.4.

Table 11.2 Information about Input variables

Input Category	Predictor Number	Abbreviation	Description	Unit	Min	Median	Mean	Max
Electrical	1	P15mP	Previous 15-Minute	kW	–11.08	0.28	–1.07	8.37
	2	PHP	Previous Hour					
	3	PDP	Previous Day					
Meteorological	4	T	Temperature	°C	4.74	20.63	20.33	33.24
	5	RH	Relative Humidity	%	26.56	80.78	76.83	100.00
	6	P	Pressure	hPa	977.1	1006.7	1006.7	1022.3
	7	WS	Wind Speed	m/s	0.06	2.72	2.94	11.31
	8	WD	Wind Direction	°	0.08	200.66	191.72	359.96
	9	R	Rainfall	kg/m^2	0	12.9e–04	49.46e–03	47.00
	10	SD	Snow Depth	m	0	0	3.99e–10	1.00e–06
	11	SWI	Short-Wave Irradiation	Wh/m^2	0	14.20	58.12	955.00
Calendar	12	MY	Month of Year	–	1	–		12
	13	WY	Week of Year	–	1	–		53
	14	DY	Day of Year	–	1	–		365
	15	DM	Day of Month	–	1	–		31
	16	DW	Day of Week	–	1	–		7
	17	HD	Hour of Day	–	1	–		23
	18	QH	Quarter of Hour	–	1	–		4
	19	TD	Type of Day	–	0	–		1

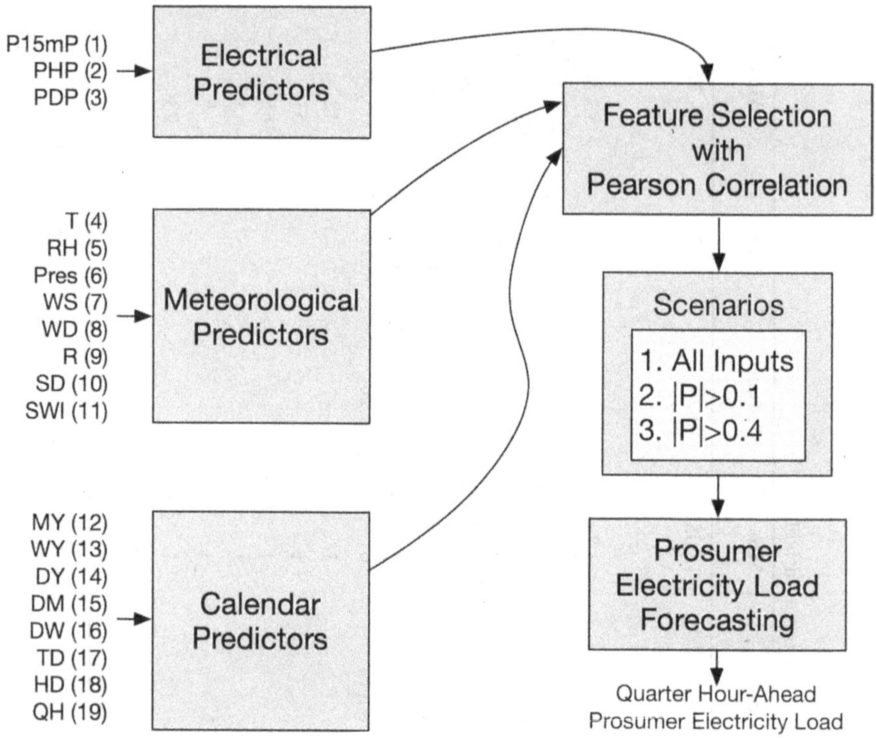

Figure 11.2 Systematic analysis of the work.

11.3.2 Methods

The selection of MLR, MLPNN, GEP, GMDHN, and GBDT is based on their proven effectiveness in forecasting research. Particularly, the implementation of both statistical and AI algorithms enhances the scope of the study.

MLR

MLR is a statistical method used to forecast the outcome of a response variable by considering several explanatory variables. An MLR model is used to represent the linear relationship between the independent variables x and the dependent variable y that will be examined [29].

$$y = b_0 + b_1x_1 + b_2x_2 + \cdots + b_ix_i \tag{1}$$

where y is the independent variable, b is the regression constant, and x referred to ith predictor [30].

MLPNN

ANN has attracted considerable interest owing to its capacity to imitate the functions of the human brain and its efficacy in resolving intricate problems.

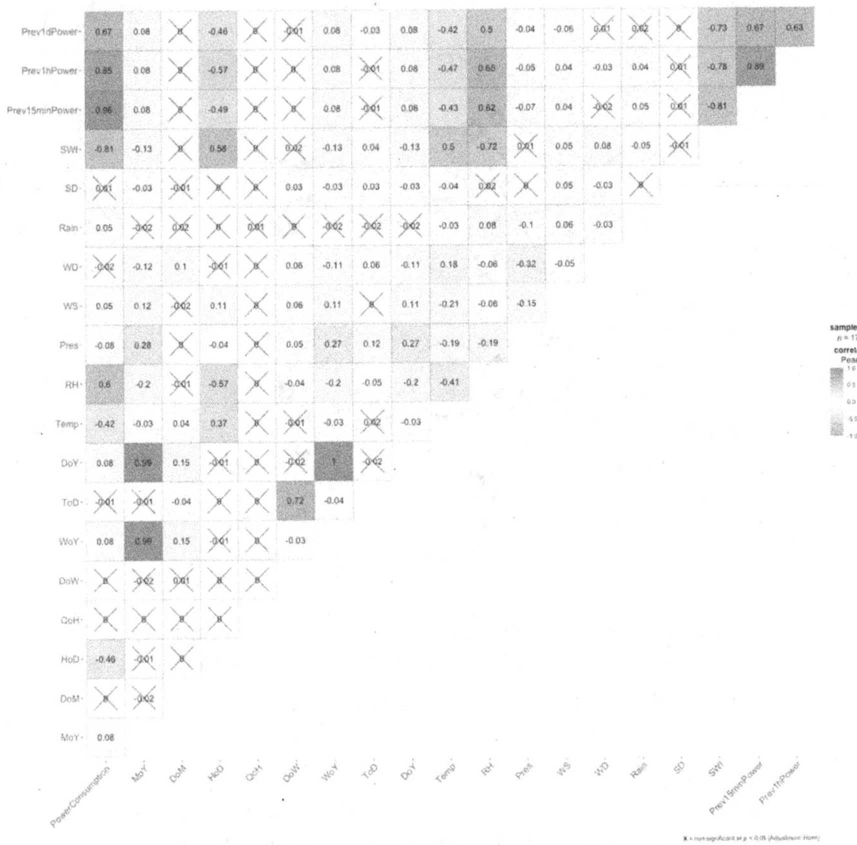

Figure 11.3 Correlation map.

These networks exhibit essential characteristics, including real-time functionality, capacity for learning, parallel processing, generalization, self-organization, stability, and adaptability. Their vast array of neural network models and training algorithms have led to their extensive application in many fields such as function estimation, prediction, pattern recognition, and control. The MLPNN network is a specific type of ANN that demonstrates exceptional performance in accurately approximating nonlinear functions. It is capable of accurately detecting complex dynamic systems without relying on explicit models [31, 32].

In particular, ANN has emerged as a promising alternative to conventional statistical modeling approaches in several scientific fields. An MLPNN is a type of neural network consisting of three layers: input, hidden, and output [33]. It can be defined as a neural network architecture that allows for customized training of biases and weights to attain a desired result. Furthermore, the weights are considered a collection of neurons that can be organized into different tandem layers [34]. A general representation of the MLPNN is given in Figure 11.4.

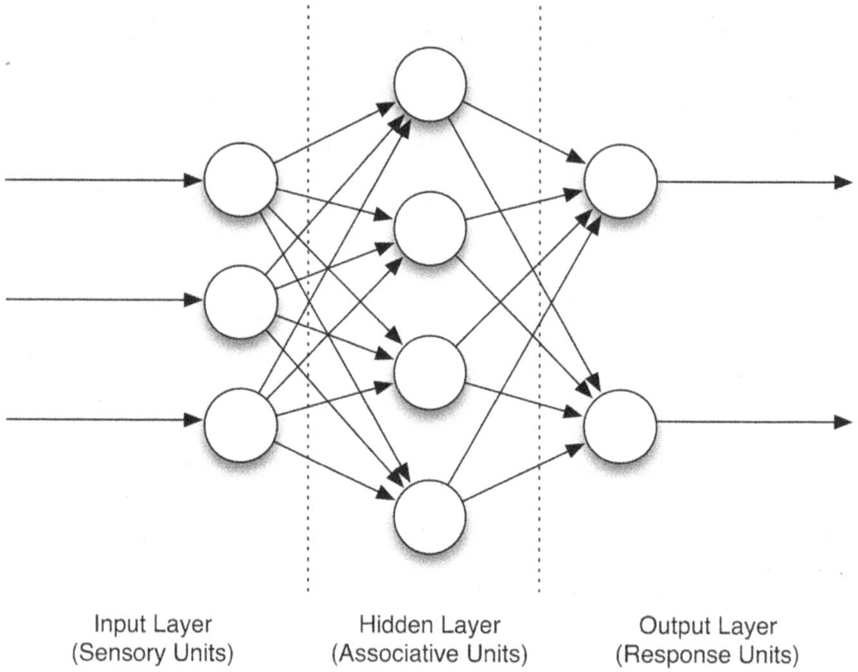

Figure 11.4 A representation of MLPNN.

GEP

GEP is a fundamental and widely recognized AI method that produces simple equations between predictor variables and target variables. GEP is an enhanced algorithm that is essentially based on genetic algorithms and programming systems [35]. The GEP framework comprises several essential components, including function and terminal sets, control parameters, fitness function, and termination conditions. Even though parse tree notation is commonly utilized in conventional genetic programming, the GEP algorithm implements a predetermined length of character strings to represent resolutions to the problems, which are subsequently rendered as parse trees [36]. The figure below depicts this GEP demonstration, known as an expression tree.

The equation belonging to expression tree indicated in Figure 11.5 is below:

$$y = a_1 * b_1 + \sqrt{a_2 - b_2} \qquad (2)$$

The representation of the GEP algorithm is depicted in Figure 11.6. In a nutshell, the algorithm initiates the process of randomly generating chromosomes in order to determine the beginning population. Next, the expression and fitness assessment of each chromosome are performed sequentially. Following that, the selection of individuals is conducted based on their fitness for reproduction and modification. The process is iterated for an indeterminate number of generations or until a solution is reached.

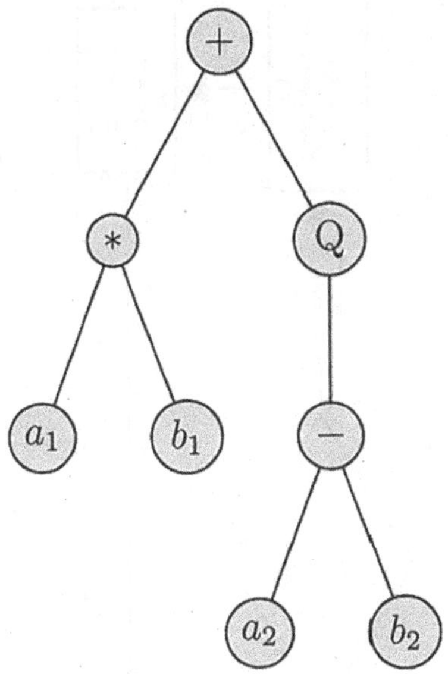

Figure 11.5 An example of expression tree [37].

GMDHN

The GMDHN is a neural network designed for modeling the self-organization of complex systems. Its fundamental principles operate as follows: Initially, the system generates a sequence of active neurons based on the cross-correlation of input units. Each neuron has the ability to choose the most suitable transfer function. Subsequently, a multitude of neurons in close proximity to the target variable are picked from the available set of neurons, and then the most advantageous combination of neurons comprising the new generation is selected. The cycle of survival and evolution continues until the subsequent generation of neurons does not surpass the preceding one, and the ideal model is determined [38–40].

During training, the GMDHN adaptively generates an ideal model that attains the highest level of accuracy while avoiding overfitting. To achieve this, GMDHN uses least squares regression to determine the most favorable mathematical correlation between input and output variables by exploiting a reference function represented as follows:

$$y = a_0 + \sum_{i=1}^{n} a_i x_i + \sum_{i=1}^{n}\sum_{j=1}^{n} a_{ij} x_i x_j + \sum_{i=1}^{n}\sum_{j=1}^{n}\sum_{k=1}^{n} a_{ij} x_i x_j x_k + \cdots \quad (3)$$

where y represents the output, $X = (x_1, x_2, \ldots, x_n)$ symbolizes the input vector and finally a represents the weight vector [38].

The quadratic representation of two variables typically employs the below equation:

$$y = a_0 + a_1 x_i + a_2 x_j + a_3 x_i x_j + a_4 x_i^2 + a_5 x_j^2 \quad (4)$$

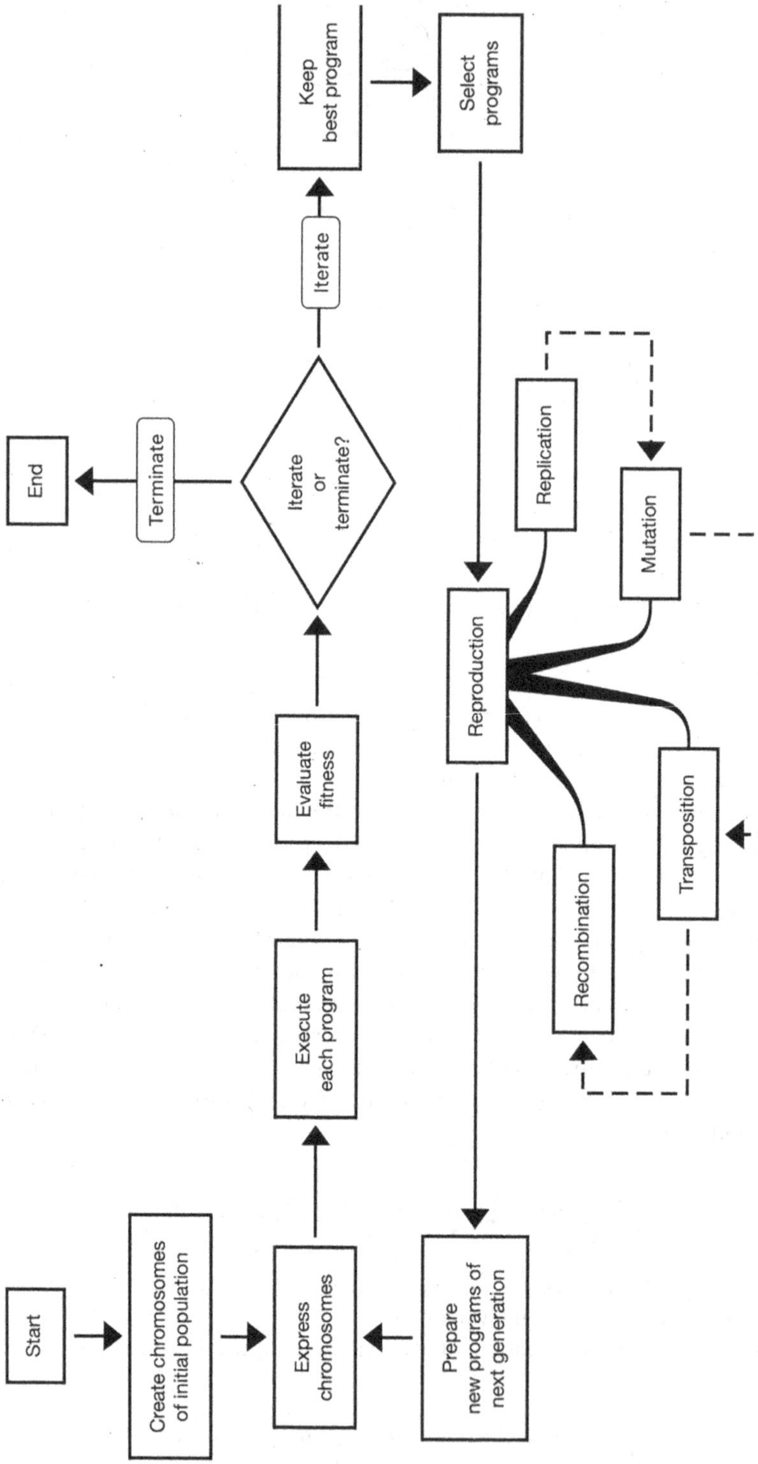

Figure 11.6 The diagram of GEP algorithm [37].

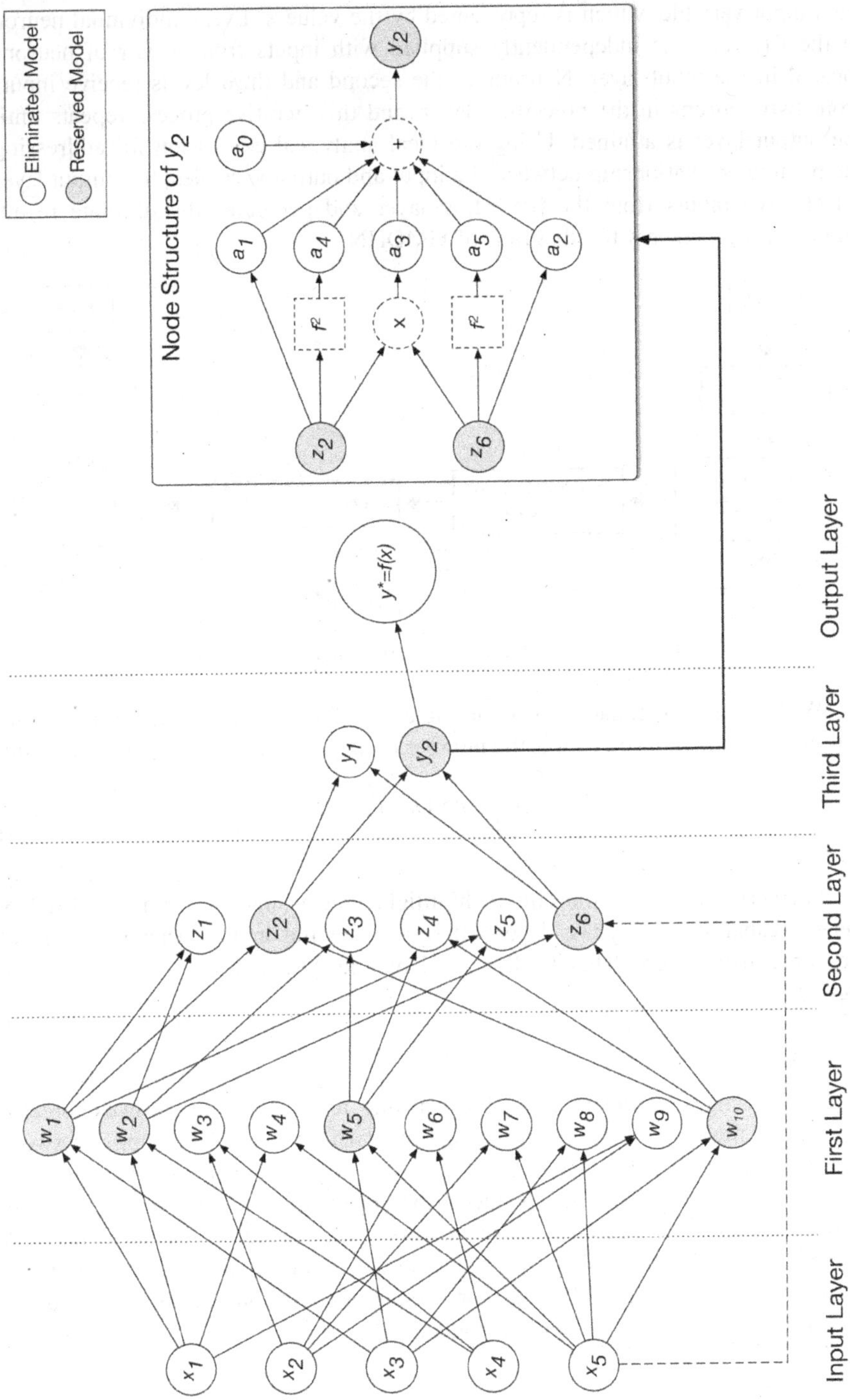

Figure 11.7 The structure of GMDHN [38].

As shown in Figure 11.7, the input layer of GMDHN has neurons that represent each input variable, which is represented by the value x. Every individual neuron in the first layer is independently supplied with inputs from a pair of neurons located in the input layer. Neurons at the second and third levels receive inputs from two neurons in the preceding layer, and this iterative process repeats until the output layer is attained. Using the ideal analytical expression for addressing the parameter relationship between the input and output variables, the output layer selects two inputs from the preceding layer and generates the ultimate result. Figure 11.8 represents the diagram of GMDHN.

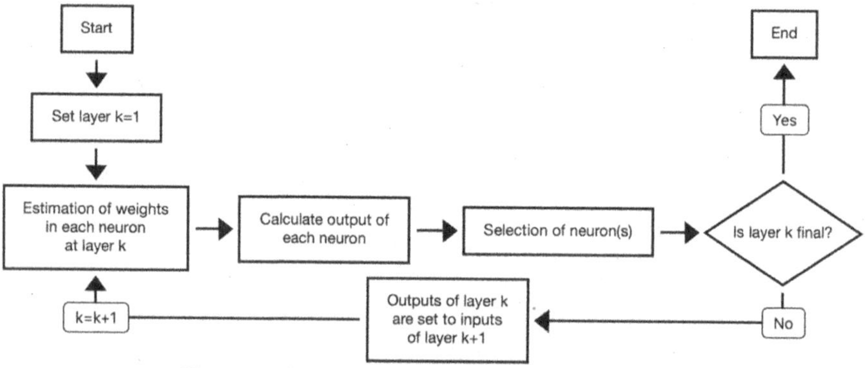

Figure 11.8 The demonstration of GMDHN [38].

With the below equation, it is possible to calculate the number of candidate neurons in the next layer, as n is the number of neurons in a layer in GMDHN [38].

$$\binom{n}{2} = \frac{n \times (n-1)}{2} \tag{5}$$

Furthermore, it is important to highlight that a single neuron in GMDHN has the capability to bypass layers directly from the input variables to one of the subsequent layers. This is illustrated by the dashed lines from x_5 to z_6 in Figure 11.7.

GBDT

GBDTs are highly efficient ensemble learning techniques. It improves forecast accuracy at the expense of some training time. GBDT comprises an upper network that directly predicts the output parameter and a bottom network that forecasts the residual between the output value of the upper network and the correct target value. This approach allows for a reduction in the residual of the upper network in the gradient direction, thereby enhancing the accuracy of the model in fitting to the actual distribution [41, 42]. For a better understanding, an illustration of GBDT by golf example is given in Figure 11.9.

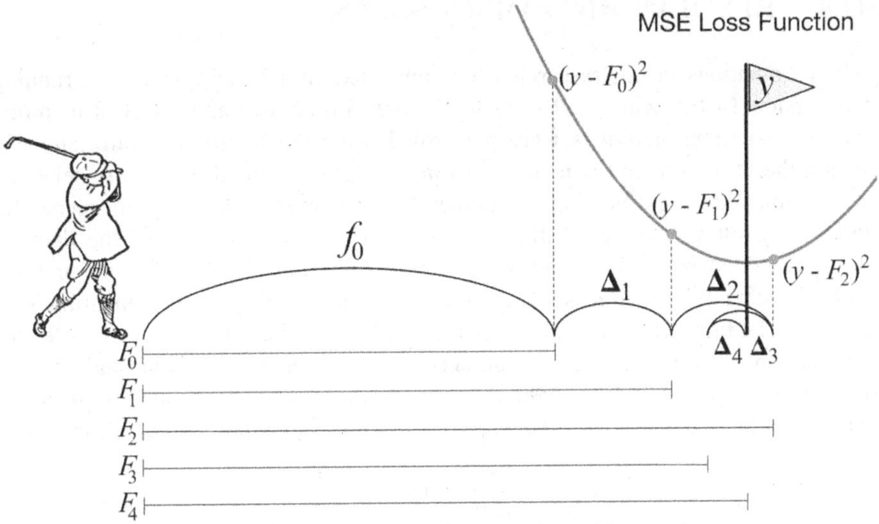

Figure 11.9 Illustration of GBDT by golf example.

Gradient boosting trains additive models in a step-by-step manner, adhering to a specific form:

$$F_m(x) = \mathrm{F}_{m-1}\,(x) + h_m(x) \tag{6}$$

where $h_m(x)$ represents the constant size of decision tree, the summation of $F_m(x)$ provides the sum of m decision trees and x is the cluster of input variables. In aim to forecast the response for the best h_m, the response $Y_{i,t+k}$ from the training set yielded as follow:

$$h_m(x_{i,\,t}) = Y_{i,t+k} - F_{m-1}\,(x_{i,t}) \tag{7}$$

where h_m represents the $r_{m,i,t}$ which is the abbreviation for the model that fits the current residuals at iteration m. This statement highlights that the present residuals refer to the negative gradients of the squared error loss function

$$r_{m,i,t} = -\frac{\partial \frac{1}{2}\left(Y_{i,t+k} - F_{m-1}\left(x_{i,t}\right)\right)^2}{\partial F_{m-1}\left(x_{i,t}\right)} \tag{8}$$

It is further shown that h_m is equivalent to the negative gradient of the squared error loss function. In GBDT, shrinkage factor, which is also known as a learning rate, is specified to adjust the contributions of each decision tree in a regularization technique used to prevent overfitting.

$$F_m(x) = F_{m-1}(x) + vh_m\,(x),\; v \in [0;1] \tag{9}$$

which smaller values of v suggested for minimizing test error [43, 44].

11.4 RESULTS AND DISCUSSION

All computations in this research were conducted on a Macintosh device running OS version 14.1.2, with a 2.4 GHz Intel Core i5 processor and 8 GB of memory. All computational activities were performed using the R programming language within the R Studio environment. Pearson correlation method for feature selection was employed to extract input parameters for a more effective and successful process, resulting in three distinct scenarios. The input variables of the data set are normalized by scaling their values between –1 and 1. Eliminating units of different data types reduces computing time and memory usage, ensuring data integrity. Additionally, this scaling approach allows for benchmarking multiple data columns in a similar manner. For an accurate assessment, R^2, nMAE and nRMSE have been implemented to evaluate the performances of the applied approaches. The performance metrics can be expressed by the following formulae [45, 46]:

$$R^2(\%) = \left(1 - \frac{\sum_{i=1}^{n}(y_i - \hat{y}_i)^2}{\sum_{i=1}^{n}(y_i - \bar{y}_i)^2}\right) \times 100 \tag{10}$$

where $\hat{y}_i$ is the predicted and y_i is the actual value. Furthermore, $\bar{y}$ can be represented as the mean of y_i and n indicates the number of observations.

$$nMAE(\%) = \frac{1}{n}\sum_{i=1}^{n}\frac{|y_i - \hat{y}_i|}{y_i} \times 100 \tag{11}$$

$$nRMSE(\%) = \frac{\sqrt{\frac{\sum_{i=1}^{n}(y_i - \hat{y}_i)^2}{n}}}{\max(y_i) - \min(y_i)} \times 100 \tag{12}$$

Similarly, within these equations, $\hat{y}_i$ is the predicted, y_i is the actual value and n represents the number of observations.

The random sample technique is applied to MLR, MLPNN, GEP and GMDHN and GBDT for model testing and assessment. Specifically, 20% of the data set is used as training data, while the remaining 80% is randomly selected as validation data.

As each approach has its own unique set of parameters and operational procedures, the parameters and results of the techniques are elaborated upon in the subsequent sections. For each method, three different scenarios were created. In the first scenario, all inputs were included, while in the second scenario, 7 inputs were chosen based on their P coefficient, which ranged from larger than 0.1 to less than –0.1. In the final scenario, inputs with P coefficients of 0.4 or higher and –0.4 or lower were selected and results were obtained applying methods with 6 inputs. In all of those scenarios, power consumption is the target variable. Specific features and measurements are detailed in the following subheadings.

11.4.1 Parameters of MLPNN

Using grid search for MLPNN, the number of neurons giving the best result between 2 and 50 is determined for Scenario 1, 2, and Scenario 3. As an activation function logistic-linear is employed and a scaled conjugate gradient algorithm is utilized for the learning algorithm.

Parameters of GEP

The model development parameters for GEP consist of a population size of 50, chromosome genes equal to 4, and a head length of 8. In the fitness function, fitness characteristics are calculated as the mean squared error (MSE). Algorithmic simplifications are conditionally permitted during computations, with the following functions allowed: addition (+), subtraction (−), multiplication (×), division (/), and square root (√). The length of the training model is 1,880 generations, and the number of evaluations for the fitness function is 118,200.

GEP models for each three scenarios is demonstrated following Figures 11.10, 11.11 and 11.12 and equations.

$$\text{Power Consumption} = \text{P15mP}\left(1 - \frac{6.257}{DY}\right) + 0.019\text{PDP} - 0.025 \qquad (13)$$

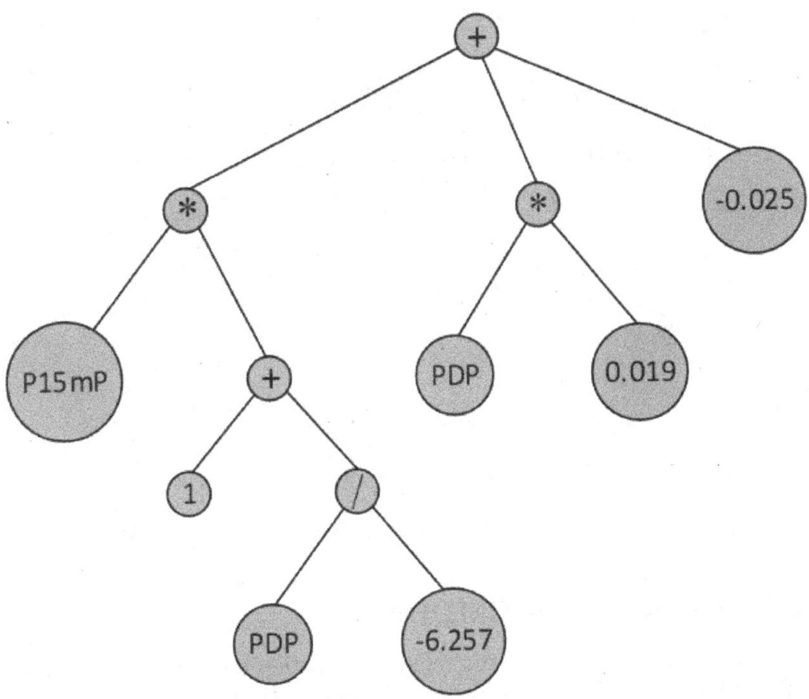

Figure 11.10 Expression tree of the GEP model for Scenario 1.

$$\text{Power Consumption} = \text{P15mP}\left(1 + \frac{1}{\text{HD} - 31.551}\right) + 0.047 \times \text{PDP} - 0.001 \times \text{SWI} \quad (14)$$

$$\text{Power Consumption} = 0.874P15mP + 0.004PDP - 0.004SWI - 0.126 \quad (15)$$

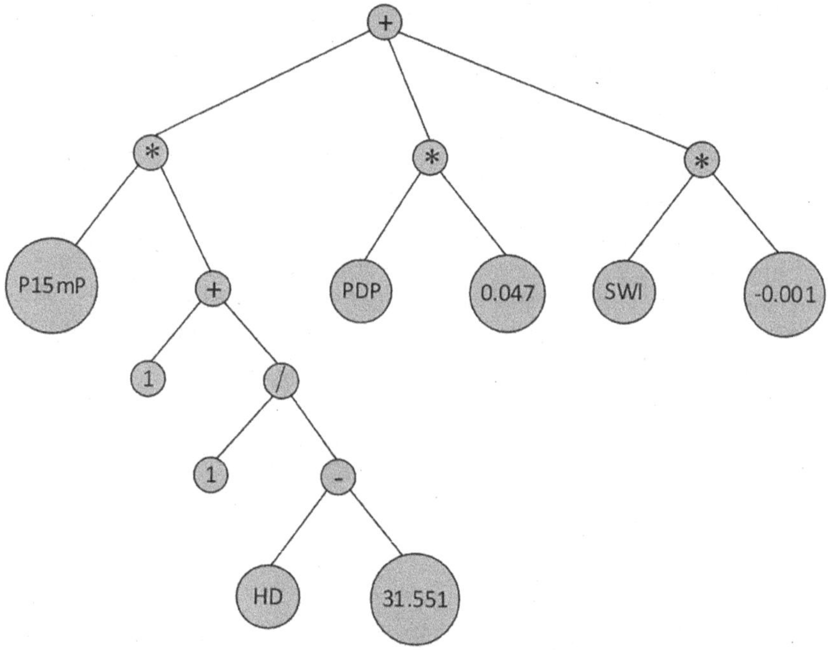

Figure 11.11 Expression tree of the GEP model for scenario 2.

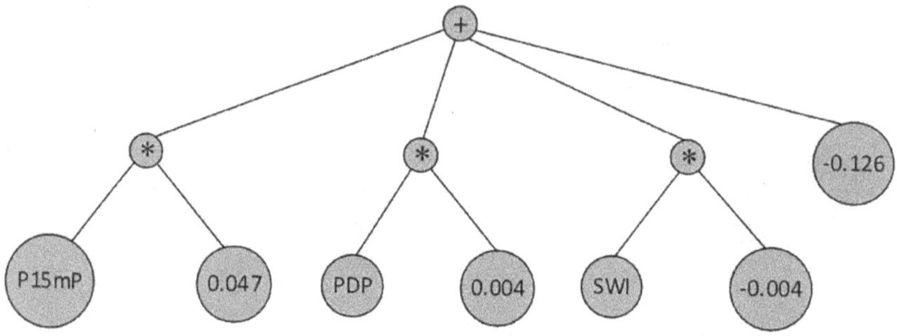

Figure 11.12 Expression tree of the GEP model for scenario 3.

11.4.2 Parameters of GMDHN

The GMDHN utilize the quadratic reference function consisting of two variables as defined in equation 4. Parameters for the GMDHN are predetermined as 20 for the number of both maximum network layers and neurons per layer. The permitted network architecture for the neurons in the subsequent layer is determined by selecting neurons from any layer and assigning them the original input variables. Additionally, 4 predictors have been used for scenario 1 which are P15mP, PHP, HD, and SWI, 6 predictors have been used for scenario 2 which are P15mP, PHP, PDP, HD, T and SWI, 3 predictors have been used for scenario 3 which are P15mP, HD, and SWI to construct the quadratic reference function.

11.4.3 Parameters of GBDT

For building the GBDT model, trees in series varies in three scenarios. 58 trees for Scenario 1, 57 trees for Scenario 2 and 56 trees for Scenario 3 have used. Depth of trees were determined as 5 and the Huber's quantile cutoff which is employed to regulate outliers during the management of forecast errors is fixed to 0.95. Furthermore, it utilizes the square error up to a specific error threshold (cutoff) and the absolute error above this threshold.

11.4.4 Overall Results

The results of the PEDF study, which covers the period between May and November 2019 and is intended to be carried out using the meteorological data set of the location of the house together with the electrical data obtained from a house located in New York, USA, are presented in detail in Table 11.2. An analysis was conducted on the performances of MLR, MLPNN, GEP, GMDHN, and GBDT models in three distinct scenarios, employing Pearson correlation as a feature selection approach. During the evaluation of these scenarios, the algorithms were compared based on R^2, nMAE, nRMSE, and run times. Table 11.3 indicates that the GBDT model achieved the highest R^2 value for Scenario 1 and the lowest margin of error in the other two error measures. The low run time of MLR can be attributed to its statistical approach characterized by low complexity. In Scenario 2, the GMDHN model attains the greatest R^2 value, whereas the GBDT model has superior performance as measured by nMAE. Among the models, MLPNN, GMDHN, and GBDT exhibit the lowest error values for nRMSE, with identical responses. The final scenario demonstrated that GBDT exhibited superior performance and a high level of accuracy in all performance metrics. Comprehensive examination of the table reveals minimal variability in the outcomes provided by the models. The only notable difference is in the relatively short run time of MLR, a statistical technique, which sets it apart from competing AI methods. Nevertheless, given that GMDHN is an AI technique, the runtime metrics are fairly satisfactory.

Figure 11.13 illustrates the R^2 performance among the three diverse scenarios examined in the study. Scenario 3 demonstrated the greatest median R^2 value, underscoring its exceptional predictive performance. Scenario 2 exhibited competitive performance, although with marginally reduced accuracy. On the contrary, Scenario 1 demonstrated more volatility and diminished average performance. The results presented here emphasize the significance of feature selection in enhancing model accuracy and computational efficiency for PEDF.

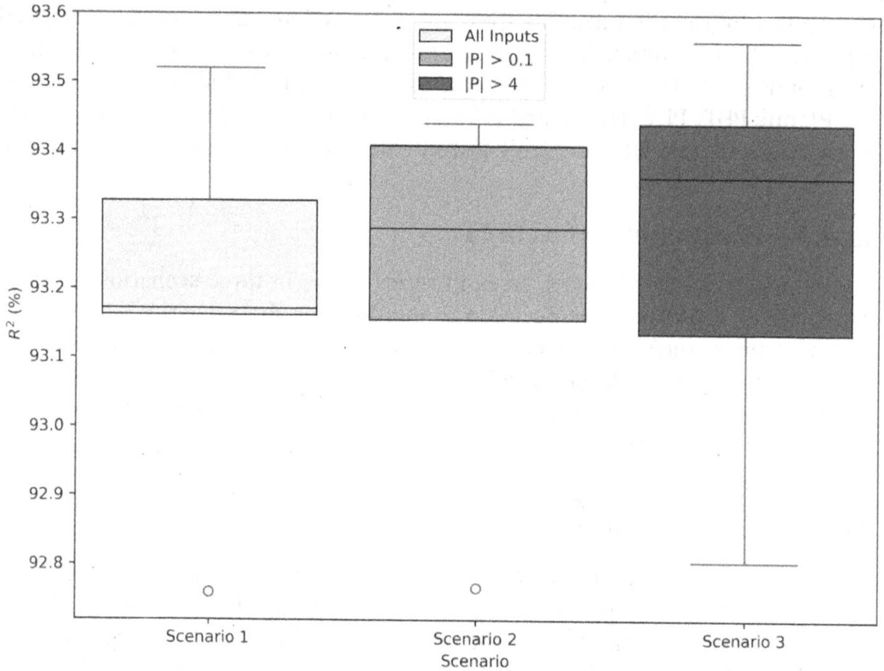

Figure 11.13 Performance of R^2 based on three scenarios.

Table 11.3 Performance metrics for three scenarios according to employed methods

	Inputs	Model	R^2 (%)	nMAE (%)	nRMSE (%)	Run Time (s)
Scenario 1	All Inputs	MLR	93.163	4.7	8.1	1.47
		MLPNN	93.172	4.8	8.1	169.20
		GEP	92.760	4.8	8.3	536.97
		GMDHN	93.328	4.7	7.9	53.62
		GBDT	93.520	**4.5**	**7.8**	10.79
		Average	93.187	4.7	8.04	154.41
Scenario 2	7 Inputs |P| > 0.1	MLR	93.156	4.7	8.1	**0.48**
		MLPNN	93.289	4.7	7.9	56.02
		GEP	92.767	4.8	8.3	499.20
		GMDHN	93.441	4.6	7.9	38.88
		GBDT	93.409	**4.5**	7.9	8.38
		Average	93.212	4.66	8.02	120.59
Scenario 3	6 Inputs |P| > 0.4	MLR	93.137	4.7	8.1	0.97
		MLPNN	93.363	4.7	7.9	78.36
		GEP	92.805	4.8	8.2	489.12
		GMDHN	93.441	4.6	7.9	31.93
		GBDT	**93.560**	**4.5**	**7.8**	6.99
		Average	93.261	4.66	7.98	121.47

11.5 CONCLUSION

Over the past few years, conventional electric power systems have undergone a significant transformation into modern electric power systems by incorporating leading technologies involving smart grids, microgrids, and the internet of energy. The aforementioned advancements enable the utilization of domestically generated electricity with minimal power loss and optimal efficiency, all aimed at achieving a more sustainable future. The integration of renewable energy sources into current electric distribution networks has contributed to the transition from the consumer concept to the prosumer model. The aim of this study is to calculate the PEDF for a specific household in New York, USA, using the prosumer framework and incorporating meteorological data. In this specific scenario, the statistical algorithm MLR is utilized, and the AI algorithms MLPNN, GEP, GMDHN, and GBDT are applied to perform the PEDF. An analysis of power-related, meteorological, and calendar parameters is conducted using a dataset that includes 19 distinct inputs with a 15-minute resolution of data. In addition, a feature selection technique, which is Pearson correlation, is incorporated to generate three distinct scenarios with various P values. The present study assesses the efficacy of the implemented models in the PEDF concept, considering different input sets. This evaluation is carried out utilizing several performance and error measures, such as R^2, nMAE, nRMSE, and run time. The results showed that all models exhibited satisfactory performance for PEDF calculation. However, when analysed individually for each scenario, the GBDT model demonstrated superior performance in Scenario 1 and Scenario 3. Accordingly, the GMDHN model demonstrates higher accuracy with minimal errors in Scenario 2. Therefore, both GBDT and GMDHN models are recommended for the PEDF concept of research through incorporating meteorological data.

This study successfully satisfies its objective, as stated in the abstract, by calculating PEDF using statistical and AI-based methods while analysing in detail the impact of various input scenarios derived from Pearson correlation. The results confirm the potential of incorporating meteorological data and scenario-based input selection to improve the accuracy of PEDF, thereby addressing a critical gap in the literature and providing useful guidelines for future research in the field.

REFERENCES

[1] Zor, K., O. Timur and A. Teke. 2017. A state-of-the-art review of artificial intelligence techniques for short-term electric load forecasting. *In*: 2017 6th International Youth Conference on Energy (IYCE). IEEE. 1–7.

[2] Schick, C., N. Klempp and K. Hufendiek. 2020. Role and impact of prosumers in a sector-integrated energy system with high renewable shares. IEEE Transactions on Power Systems. 37(4): 3286–3298.

[3] Parag, Y. and B.K. Sovacool. 2016. Electricity market design for the prosumer era. Nature Energy. 1(4): 1–6.

[4] Benti, N.E., M.D. Chaka and A.G. Semie. 2023. Forecasting renewable energy generation with machine learning and deep learning: Current advances and future prospects. Sustainability. 15(9): 7087.

[5] Dou, Y., S. Tan and Xie, D. 2023. Comparison of machine learning and statistical methods in the field of renewable energy power generation forecasting: A mini review. Frontiers in Energy Research. 11.

[6] Shohan, M., M. Faruque and S. Foo. 2022. Forecasting of electric load using a hybrid LSTM-neural prophet model. Energies. 15(6): 2158. https://doi.org/10.3390/en15062158

[7] Winter, D., R. Khatri and M. Schmidt. 2021. Decentralized prosumer-centric P2P electricity market coordination with grid security. Energies. 14(15): 4665.

[8] Bouktif, S., A. Fiaz, A. Ouni and M. Serhani. 2018. Optimal deep learning LSTM model for electric load forecasting using feature selection and genetic algorithm: Comparison with machine learning approaches. Energies. 11(7): 1636.

[9] Benti, N.E., M.D. Chaka and A.G. Semie. 2023. Forecasting renewable energy generation with machine learning and deep learning: current advances and future prospects. Sustainability. 15(9): 7087.

[10] Dewitte, S., J. Cornelis, R. Müller and A. Munteanu. 2021. Artificial intelligence revolutionises weather forecast, climate monitoring and decadal prediction. Remote Sensing. 13(16): 3209.

[11] Aderibigbe, A.O., E.C. Ani, P.E. Ohenhen, N.C. Ohalete and D.O. Daraojimba. 2023. Enhancing energy efficiency with AI: A review of machine learning models in electricity demand forecasting. Engineering Science and Technology Journal. 4(6): 341–356.

[12] Yousef, L.A., H. Yousef and L. Rocha-Meneses. 2023. Artificial intelligence for management of variable renewable energy systems: A review of current status and future directions. Energies. 16(24): 8057.

[13] Pinto, R., R.J. Bessa and M.A. Matos. 2017. Multi-period flexibility forecast for low voltage prosumers. Energy. 141: 2251–2263.

[14] Bruno, S., G. Giannoccaro and M. La Scala. 2017. Predictive control of demand and storage for residential prosumers. *In*: 2017 IEEE PES Innovative Smart Grid Technologies Conference Europe (ISGT-Europe). 1–6. IEEE.

[15] Petrican, T., A.V. Vesa, M. Antal, C. Pop, T. Cioara, I. Anghel, et al. 2018. Evaluating forecasting techniques for integrating household energy prosumers into smart grids. *In*: 2018 IEEE 14th International Conference on Intelligent Computer Communication and Processing (ICCP). 79–85. IEEE.

[16] Ruiz-Abellón, M.C., L.A. Fernández-Jiménez, A. Guillamón, A. Falces, A. García-Garre and A. Gabaldón. 2019. Integration of demand response and short-term forecasting for the management of prosumers' demand and generation. Energies. 13(1): 11.

[17] Grimaldo, A.I. and J. Novak. 2020. Combining machine learning with visual analytics for explainable forecasting of energy demand in prosumer scenarios. Procedia Computer Science. 175: 525–532.

[18] Faraji, J., A. Ketabi, H. Hashemi-Dezaki, M. Shafie-Khah and J.P. Catalao. 2020. Optimal day-ahead scheduling and operation of the prosumer by considering corrective actions based on very short-term load forecasting. IEEE Access. 8: 83561–83582.

[19] Panapakidis, I.P., N.E. Koltsaklis and G.C. Christoforidis. 2021. Forecasting methods to support the decision framework of prosumers in deregulated markets. *In*: 2021 9th International Conference on Modern Power Systems (MPS). 1–5. IEEE.

[20] Zhao, L. 2021. Machine Learning in Electricity Load Forecasting of Prosumer Buildings.

[21] Zhou, B., Y. Meng, W. Huang, H. Wang, L. Deng, S. Huang, et al. 2021. Multi-energy net load forecasting for integrated local energy systems with heterogeneous prosumers. International Journal of Electrical Power and Energy Systems. 126: 106542.

[22] Antal, M., L. Toderean, T. Cioara and I. Anghel. 2022. Hybrid deep neural network model for multi-step energy prediction of prosumers. Applied Sciences. 12(11): 5346.

[23] Jiang, Y., T. Gao, Y. Dai, R. Si, J. Hao, J. Zhang, et al. 2022. Very short-term residential load forecasting based on deep-autoformer. Applied Energy. 328: 120120.

[24] Yazdani, H., M. Doostizadeh and F. Aminifar. 2023. Forecast-aided power and flexibility trading of prosumers in peer to peer markets. IET Renewable Power Generation. 17(4): 920–934.

[25] Zhang, S., B. Wang, S. Huang, J. Shi, C. Jiang, F. Chen, et al. 2023. P2P energy Trading Based on power generation and Load forecasting of Prosumers. *In*: 3rd International Conference on Management Science and Software Engineering (ICMSSE 2023). 326–340. Atlantis Press.

[26] Kychkin, A. and G.C. Chasparis. 2024. AI-Powered Predictions for Electricity Load in Prosumer Communities. arXiv preprint arXiv:2402.13752.

[27] Dataport of Pecan Street Inc., [online] Available: https://www.pecanstreet.org/dataport/

[28] Gelaro, R., W. McCarty, M.J. Suárez, R. Todling, A. Molod, L. Takacs, et al. 2017. The modern-era retrospective analysis for research and applications version 2 (MERRA-2). Journal of Climate. 30(14): 5419–5454.

[29] Maulud, D. and A.M. Abdulazeez. 2020. A review on linear regression comprehensive in machine learning. Journal of Applied Science and Technology Trends. 1(2): 140–147.

[30] Yorat, E., N.S. Özbek, K. Zor and L. Sarıbulut. 2023. Day-ahead electricity price forecasting using artificial intelligence-based algorithms. *In*: 2023 International Conference on Innovation and Intelligence for Informatics, Computing and Technologies (3ICT). 121–126. IEEE.

[31] Afzal, S., B.M. Ziapour, A. Shokri, H. Shakibi and B. Sobhani. 2023. Building energy consumption prediction using multilayer perceptron neural network-assisted models; comparison of different optimization algorithms. Energy. 282: 128446.

[32] Xu, Y., F. Li and A. Asgari. 2022. Prediction and optimization of heating and cooling loads in a residential building based on multilayer perceptron neural network and different optimization algorithms. Energy. 240: 122692.

[33] Hasan, M.M., M.S.M. Nilay, N.H. Jibon and R.M. Rahman. 2023. LULC changes to riverine flooding: A case study on the Jamuna River, Bangladesh using the multilayer perceptron model. Results in Engineering. 18: 101079.

[34] Sreejith, S., J. Ajayan, N.U. Reddy, S.B. Devasenapati and S. Rebelli 2023. Analysis of Covid-19 CT chest image classification using Dl4jMlp classifier and Multilayer Perceptron in WEKA Environment. Current Medical Imaging.

[35] Ferreira, C. 2001. Gene expression programming: A new adaptive algorithm for solving problems. arXiv preprint cs/0102027.

[36] Sadat Hosseini, S.S. and A.H. Gandomi. 2012. Short-term load forecasting of power systems by gene expression programming. Neural Computing and Applications. 21: 377–389.

[37] Çelik, Ö., K. Zor, A. Tan and A. Teke. 2022. A novel gene expression programming-based MPPT technique for PV micro-inverter applications under fast-changing atmospheric conditions. Solar Energy. 239: 268–282.

[38] Zor, K., Ö. Çelik, O. Timur and A. Teke. 2020. Short-term building electrical energy consumption forecasting by employing gene expression programming and GMDH networks. Energies. 13(5): 1102.

[39] Zhang, S. and R. Zhang. 2023. Prediction of the thermal conductivity of rocks using group method of data handling (GMDH). Geothermics. 115: 102823.

[40] De Giorgi, M.G., M. Malvoni and P.M. Congedo. 2016. Comparison of strategies for multi-step ahead photovoltaic power forecasting models based on hybrid group method of data handling networks and least square support vector machine. Energy. 107: 360–373.

[41] Xiao, J., Y. Li, L. Xie, D. Liu and J. Huang. 2018. A hybrid model based on selective ensemble for energy consumption forecasting in China. Energy. 159: 534–546.

[42] Wu, W., J. Wang, Y. Huang, H. Zhao and X. Wang. 2021. A novel way to determine transient heat flux based on GBDT machine learning algorithm. International Journal of Heat and Mass Transfer. 179: 121746.

[43] Parr, T. and J. Howard. 2018. How to explain gradient boosting. Explained. AI.

[44] Persson, C., P. Bacher, T. Shiga and H. Madsen. 2017. Multisite solar power forecasting using gradient boosted regression trees. Solar Energy. 150: 423–436.

[45] Zor, K. and K. Buluş 2021. A benchmark of GRU and LSTM networks for short-term electric load forecasting. 2021 International Conference on Innovation and Intelligence for Informatics, Computing and Technologies (3ICT). 598–602. IEEE.

[46] Zor, K., O. Timur, Ö. Çelik, H. Yıldırım and A. Teke. 2017. Interpretation of error calculation methods in the context of energy forecasting, *In*: 12th Conference on Sustainable Development of Energy, Water and Environment Systems, Dubrovnik, Croatia. 722: 1–9.

Index

3PL 76, 77, 78, 79, 80, 81, 83, 84, 85, 93, 102

A

Anomaly Detection 5, 9, 29, 30, 33, 37, 46, 50, 55, 56, 58, 86, 140
Artificial Intelligence (AI) 1, 28 30, 49, 55, 76, 77, 82, 102, 105, 108, 109, 117, 128, 130, 136, 139, 143, 144, 148, 152, 201, 209, 214, 233, 237, 238
Artificial Neural Network (ANN/ ANNs) 2, 11, 13, 55, 58, 181, 188, 190, 192, 194, 196, 196, 202, 203, 211, 212, 213, 218, 224, 225, 227, 236, 237, 260, 264, 265
Auto-Regressive Integrated Moving Average (ARIMA) 3, 4, 5, 8, 10, 11, 76, 82, 83, 85, 86, 87, 88, 89, 90, 91, 92, 101, 102, 132, 176, 182, 218, 241, 242, 243, 244, 245, 258, 260, 261, 262

B

Blockchain technology 114, 150

C

Chatbot Technology 29, 31, 32
Computer Vision 19, 56, 58
Continuous Learning 47, 148, 178
Convolutional Neural Networks (CNNs) 1, 10, 13, 29, 31, 33, 49, 58
Correlation and Root Cause Analysis 37

D

Data Preprocessing 2, 6, 7, 148, 149, 220, 221
Deep Learning 1, 5, 8, 9, 38, 40, 47, 48, 50, 61, 73, 81, 82, 132, 133, 134, 140, 142, 146, 147, 176, 218, 236, 257, 259
Demand 1, 2, 3, 4, 5, 6, 7, 8, 9, 10, 11, 12, 13, 14, 15, 16, 17, 18, 19, 20, 21, 22, 23, 28, 29, 32, 33, 37, 44, 46, 47, 48, 49, 76, 77, 78, 79, 80, 81, 82, 83, 102, 106, 108, 113, 114, 115, 117, 118, 120, 124, 125, 126, 127, 128, 130, 131, 132, 133, 134, 135, 136, 137, 138, 139, 140, 141, 142, 143, 144, 145, 146, 147, 148, 150, 151, 152, 157, 159, 160, 201, 202, 207, 208, 209, 210, 211, 212, 213, 214, 218, 219, 220, 221, 222, 223, 224, 227, 228, 231, 237, 238, 243, 251, 255, 256, 257, 258, 259, 260
Demand Forecasting 1, 2, 3, 4, 5, 6, 7, 8, 9, 10, 11, 12, 13, 14, 15, 16, 17, 18, 19, 20, 21, 22, 23, 29, 33, 46, 48, 76, 77, 78, 79, 81, 82, 83, 102, 108, 113, 114, 115, 117, 118, 120, 124, 125, 126, 128, 130, 131, 132, 133, 134, 135, 136, 137, 138, 139, 140, 141, 142, 143, 144, 145, 146, 147, 148, 150, 151, 201, 202, 209, 218, 228, 257

E

Electricity demand forecasting 11, 201, 209, 228, 257

Electricity 11, 12, 43, 44, 45, 106, 158, 159, 160, 173, 200, 201, 207, 208, 209, 212, 214, 217, 218, 219, 222, 224, 227, 228, 230, 231, 241, 247, 248, 250, 255, 256, 257, 259, 262, 277
Energy 5, 8, 10, 12, 16, 17, 18, 19, 21, 54, 55, 56, 106, 108, 109, 112, 113, 114, 115, 118, 120, 156, 157, 158, 159, 160, 161, 162, 163, 164, 169, 170, 171, 174, 175, 180, 182, 185, 186, 188, 190, 196, 200, 217, 218, 219, 220, 221, 222, 227, 228, 230, 237, 238, 239, 244, 245, 246, 247, 248, 250, 251, 252, 255, 256, 257, 258, 259, 260, 261, 262, 277
Energy Demand Forecasting 16, 218

F

Forecast 2, 3, 4, 7, 8, 12, 13, 14, 15, 18, 21, 22, 23, 32, 37, 46, 48, 60, 79, 80, 81, 82, 84, 85, 86, 88, 89, 90, 91, 92, 93, 94, 95, 96, 97, 98, 99, 100, 101, 102, 108, 114, 115, 118, 125, 131, 132, 135, 136, 137, 139, 141, 143, 144, 145, 146, 147, 148, 152, 158, 160, 176, 179, 201, 202, 204, 205, 207, 209, 210, 211, 212, 213, 214, 218, 219, 227, 230, 231, 232, 236, 237, 238, 239, 240, 241, 243, 245, 251, 256, 257, 258, 259, 260, 261, 262, 264, 270, 271, 275
Forecast Accuracy 12, 18, 22, 81, 82, 93, 94, 95, 100, 101, 102, 143, 238, 251, 261, 270
Forecasting 1, 2, 3, 4, 5, 6, 7, 8, 9, 10, 11, 12, 13, 14, 15, 16, 17, 18, 19, 20, 21, 22, 23, 29, 33, 44, 46, 48, 49, 50, 76, 77, 78, 79, 80, 81, 82, 83, 85, 86, 87, 93, 94, 100, 101, 102, 106, 108, 110, 113, 114, 115, 117, 118, 120, 124, 125, 126, 127, 128, 130, 131, 132, 133, 134, 135, 136, 137, 138, 139, 140, 141, 142, 143, 144, 145, 146, 147, 148, 149, 150, 151, 152, 157, 175, 179, 180, 182, 188, 190, 191, 196, 201, 202, 209, 212, 218, 219, 222, 227, 228, 230, 231, 232, 236, 237, 238, 239, 240, 241, 242, 243, 244, 245, 247, 250, 251, 252, 255, 256, 257, 258, 259, 260, 262, 264

G

gen-AI 77, 81, 82, 83, 93, 102
Generative Pre-trained Transformer (GPT) 29, 31, 41, 46, 47, 49, 50, 56, 83, 95, 96, 98, 99, 101, 102

H

Hierarchical forecasting 231, 237, 239, 241, 245

I

Industry 4.0 1, 3, 6, 8, 14, 22, 55, 77, 80, 105, 106, 108, 109, 110, 111, 112, 120
Industry 4.0/5.0 120
Intelligent Data Analysis 163
Internet of Things (IoT) 12, 22, 56, 106, 111, 112, 114, 117, 132, 133, 146, 150, 151, 164, 174, 175, 176, 188, 191, 196
Inventory Optimization 18, 117, 134, 140

L

Large Language Model (LLM) 56, 59, 60, 61, 73, 83
Load forecasting 10, 180, 218, 230, 231, 236, 237, 238, 239, 245, 250, 256, 257, 259, 260, 262
Logistics 13, 16, 17, 18, 23, 60, 70, 72, 76, 77, 78, 79, 80, 81, 83, 84, 102, 106, 108, 112, 113, 114, 118, 120, 124, 125, 126, 128, 129, 130, 133, 134, 135, 141, 150, 273

M

Machine Learning (ML) 1, 2, 6, 7, 8, 9, 10, 11, 12, 13, 15, 16, 17, 18, 19, 22, 29, 30, 31, 33, 36, 37, 40, 41, 42, 49, 50, 55, 60, 70, 73, 76, 77, 78, 79, 80, 81, 82, 83, 85, 86, 88, 89, 90, 91, 92, 101, 102, 105, 106, 109, 112, 113, 114, 118, 128, 132, 133, 134, 135, 139, 140, 143, 144, 145, 146, 147, 148, 149, 151, 152, 176, 179, 180, 183, 188, 194, 196, 201, 202, 205, 211, 218, 219, 227, 228, 236, 257, 258, 259, 260, 261, 262
Manufacturing Industry 2
Microgrid 188, 255, 257, 259, 262, 277
Multiple Linear Regression 218, 224, 227

N

Natural Language Processing (NLP) 29, 30, 31, 46, 49, 50, 59, 82, 108, 133, 136, 137, 138
Neural networks 1, 2, 4, 5, 10, 11, 13, 18, 29, 31, 38, 40, 49, 50, 55, 58, 60, 70, 72, 81, 82, 102, 132, 138, 140, 147, 152, 180, 181, 182, 190, 196, 201, 202, 204, 211, 214, 218, 224, 225, 227, 236, 237, 239, 240, 243, 245, 257, 259, 265, 267
News Classification 29, 31, 38, 41, 44, 49

O

Open-Source Intelligence (OSINT) 28, 29, 30, 31, 32, 46, 47, 48, 49, 50

P

Propagation Rate 56, 59, 61, 64
Prosumer 256, 257, 258, 259, 260, 262, 277

R

Random Forest 13, 16, 17, 60, 70, 72, 146, 147, 202, 218, 224, 225, 226, 227, 228
Reinforcement Learning 11, 48, 120, 135, 140, 147, 176, 178

S

SCADA 56, 60, 61, 163, 164, 165, 166, 167, 168, 169, 171, 172, 173, 174, 196, 237
Smart grid 16, 175, 185, 186, 218, 255, 258, 277
Smart manufacturing 110
Special days 202
Supply Chain Management 2, 6, 13, 16, 18, 19, 23, 77, 81, 82, 83, 106, 119, 124, 125, 126, 127, 128, 130, 131, 133, 134, 135, 136, 147, 148, 149, 150, 151
Sustainability 23, 56, 81, 106, 108, 109, 110, 111, 112, 113, 114, 115, 118, 120, 145, 152, 196, 218, 255, 256, 257

T

Top-down 231, 232, 238, 240, 251